Cranks from Cooperstown

50 BIKE RIDES IN UPSTATE NEW YORK

Two Books in One! A How-to-Bike Instruction Manual & A Bicycle Tour Guide with 50 tear-out Cue Sheets and Maps

Andrea —

Let's Get Cranking!

Denis Savoie

The Book

Cranks from Cooperstown: 50 Bike Rides in Upstate New York

Published by:
Tourmaster Publications, L.L.C.
P.O. Box 568
Cooperstown, NY 13326

Phone:	607-547-CRANK (607-547-2726)
	888- 49-CRANK (888-492-7265)
Fax:	888- 59-CRANK (888-592-7265)
Email:	crankmail@usa.net

Library of Congress Catalog Card Number: 97-97227
ISBN 0-9662638-1-2
Printed in the United States of America
Distributed in the United States by Tourmaster Publications, L.L.C.

First Edition

Limit of Liability and Disclaimer of Warranty: The Author/Publisher has used his best efforts in preparing this book and makes no representation or warranties with respect to the accuracy or completeness of the contents of this book. The Author/Publisher assumes no liability for accidents or injuries occurring to readers who bicycle the tours described in this book.

Book Design and Maps by: Guyot Designworks
Edited by: Janet Kerr
Photos by: Frank Rollins (pages 5, 6, 7 & back cover)
          Jon Savoie (page 72)

The Facts

Fix the Facts: The roads won't change, but the road signs may. In the northeast, snowplows eat road signs for breakfast in the winter. Hunters shoot them in the fall. And teenagers tear them down in the summer. In addition, as we go to press, local road signs are being changed to implement a 911 emergency communication system. If you notice any changes or errors in this book, please contact the publisher so that future editions can be corrected.

The Definition

*The crank is your bike's heart and soul. It makes you and your bike **come alive.** Be a crank. **Join me on a Crank from Cooperstown!***

crank (krangk), *n., v.,* **-n. 1** an arm at right angles to the end of a shaft by which circular motion is imparted to the shaft. *I made my bicycle go forward by turning the crank with my pedals.* **2** *Informal, Figurative.* **a** a person with queer ideas or habits; a person possessed, as by some hobby. **b** a person who turns a bicycle's crank. SYN: a **cyclist.** a **crankmeister.** **c** a place where a bicycle goes as it's being cranked. SYN: a **bicycle ride.** a **bicycle tour.** *I went on a crank from Cooperstown.* **- v.t. 1** to work by means of a crank. **2** to speed; to accelerate. **3** *Informal, Figurative.* to go on a bike ride; to crank. *Let's get cranking.*

The Logo

Let's Get Cranking!

The Slogan

Table of Contents

Introduction

"If you build it, they will come..."

I **was thinking about you when I built this book**. I was thinking about you and your first bike. Remember the wire basket?…the bell?… the handlebar streamers?… the playing cards clothespinned to the spokes? Remember the exhilaration you felt when your parent let go, sending you on your first solo flight?

That bike gave you your first taste of freedom as you navigated the sidewalks of your block. It gave you a ticket to explore the universe. It was your sole source of transportation for years. Then your hormones kicked in; you learned how to drive the family car; and coming of age signaled the end of your bicycling career.

Many years have gone by….

You realize you aren't a kid anymore. It just isn't fun to drive all the time. You're gaining weight without really trying. Your doctor is talking about things like health maintenance. You're thinking about biking again.

There's just one problem: you don't know how! You were taught to ride your bike as a sidewalk toy; no one taught you how to drive your bike as a roadworthy vehicle. You're afraid of traffic. When you go to the bike shop you don't know if you need a mountain bike, a road bike, a touring bike, a recumbent, or a tandem. You don't recognize derailleurs, or understand what to do with all those gears. You aren't exactly sure how to perch your adult self comfortably on what appears to be a child-sized seat. And even if you do get back on the road again, you aren't sure how to bike efficiently or how to choose roads without getting lost.

Some of you are lucky. You have a bicycling friend, shop owner, or bicycle club to show you how. You've learned to use your bike for fitness, pleasure, adventure, and transportation.

Some of you are not so lucky. Local bicycling resources are not readily available. For you, the lure of the open road remains an unfulfilled dream.

I've built this book for both of you. For the novice cyclist, I've included a "how to bike" section in what is otherwise meant to be a "where to bike" book; I've included tours that are as short and as flat as the terrain allows. For the seasoned cyclist, I've included fifty long and beautiful backroads tours that are guaranteed to please.

"If you build it, they will come...

I was thinking about you when I built this book. I was thinking about you and your newest bike.

I have built it; now it's time for you to come.

Welcome!

"The road riding here rivals any eastern touring hotspot. The area is less touristy and developed than, say, Lancaster, Pennsylvania. And while the mountains may be only half as high as Vermont's, there's plenty of challenging climbing and New England hospitality."

Welcome, bicycling friend! Welcome to Cooperstown and to Leatherstocking Country, NY! Welcome to the best cycling in the East and to unspoiled, rural, "Norman Rockwell" Americana! As Bill Strickland proclaimed in his review of Cooperstown in the November 1994 issue of *Bicycling* magazine: *The road riding here rivals any eastern touring hotspot. The area is less touristy and developed than, say, Lancaster, Pennsylvania. And while the mountains may be only half as high as Vermont's, there's plenty of challenging climbing and New England hospitality.*

So move over Pennsylvania Dutch Country, and move over, Green Mountain State; here comes Cooperstown to claim its rightful place as the backroads bicycle touring capital of the East!

Cooperstown is located in Otsego County, in upstate New York. Otsego and surrounding counties geographically define Leatherstocking Country, the home of the characters immortalized by James Fenimore Cooper in his *Leatherstocking Tales.* Leatherstocking Country is a rural, scenic wonderland bordered by Albany to the east, Utica and Syracuse to the west, and Binghamton to the south.

Cooperstown is a quaint village of 2500 inhabitants nestled at the southern shore of nine-mile-long Lake Otsego. It is located in a mini-Finger-Lakes-type glacial region wedged between the Mohawk Valley and Adirondacks to the north, and the Catskills to the south. This is a land of north-south river valleys separated by east-west ridges. The scenery is spectacular. Opportunities for fishing, swimming, sailing, hiking and golfing abound. The backroads are traffic free. **And the bicycling is superb.**

Cooperstown is a center of New York State history. Prior to the 1600's, it was home to the Susquehannock and Iroquois Indians. In 1779, it hosted the Sullivan-Clinton Campaign in the Revolutionary War. Later, Cooperstown was home to Judge William Cooper, after whom it is named; and to his son, James

The Farmers' Museum

Fenimore House Museum

Lake Otsego

Fenimore Cooper. Two of James Fenimore's five *Leatherstocking Tales* take place on the shores of *The Glimmerglass*, now called Lake Otsego. All five of the *Tales* immortalized Natty Bumppo, alias the Deerslayer, alias Hawkeye (in *The Last of the Mohicans*), alias the Pathfinder, alias Leatherstocking. The bicycle tours in this book explore the landmarks associated with these historical events.

Cooperstown is known as the Village of Museums. It is the home of the Fenimore House Museum of American culture and its spectacular American Indian wing. It is also the home of the Farmers' Museum, a working recreation of a typical mid-19th century rural New York village.

Cooperstown is best known as the Home of Baseball. In the center of town is Doubleday Field where baseball was first played, and the National Baseball Hall of Fame where thousands of baseball fans flock each year (especially during the Hall of Fame Induction Ceremonies each August). If you like baseball, you'll love Cooperstown!

Cooperstown plays host to many cultural activities. It is the home of the nationally acclaimed Glimmerglass Opera Company, the Cooperstown Concert Series, Gallery 53, Cooperstown Art Association, and the Smithy-Pioneer Gallery.

Beyond the village of Cooperstown, Leatherstocking Country beckons with attractions too numerous to mention. Bike to waterfalls, gorges, nature trails and State Parks. Bike to Howe Caverns, the Fly Creek Cider Mill, historic Cherry Valley, the Mohawk River and the Erie Barge Canal. Bike to Sharon's Bath Houses, Jordanville's Russian Orthodox Monastery, Gilbertsville's polo fields, and Oneonta's National Soccer Hall of Fame.

So welcome, bicycling friend! Welcome to Cooperstown and to Leatherstocking Country, NY!

Welcome to the best bicycling in the East! Just don't tell anybody about it. We wouldn't want the secret to get out.

Welcome to the best bicycling in the East! Just don't tell anybody about it. We wouldn't want the secret to get out.

Glimmerglass Opera

Baseball Hall of Fame

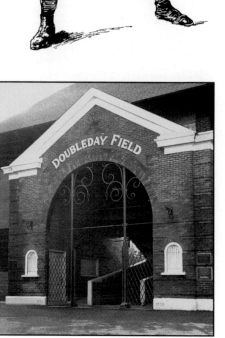

Doubleday Field

How this Book Works

This book is a bicycle guide to the scenic back roads surrounding Cooperstown, in upstate New York.

*The **fifty tours** included in this book are designed for **bicyclists of all abilities**. The rides vary from **7 to 100 miles** in length. The terrain varies from relatively flat to definitely mountainous. Each tour states the distance to be biked and rates the hills to be climbed. This makes it easy to choose a ride that's within your bicycling abilities!*

The format of the tour directions in this book is unique. Tour guides are usually **"narrative"** in format: they combine route directions with paragraphs describing local points of interest. Though this format is enjoyable and interesting, it is not user friendly; the directional information is not concise; there is no convenient way to carry the entire book on tour. Simply stated, **you can't easily bike and read at the same time!**

In contrast, organized bike tours use a **"cue sheet back-up"** format. The cue sheet offers concise, directional cues (instructions) on a single sheet of paper. It is portable and user friendly, but it provides no descriptive information about the route. The cue sheet is usually designed for "signed" routes where a cyclist follows directional arrows painted on the road. In that format, the cue sheet is used as a "back-up" to the painted arrows and does not have to be painstakingly detailed.

*This book bridges the gap between the "narrative" and "cue sheet back-up" formats by providing **greatly improved tear-out cue sheets**.* These new, improved cue sheets are sufficiently detailed for unsigned routes (no arrows painted on the road), provide at least a brief description of the area to be explored, and remain sufficiently compact and portable to be user friendly.

The organization of the tours in this book is also unique. Tour guides usually use a **"scatter"** format: single tours leave from many different starting points. The single tour option makes it difficult for cyclists of differing abilities to bike together. The scattered starts make it necessary to drive from one touring location to another.

*This book is instead organized in a **"rally"** format: rides of varying length and difficulty leave in many directions from the same starting point.* The usual rally format has been improved to provide options within options: you can frequently opt for a short, medium or longer variation of the same tour! Half of the fifty tours leave from Cooperstown. In typical rally style, the other twenty-five tours leave from "remote starts" within a 10-20 mile radius of Cooperstown. You can choose to bike or drive to a remote start. Since many of the tours interconnect, you can choose to combine a Cooperstown route with a "remote start" route. The possibilities are endless! This **improved rally format** allows you to bike for a day, week, month, or season from your "home base" in Cooperstown. It allows families, groups and clubs with members of differing abilities to bike "together." It provides a method for a novice cyclist to learn bicycle touring, and then develop the skills necessary for distance cycling.

This book has been written for your bicycling pleasure. So get on your bike and ride!

Let's Get Cranking!

Part 1: How to Bike

This primer provides you with basic bicycling instructions. With this information, you can get your bike on the road, increase your fitness level, and enjoy the longer tours included in this book.

This is a detailed instruction manual; it frequently requests your active participation.

ROAD BIKE

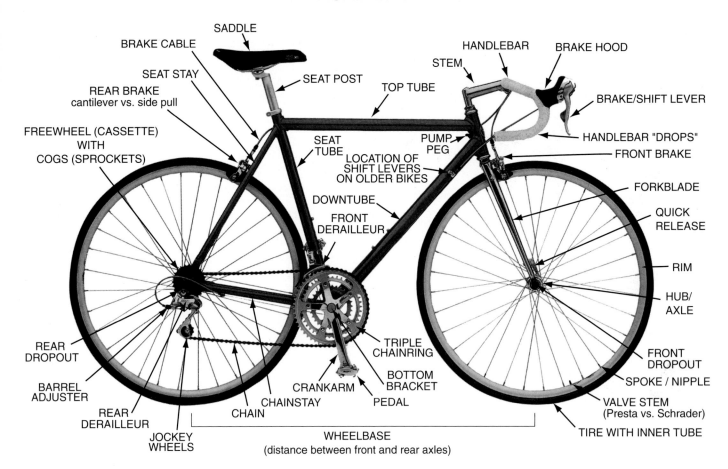

SADDLE

BRAKE CABLE

SEAT STAY

REAR BRAKE
cantilever vs. side pull

FREEWHEEL (CASSETTE)
WITH
COGS (SPROCKETS)

SEAT POST

TOP TUBE

SEAT
TUBE

LOCATION OF
SHIFT LEVERS
ON OLDER BIKES

DOWNTUBE

FRONT
DERAILLEUR

PUMP
PEG

HANDLEBAR

STEM

BRAKE HOOD

BRAKE/SHIFT LEVER

HANDLEBAR "DROPS"

FRONT BRAKE

FORKBLADE

QUICK
RELEASE

RIM

HUB/
AXLE

REAR
DROPOUT

BARREL
ADJUSTER

REAR
DERAILLEUR

JOCKEY
WHEELS

CHAIN

CHAINSTAY

CRANKARM

PEDAL

BOTTOM
BRACKET

TRIPLE
CHAINRING

FRONT
DROPOUT

SPOKE / NIPPLE

VALVE STEM
(Presta vs. Schrader)

TIRE WITH INNER TUBE

WHEELBASE
(distance between front and rear axles)

Before beginning, glance at the bicycle parts diagram above to familiarize yourself with bicycling terminology.

1. HOW TO CHOOSE THE CORRECT BICYCLE TYPE: *There are several types of bicycles. Each type is designed for a different purpose:*

• **MOUNTAIN BIKES:** *If you will be bicycling predominantly off pavement, around rocks, in mud, over the river and through the woods to Grandmother's house we go, you should choose a mountain bike. A **mountain bike** is like a **Jeep**.*

A mountain bike is constructed sturdily to survive the abuse of off-road riding. In general, this translates to a bike which is heavier than one intended for riding on pavement.

A mountain bike is designed to afford excellent traction in uneven terrain. It is equipped with wide tires from which protrude large rubber knobs to grab the soft terrain. These knobby tires are filled with very little air (40 pounds per square inch), to keep them soft, and to improve traction. The price to pay for this increased traction is increased resistance to rolling forward (**increased rolling resistance**), but this is not a significant problem at the slower speeds usually experienced with off-road travel.

FLAT
HANDLEBAR

KNOBBY TIRE

MOUNTAIN BIKE

A mountain bike is equipped with a **flat handlebar**. The flat handlebar results in a more upright riding position This upright position helps a cyclist execute the frequent fore-aft weight shifts necessary to maintain traction off-road. The upright position is not very aerodynamic; but, once again, this is not a significant problem at the slower speeds usually experienced with off-road travel.

A mountain bike has a wide range of lower (easier) gears arranged around a triple crank (three chainrings are attached to the pedals instead of two). These lower gears make it easier to climb in mountainous terrain, and to overcome the increased rolling resistance described above.

• ROAD BIKES: *If you will be bicycling predominantly on pavement, you should choose a road bike.*

Since pavement is a smooth, hard surface, a great deal of traction is not only unnecessary, it is counterproductive. For that reason, unlike a mountain bike, a road bike is designed to **minimize rolling resistance**. To that end, it weighs less and is equipped with lighter, narrower, "bald" tires, filled until they're hard with a lot of air (100 pounds per square inch).

A road bike is equipped with a **dropped handlebar**. The dropped handlebar results in a less upright riding position. Since the air trapped by a cyclist's upright body creates the greatest resistance to bicycling forward, the dropped handlebar results in a lower, aerodynamic position more efficient for the faster speeds attained on pavement. The dropped handlebar also provides more hand positions for comfort on longer rides.

There are several types of road bikes:

• *A racing bike is like a sports car*. It is designed for competition. Racing bikes are very lightweight, and are manufactured with a more upright frame geometry. This upright geometry provides a shorter front-to-back wheelbase that results in quicker, more finicky handling. Like any other thoroughbred, a racing bike wants to go fast, to corner, and to turn with little provocation. A racing bike wants to compete, and demands that you pay close attention to technique.

• *A sport-touring bike is like a sedan*. It is meant for long distance exploration in varying terrain. It is designed with lower gears, and with a more relaxed frame geometry. This relaxed geometry provides a longer front-to-back wheelbase that results in slower, more stable handling. A touring bike wants to keep tracking forward all day long, at a sufficiently fast pace, while you pay attention to the scenery.

• *A full-loaded touring bike is like a truck*. It is similar to the sport-touring model, but is designed to carry camping gear for multi-day tours.

So, which type of bike should you choose?

You should choose a bicycle designed for the type of cycling you plan to perform. The long, on-road tours described in this book are most efficiently and comfortably accomplished on a road bike equipped with gears sufficiently low (easy) for hilly terrain. If you have only a mountain bike available, decrease the rolling resistance by switching to smooth, knobby-less tires; improve the aerodynamics by lowering the handlebar (if feasible), and by installing bar-end extensions.

• **OTHER BIKES:** A **tandem bike** is a bicycle built for two. A tandem provides togetherness, even if the cyclists are of differing abilities. A **recumbent bike** is a bicycle designed so that the rider is seated, and pedals with his legs in front of him. This bike is comfortable, and is a good choice for cyclists with low back problems. A **hybrid bike** is a bicycle that combines features of both road and mountain bikes.

So, which type of bike should you choose? *You should choose a bicycle designed for the type of cycling you plan to perform. The long, on-road tours described in this book are most efficiently and comfortably accomplished on a road bike equipped with gears sufficiently low (easy) for hilly terrain. If you have only a mountain bike available, decrease the rolling resistance by switching to smooth, knobby-less tires; improve the aerodynamics by lowering the handlebar (if feasible), and by installing bar-end extensions.*

2. **HOW TO CHOOSE THE CORRECT BICYCLE SIZE:** *Choosing a properly sized bicycle frame is necessary for comfortable and efficient cycling.* Only on a properly sized frame will you be able to position your body for maximum ergonomic performance. Choosing a frame that is too small, or that you can "grow into," is uncomfortable and dangerous.

INSEAM MEASUREMENT

The frame's size is the length of its seat tube, measured from the center of the bottom bracket to the center of the top tube (assuming the top tube is horizontal). To determine your proper frame size, first obtain an accurate inseam measurement: On a hard floor (no carpet), stand with your back against a wall, in your bare feet, with your legs spread 6 inches apart. Wedge a book *firmly* up between your legs to simulate a saddle. Have a friend measure the distance from the top of the book to the floor in inches or centimeters (2.54 cm to the inch). Repeat the procedure a few times for accuracy. This is your inseam length. **Multiply your inseam length by .65 for a road bike, or by .52 for a mountain bike. This is the seat tube length which is your frame size.** Non-custom frames usually come in 19-25 inch sizes (48-63 centimeters). As a rule of thumb, a properly sized frame should allow 1 inch of crotch clearance when you stand over your road bike in shoes, and 3-4 inches of crotch clearance when you stand over your mountain bike in shoes.

3. **HOW TO FIND THE CORRECT BICYCLE POSITION:** *The manner in which you position your body on the bike is crucial for comfortable and efficient cycling. Your body is attached to the bike in three critical locations: the pedals, the saddle, and the handlebars. Minor adjustments at these three attachments can result in major ergonomic changes.*

• **THE PEDALS:** *Your foot should be firmly **attached** to the pedal, and **positioned** so that the ball of your foot is directly over the pedal axle.* This attaching and positioning can be accomplished with the use of toeclips and straps. The appropriately sized toeclip will place your foot in the proper fore-aft position, and the strap will keep it there. This attaching and positioning can also be accomplished with the use of a cleated bicycling shoe with a step-in binding. With this system, a cleat attached to the sole of a special shoe is positioned accurately beneath the ball of your foot. The cleat allows you to "click" into and out of a special "clipless" pedal much as you would step into and out of a ski binding. Cleats designed for racing bikes usually protrude from the sole, making it difficult to walk. Cleats designed for mountain bikes are usually recessed, making it easy to walk. For bicycle touring, recessed cleats are recommended. The clipless pedal system is preferable to the toeclip pedal system because it is more comfortable and efficient. The clipless system is also preferable because the cleat can be adjusted for foot rotation. This rotational adjustability properly aligns the lower leg during pedaling, and allows "float" to prevent knee pain. The clipless system is, however, more expensive than the toeclip system. Both systems position your foot properly on the pedals, and attach your foot firmly to the pedals. Attaching your foot to the pedals is necessary for efficient "spinning" which will be discussed later.

Riding a properly sized bicycle in the correct position makes all the difference.

- **THE SADDLE:** *Your saddle must be adjusted in four directions:*

    RIGHT-LEFT: *Your saddle should be directed straight forward*, pointing neither to the right nor left.

    TILT: *The front of your saddle should be horizontal, or tilted slightly upwards.* Slightly upwards prevents you from sliding forward off the saddle, but may result in a temporarily numb genital region. In this regard, millimeters matter. The front of the saddle should not tilt down. The tilted down position shifts your weight forward over the handlebars resulting in poor bike handling, and in sore neck, shoulder, arm, and hand muscles.

    HEIGHT: *The height of your saddle above the pedals determines your leg extension.* When your saddle is at the proper height, your knee should be slightly bent at the bottom of the pedal stroke (when the pedal is at 5 o'clock); and your hips should not rock up and down on the saddle, when you are viewed from behind as you pedal. **The saddle height, measured from the center of the pedal axle to the center of the depression in your saddle, should equal your inseam measurement multiplied by .885.**

    FORE-AFT: *The fore-aft position of your saddle determines the placement of your leg muscles over the pedals for maximum power and efficiency.* Note that because the seat tube is not vertical, each adjustment of seat height also changes fore-aft position; whenever you adjust one, you must adjust the other. **With your bike on a level surface, and with your foot on the ped-**

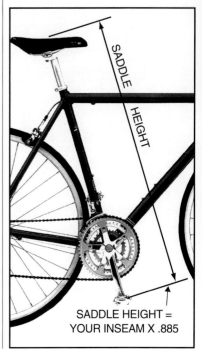

SADDLE HEIGHT =
YOUR INSEAM X .885

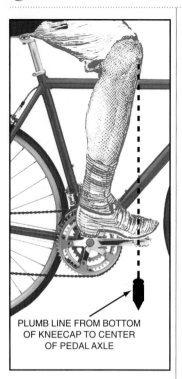

PLUMB LINE FROM BOTTOM
OF KNEECAP TO CENTER
OF PEDAL AXLE

als in a horizontal position, a plumb line dropped from the bony prominence (tibial tuberosity) below the bottom of your kneecap should bisect the pedal axle.

- **THE HANDLEBAR:** *Your handlebar must be adjusted in three ways:*
  - **HANDLEBAR REACH:** *The distance from the front of the saddle to the handlebar is the handlebar reach.* The proper handlebar reach defines the length of your "cockpit" (driving space) and ensures proper fore-aft weight distribution. If the handlebar reach is too short, your cockpit will be uncomfortably cramped, resulting in dangerous elbow-knee overlap while pedaling and turning. If the handlebar reach is too long, your cockpit will be uncomfortably stretched out, resulting in poor front wheel handling. The handlebar reach is determined by the length of the top tube on your properly sized frame, plus the length of your handlebar stem. Since the top tube length can't be changed, the only way to adjust handlebar reach is to install a different stem. Your proper handlebar reach can best be measured in a bike shop, but a rule of thumb will tell you if you are in the right ballpark: **When you are biking with your hands on the brake hoods, the handlebar should obscure your vision of the front wheel axle**.
  - **HANDLEBAR HEIGHT:** *Your dropped handlebar should be the same height as, or 1-2 inches lower than, your saddle* for aerodynamics.
  - **HANDLEBAR ROTATION:** *Rotate your dropped handlebar so that the ends are either parallel to the ground* or pointing down no more than 10 degrees.

4. **HOW TO PEDAL AND SHIFT GEARS: WARNING:** *This section may make your head spin as well as your pedals. Put your brain in gear now, so you can put your bike in gear later. This section is easier to understand if you study your bike as you read the following:*

- **PEDALING:** *If your feet are not firmly attached to the pedals, you can only move your bike forward by pushing down from 2-5 o'clock on the pedaling circle. This is very inefficient*: it uses only one leg muscle group for a short period of time; it wastes the opportunity to use other leg muscle groups during the remainder of the pedaling circle.

  If, on the other hand, your feet are firmly attached to the pedals, with either toeclips or the clipless pedals discussed above, you can move your bike forward using the entire pedaling circle. This is very efficient: it uses different leg muscle groups sequentially to push down, pull back, pull up, and push forward on the pedals. This very efficient technique, called "**spinning**," is the basis for efficient cycling. You can get a good feel for the sequential muscle actions involved in spinning, if you practice pedaling with only

SPINNING IN CIRCLES
PUSH DOWN,
PULL BACK,
PULL UP,
AND PUSH FORWARD
ON THE PEDALS.

one foot attached to a pedal (in a safe location). Hint: As you finish pushing down on the pedal, imagine scraping mud off the bottom of your shoe to initiate the pulling-back motion.

The speed at which you spin your pedals is called **cadence**. You pedal most efficiently when you maintain a relatively fast cadence. A cadence of 60 revolutions per minute (rpm) is too slow for efficient cycling; 80-90 rpm is efficient; 100 rpm is racing; 120 rpm is sprinting. Calculate your cadence by counting how often one foot reaches the top of a pedal stroke in ten seconds and multiplying by 6. With practice, spinning at an efficient cadence is easy to accomplish, as long as there is little resistance against the pedals. The resistance against the pedals is adjusted by shifting gears. *Simply stated,* **you shift gears to maintain an efficient cadence.**

"Cadence" is pedaling rpm.

- **Gears:** *Now that you know proper pedaling technique, you must learn about* **gears** *before you can understand shifting.*

Attached to your bike's right pedal are two or three chainrings, each of which has a certain number of teeth. Attached to your bike's right rear hub is a freewheel (also called a cassette), consisting of 6-9 cogs (also called sprockets); each of the cogs contains a certain number of teeth. The front chainrings are connected to the rear cogs by your bike's chain. You can move the chain from one front chainring to another by using your left shift lever, which moves the front derailleur (pronounced dee-rail- er). You can move the chain from one rear cog to another by using your right shift lever, which moves the rear derailleur. Remember "right-rear" as a mnemonic.

Your gears... they're not as complicated as you think.

Each combination of one chainring with one cog is called a gear. In the past these gears were erroneously called "speeds"; if you had two front chainrings and five rear cogs you had a "10 speed" bike. In truth, your bike has only one speed: the speed that you provide as the "motor." Modern bicycles have 2-3 front chainrings which can combine with 6-9 rear cogs to produce 12-27 "speeds", or gears!

What does each gear indicate? If a front chainring has 50 teeth, and a rear cog also has 50 teeth, the rear wheel rotates one full revolution for each pedal revolution. This 1:1 ratio propels the bicycle forward a distance equal to one circumference of its wheel.

If a front chainring has 50 teeth, but a rear cog is much smaller with only 25 teeth, the rear wheel rotates two full revolutions for each single pedal revolution. This 2:1 ratio is a "higher" gear which propels the bicycle forward a distance equal to twice the circumference of its wheel. The higher ratio demands that you push much harder on the pedals at a slower cadence, but it propels your bike forward twice as far. Remember "high-hard" as a mnemonic.

If a front chainring has 50 teeth, but a rear cog is much larger with 100 teeth, the rear wheel rotates only 1/2 revolution

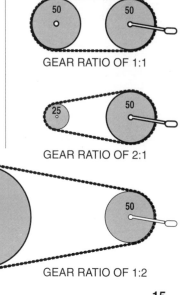

GEAR RATIO OF 1:1

GEAR RATIO OF 2:1

GEAR RATIO OF 1:2

for each single pedal revolution. This 1:2 ratio is a "lower" gear which propels the bicycle forward a distance equal to only 1/2 the circumference of its wheel. The lower ratio allows very easy pedaling at a faster cadence, but it propels your bike forward only 1/2 as far.

Note the relationship between cadence, pedaling effort, and distance traveled forward:

• If you are bicycling on flat terrain in an inappropriately high (hard) gear, your pedals will be moving inappropriately slow. You will exhaust yourself pushing the pedals against excessive resistance.

• If you are bicycling on flat terrain in an inappropriately low (easy) gear, your pedals will be spinning inappropriately fast. You will exhaust yourself spinning the pedals fast against almost no resistance. You will be moving forward at an inappropriately slow speed, wasting energy and getting nowhere fast.

• If, on the other hand, you are bicycling on flat terrain in just the right gear, your pedals will be spinning at just the right speed. You will be pedaling against just the right resistance. You will be propelling your bike forward most efficiently, for the longest period of time, at the best speed which can be maintained without tiring prematurely.

• If, while you are in just the right gear for flat terrain, a headwind or hill arrives to oppose your forward motion (and, in so doing, increases the resistance against your pedals), shift to a lower (easier) gear to maintain the same cadence.

• If, on the other hand, a tailwind or descent arrives to assist your forward motion (and, in so doing, eases the resistance against your pedals), shift to a higher (harder) gear to maintain the same cadence.

It is obvious from these examples that constantly finding the right gear provides the mechanical advantage that is crucial for efficient cycling. **But how can you tell one gear from another?** We've already learned that the ratio of the number of teeth on a front chainring, to the number of teeth on a rear cog, defines a particular gear. So a particular gear can be named by its ratio (for example 2:1), or by the front-back teeth combination (for example, 42 x 19). Most commonly, however, a gear is named by its "gear-inch." **A gear-inch is the ratio of the number of teeth on the front chainring, to the number of teeth on a rear cog, multiplied by the diameter of the wheel:**

$$\frac{\text{FRONT CHAINRING TEETH}}{\text{REAR COG TEETH}} \times \text{WHEEL DIAMETER} = \text{GEAR-INCH}$$

The term "gear-inch" is a historic throwback to the days when high-wheeled bicycles were purchased according to leg length (wheel diameter). Note that the gear-inch number multiplied by pi (3.14) equals the distance (in inches) your bike travels forward with each pedal revolution in that gear.

Example:
$$\frac{42}{19} \times 27 = 59.7 \text{ GEAR-INCHES}$$
(ROUND UP TO 60)

Now, use gear-inches to name and to diagram all the gears on a fictional bike. Assume that your fictional bike has two front chainrings; the inner chainring has 42 teeth and the outer chainring has 53 teeth. Assume that your fictional bike has 8 rear cogs, with 12, 13, 15, 17, 19, 21, 23, and 25 teeth respectively. Assume that your fictional bike is a road bike, with standard 27 inch diameter wheels; as opposed to a mountain bike, with standard 26 inch diameter wheels.

Now, make a diagram of your fictional bike's gears. Let the columns in the diagram represent the front chainrings, with the inner chainring heading the left column, and the outer chainring heading the right column. Let the rows in the diagram represent the rear cogs, with the smaller, outer cogs heading the top rows, and the larger, inner cogs heading the bottom rows. Next, fill in the gear-inch blanks. So that you don't have to do the math, refer to the convenient gear-inch charts on the next page. Make sure you use the gear-inch chart for 27 inch diameter, road bike wheels, and not the gear-inch chart for 26 inch, mountain bike wheels.

Now that your diagram is complete, and you've named all the gears on your fictional bike, make the following observations:

• Note that you shift (left-right) from one chainring *column* to another using your **front derailleur (left shift lever)**. The right, larger chainring column indicates higher gears; the left, smaller chainring column indicates lower gears.

• Note that you shift (top-bottom) from one cog *row* to another using your **rear derailleur (right shift lever)**. The upper rows indicate the smaller, outer, higher-gear cogs; the lower rows indicate the larger, inner, lower-gear cogs. Don't be confused by the fact that you shift *up* to *higher*, harder, "bigger" gears using *smaller* rear cogs; and that you shift *down* to *lower,* easier, "smaller" gears using *larger* rear cogs.

• Note that you **"double shift"** to move from 60 to 68. You first shift "up" from the small to the large chainring, using the left shift lever (front derailleur). You then shift "down" from the 19 to the 21 rear cog, using the right shift lever (rear derailleur).

• Note that the combination of the larger 53-tooth front chainring, and the smallest 12-tooth rear cog, results in the highest, hardest gear of 119 gear-inches. This is an adequate **high gear**, even for pedaling actively downhill.

• Note that the combination of the smaller 42-tooth front chainring, and the largest 25-tooth rear cog, results in the lowest, easiest gear of 45 gear-inches. This is an appropriately **low gear** for rolling terrain, but would not be adequately low for climbing in mountainous terrain. A lower gear could be created by changing to a front chainring with fewer than 42 teeth, by changing to a rear cog with more than 25 teeth, or by changing both (as long as

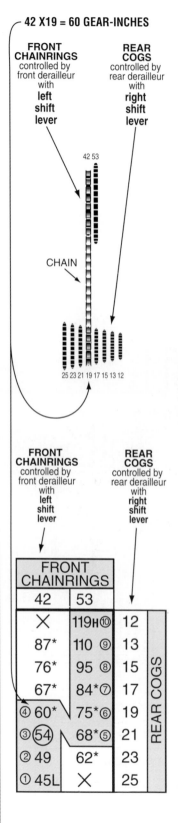

42 X19 = 60 GEAR-INCHES

| FRONT CHAINRINGS controlled by front derailleur with **left shift lever** | | | REAR COGS controlled by rear derailleur with **right shift lever** |

CHAIN

25 23 21 19 17 15 13 12

| FRONT CHAINRINGS controlled by front derailleur with **left shift lever** | | | REAR COGS controlled by rear derailleur with **right shift lever** |

FRONT CHAINRINGS		REAR COGS
42	53	
✕	119H⑩	12
87*	110 ⑨	13
76*	95 ⑧	15
67*	84*⑦	17
④ 60*	75*⑥	19
③㊿54	68*⑤	21
② 49	62*	23
① 45L	✕	25

GEAR-INCH CHART FOR 27-INCH WHEELS

Number of Teeth on Chainring

Number of Teeth on Cog	24	26	28	29	30	31	32	33	34	35	36	37	38	39	40	41	42	43	44	45	46	47	48	49	50	51	52	53	54
11	59	64	69	71	74	76	79	81	83	86	88	91	93	96	98	101	103	106	108	110	113	115	118	120	123	125	128	130	133
12	54	59	63	65	68	70	72	74	77	79	81	83	86	88	90	92	95	97	99	101	104	106	108	110	113	115	117	119	122
13	50	54	58	60	62	64	66	69	71	73	75	77	79	81	83	85	87	89	91	93	96	98	100	102	104	106	108	110	112
14	46	50	54	56	58	60	62	64	66	68	69	71	73	75	77	79	81	83	85	87	89	91	93	95	96	98	100	102	104
15	43	47	50	52	54	56	58	59	61	63	65	67	68	70	72	74	76	77	79	81	83	85	86	88	90	92	94	95	97
16	41	44	47	49	51	52	54	56	57	59	61	62	64	66	68	69	71	73	74	76	78	79	81	83	84	86	88	89	91
17	38	41	44	46	48	49	51	52	54	56	57	59	60	62	64	65	67	68	70	71	73	75	76	78	79	81	83	84	86
18	36	39	42	44	45	47	48	50	51	53	54	56	57	59	60	62	63	65	66	68	69	71	72	74	75	77	78	80	81
19	34	37	40	41	43	44	45	47	48	50	51	53	54	55	57	58	60	61	63	64	65	67	68	70	71	72	74	75	77
20	32	35	38	39	41	42	43	45	46	47	49	50	51	53	54	55	57	58	59	61	62	63	65	66	68	69	70	72	73
21	31	33	36	37	39	40	41	42	44	45	46	48	49	50	51	53	54	55	57	58	59	60	62	63	64	66	67	68	69
22	29	32	34	36	37	38	39	41	42	43	44	45	47	48	49	50	52	53	54	55	56	58	59	60	61	63	64	65	66
23	28	31	33	34	35	36	38	39	40	41	42	43	45	46	47	48	49	50	52	53	54	55	56	58	59	60	61	62	63
24	27	29	32	33	34	35	36	37	38	39	41	42	43	44	45	46	47	48	50	51	52	53	54	55	56	57	59	60	61
25	26	28	30	31	32	33	35	36	37	38	39	40	41	42	43	44	45	46	48	49	50	51	52	53	54	55	56	57	58
26	25	27	29	30	31	32	33	34	35	36	37	38	39	41	42	43	44	45	46	47	48	49	50	51	52	53	54	55	56
27	24	26	28	29	30	31	32	33	34	35	36	37	38	39	40	41	42	43	44	45	46	47	48	49	50	51	52	53	54
28	23	25	27	28	29	30	31	32	33	34	35	36	37	38	39	40	41	41	42	43	44	45	46	47	48	49	50	51	52
29	22	24	26	27	28	29	30	31	32	33	34	34	35	36	37	38	39	40	41	42	43	44	45	46	47	47	48	49	50
30	22	23	25	26	27	28	29	30	31	32	32	33	34	35	36	37	38	39	40	41	41	42	43	44	45	46	47	48	49
31	21	23	24	25	26	27	28	29	30	30	31	32	33	34	35	36	37	37	38	39	40	41	42	43	44	44	45	46	47
32	20	22	24	24	25	26	27	28	29	30	30	31	32	33	34	35	35	36	37	38	39	40	41	41	42	43	44	45	46
33	20	21	23	24	25	25	26	27	28	29	29	30	31	32	33	34	34	35	36	37	38	38	39	40	41	42	43	43	44
34	19	21	22	23	24	25	25	26	27	28	29	29	30	31	32	33	33	34	35	36	37	37	38	39	40	41	41	42	43

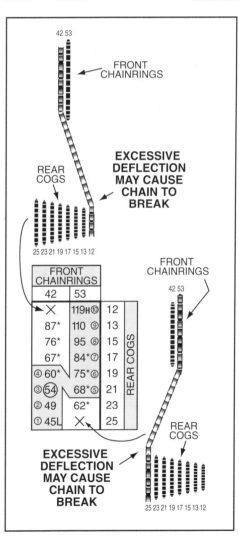

the derailleur's "capacity" for shifting to these gears is not exceeded). For mountainous terrain, including many of the tours in this book, a lower "granny gear" approaching 20 gear-inches is recommended.

• Note that gears 42 x 12 and 53 x 25 are crossed out. They represent combinations of front chainring and rear cog that bend the chain so much it might break. These **"cross-chain" gears** should not be used because they cause excessive **chain deflection**.

• Note that gears within 3 gear-inches of one another are starred. They are similar enough to be considered **duplications**. Use one or the other, but not both, when you determine a shifting sequence.

• Note that, of the 16 available gears, 2 must be ignored because of excessive chain deflection, and 4 pairs represent duplications, leaving only 10 usable gears!

• Note that 54 is circled. The circle indicates that 54 is an appropriately easy gear to use when you start moving your bike forward. Any gear in the 50-70 gear-inch range is an appropriate **"start-up" gear.**

• Note the **shifting sequence** outlined in the diagram. The goal is to shift from the lowest gear, to the highest gear, in a simple sequence which avoids chain deflection, avoids duplications, minimizes double shifting, and utilizes appropriate gear-inch differences. Gears differing from 4-8 gear-inches are called **"half-step" shifts**; they are preferable. Gears differing from 9-14 gear-

GEAR-INCH CHART FOR 26-INCH WHEELS

Number of Teeth on Cog	Number of Teeth on Chainring																													
	24	26	28	29	30	31	32	33	34	35	36	37	38	39	40	41	42	43	44	45	46	47	48	49	50	51	52	53	54
11	57	61	66	69	71	73	76	78	80	83	85	87	90	92	95	97	99	102	104	106	109	111	113	116	118	121	123	125	128
12	52	56	61	63	65	67	69	72	74	76	78	80	82	85	87	89	91	93	95	98	100	102	104	106	108	111	113	115	117
13	48	52	56	58	60	62	64	66	68	70	72	74	76	78	80	82	84	86	88	90	92	94	96	98	100	102	104	106	108
14	45	48	52	54	56	58	59	61	63	65	67	69	71	72	74	76	78	80	82	84	85	87	89	91	93	95	97	98	100
15	42	45	49	50	52	54	55	57	59	61	62	64	66	68	69	71	73	75	76	78	80	81	83	85	87	88	90	92	94
16	39	42	46	47	49	50	52	54	55	57	59	60	62	63	65	67	68	70	72	73	75	76	78	80	81	83	85	86	88
17	37	40	43	44	46	47	49	50	52	54	55	57	58	60	61	63	64	66	67	69	70	72	73	75	76	78	80	81	83
18	35	38	40	42	43	45	46	48	49	51	52	53	55	56	58	59	61	62	64	65	66	68	69	71	72	74	75	77	78
19	33	36	38	40	41	42	44	45	47	48	49	51	52	53	55	56	57	59	60	62	63	64	66	67	68	70	71	73	74
20	31	34	36	38	39	40	42	43	44	46	47	48	49	51	52	53	55	56	57	59	60	61	62	64	65	66	68	69	70
21	30	32	35	36	37	38	40	41	42	43	45	46	47	48	50	51	52	53	54	56	57	58	59	61	62	63	64	66	67
22	28	31	33	34	35	37	38	39	40	41	43	44	45	46	47	48	50	51	52	53	54	56	57	58	59	60	61	63	64
23	27	29	32	33	34	35	36	37	38	40	41	42	43	44	45	46	47	49	50	51	52	53	54	55	57	58	59	60	61
24	26	28	30	31	33	34	35	36	37	38	39	40	41	42	43	44	46	47	48	49	50	51	52	53	54	55	56	57	59
25	25	27	29	30	31	32	33	34	35	36	37	38	40	41	42	43	44	45	46	47	48	49	50	51	52	53	54	55	56
26	24	26	28	29	30	31	32	33	34	35	36	37	38	39	40	41	42	43	44	45	46	47	48	49	50	51	52	53	54
27	23	25	27	28	29	30	31	32	33	34	35	36	37	38	39	39	40	41	42	43	44	45	46	47	48	49	50	51	52
28	22	24	26	27	28	29	30	31	32	33	33	34	35	36	37	38	39	40	41	42	43	44	45	46	46	47	48	49	50
29	22	23	25	26	27	28	29	30	30	31	32	33	34	35	36	37	38	39	39	40	41	42	43	44	45	46	47	48	48
30	21	23	24	25	26	27	28	29	29	30	31	32	33	34	35	36	36	37	38	39	40	41	42	42	43	44	45	46	47
31	20	22	23	24	25	26	27	28	29	29	30	31	32	33	34	34	35	36	37	38	39	39	40	41	42	43	44	44	45
32	20	21	23	24	24	25	26	27	28	28	29	30	31	32	33	33	34	35	36	37	37	38	39	40	41	41	42	43	44
33	19	20	22	23	24	24	25	26	27	28	28	29	30	31	32	32	33	34	35	35	36	37	38	39	39	40	41	42	43
34	18	20	21	22	23	24	24	25	26	27	28	28	29	30	31	31	32	33	34	34	35	36	37	37	38	39	40	41	41

inches are called **"full-step" shifts**; they remain acceptable. Gears differing more than 15 gear-inches should be avoided. Note that alternative shifting sequences could have been chosen.

Now, it's time for you to make a gear-inch diagram for your own bike. Go to your bike and count the teeth on each front chainring. Then, count the teeth on each rear cog. Fill in these numbers on a blank gear-inch diagram. Use the two-column blank diagram if you have 2 chainrings, and the three-column blank diagram if you have 3 chainrings. Fill in the rest of the blanks by consulting the appropriate gear-inch chart. Make sure you use the gear-inch chart for 27 inch wheels if you have a road bike and the gear-inch chart for 26 inch wheels if you have a mountain bike. Do the following with your completed diagram:

- Note your unusable "cross-chain" gears.
- Label your highest and lowest gears with a "H" or "L".
- Choose and circle a start-up gear in the 50-70 range.
- Put a star next to duplicated gears with a 0-3 gear-inch difference.
- Devise a low-to-high shifting sequence for your bike. Remember that the goal is to shift from the lowest gear, to the highest gear, in a simple sequence which avoids chain deflection, avoids duplications, minimizes double shifting, and utilizes appropriate gear-inch differences (preferably 4-8 or 9-14).
- Tape a copy of your diagram to your handlebar. Use it until shifting becomes second nature. Then forget it!

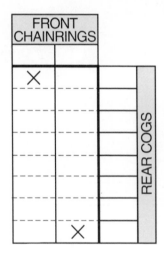

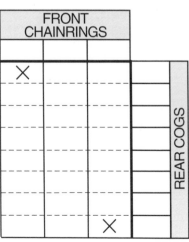

5. How to Ride Your Bike: Let's get out of the classroom and onto the bike! This section will discuss basic bicycling techniques. Since this is a bicycle touring book, the discussion will be geared (no pun intended) to road bikes, riding on pavement, in non-racing situations. Find an empty parking lot, or a deserted back road, where you can safely practice each technique. Let your body feel what the text is trying to teach. Learn by doing. Alternate performing a technique correctly, and then incorrectly, to feel the difference. Realize that once you understand a skill, you have to perform it repetitively until it becomes second nature, and until your muscle groups develop enough to respond comfortably and efficiently. Let's get cranking!

Before mounting your bike, put on your helmet! Then glance down at your chain's position on the front chainrings and rear cogs to confirm that you are in a properly low gear for starting (refer to your gear sequence chart). Throw your dominant leg over the saddle, and straddle the top tube. Secure your dominant foot in its toeclip or clipless pedal. Lift that secured foot counterclockwise up to the 2 o'clock position on the pedaling circle. Glance over your left shoulder to assess traffic. Push off with your grounded foot, while simultaneously pushing down with your secured foot to initiate a coast. While coasting, secure your remaining foot in its pedal, and then start pedaling. You may wish to assist acceleration by standing and pushing harder on the pedals for a few strokes until you feel little resistance against the pedals. Then be seated, and shift appropriately to maintain the proper cadence of 80-90 revolutions per minute against acceptable resistance. To maintain that comfortable cadence, shift frequently every time you feel more or less resistance against your pedals caused by shifts of wind or changes in terrain. It is more efficient to pedal continuously at the proper cadence in the proper gear, than to pedal and coast alternately. Bike a straight and predictable line.

*Rest your **hands** gently on the handlebar.* Don't grip it tightly. White knuckles will only tire your neck, shoulder and arm muscles. For comfortable cruising, ride with your hands on the top of your dropped handlebar, or on the brake hoods. Change your hand position frequently for comfort. Don't cock your wrists excessively for long periods of time. Move down to the bottom portion of your handlebar, the "drops", for improved aerodynamics while descending, or while fighting a headwind.

*Keep your **elbows** bent.* Locked elbows transfer your weight from the saddle, where it belongs, to the front end of the bike. Weighting the front end of the bike adversely affects steering, and results in tired neck, shoulder and arm muscles. Experiment with purposely locking your elbows, and pushing down on the handlebars. Now suddenly "unweight" the handlebar, and bend your elbows. Note how your weight is immediately transferred from your arms to your saddle. Note how your abdominal,

Put on Your Helmet!

Relax Your Hands

Bend Your Elbows

back, and buttock muscles are suddenly engaged. These muscle groups, in addition to your leg muscles, must be strengthened for comfortable and efficient cycling. Keep your elbows and knees in, towards your body, to improve aerodynamics. Your upper body is most aerodynamic when your hands are on the handlebar drops, and when your elbows are in and bent, so that your forearms are parallel to the ground.

*Keep your **neck** up*, so you can look forward down the road, and not down at your front wheel. Exercise your neck muscles frequently, in all directions, to prevent tiring.

*Keep your **back** flat.*

*Keep your **upper body** still and relaxed, without bobbing or rocking.* When viewed from behind, your legs should be a blur, but your upper body should be motionless.

*Constantly **adjust your buttocks in 3 directions** (butt in-out, butt front-back and butt right-left)*. Adjusting your butt steers your bike, and uses your cycling muscles more efficiently. Begin with your butt in a neutral position in the middle of your properly positioned saddle. In this neutral position, the quadriceps muscles in the front of your thighs, and the hamstring muscles in the back of your thighs, are being used equally.

*First let's experiment with **pelvic position**:* Without moving your butt from its neutral position on the saddle, thrust and rotate your pelvis forward toward your navel (bring your butt in). Note that with this simple maneuver you predominantly pull up on the pedals, using your hamstrings more than your quadriceps. Now rotate your pelvis back away from your navel (stick your butt out). Note that with this simple maneuver you predominantly push down on the pedals, using your quadriceps more than your hamstrings. Now return to the neutral pelvic position, and note the return to equal use of these muscle groups. **It's easy to accentuate or rest different muscle groups just by changing your pelvic rotation.**

*Next let's experiment with **fore-aft buttock position**:* From its neutral position in the center of your saddle, slide your butt to the front tip of the saddle. Note that with this simple maneuver you predominantly push down on the pedals. Now slide your butt to the back of your saddle. Note that with this simple maneuver you predominantly pull up and push forward on the pedals. **It's easy to accentuate or rest different muscle groups just by changing your fore-aft buttock position on the saddle.** Learn to use varying combinations of pelvic rotation and buttock seat position to use your leg muscles more powerfully and efficiently.

*Finally, let's experiment with **right-left buttock position**. Contrary to popular opinion, you don't **steer** your bike predominantly by turning the handlebar; you steer it predominantly by making the bike lean right or left. Bike lean is accomplished by **shifting your butt weight** to the right or to the left.* Without moving your butt from its neutral position, shift your weight onto your

Keep Your Neck Up

Keep Your Torso Still

Keep Your Back Flat

Adjust Your Butt

right buttock. Note that your bike leans and veers to the right, even though your handlebar remains straight. Now shift your weight onto your left buttock. Note that your bike leans and veers to the left, even though your handlebar remains straight. Practice quickly alternating right-left weight shifts. Note that you continue forward on a relatively straight course, even though your bike is rocking back and forth beneath you. Paradoxically, it is with constant, small weight adjustments, that you maintain a predictable, straight line course without weaving. Experienced cyclists ride "no hands" in this manner. As you practice quickly leaning the bike right and left, practice shifting your upper body so that it remains upright and vertical, as the bike rocks back and forth beneath you.

Shift Your Weight

You can also **shift your weight by pointing your knee.** While coasting, lift your right pedal to 12 o'clock, and point your right knee out away from the bike; watch your bike lean and veer to the right. While coasting, lift your left pedal to 12 o'clock, and point your left knee out away from the bike; watch your bike lean and veer to the left.

You can also **shift your weight by pushing down on the right or left side of your handlebar** *with your hands.* Push down persistently on the right side of your handlebar with your right hand. Note that your bike once again leans and veers to the right, even though your handlebar remains straight. Push down persistently on the left side of your handlebar with your left hand. Note that your bike leans and veers to the left, even though your handlebar remains straight.

Experiment with the following: While pedaling, push down on your right handlebar until the bike leans right. Then suddenly remove your weight from the **right** handlebar, keep pedaling, and watch your bike lean and veer paradoxically to the **left**! Emphasize this paradoxical turn by doing the following: While pedaling, push down on the **right** handlebar until the bike leans right. Then suddenly unweight the right handlebar while simultaneously pushing down on the **left** handlebar and watch your bike dive into a dramatic left turn. Repeat these two maneuvers, this time starting with your left handlebar. *Note that a quick turn in one direction precedes and emphasizes a turn in the opposite direction! This phenomenon is called* **countersteering**. When you quickly release a lean, your bike suddenly returns to vertical; its momentum carries it beyond vertical to a new more dramatic lean in the opposite direction. Satisfy yourself that this is true. Practice initiating both right and left turns by countersteering. Countersteering becomes even more important at higher speeds, especially when descending around sharp curves.

Practice

Use all of the above skills (shifting weight with the buttocks, knees, hands; and countersteering) to practice the following :
- Bike a narrow, straight, predictable line.

- Wobble your front wheel **quickly to dodge a stone** in your path.
- Place cones or rocks in a straight line. Practice **cutting in and out** around them slalom-style. Practice at slow speed with the cones close together. Practice at faster speeds with the cones farther apart.
- Practice **biking in circles**. Circle clockwise, then counterclockwise. Practice changing from clockwise, to counterclockwise, and vice versa. Circle fast; circle slow. Circle seated; circle standing. Circle with a large radius, then adjust to a smaller radius. Circle pedaling, and circle coasting. When you circle coasting, lift your inside pedal to 12 o'clock, point your knee to the center of the circle, keep your upper body vertical, and weight your outside pedal for stability.
- Finally, try **braking while you are in a circle**. First brake gently. Then brake emphatically. Note that you suddenly lose control of your turn. When you brake while in a turn, your bike immediately comes out of its lean and starts tracking straight ahead at a tangent to your original circle. You end up off the side of the road, instead of around the corner as intended. Learn to *brake to a comfortably slower speed* **before you enter a turn**.

Brake

Let's discuss **braking**. Remember that the right brake lever controls the rear brake (right-rear mnemonic), and that the left brake lever controls the front brake.

The more your weight is distributed over a wheel, the more that wheel can be braked. When you are not braking, 60-70% of your weight is over the rear wheel. When you are braking, momentum transfers most of your weight to the front wheel. *Since* **the weighted wheel stops better**, *your front brake is the more effective brake.*

If you emphatically apply only your rear (right) brake, momentum transfers most of your weight to your front wheel. This leaves only 20% of your weight on the rear wheel, decreasing traction and resulting in poor stopping power. The unweighted rear wheel will not stop you; it will lock and skid out of control.

If you emphatically apply only your front (left) brake, momentum will once again transfer your weight to the front wheel. If you brake too hard, you will lock up the front wheel. Since a locked wheel cannot be steered, you will once again lose control of the bike. In addition, the unweighted rear wheel may lift off the ground and flip you over the handlebars.

For a safe and controlled stop you must **apply both brakes at the same time.** Since, during braking, most of your weight is transferred to the front of the bike (making the front brake more effective), *it is appropriate to* **apply the front brake twice as hard as the rear brake.**

Practice coming to a slow, controlled stop as you would at a stop sign. Squeeze both brake levers simultaneously, front more than rear. "Feather" the brakes, applying gentle but progressive pressure with one or two fingers, until you come to a smooth stop. Remember, while stopping, that you must shift down to a lower, easier gear to get started again more easily. Remember that you must loosen one toestrap while coasting to a stop, so you can disengage that foot when you do stop.

Practice "panic" stops by sliding to the back of the saddle and applying sudden, emphatic braking power without locking the rear wheel or skidding. If your unweighted rear wheel does lose traction and starts to skid, return some weight to the *rear* wheel by applying less pressure on the *front* brake.

Descend

*Now, let's **descend**.* Practice braking to control your speed on a long, straight descent. Both braking and descending transfer your weight to the front wheel. This forward weight shift can be counterbalanced by sliding your butt to the rear of the saddle. Learn to brake intermittently on long descents. With constant braking, the brakepad friction on the rim causes excessive heat. This heat can expand the air in your tires and cause a blowout. Brake briefly, but emphatically, with both brakes to control speed; then coast until you need to slow down again. On very steep descents, when constant braking is necessary, smoothly alternate between front and rear brake, to minimize brake pad friction. Control your descending speed by making your position less aerodynamic; sit upright with your hands on the brake hoods.

Practice descending around sharp turns. Remember to brake to a comfortable speed before the turn. Then, coast through the turn with your inside pedal at 12 o'clock, your outside pedal weighted at 6 o'clock, your knee pointed to the center of the turn, and your upper body vertical over the bike.

You can minimize bike lean and "straighten the corner" by following an outside/inside/outside line. Start a left-hand turn at the right side of the road; aim for the centerline of the road at the apex of the turn (if traffic allows); then exit the turn aiming once again for the right side of the road. Start a right-hand turn at the centerline of the road (if traffic allows); aim for the right side of the road at the apex of the turn; then exit the turn aiming once again for the centerline.

Practice coasting on a moderate descent. Keep your pedals horizontal, tuck your upper body down toward the handlebar in an aerodynamic position, and push your knees against the top tube for stability. Control your speed by raising your body up into a less aerodynamic position and by braking as discussed above.

Climb

*Next, let's **climb**.* If you are new to cycling, gradually increase the miles you bike on flat and rolling terrain for 4-6 weeks to strengthen cycling muscles and to gain endurance. Then, start to train on progressively steeper and longer climbs.

As you approach a hill, anticipate the increased resistance against your pedals, and *shift down to an easier gear just before you start to climb.* Continue to shift down progressively, as necessary, to maintain a comfortable cadence around 70. Hope that you run out of hill before you run out of low gears. If, after an appropriate training and leg strengthening period, you find that your bike's low gear is consistently not low enough for comfortable climbing in your terrain, buy a smaller, inner, front chainring and/or a larger, rear cog to provide a lower "granny gear".

Climb with your hands on the brake hoods to open up your chest and to facilitate breathing. Climb predominantly in a seated position, which uses fewer muscle groups and requires less oxygen. Slide to the back of the saddle, rotate your pelvis forward (butt in), and lean your upper body forward so you can push forward on the pedals. Emphasize each forward pedal stroke by pulling that side of the handlebar toward you from the brakehood (right arm/right leg and vice versa). Periodically adjust your butt position (fore/aft and in/out) to rest different muscle groups in your legs.

Climbing in a standing position is more powerful, but it's also more strenuous. Stand periodically to stretch, and to use your leg muscles differently. Stand when you run out of low gears. To initiate a stand, shift to a slightly higher (harder) gear. Then, pull yourself up to a standing position from the brake hoods, just as your dominant foot begins its downstroke. Rock the bike gently below you with each downstroke. Shift to a lower (easier) gear before resuming a seated position.

Stand and Stretch

Concentrate on remaining aerobic (breathing heavily without gasping). Establish a rhythmic and hypnotic breathing pattern in concert with your pedal stroke. Distract yourself with a mantra ("I think I can...I think I can...") or with identifying roadside plants. Ignore the summit and concentrate on the road in front of you. Set mini-goals to the next turn, road sign, or plateau. Use a plateau, or a less-steep section, to "recover." When climbing around a corner, choose the "flattest" line. Forget about speed and concentrate on endurance. Set your own pace. Take your time. Climb with a positive attitude. Enjoy the effort. Anticipate the sense of accomplishment which will occur at the summit. Know that you will be worthy of the upcoming vista and of the exhilarating descent to follow. Climb with a passion. Love the hill. Let your love of the hill free you to explore everywhere on your bike, without fear of terrain. And remember, there is no hill that you can't walk!

Back on the flats, let's discuss **acceleration**. Even a leisurely touring cyclist should learn how to sprint out of harm's way, if only to beat Rover to the edge of his territory. (We'll talk more about dealing with dogs later.) Of course, this same skill will help you beat your riding companion when he says, "Race you to the next road sign."

Accelerate

To accelerate from a comfortable cruising speed, grasp the brakehoods while you shift up to a higher, harder gear. Then, pull yourself up to a standing position from the brakehoods, just in time to push down on your dominant pedal with your entire weight and power. Progressively and quickly increase your cadence. Emphasize the power of each downward pedal stroke by pulling up on the same side of the handlebar. Let the bike rock back and forth beneath you, as your standing body remains upright. When you've reached maximum cadence for that gear, be seated; move your hands to the drops; keep your elbows in and bent to lower your upper body into a more aerodynamic position. If possible shift up again, and spin as fast as you can. Continue to emphasize the power of each downstroke by pulling the same side of the handlebar towards you with your hands in the drops. Once the sprint is over, coast, shift to a lower, easier gear and recuperate.

Wind and Rain

*Let's talk about the **wind**.* When you bike forward, you create your own wind. Seventy percent of the resistance to moving forward is caused by your upright body catching the wind you have created. A strong **headwind** (wind coming towards you) significantly increases your resistance to moving forward. This impedes your forward progress, just as gravity does when you climb. It is exhausting to fight a relentless headwind. You can decrease the resistance to moving forward by assuming a more aerodynamic position: move your hands down to the drops, bend your elbows, and lower your shoulders down towards the handlebars. Shift to a lower, easier gear and maintain a comfortable cadence.

A **tailwind** (wind coming from behind) assists your forward progress, just as gravity does when you descend. Take advantage of its assistance by sitting upright and using your upper body as a sail. Shift up to a higher gear and enjoy!

If it's possible, plan your circular tour so that you bike into a headwind at the beginning of a ride, when you are fresh. Then you'll have the assistance of a tailwind to blow you back home when you are fatigued.

A **crosswind** (wind coming from the side) affects bike handling. You must adjust bike lean into the crosswind just to maintain a straight line forward. This is particularly difficult if the crosswind comes in gusts. Be especially careful if a crosswind comes from the left: if a crosswind comes from the left, you will be leaning to the left, toward traffic, to maintain a straight line forward. As a vehicle overtakes you and blocks the wind, your lean to the left steers you toward the overtaking vehicle. The secret to safe bike handling in a crosswind is to keep your elbows bent, your arms relaxed, and your grip on the handlebar loose, so you can quickly adjust steering in response to gusts.

*There are times when you will be riding in the **rain**. Rain **decreases traction and braking efficiency.*** Slow down, especially around corners. Remember to brake to a slower speed before the corner. Decrease bike lean and keep your bike more vertical. Anticipate the need for a longer stopping distance. Tend to use your rear brake more than usual, since it's easier to control a skidding rear wheel than a skidding front one. When descending, apply your brakes slightly to keep water off your rims. Be particularly careful crossing slippery, wet, metal surfaces such as grates, manhole covers, steel deck bridges and railroad tracks (railroad tracks should always be crossed at right angles, even when they are dry). Painted surfaces, such as the white line at the side of the road and turn lane arrows, are also slippery when wet.

6. How to Drive Your Bike: *When you were a child, you learned to* **ride** *your bike as a toy on the sidewalk. Now you must learn to* **drive** *your bike as a vehicle on the road.* In all 50 states, you, as the driver of a bike, have the same rights and duties as the driver of a motorized vehicle. You have the right to drive your bike on the road with a motorist, and you have the responsibility to follow the same rules as a motorist. That means that you ride with traffic, on the right side of the road; and not against traffic, on the left side of the road. That means that you stop at stop signs, and that you hand signal all turns. *That means that you* **follow all the rules in the driver's manual.**

Drive Your Bike

All vehicles are not created equal. Compared to a car, your bicycle is slow-moving, small, and narrow. Because you are slow, small, and narrow, you are required to share the road by riding "as near to the right side of the road as practicable." That makes sense as long as you share the road by riding as far to the right side of the road as is safe. To ride safely with traffic, you must ride your small and narrow vehicle in a road position where you are visible to a motorist. *Only if you are apparent and visible in the traffic lane will you be treated as a slow-moving vehicle, like a tractor or horse buggy, that is sharing the road.* Proper visibility is accomplished by proper lane position.

Share the Road

The very edge of the road is the most hazardous. That is where the pavement cracks and crumbles. That is where an uneven shoulder changes to treacherous sand or grass. That is where debris, glass and roadkill end up. That is where metal drainage grates are placed. That is where the raised and slippery white line at the edge of the road is painted. That is where cars are parked, ready to open their doors in your path. That is where you are least visible to an overtaking motorist trying to squeeze by you without leaving his lane. The very edge of the road is just not a safe place to be.

Your proper lane position is 1 or 2 feet to the left of the white line painted at the edge of the road. When you are cycling in this position, an overtaking motorist will see you, will define you as a vehicle, and will make a conscious decision about passing you safely – just as he would with any other slow-moving vehicle. This is a safe and defensive posi-

Maintain Proper Lane Position

tion; it is not meant to be offensive, though some motorists may interpret it as such. The degree to which you represent a partial obstruction to a motorist in this position depends on the width of the lane. On a wide road with 12 foot lanes, your safe lane position places you just to the right of traffic; this position does not impede a motorist's progress. On a narrow road, your safe lane position overlaps with a motorist's right tire track; this position requires him to slow down and decide when it is safe to veer into the opposite lane to pass you.

You may, of course, gently alter your lane position as circumstances dictate. If there is a wide, paved, well-maintained shoulder to the right of the white line, you may choose to ride there. If there is oncoming traffic on a narrow road, you may choose to move farther left toward the center of the lane, forcing a motorist to wait until it's safe to pass you.

Remember to ride a straight and predictable course, without swerving, so the motorist can make proper decisions about you. Make lane adjustments gradually and only after glancing behind to check traffic, just as you would in your car. Take time now, in a safe location, to practice turning your head to look over your left shoulder, for one second, without swerving. Develop the same skill for looking over your right shoulder. *You should never make any sideways motion without first **looking behind**.* Learn to glance behind by turning your head, even if you use a rear-view mirror (recommended) mounted on your helmet or handlebar. Use the mirror to scan, but use your head before moving.

Cyclists are understandably worried about car-bike accidents, especially from behind. In reality, the statistics cited in John Forester's *Effective Cycling* show these accidents to be uncommon. 50% of bicycle-related accidents involve only the cyclist himself, when he falls for one reason or another. In addition, bike-bike collisions and car-bike collisions are equal, each accounting for only 17% of bicycle-related accidents. When car-bike collisions do occur, the cyclist is either disobeying a rule of the road or is performing a normal roadway activity improperly over 50% of the time Of the car-bike collisions which occur, few involve a motorist overtaking from behind, and the majority of these are caused by the cyclist swerving in front of the car. The vast majority of car-bike collisions occur while turning and while crossing lanes, especially in urban settings. Car-bike collisions are caused in the following order: 25% failure to yield to crossing traffic; 17% cycling against the flow of traffic; 13% failure to yield when changing lanes; 8% motorist left turn in front of a cyclist while traveling in opposite direction; 7% riding on the sidewalk; 5% motorist right turn in front of a cyclist while traveling in the same direction; 4% a motorist restarts from a stop sign.

Here's the take home message: 1) You can most frequently stay out of harm's way by developing good cycling skills and by following the rules of the road. 2) Car-bike collisions from behind are infrequent. They can

Be Predictable

Look Behind You!

Avoid Accidents

be minimized by maintaining proper lane position and by glancing behind. 3) Car-bike collisions on rural roads such as those described in this book are rare. 4) The car-bike collisions which do occur can be minimized by caution, and by maintaining proper lane position while turning and while crossing lanes at intersections.

When you approach an intersection, position yourself according to your destination: stay next to the curb if you will turn right; stay in the center of the lane if you will go straight; stay next to the centerline if you will turn left. Yield to crossing traffic. Yield to traffic when you are changing lanes. Establish eye contact with motorists. Hand signal turns and lane changes. Be defensive. Anticipate motorist error and plan evasive action. If you ride safely and know where potential motorist dangers exist, you can bike without fear on the roadway. More detailed explanations of these crucial safety issues can be found in John Forester's *Effective Cycling* "bible" listed in the **Part 2: Where to Find More Information.**

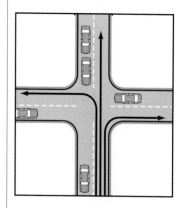

7. How to Handle Road Hazards: *You can't handle a road hazard that you don't see.* Look down the road far enough to identify a road hazard in time to deal with it safely. Many road hazards can be avoided with a safe swerve. Remember that a motorist expects you to follow a straight and predictable line. Remember never to make a sideways move without first glancing behind. Remember never to swerve into traffic. If necessary, stop before you reach a road hazard, let the traffic pass, and then deal with the hazard safely.

Road Hazards

> **Glass:** *Broken glass is the most common cause of flat tires.* If, by chance, you do ride through glass, stop immediately. Lift and spin each wheel to wipe debris off the tires with your gloved palm.
>
> **Sand:** *Even a thin layer of sand on the road can result in a loss of traction* when you are stopping or turning. On corners, slow down by braking before the turn and before the sand. Try to go through the sandy corner as straight and upright as possible, with minimal use of the front brake. Sand on a straightway is a minor problem unless it is deep enough to turn your front wheel. If you must bike through a long, straight, sandy section, keep pedaling, remain seated, and keep your weight back.
>
> **Rocks:** *Hitting a rock with your wheel can result in loss of bike control and a flat tire as well.* A single rock is easy to miss; a group of rocks is not. If you encounter a group of rocks, swerve around the entire group, if it is safe to do so. If it's not safe to swerve, you have two choices: if the rocks are widely spaced, try to steer through them without hitting one with your front wheel;

if the rocks are tightly spaced, stop before you reach them, and walk around.

OIL: *Be especially careful during the first few minutes of a rainstorm.* At that time, a thin layer of oil comes to the surface of pavement making it very slippery. In dry conditions, patches of oil from cars can be slippery, especially on corners.

PAINTED SURFACES: *Paint on pavement is slippery when wet.* Avoid the painted lines and arrows on the road when it's raining.

UNEVEN ROAD SURFACES: *A crash may occur if your front wheel slams against an elevated road surface (a "step-up"), or drops into a depressed road surface (a "step-down").* An uneven road surface may be perpendicular to your direction of travel, such as the step-up encountered at the beginning of a bridge; or, it may be parallel to your direction of travel, such as the step-down encountered where the edge of the pavement meets a lower shoulder.

> *Perpendicular step-ups offer little difficulty, as long as you don't slam into them with weighted wheels.* Instead, stand before the impact, keep your pedals horizontal, bend your elbows and knees and help your front wheel over the step-up by pulling up hard on the handlebars.

> *Parallel step-ups can catch your front wheel, causing a crash.* If you are biking on a shoulder which is lower than the road, you have three options: a) if the shoulder is smooth and wide enough, you can temporarily remain there, while patiently looking for a place where pavement and shoulder become even with one another; b) if traffic and space allow, you can countersteer to cross the step-up as close to a right angle as possible (in effect turning the parallel step-up into a perpendicular step-up; c) if neither of the above options is safe, you can stop, dismount, and manually place your bike up on the higher surface.

> *A pothole is a good example of a dangerous step-down.* A pothole can cause loss of bike control, a flat tire, and a dented rim. A water-filled pothole is particularly dangerous, because you can't judge its depth or its contents.

> *A railroad track is a good example of a dangerous step-up;* the metal track is frequently elevated above the pavement surface. Cross railroad tracks at a right angle, even when they are not perpendicular to the road. Be especially careful when it's raining, since the elevated metal tracks will also be slippery.

METAL SURFACES: *Steel deck bridges, railroad tracks, manhole* *covers, and **metal grates** are all slippery when wet.* Metal grates for water runoff are most dangerous when their open slats are parallel to the side of the road; in this position, the slat can instantly trap your front wheel, and send you over the handlebars.

DOGS: *Rover is instinctively territorial; he gives chase to protect his yard.* Rover is instinctively a hunter; he gives chase to hamstring his prey's rapidly moving feet from behind. Rover is also easily startled; he may give chase to protect himself. When you are on a bike, Rover does not see you as a kind, domineering human like his master; he sees you, your bike, and your spinning feet, as a startling, invading, vehicular prey. You can avert most of Rover's chases by avoiding his startle reflex, by coasting or pedaling slowly, and by identifying yourself as human. To this end, get in the habit of seeing Rover before he sees you. Gently inform him of your presence by speaking to him in a kind and friendly manner before you reach his territory ("Hey, nice puppy...What a good dog!"). Listen for the reassuring sound of a chain securing Rover to his post. If he's unfettered, read his body language. If his

Show No Fear!

ears go down and his tail starts to wag, the chase is off. If his ears go up and his body tightens ready to spring, it's time for you to act more authoritatively, as his master. Point a finger straight at him and sternly yell, "NO!" These behaviors ward off most chases. If Rover persists, decide whether you should stop or whether you should outsprint him to the end of his property.

Rover's danger is not as much in his teeth (it's hard for him to bite your spinning feet) as it is in your cycling behavior when you are frightened by his pursuit. The danger comes from swerving into traffic, or off the road, as you try to outmaneuver him. The danger comes from running into Rover himself and losing control of your bike. Remember to bike a straight and predictable line. Make no sideways movement without first glancing behind. Avoid colliding with Rover's body. If necessary, dismount and use your bike as a physical shield between you and the dog, as you walk to the end of his property. If it's safe to do so, consider moving to the other side of the road; Rover has probably been taught not to go there, and he probably does not consider it part of his domain. Show no fear. Offer him some food (some cyclists routinely carry dog biscuits for this purpose). If necessary, wield your pump, and squirt your water bottle as weapons. Some cyclists carry irritant sprays such as HALT! as an additional deterrent.

Roadkill: *Fear the flattened fauna.*

Pedestrians: *Pedestrians in crosswalks are expected;* they have the right of way. Pedestrians jaywalking, or entering a roadway from between parked cars, are not expected; they are a potential hazard.

Cars: *We've already discussed moving cars as traffic hazards. Parked cars can also be hazardous.* Parked cars may be preparing to enter traffic; watch for brake lights and turning front wheels. They may be parked on the shoulder partially obstructing your lane. They may have occupants about to open the car door into your path. Look into the car's rear window and rearview mirror to spot occupants preparing to leave. Bike a safe and predictable line two or three feet to the left of parked cars, without swerving in and out between them.

**Riding
With Friends**

8. How to Ride in a Group: *When you are riding with a group of cyclists, you must ride safely in the group to avoid bike-bike as well as car-bike accidents.* Ride in a straight and predictable manner at a constant speed. Pass other cyclists on the left and announce "on your left" as you do so. Communicate with group members, as well as with motorists, by vocal and hand signals. Signal and state your intention to turn right or left. Signal and state your intention to slow, to stop, or to change road lane position. If you are at the front of the group, point to and announce road hazards such as glass, sand, gravel, drainage grates, potholes, and bumps. Do not announce "clear" at an intersection, since the intersection may no longer be clear of cross traffic when the next cyclist arrives. Do announce "car up" to alert the group of oncoming traffic. If you are at the back of the group, do announce "car back" to warn the group of overtaking traffic from behind. Though you may ride double file on lightly traveled back roads, scan for traffic and then ride single file to let cars pass. On narrow roads, especially when riding uphill, leave gaps for cars to pass between every 3 or 4 cyclists. If you stop for a rest, or for a mechanical problem, move off the road so as not to impede traffic.

**A Pre-Ride
Quick Check**

9. How to Inspect Your Bike Before Each Ride: *Bonnie McClun, an Effective Cycling Instructor for the League of American Bicyclists, suggests the ABC Quick Check:*

A: Check the **air** in your tubes, and the general condition of your tires. Air slowly diffuses out of normal inner tubes. Check the air pressure once or twice weekly. Maintain an air pressure of 90-100 pounds per square inch (psi) in road bike tires. Lower air pressure increases rolling resistance and wastes your energy. Lower air pressure also causes "snakebite" flat tires when the rim of your wheel pinches the poorly inflated tube. Check your tires for bulges and for worn spots.

B: Check that both your front and rear **brakes** function properly.

C: Check that the **crankset** and bottom bracket are tightly adjusted.

QUICK: Check that **quick-releases** of wheels, brakes and seatposts are tightly engaged. BICYCLING magazine emphasizes that *a tight and properly adjusted quick-release starts to exert pressure against your palm when it is half-closed; it exerts enough pressure to leave an impression on your palm when it is fully closed.*

CHECK: Check, during a practice ride around the parking lot, that **both derailleurs**, and **both shift levers**, are working properly.

In addition, periodically check your **chain** for proper lubrication. Also, lift each wheel and watch it spin between the brake pads to ensure that it is not wobbling laterally from side to side; a wobbling wheel is **"out of true"** and needs spoke adjustment.

10. HOW TO REPAIR YOUR BIKE: *Learn enough about bike repair to get home if a breakdown occurs:*

- **HOW TO FIX A FLAT TIRE:** *A bicycle tire is inflated by means of an inner tube.* If a sharp object penetrates the outer tire and punctures the inner tube, a flat tire results. The outer tire is usually not damaged and does not usually need repair. On rare occasions, the outer tire will be gashed, resulting in a hole through which the inflated inner tube may protrude. If this occurs, the outer tire can be repaired temporarily by placing "boot" material, such as a dollar bill or some other type of thin fabric-like material, between the outer tire and the inner tube. Most of the time, repairing or replacing the punctured inner tube is all that is necessary. To fix a punctured inner tube, do the following:

  - **Open the brakes.** For sidepull brakes, open the quick-release on the brake itself or on the brake lever. For cantilever brakes, squeeze the brakepads together, and unhook the transverse cable from the brakearm that has a slot.

  - **Remove the wheel.** If the *front* tire is flat, open the front wheel quick-release, lift the front wheel off the ground by the handlebar, remove the wheel with your other hand, and lay the bike down on its non-derailleur left side. If the *rear* tire is flat, shift to the smallest rear cog, lift the chain onto the right chainstay's chain-holder peg (if your bike has one), open the rear wheel quick-release, lift the rear wheel off the ground by the saddle, remove the wheel with your other hand, and lay the bike down on its left, non-derailleur side.

  - **Release air from the tube.** Deflate the tube completely by depressing the valve stem. The tip of the thin, non-automotive, Presta-type valves must first be unscrewed.

Basic Repairs and Adjustments

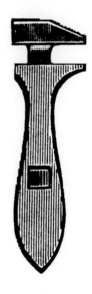

Fix a Flat

- **Remove the tire.** Pry one tire bead off the rim using tire levers: Hold the wheel upright. Start opposite the stem. Slide the flat end of a tire lever between the rim and the tire. Pull the lever down to pry a section of tire bead off the rim; hook the other end of that lever to a spoke. Slide a second tire lever between the rim and the tire, a few inches away from the first one. Pull that second lever down to pry an additional section of tire bead off the rim; hook the other end of that lever to a spoke. Remove the first lever. Repeat the process, alternating the levers, until you can slide one lever around the rim, freeing the entire bead. Leave the other bead on the rim; do not remove the entire tire.

- **Remove the tube:** Reach inside the rim and extract the deflated tube. Momentarily leave the stem in place. Use a pump to inflate the *tube* sufficiently to find the location of the leak. Inspect the *tire* at this location to ensure that the penetrating object is no longer present. Wipe the inside of the tire with a rag to see if it catches on any foreign object; remove any debris. Now, remove the tube.

- **Replace the tube:** The fastest way to fix a flat is to replace the punctured tube with a spare tube. The punctured tube can be repaired, either at home, or on the road, by using a patch repair kit. Insert the new tube's valve stem through the hole in the rim, inflate the tube just enough to give it some form, and place it inside the tire.

- **Replace the tire:** Beginning at the valve stem, *use your hands to replace the tire bead*. Don't pinch the tube. Expect the last section to be tight. Use a tire lever only as a last resort; it may puncture the newly replaced tube! Never use a screwdriver as a tire lever for the same reason..

- **Inflate the tire.** Use the pump to inflate the tube to 90-100 pounds per square inch. Be careful not to wiggle the valve stem back and forth as you pump; this can break the stem and give you another flat tire! Spin the inflated tire to ensure that it is evenly "seated" on the rim without any bulges.

- **Install the wheel**. To insert a *front* wheel, lift the bike up by the handlebar. Place the wheel between the front forkblades with the quick-release lever on the left. Insert the axle securely in the dropouts, center the wheel, and close the wheel's quick-release. Close the brakepads. Re-center the wheel between the brakepads, if necessary. Spin the installed front wheel to make sure it moves freely. To insert a *rear* wheel, lift the bike up by the saddle. Place the wheel between the rear chainstays with the quick-release lever on the left. Place the freewheel inside the chain, just above the rear derailleur. Engage the chain on the smallest cog. Insert the axle securely in the dropouts, center the wheel, and close the

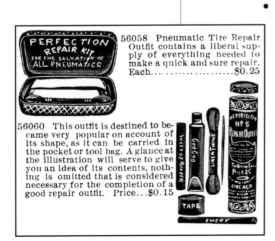

wheel's quick-release. Remove the chain from its chainstay peg. Close the brakepads. Re-center the wheel between the brakepads, if necessary. Spin the installed rear wheel to make sure it moves freely. *Remember that a tight and properly adjusted quick-release lever starts to exert pressure against your palm when it is half-closed; it exerts enough pressure to leave an impression on your palm when it is fully closed.*

- **HOW TO ADJUST THE BRAKES:** *Well-maintained brakes rarely fail en route.*

  Sometimes it is necessary to make *minor adjustments* in the distance between the brakepads. A minor increase in the brakepad distance is necessary when an out-of-true wheel rubs against a brakepad (and you don't have a spoke wrench with you to correct the situation). A minor decrease in the brakepad distance is necessary when a new brake cable stretches; the longer cable spreads the brakepads farther apart, resulting in poor braking power. These minor adjustments are accomplished by turning the barrel adjuster, on the brake cable, clockwise or counterclockwise. As you do so, watch the brakepads move closer to, or farther away from, the rim.

  Sometimes it is necessary to temporarily make *major adjustments* in the distance between the brakepads. Increasing the brakepad distance is usually necessary to remove a wheel when repairing a flat tire. Increasing the brakepad distance may also be necessary to accommodate the extremely out-of-true wheel which occurs when you break a spoke (and, once again, you don't have a spoke wrench with you to correct the situation). On a sidepull brake, the brakepad distance is easily increased by opening the quick-release at the brake itself, or at the brake lever. On cantilever brakes, the brakepad distance is easily increased by squeezing the brakepads together, and unhooking the transverse cable from the brakearm that has a slot. Realize that brakes with opened brakepads are not effective brakes and act accordingly.

- **HOW TO ADJUST THE DERAILLEURS:** *When shifting is noisy, or when the chain overshifts and falls off, a derailleur needs adjustment.*
  - **Front derailleur:** The front loop of the bicycle's chain moves within the confines of the front derailleur's rectangular cage. When the front derailleur is shifted, the rectangular cage moves right or left above the chainrings, guiding the chain from one chainring to another. The front derailleur has 2 adjustment screws:

    The *"high"* (H) adjustment screw limits or extends the distance the front derailleur cage travels *away from the bike* when you shift to the *large* chainring. Tightening the (H) screw clockwise limits the cage's lateral travel; loosening the (H)

Adjust the Brakes

Adjust the Derailleurs

screw counter-clockwise extends the cage's lateral travel. If, when you shift to the large chainring, the chain "overshifts" and falls laterally off the chainring away from the bike, tighten the (H) screw to limit the cage's lateral travel. If, when you shift to the large chainring, the chain "undershifts" and does not reach the large chainring, loosen the (H) screw to extend the cage's lateral travel. Adjust the (H) screw only after you have shifted to high gear (the large front chainring and the smallest rear cog).

The "*low*" (L) adjustment screw limits or extends the distance the front derailleur cage travels *towards the center of the bike* when you shift to the *small* chainring. Tightening the (L) screw clockwise limits the cage's central travel; loosening the (L) screw counter-clockwise extends the cage's central travel. If, when you shift to the small chainring, your chain "overshifts" and falls centrally off the chainring onto the bottom bracket, tighten the (L) screw to limit the cage's central travel. If, when you shift to the small chainring, the chain "undershifts" and does not reach the small chainring, loosen the (L) screw to extend the cage's central travel. Adjust the (L) screw only after you have shifted to low gear (the smallest front chainring, and the largest rear cog).

• **Rear derailleur:** The rear loop of the bicycle's chain moves within the confines of the 2 "jockey wheels" in the rear derailleur's cage. When the rear derailleur is shifted, the jockey wheel cage moves right or left below the freewheel cogs, guiding the chain from one cog to another. The rear derailleur has 2 adjustment screws:

The "*high*" (H) adjustment screw limits or extends the distance the rear derailleur cage travels *away from the bike* when you shift to the *smallest freewheel cog*. Tightening the (H) screw clockwise limits the cage's lateral travel; loosening the (H) screw counter-clockwise extends the cage's lateral travel. If, when you shift to the smallest cog, the chain "overshifts" and falls laterally between the cog and the chainstay, tighten the (H) screw to limit the lateral travel. If, when you shift to the smallest cog, the chain "undershifts" and does not reach the smallest cog, loosen the (H) screw to extend the cage's lateral travel. Adjust the (H) screw only after you have shifted to high gear (the large front chainring and the smallest rear cog). The rear derailleur on bikes with **indexed shifting** has a convenient barrel adjuster on the rear derailleur cable. In effect, the barrel adjuster fine-tunes the "high" adjustment. Turning the barrel adjuster *counterclockwise*, when viewed from behind, limits the cage's lateral travel; this moves the chain closer to the next largest cog. Turning the barrel adjuster clockwise, when viewed from behind, extends the cage's lateral travel; this moves the chain towards the chainstay.

The "*low*" (L) adjustment screw limits or extends the distance the rear derailleur cage travels *towards the center of the bike* when you shift to the *largest freewheel cog*. Tightening the (L) screw clockwise limits the cage's central travel; loosening the (L) screw counter-clockwise extends the cage's central travel. If, when you shift to the largest cog, the chain "over-shifts" and falls off the cog centrally toward the spokes, tighten the (L) screw to limit central travel. If, when you shift to the largest cog, the chain "undershifts" and does not reach the large cog, loosen the (L) screw to extend its central travel. Adjust the (L) screw only after you have shifted to low gear (the small front chainring and the largest rear cog).

- **HOW TO ADJUST THE SPOKES:** *When its spokes are properly tightened, a wheel is said to be "true"; its rim does not wobble laterally from side to side.* When spokes are loose or broken, a wheel is said to be "out of true"; a section of the rim is to the right of, or to the left of, center. Spin a wheel and watch the gap between the brakepad and the rim; the gap should remain constant. If the gap varies, the wheel is out of true. If the wheel is significantly out of true, the rim will strike the brakepad and slow the bike down. If the wheel is extremely out of true, the rim will wedge between the brakepads and stop the bike completely. You should know how to true the wheel enough to get you home:

  - Spin the wheel to identify how many spokes are involved in the problem area. Use a brakepad as a reference.
  - Note that the spokes alternate going to the right side and to the left side of the hub. If a rim section is pulled laterally toward the right brakepad, first loosen the spokes in that section, which go to the right hub flange. Then, pull the rim back to center, by tightening the alternate spokes in that section, which go to the left hub flange.
  - *A spoke is loosened or tightened by turning the spoke nipple at the rim with a properly sized spoke wrench* You should carry a spoke wrench in your tool kit. Always turn the spoke nipples when they are at the *top* of the rim. In that position, *a clockwise turn tightens the spoke*. Tighten and loosen the appropriate spoke nipples by no more than 1/4 or 1/2 turn at a time. To judge your progress, spin the wheel after each minor sectional adjustment.
  - If you don't have a spoke wrench; or, if, despite your best efforts, the rim continues to strike a brakepad, open the

Adjust the Spokes

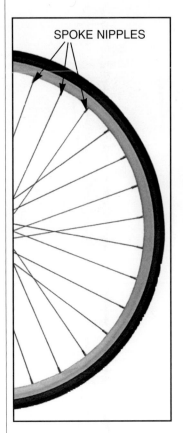

SPOKE NIPPLES

brakepads, as a last resort, to get home. Realize that brakes with opened brakepads are not effective brakes and act accordingly.

- If a spoke is broken, unscrew it from its nipple, or wrap it around a neighboring spoke. Remember that the above adjustments are temporary solutions. The spoke should be replaced and the wheel should be properly trued once you get home.

- **HOW TO FIX A BROKEN CHAIN:** *A properly maintained and properly shifted chain rarely breaks.* If a chain does break, fix it with a simple chain tool. Your dealer will show you how to use the chain tool to remove the faulty link and to reassemble the chain.

Eat and Drink

11. **HOW TO EAT AND DRINK WHILE YOU RIDE:** *While you bike, you **lose water** and electrolytes (such as sodium and potassium) in your sweat. You also **use sugar** (glucose and chains of stored glucose called glycogen) for energy. If you fail to adequately replace fluids, you will become dehydrated and you may experience heat exhaustion. If you fail to replace glucose calories, you will experience "the bonk", a low blood sugar state in which you feel weak, tired, dizzy, irritable, disoriented and rubber-legged. Dehydration and the bonk can be avoided by **drinking before you're thirsty and eating before you're hungry.***

Expect to lose one or two quarts of sweat every hour while you bike! To replace this fluid loss, bring 2, full, water bottles with you on every ride. Start sipping 15 minutes after you start and continue to sip every 15 minutes thereafter. Consume at least 1 water bottle per hour; more if it's hot and humid. Drink enough to pass at least a few ounces of light-yellow colored urine every 2 to 4 hours; no urine, or a few drops of dark-orange urine, indicates inadequate hydration. Refill your water bottles as often as necessary to maintain proper hydration. If you bike for 90 minutes or less, water replacement is all that is necessary. If you bike for longer than 90 minutes, glucose and electrolyte replacement are also necessary. For these longer rides, fill your water bottles with any commercial sports drink. Since your exercising stomach can better absorb a weak glucose solution, consider adding water to dilute the sports drink (or orange juice) by 50%. Some sports drinks can be purchased as a powder, which can be carried in a Ziploc bag to mix with water en route.

Expect to burn approximately 500 calories per hour while you bike! You should replace at least half of these calories to continue cycling efficiently. Consider adding solid food calories on rides lasting more than three hours. Traditional, solid, high carbohydrate, cycling foods include bananas, fig bars, dates, bagels, and commercial high energy bars (or gels). These foods are usually carried in the back pockets of cycling shirts, where they are conveniently accessible. Hint: Smaller food items, such as fig bars and dates can be carried in Ziploc bags. Hint: To peel a banana with one hand, hold it by the stem, bite off the opposite end, and peel it with your teeth.

During a ride, avoid overeating at rest stops and avoid foods high in fat.

Within 1 or 2 hours after a ride, drink water until you pass urine. Eat a meal high in carbohydrates, such as pasta or potatoes. This post-ride "carbo-loading" replaces used glycogen stores, so you can ride far again tomorrow!

12. HOW TO RIDE FAR: *Though you should set a goal to ride a century (a 100 mile day trip), realize that your goal may not be reached during your first cycling season. Distance cycling is learned in stages.*

Bike Far

First, concentrate on **time and frequency**, not on distance. Try to bike regularly, 5-6 times a week. Plan longer rides when more time is available on your day off. Gradually work up to biking 2 hours non-stop, on relatively flat terrain, at a comfortable speed. Remember to spin an easy gear. During this stage, concentrate on developing proper cycling technique, on establishing aerobic physical fitness, and on strengthening cycling-specific muscles.

Next, start to increase **speed**. Aim at maintaining an average speed of 15-16 miles per hour. Later, periodically try to maintain 17, or even 18, miles per hour. Vary your pace from day to day. Challenge yourself with a fast ride one day, a slow recuperative ride another day, and a moderate ride the next.

After 4-6 weeks, leave the flatlands and start training on **hills**. Start with rolling hills; then graduate to longer and steeper ones.

Once you feel comfortable biking nonstop for 2 hours at a 15 (or more) mile per hour pace in varying terrain, start to increase **distance**. Your total weekly distance, and your longest weekly ride, should not increase by more than 10%. Once you can bike a 75 mile ride, you can probably bike your first century.

Time your century properly. A 10 mph century will take 10 hours on the bike, plus additional time for rest and food stops. A 12.5 mph century will take 8 hours. A 14.3 mph century will take 7 hours. A 16.7 mph century will take 6 hours. Choose your century properly; the first one should be relatively flat.

Use the same bike and clothes for the century that you use for your training rides. The day of the century is not the day to try a new saddle or saddle position.

Remember to hydrate constantly. Eat frequent mouthfuls of high carbohydrate, low fat foods.

Rest no longer than 5 or 10 minutes at a time, so you don't get stiff. Stretch frequently on the bike. Bike at your own pace. Bike faster while you're fresh during the first 50 miles, so you can slow down the pace when you're tired later on. Remember to spin in an easy gear. Be confident. Be proud. Enjoy!

Bike Clothes

Wear a Helmet!

The almost universal use of the wheel as a means of pleasure has developed a great demand for strongly made, neat and tasty clothing, which has enough uniform appearance to distinguish the wearer as a rider, at the same time makes a neat business or street suit. Our goods are selected and made up with this view, and we can assure riders that nothing in the market is better made or more tasty in shape.

56001 Extra Fine Wool Cassimere, very dressy in small gray or brown checks, coat, four button sack, two lower, one cash and one pump pockets. Pants bloomer, two hip pockets with buttoned flap.
Price, per suit............................$9.33
Price, coat separate.......................5.66
Price, pants separate......................3.67
56003 Fine Woolen Mixture in gray and brown, gray and black checks and plain black, rich and handsome, coat, four button sack, with two lower, one cash and one pump pockets. Pants bloomer with two hip pockets, with buttoned flap. Price, per suit................$7.33
Price, coat separate.......................4.67
Price, pants separate......................2.66
56005 Brown Check Imitation Scotch Tweed, medium weight, very handsome in coloring and designs, coat three-button sack, with four patch pockets. Pants bloomer, reinforced seat, two hip pockets.
Price, per suit....... ....$5.33
Price, coat separate................ ....3.16
Price, pants separate 2.17
56007 Same as No. 56005, but is gray mixed.
Price, per suit........................5.33
Price, coat separate......................3.16
Price, pants separate.....................2.17
56009 Light Brown Mixed Chevoit, neat, strong and good wearing. Coat, three-button sack, four patch pockets, buckles and straps at knee.
Price, per suit....... ....4.66
Price, coat separate..... .. ..2.66
Price, pants separate. 2.00
56011 Same as No. 56009, but is oxford or black mixed.
Price, per suit..........................4.66
Price, coat separate......................2.66
Price, pan s separate.... .. ..2.00

13. **WHAT TO WEAR WHEN YOU BIKE:**

- **Helmet:** *The good news, as we've already discussed, is that if you develop good biking skills, and if you follow the vehicular rules of the road, you minimize the chance of an accident. The bad news is that if an accident does occur, both death and permanent disability result from brain damage 75% of the time.* Wearing a helmet significantly reduces the chance of brain damage should an accident occur. Enough said. This is truly a no-brainer. *WEAR A HELMET.* Period. Today's helmets are lightweight, cooler than your bare head and fashionable. Choose a helmet which is an approved model and which fits snugly. Adjust the helmet properly, so that it is worn horizontally, covering your forehead. The chin strap should fit snugly, to prevent the helmet from moving should you crash.

- **Cycling Eyewear:** Cycling sunglasses provide protection from the sun, from UV light, and from glare. They also provide protection from airborne debris (You haven't felt pain until a bug bounces off your eyeball at 40 miles per hour). Choose a wraparound model, which won't interfere with your peripheral vision.

- **Cycling Shirt:** You can wear any shirt to bike, but cycling shirts are specifically designed for the sport. They are longer in the back to prevent riding up when you bend forward on the bike. They are made of nonabsorbent, wicking fabrics to move sweat away from your skin. They have a front zipper to aid ventilation. They have 3 convenient rear pockets to hold food, maps, and other cycling necessities. They are brightly colored to ensure high visibility in traffic.

- **Cycling Shorts:** As with cycling shirts, cycling shorts are specifically designed for the sport. They are designed to fit properly in the bent forward riding position. They are made of tight-fitting, stretch fabric which moves with you so as not to bunch, crease, pinch, bind or cause friction. They have a padded, seamless crotch to increase saddle comfort, and to decrease the possibility of saddle sores. Cycling shorts are usually worn without undergarments (though these are available). Wash your shorts often to ward off bacteria and saddle sores.

- **Cycling Gloves:** Cycling gloves have comfortable padded palms. They distribute handlebar pressure across your palm, decreasing soreness and nerve compression. They protect your outstretched hands should you fall. They can be used to brush road debris, such as glass, from your tires safely. Cycling gloves leave your fingers free for proper dexterity. They frequently have an absorbent, terry cloth section near the thumb, for wiping your eyes and nose.

- **Cycling Shoes:** Cycling shoes are designed with a **stiff sole** to transfer power more efficiently to the pedals as you push them down and pull them up. These stiff soles also help to prevent numb feet from pedal pressure. Some cycling shoes have **ridged, stiff soles** designed to be used with a standard pedal and toeclip system. Racing shoes and off-road shoes have **cleated, stiff soles** designed to be used with special step-in pedal systems resembling a ski binding. The step-in pedal systems are more efficient and comfortable (but also more expensive) than the toeclip system. Racing cleats protrude from the sole, making it difficult to walk. Off-road cleats are recessed, making it easy to walk. Recessed cleats are obviously preferable for the type of bicycle touring described in this book.

- **Cycling Socks:** Though socks specifically designed for cycling are available, any short, thin athletic sock make of a non-absorbent wicking material will do.
- **Cool Weather Apparel:** *Since bicycling creates its own wind, wind chill begins at the relatively warm temperature of 60 degrees.* A longsleeve, windbreaker jacket is lightweight and is sufficiently compact to be stored in a rear pocket or expandable seat pack when it's no longer needed. If your windbreaker is waterproof (but breathable), as well as windproof, it can double as a raincoat. Removable arm and leg warmers are also available.

Bike Accessories

14. WHAT BICYCLING ACCESSORIES TO BUY:
- **Tool Kit:** Your on-road minimal tool kit should include 2 tire levers to help remove a tire; a patch kit to repair a tube; "boot" material such as a dollar bill, or piece of canvas to temporarily repair a cut in a tire; flat-head and Phillips screwdrivers; 4, 5, and 6 mm Allen wrenches; and an appropriately sized spoke wrench. Consider including a chain tool. These tools can be purchased as a convenient and compact combination multi-tool. Keep your toolkit handy in a Ziploc bag in your seat pack. You should also carry a spare tube (stuffed under your saddle).
- **Frame Pump :** You need a pump to inflate the tube after you change a flat. A long pump which fits your frame (usually under the top tube) is recommended. Smaller mini-pumps are available, but are designed for the lower pressures used in off-road tubes, and not for the higher pressures used in on-road tubes.
- **Water Bottles and Cages:** You will need 2 water bottles, and 2 cages to hold the bottles on your bike (usually on the down tube and seat tube). Choose large, instead of standard, size bottles. Choose wide-mouth bottles, which are easier to fill with water and ice.
- **Seat Pack:** A small pack which attaches under your saddle is a very convenient place to store your tool kit, wallet, identification, keys, and change for a phone call. The pack allows you to use the pockets in your cycling shirt for more immediately needed articles, such as food and maps. Some seat packs have zippered compartments; they can expand to a larger size, if necessary, to accommodate additional items, such as a windbreaker or raincoat.
- **Lock:** Various locks are available to protect your bike should you leave it unattended.

- **Cycling Computer:** For as little as $25-$30, a bicycling computer measures current speed, average speed, maximum speed, trip odometer, total odometer, elapsed time, and current time. Some also measure cadence. For bicycling the tours described in this book, a cycling computer is a necessity.
- **Cue Sheet Holder:** A cue sheet holder attaches the cue sheet to your handlebar, where you can conveniently read it without using your hands. For biking the tours described in this book, a cue sheet holder is a necessity. See information for obtaining a cue sheet holder in **Part 3: How to Use This Book**.
- **Rearview Mirror:** Attach a rearview mirror to your helmet or handlebar. Use it to scan behind, but never make a sideways move without first glancing back over your shoulder.
- **Lights:** Bicycle tail lights and headlights of varying power (and cost) are available. Never ride beyond dusk without a light. *Do not rely on reflectors or on reflective articles of clothing for visibility at night.*

How Much Stuff Should I Bring On a Bike Tour?

15. WHAT TO BRING ON A RIDE:
  - **Directions:** Cycling computer, cue sheet, cue sheet holder, county map(s).
  - **Tool Kit:** Tire levers, patch kit, boot material, spare tube (can be stuffed under your seat), pump, combo tool with appropriate screwdrivers and Allen keys, spoke wrench. Consider a chain-breaker.
  - **Food/Drink:** 2 full water bottles, bananas, Fig Newtons, energy bars/gels. Consider sport drink powder in a Ziploc bag.
  - **Money.**
  - **Clothing:** Proper bicycle clothing including helmet, goggles, gloves. Consider extra layer (windbreaker vs rain gear).
  - **Identification and Emergency Phone Number(s).**
  - **First Aid:** Sunblock, antibacterial ointment, personal prescriptions.

Part 2: Where to Find more Information

*Part One has shown you how to bike; let Part Two show you where to **find more information** about **bicycling** in general and about **Cooperstown** and Leatherstocking Country in particular.*

Where to Find More Information About Bicycling

Bicycling the Internet

- **The WWW Bicycle Lane:** www.cs.purdue.edu/homes/dole/bike.html
- **The Cyberider Cycling WWW Site:** http://blueridge.infomkt.ibm.com.bikes/
- **The Global Cycling Network:** http://cycling.org
- **The Virtual Breakaway:** http://www bikeride/breakaway.html
- **The WWW Bike Repair Shop:** www.uidaho.edu/~baile934/
- **Bicyclopedia:** www.homepage.interaccess.com/~opcc/bc/
- **The Yahoo Cycling Search Engine:** http://www.yahoo.com.
  Type "cycling" in the search box for many web sites to explore.
- **The AOL Cycling Sites:** Keyword BIKENET on AOL to visit the online sites of the Adventure Cycling Organization, the U.S. Cycling Federation, Bicycle Federation of America, and the International Mountain Bicycling Association.
- **The Adventurous Traveler Bookstore:** www.adventuroustraveler.com
  Click on "browse by activity," then "biking."
- **Amazon Internet Bookstore:** www.amazon.com. Click on "browse subjects," then "sports & outdoors," then "individual sports," then "cycling."
- **Barnes & Noble Internet Bookstore:** www.barnesandnoble.com.
  At "browse subjects," choose and go to "sports and adventure," then "search sports and adventure," then "cycling."
- **Pete & Ed Books:** www.a1.com/pebooks/books.html

Bicycling Books

- *Effective Cycling, 6th edition.* John Forrester. MIT Press. 1993.
- *Richard's Cycling for Fitness.*
  John Schubert. Ballantine Books. 1988
- *The Bicycle Fitness Book.*
  Rob Van der Plas. Bicycle Books, Inc. 1990. 800-468-8233, 715-294-3345.
- *Fitness Cycling.* E. Burke & C. Carmichael. Human Kinetics Publishers. 1994. www.humankinetics.com. 800-747-4457
- *BICYCLING magazine's Training for Fitness and Endurance.*
  By the editors of BICYCLING magazine. Rodale Press. 1990. 800-848-4735.
- *BICYCLING magazine's 600 Tips for Better Bicycling.*
  By the editors of BICYCLING magazine. Rodale Press. 1991. 800-848-4735.
- *BICYCLING magazine's Complete Guide to Bicycle Maintenance and Repair.*
  By the editors of BICYCLING magazine. Rodale Press. 1994. 800-848-4735.
- *Cuthbertson's All-In-One Bike Repair Manual.*
  Tom Cuthbertson. Ten Speed Press. 1996.
- *Bicycle Repair Step-by-Step.*
  Rob Van der Plas. Bicycle Books, Inc. 1994. 800-468-8233, 715-294-3345.
- *Greg LeMond's Complete Book of Bicycling.* LeMond and Gordis. Paperback. 1990.

- *Sloane's Complete Book of Bicycling,* **25**[th] **Anniversary**.
  Eugene Sloan. Simon & Schuster. 1995.
- **Adventurous Traveler Bookstore (catalog)**. This is a mail-order and on-line catalog of outdoor travel books, including bicycling, with state-by-state, national, and international listings. PO Box 64769, Burlington, VT 05406-4769. www.adventuroustraveler.com.
  800-282-3963. 802-860-6776.
- *Cycling in Cyberspace.* Michelle Kienholz, Robert Pawlak.
  Bicycle Books. 1996.

- *BICYCLING.* 33 E. Minor St., Emmaus, PA 18098. 610-967-5171.
  www.bicyclemagazine.com also, keyword BICYCLING on AOL.
  BICYCLING is the most widely read general-bicycling magazine in the United States.
- *Bicyclist*. PO Box 52712, Boulder, CO 80328-2712. 800-825-0484.
  www.bicyclist.com. *Bicyclist* (previously called *Bicycle Guide)* is a magazine devoted to on-road bicycling topics.
- *Mountain Bike.* Box 7347, Red Oak, IA 51591-0347. 800-666-1817.
  Mountain Bike is a magazine devoted to off-road bicycling topics.
- *Bicycle USA.* *Bicycle USA* is the magazine received by members of the League of American Bicyclists (See Bicycle Organizations).
- *Adventure Cyclist.* *Adventure Cyclist* is the magazine received by members of the Adventure Cycling Association (See Bicycle Organizations).

Bicycling Magazines

- **Performance Bicycle:** Box 2471, Chapel Hill, NC 27514.
  www.performancebike.com. 800-727-2453.
- **Bike Nashbar:** 4111 Simon Rd., Youngstown, Ohio 44512-1343.
  www.nashbar.com. 800-NASHBAR.

Bicycling Mail-Order Catalogs

- **League of American Bicyclists (LAB):** The League of American Bicyclists (LAB), formerly called the League of American Wheelmen, was established in 1880. It is a non-profit organization devoted to protecting bicyclists' rights and promoting bicyclists' interests through national advocacy, grassroots organizing, and educational programs. Its presence in Washington, DC keeps you and your bike on the road. Its *Effective Cycling* program teaches safe cycling to children and to adults nationwide. Members receive the organization's *Bicycle USA* magazine and its annual *Almanac* which lists state-by-state bicycle-related information. Members can attend the National and the Great Eastern Rallies (GEAR) where a thousand vacationing cyclists convene at a college campus for daily bicycle tours, seminars on bicycle-related topics, and evening entertainment. **If you own a bicycle, you should belong to this organization.** 1612 K Street NW, Suite 401, Washington, D.C. 20006.
  www.bikeleague.org. Email:BikeLeague@aol.com. 202-822-1333.

Bicycling Organizations

- **Adventure Cycling Association:** The Adventure Cycling Association, formerly called Bikecentennial, is the largest bicycle touring organization in the country. It is a non-profit, membership-supported organization devoted to bicycle travel. The Adventure Cycling Association develops scenic, low-traffic, transcontinental on-road and off-road bicycling routes. It sells maps for those routes and leads rides over those routes. Members receive the Association's *Adventure Cyclist* magazine. Members also receive *The Cyclists' Yellow Pages*, a resource for state, national, and international bicycle-related information. Anyone interested in bicycle touring should belong to this organization. Box 8308, Missoula, MT 59807. www.adv-cycling.org/. Email:acabike@aol.com. 406-721-1776
- **New York Bicycling Coalition (NYBC):** The New York Bicycling Coalition is the local bicycle advocacy organization. c/o Ann Sullivan, 646 9th Ave., Apt 3RS, New York, NY 10036. ann@panix.com. 212-757-9418
- **United States Cycling Federation (USCF):** The USCF is the governing body of competitive cycling in the United States. It is the parent company of the National Off-Road Bicycling Association (NORBA). One Olympic Plaza, Colorado Springs, CO 80909. www.usacycling.org. Email: uscf@usacycling.org. 719-578-4596.
- **National Off-Road Bicycling Association (NORBA):** NORBA is the national association and governing body for mountain bike racing in the United States. It is a member of the USCF. One Olympic Plaza, Colorado Springs, CO 80909. www.usacycling.com. Email: norba@aol.com. 719-578-4717.
- **International Mountain Bicycling Association (IMBA):** IMBA promotes environmentally sound and socially responsible trail cycling. It works to keep public lands open to cyclists. PO Box 7578, Boulder, CO 80306-7578. www.outdoorlink.com/imba. Email: IMBA@aol.com. 303-545-9011.

Where to Find More Information About Cooperstown

Local Internet

• www.cooperstown.net. and www.cooperstown.com.

Travel

• **By Car:** Directions are located in **Part 5: How to Get Here.**
• **By Bus:** Adirondacks Trailways and Pine Hill Trailways. 800-858-8555.
• **By Train:** Amtrak. 800-872-7245.
• **By Plane:** Major airports are located in Albany (518-869-9611),
   Syracuse (315-454-4330), and Binghamton (607-763-4471).

Accommodations

• Check with the Chambers of Commerce listed below for motels, B & B's,
   and campgrounds. Reservations should be made far in advance.

Local Chambers of Commerce

• **Cooperstown Chamber of Commerce**: Visit the Tourist Information Center,
   31 Chestnut Street, Cooperstown, NY 13326. 607-547-9983.
   www.cooperstown.net.
• **Otsego County Chamber of Commerce**: 800-843-3394 or 607-432-4500.
   www.wpe.com/otsego/otsego.html.
• **Herkimer County Chamber of Commerce**: 315-866-7820.
• **Montgomery County Chamber of Commerce**: 518-842-8200.
• **Schoharie County Chamber of Commerce**: 800-41-VISIT.
• **Central Leatherstocking Country, NY**: 800-233-8778.
• **I LOVE NY**: 800-CALL-NYS.

Local Maps

• **Otsego County**: County Office Building, 197 Main St.,
   Cooperstown, NY 13326. 607-547-4220.
• **Herkimer County**: County Highway Dept., PO Box 167,
   Herkimer, NY 13350. 315-867-1191.
• **Montgomery County**: County DPW, PO Box 1500, Fonda, NY 12068-1500.
   518-853-3814.
• **Schoharie County**: County DPW, PO Box 249, Schoharie, NY 12157.
   518-295-7102.
• **Other New York State and County maps**: Map information Unit, NYS
   Dept. Of Transportation, State Campus, Building 4, Room 105,
   Albany, NY 12232. 518-457-3555.
• **New York State Atlas & Gazetteer**. DeLorme Mapping, Box 298,
   Freeport, ME 04032. www.delorme.com.
   Email: sales@delorme.com. 800-452-5931.

Local Bicycle Shops

• **Cooperstown Bicycle Shop**. 21 Railroad Ave., Cooperstown, NY.
   607-547-BIKE. Hours: Mon.-Fri. 8-6, Sat-Sun 9-12. Call for assistance off
   hours. Bicycle rentals available. **Directions from the Clark Sports**

Center: Left leaving the Clark Sports Center on Susquehanna Ave. Right at third stop sign onto Chestnut St. and immediate left onto Leatherstocking Street. Left on Railroad Ave.

- **Hawk Mountain Sports.** Middlefield Center Rd., Cherry Valley, NY. 607-264-3270. Limited bicycle rentals. Hours: Mon.-Fri. 10am-7pm, Wed. closed, Sat. 9am-4pm, Sun. 12 noon-3pm.
- **Sport Tech.** 166 Main St., Oneonta, NY. 607-432-1731. Hours: Mon.-Fri. 10am-7pm, Thurs. 10am-8pm, Sat. 10am-5pm, Sun. 12 noon-4pm.
- **True Value Hardware.** 12 Willett St., Fort Plain, NY. 518-993-3455. Hours: Mon.-Fri. 7:30am-5:30pm, Sat. 7:30am-4pm, Sun. 9am-1pm.
- **Jim's Bicycle.** State Route 7, Unadilla, NY. Mon.-Fri. 9am-5pm. 607-369-9178.
- **Dave's Bike Barn.** 35 Cartwright Ave., Sidney, NY. Mon.-Fri. 12 noon-6pm, Thurs. 12 noon-8pm, Sat. 12 noon-4pm. 607-563-8544.
- **Dan's Bike Shop.** 203 W. Main St, Amsterdam, NY. Mon.-Fri. 9am-5pm (closed if it rains). 518-842-6434.

Local Bicycle Clubs

- **Mohawk-Hudson Cycling Club.** PO Box 12575, Albany, NY 12212-2575. www.albany.net/~kormisto/index.htm. 518-437-9579.
- **Onondaga Cycling Club.** PO Box 6307, Teall Station, Syracuse, NY 13217-6307. www.cny.com/OCC. 315-469-8974.
- **Mohawk Valley Bicycling Club.** PO Box 898, New Hartford, NY 13413. 315-736-2739.
- **Southern Tier Bicycling Club.** 4009 Drexel Drive, Vestal, NY 13850-4016. www.cycling.org/org/id/331.html. 607-722-6005.
- **Upper Susquehanna Pedalers and Paddlers.** Box 167, Laurens, NY 13796. 607-432-2947.
- **Sullivan County Bicycle Club.** c/o Steve Katz, 399 Mongaup Rd., Monticello, NY 12701. 914-794-3000 ext. 3560.
- **Mid-Hudson Bicycle Club.** Box 1727, Poughkeepsie, NY 12601. www1.mhv.net/~mhbc/. 914-679-3435.
- **Saratoga Freewheelers.** Paradox Bicycle Center, 138 Church St., Saratoga Springs, NY 12866. 518-583-7706.
- **Adirondack Region Bike Club.** High Peaks Cyclery, 331 Main St., Lake Placid, NY 12946. www.northnet.org/gemboy/arbc.html. 518-523-3764.
- **Cranks from Cooperstown.** Coming soon!

Books of Local Interest

- *The Leatherstocking Tales.* James Fenimore Cooper. Published between 1823-1841. Listed below in order of the hero's age (Natty Bumppo, alias the Deerslayer, alias Hawkeye, alias the Pathfinder, alias Leatherstocking):
  - *The Deerslayer.* (age 22-24). 1841.
  - *The Last of the Mohicans.* (age 35-37). 1826.
  - *The Pathfinder.* (age 37-39). 1840.

- *The Pioneers.* (age 71-72). 1823.
- *The Prairie.* (age 80-83). 1827.
- *A Guide in the Wilderness.* Judge William Cooper. Published in 1810. 5th printing by Freeman's Journal. 1965. (Hard to find)
- *William Cooper's Town: Power and Persuasion on the Frontier of the Early American Republic.* Alan Taylor. Alfred Knopf. 1995.
- *Cooperstown.* Louis C. Jones. New York State Historical Association. 1982. (Hard to find)
- *Main Street Cooperstown: A Mile of Memories.* New York State Historical Association. 1992. (Hard to find)
- *Walking Tour of Historic Cooperstown.* David O'Connor. Molly Yes Press. 1983. (Hard to find)
- *The Smith and Telfer Photographic Collection.* New York State Historical Association. 1978. (Hard to find)
- *Freelance Writer.* Jane Johngren. JayJay Publishing. 1995.
- *Whatever Happened to the Hall of Fame?: Baseball, Cooperstown, and the Politics of Glory.* Bill James. Paperback. 1995.
- *Susquehanna, River of Dreams.* Susan Q. Stranahan. Johns Hopkins University Press. 1993.
- *The Artificial River-The Erie Canal and the Paradox of Progress.* Carol Sheriff. Hill and Wang. 1996.
- *Drums Along the Mohawk.* Walter D. Edmonds. Buccaneer Books. 1996.
- *Roadside Geology of New York.* Bradford B. Van Diver. Mountain Press Publishing Co. Missoula. 1985.

Part 3: How to Use This Book

Now the fun begins! This section shows you how to use this book and how to read the new, improved tear-out Cue Sheets.

			Glimmerglass "C"			Miles	43		Tour
						Rating	Moderate		2C
			Start: Clark Sports Center. Ballfield Exit.			Climb	2200' @ 51 ft/mi		

•	0.0	R		UM 52		0.1
•	0.1	L		UM Brooklyn Ave		0.4
	0.5	L	SS	Mill St		0.2
••	0.7	R	SS	River St		0.3
•	1.0	S	SS	TRO River X Main ☞ L 0.1 FOOD		0.1
••	1.1	L		Lake St (UM 80) ⚠ Summer		8.5
•	9.6	S		TRO UM 80 @ Opera 🖐		1.9
	11.5	R		Public Landing ☞ L 0.7 80 FOOD		0.7
	12.2	L	SS	UM 53		1.7
	13.9	L		Continental ⊘ Dean Rathbun		1.8
	15.7	S	SS	Fassett Rd X 20 ⚠		1.3
	17.0	S	YS	UM 30		0.7
	17.7	BR		TRO UM 30 ⊘ Willsey Hill Rd		5.6
•	23.3	L	SS	80 FOOD		0.6
•	23.9	BL		TRO 80 ⊘ Chyle Rd		1.4
	25.3	L		Willsey Hill Rd		0.7
	26.0	R		Hinds Rd		1.2
	27.2	BL		TRO UM Hinds Rd ⊘ Domion Rd		1.4
	28.6	L	SS	20 ⚠		2.0
•	30.6	R		31		4.1
				FOOD		
•	34.7	S		TRO 31 ☞ R Glimmerglass Park		2.4
••	37.1	S		Steel Deck Bridge ⚠		4.9
	42.0	L		River St ☞ S 0.1 FOOD		0.3
	42.3	L	SS	Atwell		0.1

42.4	R		Brooklyn Ave	0.5
42.9	R	SS	UM 52	0.1
43.0	L		Clark Sports Center	

🖐 Opera: Tours 25A,B,C,D,E
@ 9.6 (Opera crosswalk) join
Tours 25A,B,C,D,E @ cue 0.0

R	Right	S	Straight	SS	Stop Sign	UM Unmarked Road	⊘ Do Not Take
L	Left	TRO	To Remain On	SL	Stop Light	26 County Route	☞ Detour Off
BR	Bear Right	X	Cross			28 State Route	🖐 Combine With
BL	Bear Left	⚠	Caution	YS	Yield Sign		

The front of each Cue Sheet is divided into 4 quadrants showing:

- *Tour Directions*
- *Points of Interest*
- *Route Descriptions*
- *Bike Shops*
- *and more...*

All of which are explained in detail in this section.

Mile	•POINTS OF INTEREST	#
0.0	Clark Sports Center	1
0.4	Deer Park (fenced enclosure @ fire hydrant) on L	2
0.7	Bassett Healthcare/Emergency Rm @ Atwell/River	3
0.8	Christ Church Historic Cemetery L	4
1.0	Cooperstown Main St ☞ L (or S @ 42.0)	17
1.1	Susquehanna Headwaters ☞ S downstairs	5
1.2	Chief Uncas Tour Boat ☞ R SS 0.1 Fair St	6
1.3	Lakefront Park/Restroom ☞ R SS 0.1 Pioneer	11
1.5	Otesaga Resort Hotel & Golf Course on R	12
2.3	Farmers' Museum L	14
2.3	Fenimore House Museum R	13
4.6	Three Mile Point Swim	22
9.6	Glimmerglass Opera & Goodyear Nature Trail	23
23.3	Owen D. Young Marker & Nature Trail ☞ R 0.1	24
23.9	Rainbow Trout Fish Hatchery ☞ BR 0.1	68
32.6	Diamond Tee Sport Center. Mini-golf	25
34.7	Glimmerglass State Park & Hyde Hall Landmark	21
37.1	East Lake Road Hiking Trail (on L after bridge)	20
41.1	Fairy Springs Swim	19
41.8	Indian Grave @ Estli/ Main	18

TOUR DESCRIPTION

The Glimmerglass Series explores the perimeter of beautiful Lake Otsego, the tranquil headwaters of the mighty Susquehanna River, and the famed "Glimmerglass" in James Fenimore Cooper's *Leatherstocking Tales*. An early morning departure is recommended to avoid traffic during the summer tourist season.

Glimmerglass "C" explores the lake's entire circumference. It adds 12 miles and an 800 foot climb to the Glimmerglass "B" tour. The extension skirts the edge of the highlands overlooking the Mohawk Valley. From this vantage point, excellent views of the Valley and the Adirondacks can be enjoyed.

Visit the charming village of Van Hornesville. Picnic and hike at the Woodruff Nature Trail. Swim at Glimmerglass State Park. Plan time to visit the many points of interest along the way.

COUNTIES
Otsego, Herkimer

BIKE SHOP
@ 0.0 ☞ L 1.0 Cooperstown Bicycle. See map.

Let us know what you think of this tour! Email: crankmail@usa.net

©1998 Tourmaster Publications, Inc.

Climb Rating in feet per mile climbed: 0-45 = Easy, 45-60 = Moderate, 60+ = Difficult

*The **Cue Sheets** and detailed **Tour Maps**, with their simple symbols, **come alive** when you and your bike are **on the road again!***

<u>Let's Get Cranking!</u> →

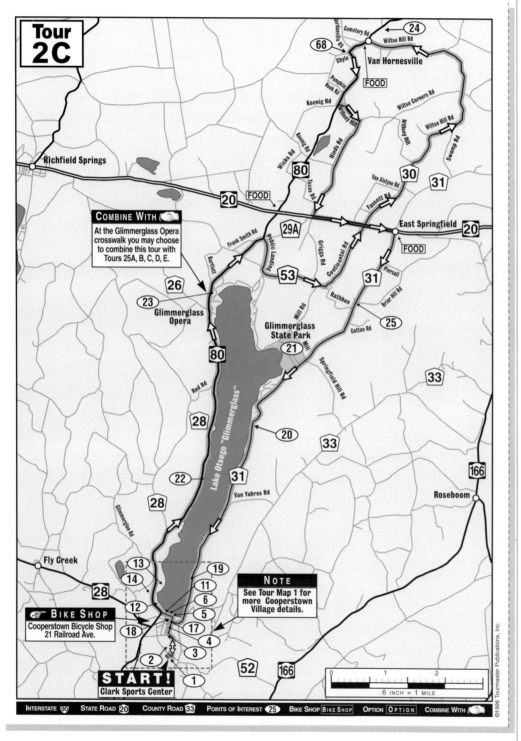

Tour 2C

- Jordanville Rd
- Cemetery Rd
- 24
- 68
- Wiltse Hill Rd
- Chyle
- Van Hornesville
- FOOD
- Pumpkin Hook Rd
- Koenig Rd
- Wiltsey Hill
- Wiltse Corners Rd
- Wicks Rd
- Koenig Rd
- Hinds Rd
- Wiltsey Hill
- Wiltse Hill Rd
- 80
- Texas Rd
- Swamp Rd
- Richfield Springs
- Van Alstyne Rd
- 30
- 31
- 20
- FOOD
- Fassett Rd
- **COMBINE WITH**
  At the Glimmerglass Opera crosswalk you may choose to combine this tour with Tours 25A, B, C, D, E.
- Frank Smith Rd
- 29A
- East Springfield
- 20
- public Landing
- FOOD
- Bartlett
- Griggs Rd
- Continental Rd
- Piersall
- 26
- 53
- 31
- Briar Hill Rd
- 23
- Glimmerglass Opera
- Rathbun
- 25
- Mill Rd
- Glimmerglass State Park
- Cotton Rd
- 80
- 21
- Mill Rd
- 33
- Red Rd
- Springfield Hill Rd
- 28
- 166
- 20
- 33
- 22
- 31
- Roseboom
- 28
- Van Yahres Rd
- Glimmerglen Rd
- Fly Creek
- 13
- 19
- 14
- 11
- 28
- 12
- 6
- **NOTE**
  See Tour Map 1 for more Cooperstown Village details.
- 5
- **BIKE SHOP**
  Cooperstown Bicycle Shop
  21 Railroad Ave.
- 18
- 17
- 4
- 2
- 3
- **START!**
  Clark Sports Center
- 1
- 52
- 166
- 0   1   2
- .6 INCH = 1 MILE

Lake Otsego "Glimmerglass"

©1998 Tourmaster Publications, Inc.

| INTERSTATE 90 | STATE ROAD 20 | COUNTY ROAD 33 | POINTS OF INTEREST 25 | BIKE SHOP BIKE SHOP | OPTION OPTION | COMBINE WITH |

The back of each Cue Sheet is a detailed map of the tour

Find These Five Tools in Part 4

Tear Out the Perforated Tour Summary Charts on Page 89

1. **HOW ARE THE TOURS ARRANGED?:** *The rides in this tour guide are arranged in a bicycle rally format.* Half of the tours leave from, and return to, the same "home base" at the Clark Sports Center in Cooperstown, N.Y. The other half of the tours leave from, and return to, "remote starts" in communities within a 10 to 20 mile radius of Cooperstown. You can choose to bike, or to drive, to a remote start. Since many tours interconnect, you can also choose to combine a Cooperstown tour with a remote tour, thereby creating a longer ride. The 50 tours vary in direction explored, in distance traveled, and in feet climbed. Whenever possible, a tour is offered as a series to provide short, medium, and longer variations of the same basic ride. This series format allows you to choose a tour variation compatible with your bicycling ability and with your time availability. The series format also allows bicyclists of differing abilities to bike "together", to explore the same area on different roads, and to meet at a mutual point of interest such as a State Park.

2. **HOW TO USE THE FIVE TOUR SELECTION TOOLS:** *This book provides five tools to help you choose a tour: a Topographic Map, a Tour Descriptions narrative, a Points of Interest information section, Tour Summary Charts, and an Overview Map. Find these five tools in* **Part 4: How to Choose A Tour** *and review them as you read the following:*

- **TOPOGRAPHIC MAP:** *The Topographic Map provides a visual summary of the hills and valleys in this region.*

- **TOUR DESCRIPTIONS:** *The Tour Descriptions section provides narrative information about each tour's route.* Scan this section to discover which tours visit areas you would like to explore.

- **POINTS OF INTEREST:** *The Points of Interest section numbers and describes the historic, natural, and man-made attractions on the tours.* If a particular Point of Interest appeals to you, choose a tour in which it is included.

- **TOUR SUMMARY CHARTS:** *The Tour Summary Charts compare all the rides in a compact format.* The Tour Summary Charts number and name each tour (e.g. Tour 4: Elk Creek Valley). They indicate if a tour is a member of a series (e.g. Tour 3C: Red Creek Valley-C). The charts also indicate, and compare, starting location, direction explored from Cooperstown, distance biked, tour interconnections, and climbing difficulty. Climbing data includes the total-feet-climbed and the feet-climbed-per-mile. A tour's climbing is rated "easy" if 0-45 feet-per-mile are climbed, "moderate" if 45-60 feet-per-mile are climbed, and "difficult" if more than 60 feet-per-mile are climbed. Interpret these climb ratings with your abilities in mind: an "easy" 0 feet-climbed-per-mile tour is flat; an "easy" 45 feet-climbed-per-mile tour is not. Remember that climbing is part of the sport. The tours with the most spectacular views and with the most exhilarating descents are the tours with the most demanding climbs. Learning to love climbing is a matter of attitude, pacing, conditioning, and gearing. Review the climbing instructions in **Part One: How to Bike**.

- **OVERVIEW MAP:** *The Overview Map provides a visual summary of where the rides go, how they overlap, and how they interconnect.* Note the "home base" in Cooperstown (Clark Sports Center). Note the "remote starts" in Springfield (Glimmerglass Opera), Sprout Brook (General Store), Cherry Valley (Village Parking Lot), Milford (ONC Boces), Laurens (American Legion), and Schuyler Lake (Post Office). Note that each tour is numbered (e.g. Tour 8), and that members of a series are identified by an alphabetical suffix (e.g. Tour 9A, 9B, 9C and 9D). Note that some tours don't overlap at all, that other tours overlap a little, and that tours which are members of a series overlap a lot (by definition). Note that most tours are circular, but that 2 are "outback" routes (Tour 2A and Tour 7). Outback routes travel out to a turn-around point, and then travel back using the same roads. Note that some Cooperstown tours connect with some remote start tours.

Tear Out the Overview Map on Page 91

3. WHAT OTHER FACTORS INFLUENCE TOUR SELECTION?:

- **CHOOSE A TOUR THAT IS COMPATIBLE WITH YOUR** *BICYCLING ABILITY* **AND WITH YOUR** *TIME AVAILABILITY.* You know how far (distance) you can comfortably ride. You should be able to ride three times as long (in time) as your usual training ride. If you can comfortably bike for a hour, you can probably bike for three hours in similar terrain, though probably at a slower pace. Most fit cyclists can maintain an average touring speed of 10-15 miles-per-hour in relatively flat terrain. Allow additional time for food stops, difficult terrain (as judged by the tour's climb rating), visits to Points of Interest, mechanical difficulties, headwinds, swimming, and just plain admiring the scenery.

Consider Your Time, Biking Ability, and Interests

- **CHOOSE A TOUR COMPATIBLE WITH** *YOUR INTERESTS.* Do you want to go far climbing a lot of hills; or do you want to bike a few flat miles while visiting museums and antique shops? Do you want to see natural wonders like caverns, gorges and waterfalls, or do you want to visit places of historical interest?

- **CHOOSE A TOUR COMPATIBLE WITH** *YOUR GROUP'S INTERESTS AND ABILITIES.* Are your group members of similar, or differing, abilities? If they are of differing abilities, decide if you will bike separately on different tours in different directions, or "together", in the same direction, but on different tours within the same series.

• CHOOSE A COMBINATION OF TOURS BASED ON *HOW MANY DAYS* YOU WILL BE IN THE AREA. If you have time for more than one tour, minimize tour overlap by choosing tours which explore in different directions, and by not choosing rides from within the same series (since these purposely overlap). Compare individual tour maps to ensure that overlap is minimal.

Let the Author Help You Choose a Tour

4. WHAT TOURS DOES THE AUTHOR RECOMMEND?:
   • FOR *CASUAL CYCLISTS* WANTING SHORT, RELATIVELY FLAT RIDES:

   TOUR 1: THE COOPERSTOWN VILLAGE PATHFINDER

   This tour is short, easy and visits many local attractions, but is heavily congested during the summer tourist season.

   TOUR 2A: GLIMMERGLASS "A"

   This is a moderate outback route. Any outback can be shortened by turning around at any point.

   TOUR 6: BEAVER MEADOW

   This tour is short, easy, scenic, rural, and free of traffic. Tours 1 & 6 can easily be combined.

   TOUR 7: SUSQUEHANNA RIVER OUTBACK

   This is an easy outback route. Combine it with any of the easy Cherry Valley Flats Tours: 17ABCD.

   Tours 9ABCD: OAKS CREEK

   This is an easy series designed for beginning cyclists. Tours 9C and 9D visit the Fly Creek Cider Mill.

   • FOR *EXPERIENCED CYCLISTS* WHO ENJOY A GOOD CLIMB:

   DAY ONE:

   • If you only have *one day* available to bike, choose **Tour 2C: Glimmerglass "C"**, followed by **Tour 1: The Cooperstown Village Pathfinder** which visits local attractions. • If you have *more than one day* available, on Day One choose **Tour 11B: Fly Creek Valley "B"** (which you can combine with Tours: 25ABCDE if so desired) followed by **Tour 1.**

   DAY TWO:

   Tour 3C: Red Creek Valley "C" (which you can combine with Tours: 15ABCD, 16ABC) or **Tour 3A: Red Creek Valley "A"** (which you can combine with Tours: 12ABC, 13, 14).

   DAY THREE:

   Tour 8: Gilbert Lake State Park (you can combine with Tours: 21ABC).

   DAY FOUR:

   Tour 5: The Cherry Valley Mountaineer (which you can combine with Tours: 18AB).

   ADDITIONAL DAYS:

   Choose from the author's recommendations for the *best remote starts*:
   a) *Long rides:* **Tours 12C, 15D, 16C.** b) *Short rides:* **Tours 13, 24.**

5. HOW TO READ THE CUE SHEET: *The cue sheet is the heart and soul of this book. It give "cues" (instructions) about where to turn. In other words, the cue sheet provides a compact list of directions for your ride.* The cue sheets in this book are designed to be used without confirmatory arrows painted on the pavement. To this end, they offer more cues than usual to help you turn at the proper places. A cue sheet is provided for each tour in this book. The cue sheet provides *directions* for a tour on one side of the page and a *map* of that tour on the other side of the page. The cue sheets in this book are located in **Part Six: Where to Bike**.

Learn to Read the Cue Sheet

- **THE BOX AT THE TOP OF THE CUE SHEET** *STATES THE NAME AND THE NUMBER OF THE TOUR.* The tour number is colored black if a tour departs from the

Clark Sports Center, in Cooperstown; and gray, if a tour departs from a "remote start." Directions to the Clark Sports Center and to each remote start can be found in **Part Five: How to Get Here.** The box at the top of the cue sheet also states the specific starting location, the distance to be biked in miles, and the feet to be climbed.

- **REFER TO THE BOX AT THE BOTTOM OF THE CUE SHEET** *TO HELP YOU INTERPRET THE CLIMB RATING.* Review the climb rating explanation on page 52.

Climb Rating in feet per mile climbed: 0-45 = Easy, 45-60 = Moderate, 60+ = Difficult

- **THE BOX IN THE MIDDLE OF THE CUE SHEET** *LISTS THE SYMBOLS USED IN THE CUE SHEET DIRECTIONS.* Many are self-explanatory, but note the following

R	Right	S	Straight	SS	Stop Sign	UM	Unmarked Road	⊘	Do Not Take
L	Left	TRO	To Remain On	SL	Stop Light	26	County Route	☞	Detour Off
BR	Bear Right	X	Cross	YS	Yield Sign	28	State Route		Combine With
BL	Bear Left	⊻	Caution						

clarifications: To "bear" right, or left, means to turn less than 90 degrees. The "unmarked" symbol **UM** indicates that there is no road sign confirming a road name at that particular location. The "do not take" symbol ⊘ helps confirm your present location by identifying roads to avoid. The "county route" 26 and "state route" 28 symbols also help confirm your present location by differentiating between minor 26 roads and major 28 roads. The "detour" symbol ☞ 0.3 directs you to side trips off the main route and states the one-way distance involved in that side trip. Detours indicate FOOD stops or Points of Interest ① not far off the main route. Note that the extra distance accumulated by the detour will not be reflected in the cue sheet's total accumulated mileage column, but will be reflected on your odometer's total mileage reading. The "combine with" symbol indicates if a tour can be extended by combining it with another tour. When tours can be combined, the 🤝 symbol will appear in three locations: 1) at the top of the cue sheet after the "miles" number, 2) within the cue sheet directions at the place where the connection occurs, and 3) at the bottom of the cue sheet followed by a list of those tours with which you can combine. On rare occasions, you will be offered an option to either shorten or lengthen your tour. On these occasions an **OPTION** symbol will be used in a manner similar to the 🤝 symbol.

- THE CUE SHEET IS DIVIDED INTO *4 QUADRANTS*. It is designed to be folded in 4 so that only 1 quadrant shows at a time. The quadrants provide compact route directions using the symbols discussed above. The quadrants also list Points of Interest along the way, provide a brief narrative description of the tour, and provide ancillary information such as bike shops, counties, tour combinations and route options. *The quadrants containing directional instructions are divided into columns.* From left to right the columns indicate the total accumulated mileage, the direction to turn at that mileage, the presence (or absence) of a traffic sign at that location, the name of the road onto which you turn, and the distance to the next direction (the next leg distance). For example:

▷ **At total mileage 1.0**, go straight at the stop sign to remain on River Street. Cross Main Street. (Signs marking both River Street and Main Street are present at this location.) If you want to, detour left 0.1 mile off the main route for food. Then return to this location and proceed 0.1 miles.

▷ **At total mileage 9.6**, go straight to remain on unmarked State Route 80 at the Opera site. (Unmarked means there is no sign confirming State Route 80 at this location. The presence of the Opera site confirms your location.) If you want to, combine with one of the tours which leave from the Opera site. (See 🤝 below). Then return to this location and proceed 1.9 miles.

▷ **At total mileage 17.7**, bear right to remain on unmarked County Route 30. Do not turn onto Willsey Hill Road. (Note that though there is no sign to confirm that you are on County Route 30, the presence of the Willsey Hill Road sign confirms that you are bearing right at the correct location.) Then proceed 5.6 miles.

▶ 🤝 **Opera 25A,B,C,D,or E:** at total mileage 9.6 on Tour 2C you may extend today's biking distance by combining with Tour 25A, 25B, 25C, 25D, or 25E all of which start from and return to the Opera site. To do so, switch to a Tour 25 cue sheet and start at its total mileage 0.0 instruction which begins at the Opera crosswalk. Upon your return, switch back to the original Tour 2C cue sheet and proceed from total mileage 9.6.

- **NOTE THE FOLLOWING HINTS:**
  - Always read an **entire line** of directions before acting, since that line may include more than one instruction.
  - The cue sheet is meant to be used with a **cycling computer** which measures distance. Despite the accuracy of your cycling computer, assume that your computer's total odometer reading will differ from the cue sheet's total accumulated mileage (left hand shaded column). This difference occurs for a variety of reasons including computer calibration, tire inflation, riding style, detours, erroneous turns, and side trips. These odometer discrepancies will be minimized if you add each, shorter, **next-leg distance** (right hand shaded column) to your current odometer reading.
  - The **next-leg distance** also helps you to relax or to be attentive. If the next leg proceeds for 10 miles to a stop sign, relax until the stop sign appears. If, on the other hand, the next leg proceeds only 0.4 miles to an unmarked turn, be very attentive for the proper turn.
  - The **FOOD** symbol is easy to spot at the end of the directions line. It indicates the presence of a convenience store, or mini-mart, where drinks or snacks can be purchased, water bottles can be filled, and bathrooms can be used. On some tours, the food stops are few and far between. **Scan the cue sheet for food stops before you leave**, to insure that you carry sufficient fluids and calories with you.
  - All routes remain **on pavement** unless specifically stated otherwise. If you turn onto a gravel road, you've probably made a mistake.

- *ANOTHER CUE SHEET QUADRANT LISTS THE POINTS OF INTEREST.*

Use a Cycling Computer

Mile	•POINTS OF INTEREST	#
0.0	Clark Sports Center	①
0.4	Deer Park (fenced enclosure @ fire hydrant) on L	②
0.7	Bassett Healthcare/Emergency Rm @Atwell/River	③
0.8	Christ Church Historic Cemetery L	④
1.0	Cooperstown Main St ☞ L (or ☞ S @ 42.0)	⑰
1.1	Susquehanna Headwaters ☞ S downstairs	⑤
1.2	Chief Uncas Tour Boat ☞ R SS 0.1 Fair St	⑥
1.3	Lakefront Park/Restroom ☞ R SS 0.1 Pioneer	⑪
1.5	Otesaga Resort Hotel & Golf Course on R	⑫
2.3	Farmers' Museum L	⑭
2.3	Fenimore House Museum R	⑬
4.6	Three Mile Point Swim	㉒
9.6	Glimmerglass Opera & Goodyear Nature Trail	㉓
23.3	Owen D. Young Marker & Nature Trail ☞ R 0.1	㉔
23.9	Rainbow Trout Fish Hatchery ☞ BR 0.1	㉘
32.6	Diamond Tee Sport Center. Mini-golf	㉕
34.7	Glimmerglass State Park & Hyde Hall Landmark	㉑
37.1	East Lake Road Hiking Trail (on L after bridge)	⑳
41.1	Fairy Springs Swim	⑲
41.8	Indian Grave @ Estli/ Main	⑱

◁ The **oval numbers** in the shaded, right-hand column of the Points of Interest quadrant correspond to the numbers in the Points of Interest information section of the book. They also correspond to the numbers locating the Points of Interest on the cue sheet map.

▶ The numbers in the shaded left-hand column indicate the mileage at which a Point of Interest is located on the tour. Frequently that location will occur between cue sheet directions. Because of space limitations, most Points of Interest are not specified in the cue sheet direction lines. For that reason, it is recommended that you **review the Points of Interest quadrant before you leave**.

Choose Your Points of Interest

Mile	•POINTS OF INTEREST	#
23.9	Rainbow Trout Fish Hatchery ☞ BR 0.1	68

Mile				
• 0.0 R		UM 52		0.1
• 0.1 L		UM Brooklyn Ave		0.4
0.5 L	SS	Mill St		0.2
•• 0.7 R	SS	River St		0.3
• 1.0 S	SS	TRO River X Main ☞ L 0.1 FOOD		0.1
•• 1.1 L		Lake St (UM 80) ⚠ Summer		8.5
• 9.6 S		TRO UM 80 @ Opera		1.9
11.5 R		Public Landing ☞ L 0.7 80 FOOD		0.7
12.2 L	SS	UM 53		1.7
13.9 L		Continental ⊘ Dean Rathbun		1.8
15.7 S	SS	Fassett Rd X 20 ⚠		1.3
17.0 S	YS	UM 30		0.7
▶ 17.7 BR		TRO UM 30 ⊘ Willsey Hill Rd		5.6
▶ • 23.3 L	SS	80	FOOD	0.6
▶ ⊙23.9 BL		TRO 80 ⊘ Chyle Rd		1.4
25.3 L		Willsey Hill Rd		0.7
26.0 R		Hinds Rd		1.2
27.2 BL		TRO UM Hinds Rd ⊘ Domion Rd		1.4
28.6 L	SS	20 ⚠		2.0
• 30.6 R		31	FOOD	4.1
• 34.7 S		TRO 31 ☞ R Glimmerglass Park		2.4
•• 37.1 S		Steel Deck Bridge ⚠		4.9
42.0 L		River St ☞ S 0.1 FOOD		0.3
42.3 L	SS	Atwell		0.1

◀ Choose those Points of Interest which you would like to explore. Indicate your choices by circling the dot (or dots) to the left of the appropriate cue sheet direction line. (*Two* dots indicate *two or more* Points of Interest.) Your circled dots will serve as a reminder that a Point of Interest is coming up. This exercise is particularly important since the Points of Interest quadrant is hidden from your view when the cue sheet is folded in four.

Note:

▸ There is no dot before 17.7 because there is no Point of Interest between 17.7 and 23.2.

▸ There is a dot before 23.3 because there is a Point of Interest between 23.3 and 23.8. The dot is not circled because the cyclist does not want to stop at the Owen D. Young Marker and Nature Trail.

▸ There is a dot before 23.9 because there is a Point of Interest between 23.9 and 25.2. The dot is circled because the cyclist does want to stop at the Rainbow Trout Fish Hatchery.

Bycue

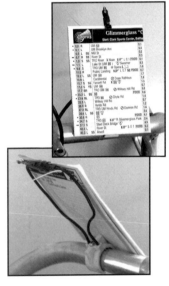

Ultimate Map Clip

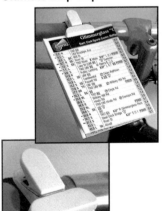

6. **HOW TO USE THE CUE SHEET:** *The cue sheet is designed to be **folded in 4** so that only one quadrant is visible at a time.* First fold the cue sheet in half from top to bottom, so that the two top quadrants show. Then fold the cue sheet in half from right to left, so that the left upper quadrant (mile 0.0) shows on one side, and the right upper quadrant shows on the other side. Attach the compactly folded cue sheet to a **cue sheet holder**. Mount the cue sheet and holder on your handlebar, where each line of directional information can be read easily. If you first insert the folded cue sheet in a Ziploc bag, you preserve it for future use, keep it from flapping in the breeze, and protect it from inclement weather and sweat. The Ziploc bag also helps secure the cue sheet to its holder without damage.

7. **WHAT CUE SHEET HOLDERS ARE AVAILABLE?:** *There are two commonly used cue sheet holders: **Bycue** and **The Ultimate Map Clip**. Bycue* attaches the cue sheet more securely than *The Ultimate Map Clip*. This more secure attachment offers additional insurance against the inadvertent loss of the cue sheet en route, but tends to damage the cue sheet, unless the cue sheet is placed in a Ziploc bag. *Bycue* positions the cue sheet on the far side of the handlebar where it's easier to read and provides support for the cue sheet to prevent flapping in the breeze. *The Ultimate Map Clip* is less expensive, less bulky, and less damaging to the cue sheet; but it works best when the cue sheet is positioned on the near side of the handlebar, where it's more difficult to read.

• **Bycue**: $8.95.

    tdmbear@fred.net.   301-696-9252.   800-522-2640.

• **Ultimate Map Clip**: $6.95

    smpcycle@snet.net.   www.webship.com/smpcycle   800-724-4402.

8. HOW TO USE THE CUE SHEET MAP: *A tour map is provided on the back of each cue sheet.* The map indicates the tour's starting location, highlights the route, locates the Points of Interest, depicts route options, and shows where tours can be combined. The tour map is not intended to be your primary source of route information; the cue sheet directions are much more specific and reliable in this regard. **The tour map is intended to be a back-up** source of information. It is advisable to bring more detailed **county maps** with you. It is for this reason that the cue sheet lists the counties visited in each tour (see the appendix for information about ordering New York State county maps). These maps can be helpful when a cue sheet turn is in doubt. They can help you get back on route if an erroneous turn has already been made. They can help you custom design a shorter way home if mechanical difficulties, inclement weather, or time constraints demand.

Bring County Maps Too

Tour 2C

Cemetery Rd · McDannville Rd · 24 · 68 · Wiltse Hill Rd · Chyle · Van Hornesville · FOOD · Pumpkin Hook Rd · Koenig Rd · Wiltse Corners Rd · Wilbsey Hill · Koenig Rd · Hinds Rd · Wilbsey Hill · Wiltse Hill Rd · Wicks Rd · 80 · Swamp Rd · Richfield Springs · Van Alstyne Rd · 30 · 31 · 20 · FOOD · Texas Rd · Fasett Rd · East Springfield · 20 · 29A · FOOD

COMBINE WITH At the Glimmerglass Opera crosswalk you may choose to combine this tour with Tours 25A, B, C, D, E.

Frank Smith Rd · Public Landing · Griggs Rd · Continental Rd · Piersall · 53 · 31 · 26 · Bartlett · 23 · Glimmerglass Opera · Rathbun · Mill Rd · Glimmerglass State Park · 21 · Briar Hill Rd · 25 · Cotton Rd · 80 · 33 · Red Rd · Springfield Hill Rd · 28 · 20 · 33 · 166 · Lake Otsego "Glimmerglass" · 22 · 31 · Van Yahres Rd · Roseboom · 28 · Glimmerglen Rd · Fly Creek · 13 · 19 · NOTE See Tour Map 1 for more Cooperstown Village details. · 14 · 11 · 6 · 28 · 12 · 5 · BIKE SHOP Cooperstown Bicycle Shop 21 Railroad Ave. · 18 · 17 · 4 · 2 · 3 · START! Clark Sports Center · 1 · 52 · 166

0 · 1 · 2 · .6 INCH = 1 MILE

INTERSTATE 90 · STATE ROAD 20 · COUNTY ROAD 33 · POINTS OF INTEREST 25 · BIKE SHOP BIKE SHOP · OPTION OPTION · COMBINE WITH

©1998 Tourmaster Publications, Inc.

The 50 tours in Part 6 explore an area of upstate New York composed of beautiful north-south river valleys separated by east-west ridges. The scenery is spectacular, the backroads are traffic-free, and the bicycling is superb! Tour climbs range from 300' to 6500'.

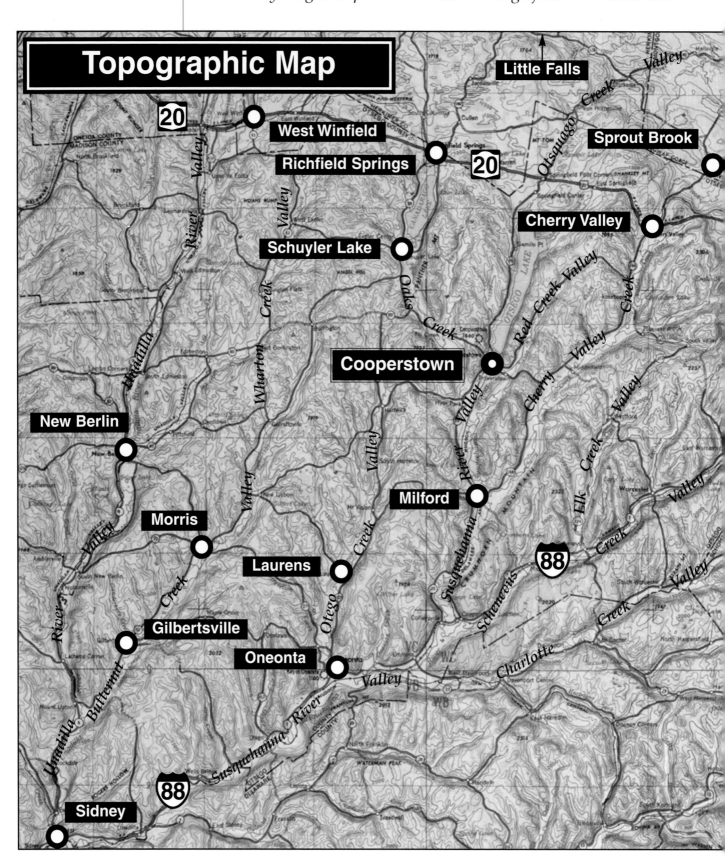

Topographic Map

Little Falls

20

West Winfield

Richfield Springs

20

Sprout Brook

Cherry Valley

Schuyler Lake

Cooperstown

New Berlin

Milford

Morris

88

Laurens

Gilbertsville

Oneonta

88

Sidney

Part 4: How to Choose a Tour

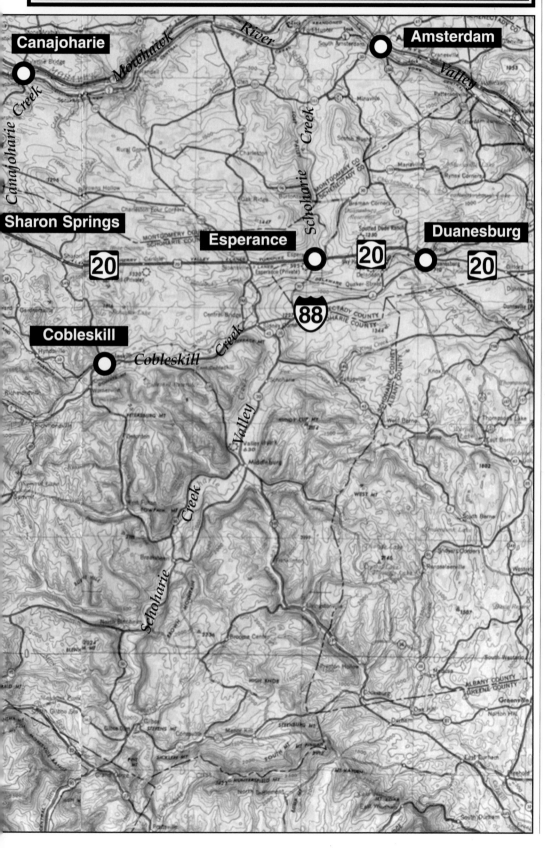

*Part Four provides you with **five tools** to help you **choose a tour**:*

- **Topographic Map**
  page 60

- **Tour Descriptions**
  page 62

- **Points of Interest**
  page 73

- **Tour Summary Charts**
  page 89

- **Overview Map**
  page 91

 = Combines With

Tour Descriptions

Tour 1

Cooperstown Village Pathfinder • 7 miles / Easy 300' climb

The Cooperstown Village Pathfinder is a short and leisurely exploration of Cooperstown's quaint and historic streets. The Pathfinder can serve as a brief introductory ride or as a day trip to the local points of interest.

Plan time to visit the Baseball Hall of Fame. Enjoy the Fenimore House Museum's American Folk Art collection and its American Indian wing. Stroll though the 19th century streets of The Farmers' Museum. Shop on Cooperstown's Main Street. Picnic at Lakefront Park. Enjoy the views of Lake Otsego from the deck of the Chief Uncas Tour Boat.

Take a trip back in time to the days of James Fenimore Cooper and his Leatherstocking Tales. Enjoy this remnant of unspoiled Americana.

Tours 2A,B,C,D

The Glimmerglass Series explores the perimeter of beautiful Lake Otsego, the tranquil headwaters of the mighty Susquehanna River, and the famed "Glimmerglass" in James Fenimore Cooper's *Leatherstocking Tales*. An early morning departure is recommended to avoid traffic during the summer tourist season.

Tour 2A

Glimmerglass A • 16 miles / Moderate 1000' climb

Glimmerglass "A" is an outback tour which explores the eastern shore of Lake Otsego. It provides the most direct route for a day swimming and picnicking at Glimmerglass State Park. Meet at the park with friends biking the longer Glimmerglass tours. Since this is an outback route, turn around anytime for a shorter ride. Plan time to visit the village of Cooperstown.

Tour 2B

[ ] 25ABCDE

Glimmerglass B • 31 miles / Moderate 1400' climb

Glimmerglass "B" explores the lake's entire circumference. The route travels north following the lake's western shore on more heavily traveled State Route 80. After climbing east over "The Sleeping Lion," Mount Wellington, the tour returns to Cooperstown following the rolling and lightly traveled East Lake Road.

Plan time to visit the many points of interest along the way. Swim and picnic at Glimmerglass State Park.

Tour 2C

[ ] 25ABCDE

Glimmerglass C • 43 miles / Moderate 2200' climb

Glimmerglass "C" explores the lake's entire circumference. It adds 12 miles and an 800 foot climb to the Glimmerglass "B" tour. The extension skirts the edge of the highlands overlooking the Mohawk Valley. From this vantage point, excellent views of the Valley and the Adirondacks can be enjoyed.

Visit the charming village of Van Hornesville. Picnic and hike at the Woodruff Nature Trail. Swim at Glimmerglass State Park. Plan time to visit the many points of interest along the way.

Glimmerglass D • 62 miles / Moderate 3200' climb

Tour 2D

 Tours 25ABCDE

Glimmerglass "D" explores the lake's entire circumference. It adds 19 miles and a 1000 foot climb to the Glimmerglass "C" tour. The extension follows the Otsquago Creek from Van Hornesville down to the Mohawk Valley at Fort Plain. Then it climbs back to Lake Otsego. Though the climb rating for the entire tour is moderate at 52 feet per mile, an eleven mile segment is difficult, climbing 145 feet per mile!

While in Fort Plain, visit Lock 15 of the New York State Barge Canal. Swim and picnic at Glimmerglass State Park. Plan time to visit the many other points of interest along the way.

The Red Creek Valley Series explores the first valley east of Lake Otsego.

Tours 3A,B,C

Red Creek Valley A • 31 miles / Moderate 1700' climb

Tour 3A

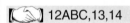 12ABC,13,14

Red Creek Valley "A" descends into the historic village of Cherry Valley before returning to Cooperstown following the eastern shore of Lake Otsego. Plan time to visit the Cherry Valley Museum. Learn about the Cherry Valley Massacre. Swim and picnic at Glimmerglass State Park.

Red Creek Valley B • 44 miles / Difficult 2700' climb

Tour 3B

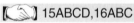 15ABCD,16ABC

Red Creek Valley "B" adds 13 miles and a 1000 foot climb to the Red Creek Valley "A" tour. The extension visits the highlands overlooking the Mohawk Valley, descends briskly to Sprout Brook and Salt Springville, then climbs up to Springfield before returning home via the eastern shore of Lake Otsego.

Visit the Cherry Valley Museum. Learn about the Cherry Valley Massacre. Plan time for a leisurely home cooked breakfast at the Breakfast House. Explore Judd Falls. Swim and picnic at Glimmerglass State Park.

Red Creek Valley C • 62 miles / Difficult 3800' climb

Tour 3C

15ABCD,16ABC

Red Creek Valley "C" adds 18 miles and an 1100 foot climb to the Red Creek Valley "B" tour. The extension visits additional highlands overlooking the Mohawk Valley and descends to the charming village of Van Hornesville before returning home via the eastern shore of Lake Otsego.

Visit the Cherry Valley Museum. Learn about the Cherry Valley Massacre. Plan time for a leisurely home cooked breakfast at the Breakfast House. Explore Judd Falls. Picnic and hike at the Woodruff Nature Trail. Swim and picnic at Glimmerglass State Park.

Elk Creek Valley • 35 miles / Difficult 3000' climb

Tour 4

This beautiful and challenging tour explores Elk Creek Valley, the third valley east of Lake Otsego. Leave the Susquehanna River Valley to visit the Red Creek Valley, the Cherry Valley and the Elk Creek Valley with four major climbs along the way. This is a relatively short, but sweet, climber's delight.

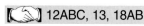

Tour 5

 12ABC, 13, 18AB

Cherry Valley Mountaineer • 61 miles / Difficult 5200' climb

The Cherry Valley Mountaineer climbs the scenic ridges surrounding the Cherry Valley Flats series (Tours 17ABCD). The seven major climbs are thankfully separated by miles of relatively flat terrain, but this remains a very challenging ride. Climbers, enjoy! Flatlanders, beware! Tour options are available to eliminate some of the climbs if your legs tire out.

The Cherry Valley Mountaineer is also offered as a remote start from ONC Boces Occupational Center in Milford (Tour 19).

Tour 6

Beaver Meadow • 7 miles / Easy 300' climb

The Beaver Meadow Tour is a short and easy loop on lightly traveled, relatively flat backroads. This ride is a good choice for beginning cyclists. It is a great warm-up ride which can be combined with the Cooperstown Village Pathfinder for an excellent introduction to Leatherstocking Country. Keep an eye out for the beaver pond!

Tour 7

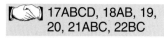 17ABCD
18AB, 19, 20

Susquehanna River Valley Outback • 33 mi. / Easy 1200' climb

The Susquehanna River Valley Outback Tour explores the eastern bank of the Susquehanna River from Cooperstown to Cooperstown Junction.

This flat and scenic tour is an excellent training ride for beginning cyclists. Since this is an outback route, turn around anytime for a shorter ride. Alternatively, extend the route by adding the Schenevus Creek Valley option, or by combining with any of the Milford remote start tours.

Tour 8

17ABCD, 18AB, 19, 20, 21ABC, 22BC

Gilbert Lake • 49 miles / Difficult 3500' climb

The Gilbert Lake Tour climbs west out of the Susquehanna River Valley and descends into the Otego Creek Valley. It then climbs out of the Otego Creek Valley and descends into the Butternut Valley. The return trip traverses the same ridges via a more southerly route.

Visit the villages of Hartwick, Laurens and Milford. Swim and picnic at Gilbert Lake State Park.

Tours 9A,B,C,D

The Oaks Creek Series is an easy practice series for beginning and casual cyclists. The distances are short and slowly progressive. The routes are flat to rolling with an occasional short "practice" hill. The tours provide traffic experience by crossing and riding a short distance on State Route 28. The "D" option even provides practice riding a short distance on gravel.

Tour 9A

Oaks Creek A • 9 miles / Easy 400' climb

Oaks Creek "A" rides to the first bridge crossing Oaks Creek at Toddsville.

Tour 9B

Oaks Creek B • 12 miles / Easy 500' climb

Oaks Creek "B" adds 3 miles and a 100 foot climb to Oaks Creek "A". The extension rides to the second bridge crossing Oaks Creek at Fork Shop Road.

Oaks Creek C • 16 miles / Easy 600' climb

Tour 9C

Oaks Creek "C" adds 4 miles and a 100 foot climb to the Oaks Creek "B" tour. The extension rides to the third bridge crossing Oaks Creek at Allison Road and then proceeds to the Fly Creek Cider Mill.

At the Cider Mill you can drink fresh cider as you watch it being made. You can snack on apples, cheeses, and homemade goodies. You can browse in the craft shop, picnic by the mill pond, and, if your timing is right, polka at the Applefest Weekend in late September.

Oaks Creek D • 18 miles / Easy 700' climb

Tour 9D

Oaks Creek "D" adds 2 miles and a 100 foot climb to the Oaks Creek "C" tour. It rides to the fourth bridge crossing Oaks Creek at Hoke Road, provides practice riding a short distance on gravel, and then proceeds to the Fly Creek Cider Mill.

At the Cider Mill you can drink fresh cider as you watch it being made. You can snack on apples, cheeses, and homemade goodies. You can browse in the craft shop, picnic by the mill pond, and, if your timing is right, polka at the Applefest Weekend in late September.

Mount Otsego • 19 miles / Difficult 1500' climb

Tour 10

This hilly route explores the ridges west of Lake Otsego with visits to Leatherstocking Falls and to the old Mount Otsego ski area.

The Mount Otsego ski area was a source of community pride and comraderie before it was insuranced out of existence twenty years ago. In its heyday it boasted the longest rope tow in the East. Legend has it that on particularly inclement snowdays, the school bus would transport children to ski at Mount Otsego since school had been closed for the day.

Though this tour is short, the climbs and the uphill gravel sections make it very challenging. The vistas and descents are your rewards.

The Fly Creek Valley Series explores the first valley west of Lake Otsego. An early morning departure is recommended to avoid traffic during the summer tourist season. Take time to explore the Fly Creek Cider Mill. At the Cider Mill you can drink fresh cider as you watch it being made. You can snack on apples, cheeses, and homemade goodies. You can browse in the craft shop, picnic by the mill pond, and, if your timing is right, polka at the Applefest Weekend in late September. Enjoy the many other attractions along the way.

Tours 11A,B

Fly Creek Valley A • 30 miles / 1700' Moderate climb

Tour 11A

Fly Creek Valley "A" follows the western shore of Lake Otsego and then climbs to explore the definitely rolling terrain of the beautiful Fly Creek Valley.

 25ABCDE

Fly Creek Valley B • 40 miles / 2700' Difficult climb

Tour 11B

Fly Creek Valley "B" adds 10 miles and a 1000 foot climb to the Fly Creek Valley "A" tour. Explore the rolling backroads of Christian Hill.

 25ABCDE

T O U R S S T A R T I N G F R O M C H E R R Y V A L L E Y

Tours 12A,B,C   ***The Sharon Springs Series*** explores northwestern Schoharie County.

Tour 12A

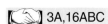 3A, 16ABC

Sharon Springs A • 22 miles / Difficult 1600' climb

Sharon Springs "A" climbs to the highlands overlooking the Mohawk Valley, travels east to Sharon Springs' historic bath houses, plummets to the village of Ames, travels west over flat valley roads to Sprout Brook, and then climbs back to Cherry Valley.

Plan time to visit the museums in Cherry Valley and Sharon Springs. Explore Judd Falls.

Tour 12B

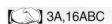 3A,16ABC

Sharon Springs B • 54 miles / Difficult 4000' climb

Sharon Springs "B" adds 32 miles and a 2400 foot climb to the Sharon Springs "A" tour. The extension follows scenic backroads to Little York, Bear Swamp and Onderdunk.

Plan time to visit the museums in Cherry Valley and Sharon Springs. Explore Judd Falls.

Tour 12C

 3A,16ABC

Sharon Springs C • 70 miles / Difficult 5000' climb

Sharon Springs "C" adds 16 miles and a 1000 foot climb to the Sharon Springs "B" Tour. The extension visits Howe Caverns, Secret Caverns, the Iroquios Indian Museum and the Caverns Creek Grist Mill Museum. You can also explore Judd Falls and visit the museums in Cherry Valley and Sprout Brook. Plan a full day for this excellent adventure.

Tour 13

 3A,15ABCD,16ABC

Judd Falls • 14 miles / Difficult 1400' climb

The Judd Falls tour is short, but it claims to deliver more scenic vistas per mile than any other tour in this book.

Climb from Cherry Valley to the highlands overlooking the Mohawk Valley. Then enjoy a 5 mile descent to Sprout Brook before climbing back to Cherry Valley following the western edge of the Judd Falls Gorge.

Plan time to explore Judd Falls.

Tour 14

🤝 3A

Belvedere Lake • 18 miles / Difficult 1900' climb

The Belvedere Lake tour is a climber's delight. Climb to the Cherry Valley Gorge and to spectacular views at the summit of East Hill. Descend to Pleasant Brook and then climb to the heights above Belvedere Lake before descending on gravel back to Cherry Valley. Look for ostriches along the way.

T O U R S S T A R T I N G F R O M S P R O U T B R O O K

Tours 15A,B,C,D   ***The Canajoharie Gorge Series*** explores the hills and valleys east of Sprout Brook. A visit to spectacular Canajoharie Gorge in Wintergreen Park is the highlight of these tours. After entering Wintergreen Park, notice a parking area on the right *before* the road descends. Walk the footpath to the right beyond the parking area for excellent views down to the Gorge. Continue on the gravel trail beyond a wooden bridge until the footpath becomes paved. The paved section leads to a deck overlooking Canajoharie Falls. After returning to the parking area, turn right and bike downhill to water level where you can picnic before completing your tour.

Canajoharie Gorge A • 19 miles / Moderate 1100'climb

Tour 15A

[🤝] 3BC

Canajoharie Gorge "A" is the shortest and most direct route to Canajoharie Gorge in Wintergreen Park.

NOTE: For planning purposes, groups with members simultaneously biking different Canajoharie Gorge tours should note that Tour "A" is the only ride in this series that circles clockwise.

Canajoharie Gorge B • 41 miles / Moderate 2300' climb

Tour 15B

[🤝] 3BC

Canajoharie Gorge "B" adds 22 miles and a 1200 foot climb to the Canajoharie Gorge "A" tour. The extension climbs Latimer Hill and Corbin Hill for views of the Mohawk Valley before joining the other tours at Canajoharie Gorge in Wintergreen Park.

Canajoharie Gorge C • 58 miles / Difficult 3800'climb

Tour 15C

[🤝] 3BC

Canajoharie Gorge "C" adds 17 miles and a 1500 foot climb to the Canajoharie Gorge "B" tour. The extension provides an exhilarating 5 mile descent to the Schoharie Creek then climbs to impressive views of the Mohawk Valley before joining the other tours at Canajoharie Gorge in Wintergreen Park.

Canajoharie Gorge D • 78 miles / Difficult 5000' climb

Tour 15D

[🤝] 3BC

Canajoharie Gorge "D" adds 20 miles and a 1200 foot climb to the Canajoharie Gorge "C" tour. The extension explores east of the Schoharie Creek, touches the outskirts of Amsterdam, and visits the Schoharie Crossing Historic Site near Lock 12 of the New York State Barge Canal. It then passes through the tranquil grounds of the Auriesville Martyrs' Shrine before joining the other tours at Canajoharie Gorge in Wintergreen Park.

The Otsquago Creek Series explores the hills and valleys west of Sprout Brook.

Tours 16A,B,C

Otsquago Creek A • 19 miles / Difficult 1500' climb

Tour 16A

[🤝] 3BC,12ABC

Otsquago Creek "A" explores the hilly backroads of southwestern Montgomery County. This tour is short and scenic.

Otsquago Creek B • 44 miles / Difficult 3500' climb

Tour 16B

[🤝] 3BC,12ABC

Otsquago Creek "B" adds 25 miles and a 2000 foot climb to the Otsquago

Creek "A" tour. The extension provides incredible panoramas of the Mohawk Valley before descending to the Mohawk River via beautiful Nowadaga Creek. Plan time to visit New York State Barge Canal Lock 16.

Save some energy for climbing back to Sprout Brook.

Tour 16C

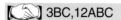 3BC,12ABC

Otsquago Creek C • 56 miles / Difficult 4000' climb

Otsquago Creek "C" adds 12 miles and a 500 foot climb to the Otsquago Creek "B" tour. The extension visits Little Falls, Moss Island's impressive glacial potholes, New York State Barge Canal Lock 17 (the world's highest canal lift lock), the historic home of Revolutionary War hero General Nicholas Herkimer, beautiful Nowadaga Creek, and New York State Barge Canal Lock 16.

Plan a full day to enjoy this excellent adventure. To save time and energy, consider abbreviating the tour by asking a non-biking driver to pick you up at mile 28.2, the Herkimer Home Historic Site on State Route 169.

TOURS STARTING FROM MILFORD

Tours 17A,B,C,D

The Cherry Valley Flats Series explores the periphery of the flat and fertile Cherry Valley, the second valley east of Lake Otsego.

Tour 17A

 8

Cherry Valley Flats A • 9 miles / Easy 300' climb

Cherry Valley Flats "A" explores north to Westville.

Tour 17B

 8

Cherry Valley Flats B • 12 miles / Easy 400' climb

Cherry Valley Flats "B" explores north to Norton Cross Road.

Tour 17C

 8

Cherry Valley Flats C • 18 miles / Easy 600' climb

Cherry Valley Flats "C" explores north to Middlefield.

Tour 17D

 8

Cherry Valley Flats D • 29 miles / Easy 1000' climb

Cherry Valley Flats "D" explores north to Roseboom and Pleasant Brook.

Tours 18A,B

The Spring Brook Series explores the hills and valleys south and west of Milford.

Tour 18A

Spring Brook A • 14 miles / Moderate 600' climb

Spring Brook "A" follows the Susquehanna River Valley south, then gradually climbs west up the Spring Brook Valley before descending briskly back to Milford. Plan time to tour the Milford Depot Railway Museum and the Cooperstown Brewery.

Tour 18B

Spring Brook B • 20 miles / Difficult 1300' climb

Spring Brook "B" adds 6 miles and a 700 foot climb to the Spring Brook "A" tour. The extension climbs to secluded Arnold's Lake and then visits impressive wetlands before descending to Milford. Plan time to tour the Milford Depot Railway Museum and the Cooperstown Brewery.

Cherry Valley Mountaineer • 60 miles / Difficult 5200' climb

Tour 19

 12ABC,13

The Cherry Valley Mountaineer climbs the scenic ridges surrounding the Cherry Valley Flats series (Tours 17ABCD). The seven major climbs are thankfully separated by miles of relatively flat terrain, but this remains a very challenging ride. Climbers, enjoy! Flatlanders, beware! Tour options are available to eliminate some of the climbs if your legs tire out.

The Cherry Valley Mountaineer is also offered as a Cooperstown start from the Clark Sports Center (Tour 5).

Crumhorn Mountain • 14 miles / Difficult 1400' climb

Tour 20

The Crumhorn Mountain Tour is a climber's delight. Climb up Hooker Mountain, descend for a while, and then climb up Crumhorn Mountain before diving back to the Cherry Valley. Can you say, "switchback?" This short, demanding tour ascends two of the seven climbs in the Cherry Valley Mountaineer (Tours 5 and 19).

T O U R S   S T A R T I N G   F R O M   L A U R E N S

The Southwest Hills and Valleys Series explores the southwestern corner of Otsego County.

Tours 21A,B,C

Southwest Hills and Valleys A • 23 miles / Difficult 2000' climb

Tour 21A

 8

Southwest Hills and Valleys "A" explores more hills than valleys. After a few warm-up miles along the flat Otego Creek Valley, the tour climbs up Mill Creek to Maple Grove and beyond before descending to Laurens.

Southwest Hills and Valleys B • 50 miles / Difficult 3700' climb

Tour 21B

 8, 22C

Southwest Hills and Valleys "B" has its ups and downs. It goes up Mill Creek, then down the west branch of the Otsdawa Creek to the Susquehanna River Valley. It climbs up Sand Hill Creek, then down Cahoon Creek to the Butternut Valley. Then it climbs up to Maple Grove and beyond, before descending to the Otego Creek Valley in Laurens. The ups and downs are long, but gentle. Relax. Pace yourself. Persevere. Enjoy this beautiful tour.

Southwest Hills and Valleys C • 57 miles / Moderate 2700' climb

Tour 21C

 8, 22C

Southwest Hills and Valleys "C" visits the four river valleys in this region. Follow the Otego Creek Valley to the Susquehanna River Valley to the Unadilla River Valley to the Butternut Creek Valley before climbing back to Laurens. Visit Oneonta, Sidney and Gilbertsville along the way. Consider a side trip to the Soccer Hall of Fame.

Tours 22A,B,C   *The Butternut Valley Series* explores the beautiful Butternut Valley region of southwestern Otsego County.

Tour 22A

Butternut Valley A • 31 miles / Moderate 1800' climb

Butternut Valley "A" explores the northern third of the Butternut Valley from Burlington to Garrettsville.

Tour 22B

8

Butternut Valley B • 53 miles / Moderate 3100' climb

Butternut Valley "B" adds 22 miles and a 1300 foot climb to the Butternut Valley "A" tour. The extension explores the middle third of the Butternut Valley from Garrattsville to Morris.

Tour 22C

8, 21BC

Butternut Valley C • 68 miles / Moderate 3900' climb

Butternut Valley "C" adds 15 miles and an 800 foot climb to the Butternut Valley "B" tour. The extension explores the southern third of the Butternut Valley from Morris to Gilbertsville.

Tours 23A,B   *The Unadilla River Valley Series* explores the northern portion of the meandering Unadilla River which delineates the western border of Otsego County. Be forewarned that both rides in this series purposely seek out memorable climbs.

Tour 23A

Unadilla River Valley A • 31 miles / Difficult 2700' climb

Unadilla River Valley "A" climbs from Canadarago Lake's Oak Creek Valley, drops down to the Wharton Creek Valley, then climbs up to Plainfield Center before descending to the Unadilla River Valley. The return trip starts with a memorable climb up to Summit Lake, dives back to the Wharton River Valley, and then switchbacks up 800 feet in 3 miles before a final, exhilarating descent.

Tour 23B

Unadilla River Valley B • 49 miles / Difficult 3700' climb

Unadilla River Valley "B " adds 18 miles and a 1000 foot climb to the Unadilla River Valley "A" tour. The extension explores an additional ten miles of the relatively flat Unadilla River Valley before returning via a memorable climb from South Edmeston to Edmeston. As with the "A" tour, the grand finale includes an 800 foot switchback climb in 3 miles before a final, exhilarating descent.

Tour 24

Canadarago Lake • 16 miles / Difficult 1100' climb

This short, scenic tour explores the perimeter of Canadarago Lake. The first half warms up along the Lake's relatively flat eastern shore. The second half climbs to three summit vantage points far above the Lake's western shore. The incredible views are well worth the incredible climbs.

TOURS STARTING FROM SPRINGFIELD (OPERA)

The Monastery Meander Series explores the rolling hills and farmlands of southern Herkimer County. These tours purposely wander, so pay close attention to the cue sheet. **Note that people wearing shorts are not permitted on the Monastery premises.** This series is designed as a mini-rally offering quarter century (25 mile), half century (50 mile), metric century (62 mile), three-quarter century (75 mile), and full century (100 mile) tours. For the brave and foolhardy, an additional 8.7 mile option offers a hair-raising 6.5 mile descent followed by a gut-wrenching 600 foot additional climb in 2.2 miles.

Tours 25A,B,C,D,E

Monastery Meander A • 25 miles / Moderate 1300' climb

Monastery "A" is a leisurely quarter century ride to Jordanville. Discover a Russian Orthodox Monastery. Hike the Nature Trails behind the Glimmerglass Opera building and the Owen D. Young Central School. Enjoy the Rainbow Trout Fish Hatchery.

Tour 25A

2BCD,11AB

Monastery Meander B • 50 miles / Difficult 3500' climb

Monastery "B" is a half century ride. It adds 25 miles and a 2200 foot climb to the Monastery "A" tour. Discover a Russian Orthodox Monastery. Hike the Nature Trails behind the Glimmerglass Opera building and the Owen D. Young Central School. Enjoy the Rainbow Trout Fish Hatchery.

Tour 25B

2BCD,11AB

Monastery Meander C • 62 miles / Difficult 4300' climb

Monastery "C" is a metric century ride (100 kilometers equals 62 miles). It adds 12 miles and an 800 foot climb to the Monastery "B" tour. Discover a Russian Orthodox Monastery. Hike the Nature Trails behind the Glimmerglass Opera building and the Owen D. Young Central School. Enjoy the Rainbow Trout Fish Hatchery.

Tour 25C

2BCD,11AB

Monastery Meander D • 75 miles / Difficult 5100' climb

Monastery "D" is a three-quarter century ride. It adds 13 miles and an 800 foot climb to the Monastery "C" tour. Visit Millers Mills. Discover a Russian Orthodox Monastery. Hike the Nature Trails behind the Glimmerglass Opera building and the Owen D. Young Central School. Enjoy the Rainbow Trout Fish Hatchery.

Tour 25D

2BCD,11AB

Monastery Meander E • 100 miles / Difficult 6500' climb

Monastery "E" is a century ride. It adds 25 miles and a 1400 foot climb to the Monastery "D" tour. Visit Millers Mills. Discover a Russian Orthodox Monastery. Hike the Nature Trails behind the Glimmerglass Opera building and the Owen D. Young Central School. Enjoy the Rainbow Trout Fish Hatchery.

Tour 25E

2BCD,11AB

Just a few of the many fascinating Points of Interest...

left:
The Indian Hunter Statue, Cooperstown
right:
Clark Sports Center (CSC), the starting point for all tours leaving from Cooperstown.

left:
The Major's Inn, Gilbertsville
right:
Main Street, Cooperstown

left:
Lock 17 on the NYS Barge Canal, Little Falls

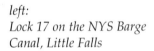

left and right:
The Russian Orthodox Monastery, Jordanville

Read about these and other places to visit in the Points of Interest Section.

72

Points of Interest

*The Cooperstown area is blessed with a rich history, an abundance of natural wonders, and a host of man-made attractions. **While you enjoy the scenic backroads on your bike, plan time to enjoy the many Points of Interest along the way.***

In this section you will learn more about the Points of Interest mentioned and numbered in the cue sheets and maps. Scan this information to get an overall feel for the area. If a particular Point of Interest appeals to you, choose a tour in which it is included. From the cue sheet, refer to this section for more detailed information.

*It would be impossible to mention all the Points of Interest in Leatherstocking Country. This section lists some of the available options, in no particular order. Other Points of Interest can be discovered at the Chamber of Commerce Visitor's Information Center, at 31 Chestnut Street, in Cooperstown; or at the Chambers of Commerce in Otsego, Herkimer, Montgomery and Schoharie Counties. See **Part 2: Where to Find More Information** for additional Chamber of Commerce information.*

Some of the information in this section is extracted and expanded from local brochures, pamphlets, and plaques.

The Clark Sports Center (CSC) is a multi-purpose, family oriented, health, fitness, and recreation facility on Susquehanna Avenue (County Route 52), in Cooperstown. **All Cooperstown bicycle tours leave from, and return to, the CSC. See Part 5: How to Get Here** for directions to the CSC and from the CSC to tours which leave from different communities (remote starts). The management of the CSC welcomes bicyclists to park, use restrooms, fill water bottles, use the phone, leave messages, and request emergency assistance free of charge. Use of other CSC facilities, including locker rooms and showers, necessitates a day fee.
- **Call: 607-547-2800**
- **Tours: 1-11**

(1)

Clark Sports Center (CSC)

Across from the Clark Sports Center (CSC), behind the stone wall, is the site of Iroquois Mansion, the home of the late F. Ambrose Clark. Though the mansion itself has been demolished, the Clark family maintains the herd of English Fallow deer which were part of the original estate. The deer can be viewed in the fenced enclosure on Susquehanna Avenue (left 0.2 mile leaving the CSC), or on Brooklyn Avenue (right 0.1 mile leaving the CSC; then left on Brooklyn Avenue 0.2 miles, to the fenced enclosure, behind the fire hydrant on the left).
- **Tours: 1, 2BCD, 3ABC, 10, 11AB**

  (also, ☞ **L 0.2 leaving Clark Sports Center on all Cooperstown tours.)**

(2)

Deer Park

Bassett Healthcare is a rural healthcare network, referral center, research center, and teaching hospital based in Cooperstown. The Mary Imogene Bassett Hospital, Emergency Room, and Clinic are located at the corner of Atwell and River Streets. Seek medical care at this location, if necessary.
- **Call 607-547-3456**
- **Tours: 1, 2BCD, 3ABC, 10, 11AB**

(3)

Bassett Healthcare Emergency Room

4

Christ Church Historic Cemetery

The graves in the Christ Church cemetery date back to the settling of Cooperstown in the late 1700's. The Cooper family graves are enclosed behind the iron railing. James Fenimore Cooper was buried here in 1861.
- **Tours: 1, 2BCD, 3ABC, 10, 11AB**

5

Stop at the intersection of River and Lake Streets in Cooperstown. Walk between the stone pillars and down the stone stairs to a breathtaking view of nine-mile-long Lake Otsego:

Sleeping Lion

- At the far end of the lake is Mount Wellington, named "The Sleeping Lion" because of its profile as viewed from this location.

Kingfisher Tower

- In the distance, on the right shore of the lake, is Kingfisher Tower. "In 1876, Henry J. Hardenburgh, who would later gain fame as the architect of the Dakota Apartments and the Plaza Hotel in New York City, was commissioned by Edward Clark to design this 60 foot tall medieval Gothic tower… simply by a desire to beautify the lake. "

Council Rock

- To the immediate right, here at the southern outlet of the lake, is Council Rock, a famous meeting place of the Mohican Indians. The rock itself is variably visible, depending on the water level.

Clinton's Dam

- Also to the right, across the Susquehanna River, is a boulder with a cannon, at the site of Clinton's Dam. The plaque reads that in July, 1779, during the Revolution, "General James Clinton built a dam to raise the level of Lake Otsego, and furnish water for navigation of the Susquehanna River. On August 8th, the dam was broken; and, the next day, 208 bateaux, heavily laden with the baggage and stores of the army, moved down the stream, while the army marched along the banks to join the main army of General John Sullivan, at Tioga Point (Athens, PA)." The Sullivan-Clinton expedition devastated Indian lands, checked the aggression of the English, and secured the frontier, extending westward the dominion of the United States. Each year, over the Memorial Day weekend, the expedition is remembered by the General Clinton Canoe Regatta, a demanding 70 mile race from Lake Otsego down the Susquehanna River to Bainbridge.

Susquehanna River Headwaters

- From where you stand, the Susquehanna River meanders 444 miles to Havre de Grace, Maryland where it, along with the Potomac, Rappahannock, York, and James Rivers, empties into, and helps to create, the Chesapeake Bay.
  - **Tours: 1, 2BCD, 3ABC, 10, 11AB**

6

Chief Uncas Tour Boat

Classic Boat Tours provides tours around beautiful Lake Otsego aboard a "fully restored classic launch." Hourly tours are available daily in July, August and early September from 10am-6pm . Cost is $8.50 for adults and $5.00 for children 3-12. Classic Boat Tours is located at the end of Fair Street, on the lake, in Cooperstown.
- **Call: 607-547-5295**
- **Tours: 1, 2BCD, 10, 11AB**

(7)

Cooperstown Village Office & Police

The Cooperstown **Village Police** can be found downstairs, at the rear of the Village Library building, at 22 Main Street, in Cooperstown. The Library building also houses the Cooperstown Art Association and is open daily 11am-4pm, Sunday 1pm-4pm.
- **Village Police: 607-547-2500**
- **Tour: 1**

(8)

National Baseball Hall of Fame and Museum

Wherever you travel in the USA, if you say, "Cooperstown", someone will say, "Hall of Fame." The Baseball Hall of Fame, on Main Street in Cooperstown, is very simply "…the best known sports shrine in the world." This is baseball Mecca. This is a baseball fan's "Field of Dreams - the bastion of individual athletic honor and achievement." Thousands flock to Cooperstown, on the last Monday in July (or on the first Monday in August), for the annual Baseball Hall of Fame Exhibition Game played on Doubleday Field. The Hall of Fame Induction Ceremony is held on the Sunday before the Game. Since the Induction Ceremony is held on the grounds of the Clark Sports Center, where all Cooperstown bicycling tours start, and since the usually tranquil roadways are flooded with avid baseball fans, Hall of Fame Weekend is not the time to plan your Cooperstown bicycling trip. The National Baseball Hall of Fame and Museum is open seven days a week, year round except Thanksgiving, Christmas, and New Year's Day. The hours of operation are from 9am-9pm from May 1 through September 30, and from 9am-5pm October 1 through April 30. Admission: adults $9.50, seniors $8.00, children $4.00.
- **Call: 607-547-7200**
- **www.enews.com/bas_ball_fame**
- **Tour: 1**

(9)

Cooper Park

In the center of Cooper Park is a statue of James Fenimore Cooper, sculpted by Victor Salvatore. The plaque on the statue reads: "On this site stood Otsego Hall, built by William Cooper, the founder of Cooperstown, in 1798, the home of James Fenimore Cooper where he lived from 1834 to the day of his death, destroyed by fire in 1853."
- **Tour: 1**

(10)

Smithy-Pioneer Gallery

The Smithy is the oldest building in Cooperstown. Judge William Cooper, the founder of Cooperstown, built the Smithy to house a blacksmith shop in 1786. Currently, the first floor site of the former blacksmith shop is used for contemporary art exhibitions, pottery classes, and special events. The second floor exhibits the work of local artists in the Pioneer Gallery. The third floor former Masonic Hall is dedicated to history exhibitions. The Smithy is located at 55 Pioneer Street in Cooperstown. It is open Tuesday to Saturday from 10am-5pm and Sunday from 1pm-5pm. Admission is free.
- **Call: 607-547-8671**
- **Tour: 1**

11 — Lakefront Park (restrooms)

Lakefront Park is a village green at the end of Pioneer Street, in Cooperstown. Enjoy magnificent views of nine-mile-long Lake Otsego at this scenic location. Eat a picnic lunch and bask in the sun. Hear a concert by the Cooperstown Community Band in the bandstand. See the statue of the Indian hunter and his dog, sculpted by John Quincy Adams Ward. This statue is a copy of the original, which can be found in Central Park, New York City. Public restrooms are available.

- **Tours: 1, 2BCD, 10, 11AB**

12 — Otesaga Resort Hotel / Leatherstocking Golf Course

The Otesaga Hotel is a stately and impressive landmark which has graced the shores of Lake Otsego since 1909. It is a member of the prestigious Historic Hotels Of America. The Hotel's Leatherstocking Golf Course (public welcome) is a PGA Course, which was designed by Devereux Emmet in 1909. The Leatherstocking Course is one of the most challenging and scenic golf courses in the East. It has been rated "Four Stars" by Golf Digest's 1996-97 "Places to Play." The Otesaga Hotel is located at 60 Lake Street, in Cooperstown. It is open April until October.

- **Reservations: 800-348-6222; Information: 607-547-9931**
- **www.otesaga.com**
- **The Leatherstocking Golf Course is located adjacent to the Hotel: 607-547-5275.**
- **Tours: 1, 2BCD, 10, 11AB**

13 — Fenimore House Museum

The Fenimore House Museum houses a spectacular collection of American Folk Art, including historic photographs and artifacts relating to James Fenimore Cooper. The Museum includes the impressive American Indian Wing, which exhibits 750 objects from the Eugene and Clare Thaw Collection of American Indian Art. Eat lunch at the Fenimore Café. Browse in the museum gift shop. The Fenimore House Museum is located on Lake Street (State Route 80) across from the Farmers' Museum, one mile north of Cooperstown. Admission: $9.00 adult, $4.00 children 7-12. Hours of Operation: April, 10-4 Tuesday-Sunday; May, 10am-4pm daily; June-Labor Day, 9am-5pm daily; September & October, 10am-4pm daily; November, 10am-4pm Tuesday-Sunday; December, 10am-4pm Friday-Sunday. Closed Thanksgiving, Christmas, and New Year's Day.

- **Call 607-547-1400 (607-547-1500 for recorded information).**
- **www.cooperstown.net/nysha**
- **Tours: 1, 2BCD, 10, 11AB**

14 — The Farmers' Museum

Historic buildings were moved to The Farmers' Museum to recreate an 1800's Village Crossroads. Turn the clock back to visit the country store, pharmacy, blacksmith shop, and Bump Tavern. Watch villagers cook, farm, weave and print with old-time skills. Watch a game of town ball. See the Cardiff Giant, the greatest hoax of the century. Enjoy the ever-changing hands-on activities and special events. Eat lunch and have a milkshake at The Herder's Cottage. Browse in the gift shop. The Farmers' Museum is located on Lake Street (State Route 80) across

from the Fenimore House Museum, one mile north of Cooperstown. Admission: $9.00 adult, $4.00 children 7-12. Hours of Operation: April, 10am-4pm Tuesday-Sunday; May, 10am-4pm daily; June-Labor Day, 9am-5pm daily; September & October, 10am-4pm daily; November, 10am-4pm Tuesday-Sunday; December, 10am-4pm Friday-Sunday. Closed Thanksgiving, Christmas, and New Year's Day.
• **Call 607-547-1450 (607-547-1500 for recorded information).**
• **Tours: 1, 2BCD, 10, 11AB**

The Cooperstown Chamber of Commerce maintains this Tourist Information Center at 31 Chestnut Street, not far from the traffic light, in Cooperstown. Stop by for a Visitor's Guide, brochures, maps, additional information about local attractions, directions, or just to use the restroom.
• **Call: 607-547-9983**
• **Tour: 1**

15

**Tourist
Information Center
(restrooms)**

The outside world quibbles about the origin of baseball. The modern day theory professes that baseball evolved from "rounders", a game invented in England in the 1600's and later played in the American colonies as "town ball". But to Cooperstonians there is nothing about which to quibble. Baseball was invented by Abner Doubleday (1819-1893) in Phinney's cow pasture, now known as Doubleday Field, in 1839. Period. End of discussion. Doubleday Field remains an active ballpark. It is the site of the annual Hall of Fame Exhibition Game held in late summer (see point of interest #8). After you visit Doubleday Field, proceed through the parking lot to the Main Street entrance where you will find the statue of "The Sandlot Kid", sculpted by Victor Salvatore.
• **Tour: 1**

16

Doubleday Field

Main Street, Cooperstown, is very simply a nice place to be. Norman Rockwell would agree. Stop at the Chamber of Commerce Tourist Information Center (point of interest # 15) for more detailed brochures and maps. Then, take your time exploring two blocks jam-packed with attractions. Visit the antique galleries, art galleries, craft stores, baseball memorabilia shops, restaurants, pubs, and the National Baseball Hall of Fame. Look for "The Ironclad Building", at 88 Main Street, so constructed after Main Street was destroyed by fire in 1862. On Saturdays, from 8am-1pm, stop at the Farmers' Market for fresh produce, local crafts, and home-made delicacies. Enjoy vintage small town America.
• **Tours: 1, 2ABCD, 3ABC, 10, 11AB**

17

**Cooperstown
Main Street
(commercial district)**

The historic marker reads: "Indian remains excavated in this field were reburied in 1874 at the base of this mysterious mound." The tablet on the mound contains this poem by the Reverend W.W. Lord: "White man, greeting. We, near whose bones you stand, were Iroquois. The wide land, which is now yours, was ours. Friendly hands have given back to us enough for a tomb."
• **Tours: 1, 2ABCD, 3ABC, 10, 11AB**

18

Indian Grave

19

Fairy Springs Park

Swim in Otsego Lake and picnic at this Cooperstown Village Park on the East Lake Road (County Route 31). Open Memorial Day to Labor Day. No charge for cyclists. ($5.00 car fee for non-residents)
- 607-547-2150
- **Tours: 2ABCD, 3ABC**

20

East Lake Hiking Trail

Beautiful, blazed hiking trails begin and climb uphill at the lower end of the steel deck bridge on the East Lake Road, County Route 31, north of Cooperstown. Respect this private property. Walk at your own risk, as you enjoy these trails.
- **Tours: 2ABCD, 3ABC**

21

Glimmerglass State Park (restrooms)

Hyde Hall

Glimmerglass State Park is located on the northeastern shore of Lake Otsego. The 600 acre park lands were originally owned by Lieutenant George Clarke, Governor of the State of New York from 1736-1744. The lands were later inherited by his great grandson George Hyde Clarke. The estate included Hyde Hall Mansion which is a National Historic Landmark. Hyde Hall is currently being restored to its original splendor as the finest example of neoclassic country mansions in the United States. The Hyde Hall Visitors Center is open 7 days a week. Tours are available Friday-Monday from 10am-6pm for $5.00.

For the bicycle rides described in this book, access to Hyde Hall is from within Glimmerglass State Park; ignore alternative directions provided on Hyde Hall roadway signs. Activities at Glimmerglass State Park include swimming, fishing, picnicking, hiking and camping. A concession stand is open from mid-June through Labor Day. Glimmerglass State Park is located on the East Lake Road, County Route 31, north of Cooperstown. It is open year round. Vehicle day use fee is $5.00. There is no charge for cyclists.
- **State Park Call: 607-547-8662**
- **Camping reservations call 1-800-456-CAMP**
- **Hyde Hall Call: 607-547-5098**
- **Tours: 2ABCD, 3ABC**

22

Three Mile Point

Swim in Otsego Lake and picnic at this Cooperstown Village Park on the West Lake Road (State Route 80). Open Memorial Day to Labor Day. No charge for cyclists. ($5.00 car fee for non-residents)
- **Call: 607-547-2777**
- **Tours: 2BCD, 11AB**

23

Glimmerglass Opera

Cooperstown is home to the internationally acclaimed Glimmerglass Opera. The 900-seat Alice Busch Opera Theater was designed specifically for opera by Hugh Hardy. It was built in 1987 on the northwestern shore of Lake Otsego, in a delightfully rural setting. Each summer season the productions are performed in repertory. The Goodyear Swamp sanctuary is located behind the Opera Theater, on the shore of the lake. Explore this beautiful five-acre wetland on walkways elevated over the water. A self-guided tour book is provided at the trailhead.

Goodyear Swamp Nature Trail

Directions to the Goodyear Swamp trailhead: Stand facing the Opera Theater at the crosswalk on State Route 80. Walk right a few yards; then turn left, on the gravel entrance road, until you come to the trailhead. **All Springfield "remote start" bicycle tours leave from, and return to, the crosswalk on State Route 80, at the Glimmerglass Opera.** Directions from the Clark Sports Center in Cooperstown, to the Glimmerglass Opera in Springfield, are provided in **Part 5: How to Get Here**. The Opera management welcomes you to park in the gravel parking lot across from the Opera Theater.
- **Call 607-547-2255 for information.**
- **www.cooperstown.net/glimmerglass**
- **Tours: 2BCD, 25ABCDE & detour on Tours 11AB**

24 Owen D. Young Marker

Woodruff Outdoor Learning Center Nature Trail

Owen D. Young (1874-1962) was born and educated in Van Hornesville. After a successful career in Law, he was chairman of the board of directors of the General Electric Corporation from 1922 until 1939. He also organized the Radio Corporation of America, RCA, for which he was also chairman of the board. He was perhaps best known for his efforts to solve reparations issues after World War I. The beautiful stonework building of the Van Hornesville Central School was his gift to the community.

Turn into the paved schoolyard, and bear left, downhill, on gravel for a few yards, to the Robert B. Woodruff Outdoor Learning Center. Here you will find idyllic hiking trails meandering through the woods, and following a cascading stream which eventually empties into the Otsquago Creek. This is a definite stop for a picnic lunch. Restrooms are available. Bicycles are not allowed on the walkways.
- **Tours: 2CD, 3C, 25ABCDE**

25 Diamond Tee Sport Center

The Diamond Tee Sport Center boasts a golf driving range, a batting range, and a miniature golf course. It is open 7 days a week during the summer season. It is located on the East Lake Road, County Route 33, two miles north of Glimmerglass State Park.
- **607-264-3394**
- **Tours: 2BCD, 3ABC**

26 Windfall Dutch Barn

The Windfall Dutch Barn in Salt Springville is a restoration of a New World Dutch barn dating back to the 18th century. The Barn is used for arts programs, including bluegrass concerts, contra dancing, country music, poetry readings, fiddling, and quilt shows. It is the site of the annual Goodyear Memorial Concert.
- **Call 607-264-3996 for a program list.**
- **Tours: 2D, 3BC, 16AB**

27 CV Massacre Alden Monument

The sign reads: " November 7, 1778. This monument marks the spot where Colonel Ichabod Alden, commander of the Fort, was tomahawked as he ran toward the Fort on the day of the Massacre." Read point of interest # 29, The Cherry Valley Museum, for more information about the Cherry Valley Massacre.

The monument is located on State Route 166 just south of Cherry Valley.
- **Tours: 3ABC, 5, 14**

Cherry Valley Massacre: Historic Cemetery

The sign reads "The remains of the settlers killed in the massacre in 1778 are buried here." Read point of interest #29, The Cherry Valley Museum, for more information about the Cherry Valley Massacre. The Cemetery is located on State Route 166 in the village of Cherry Valley.
- **Tours: 3ABC, 5, 14**

Cherry Valley Museum

The frontier headed westward from Albany following the overland route separating the Susquehanna River Valley from the Mohawk Valley. As the first settlement in this area, Cherry Valley was the furthermost post on the western frontier of the U.S. During the Revolution, the frontier settlements were plagued by British Tory and Indian raids from Canada. The most famous of these raids was the Cherry Valley Massacre of 1778. The museum flyer states that "… a force of 700 Rangers and Savages, under the command of Captain Walter Butler and Chief Joseph Brant, skulked in from the south… ruthlessly killing thirty-two inhabitants, mostly women and children." In 1779, the Cherry Valley Turnpike began the stagecoach era, which further encouraged western migration. In the early 1800's, Samuel F.B. Morse lived in Cherry Valley, working on the telegraph and Morse Code. Watch the 30 minute video on the history of the village. Walk or bike the village walking tour. The Cherry Valley Museum is located at 49 Main Street, in Cherry Valley. Open daily, May 30 through October 15, 10am- 5pm. Admission: adult $2.00, senior $1.50, groups of ten $1.00 each.
- **Call: 607-264-3303**
- **Tours: 3ABC, 5, 12ABC, 13, 14**

---

30 Pleasantview Breakfast House

The Breakfast House is a structural duplication of the Bump Tavern at the Farmers' Museum in Cooperstown. It boasts a 75 mile view of the Mohawk Valley and the Adirondack Mountains. This is a wonderful place to stop for a leisurely, home cooked breakfast in a delightful, rural setting. Cottages are available. The Breakfast House is located on County Route 54, two miles north of Cherry Valley. Hours of operation: 8am-11am Tuesday to Friday, 8am-12am Saturday, 8am-1pm Sunday. Closed Mondays.
- **Call 607-264-3980**
- **Tours: 3BC, 12ABC, 13**

Judd Falls

The Mohawk Indians named this beautiful 135 foot waterfall "Tekaharawa, The Place of High Waters." In later years, the falling water powered the Judd Iron Works and was renamed "Judd Falls." Judd Falls is located at the intersection of State Routes 20 and 166 just north of Cherry Valley. The falls are most impressive during the spring runoff. Exercise caution exploring this natural wonder.
- **Tours: 3BC, 12ABC, 13**

Henry John Kaiser (1882-1967) was born in this humble home, in the rural village of Sprout Brook. Though he first became prominent as a builder of ships during World War II, he later became famous as a builder of cars. He started the Kaiser-Fraser corporation, which bought Willys-Overland Motors, which later became the Kaiser-Jeep Corporation, which was sold to American Motors at the time of his death.
- **Tours: 3BC, 12ABC, 13, 15ABCD, 16AB**

32

Henry J. Kaiser Birthplace

Your eyes are not deceiving you. This really is a deer farm. Look for the deer at the crest of the hill 1.5 miles south of State Route 165 (4.7 miles north of Westford) on County Route 34.
- **Tour: 4**

33

English Fallow Deer Farm

Belvedere Lake is a private campground on Gage Road between Cherry Valley and Roseboom. A camp store is available for refreshments. Swimming and picnicking are available for a $5.00 day-use fee.
- **Call: 607-264-8182**
- **Tour: 14**

34

Belvedere Lake

Beer is not new to Otsego County. In the mid-1880's, half the hops grown in the United States were grown within a 40 mile radius of Cooperstown. A blight wiped out the crops at the end of the century. In more recent years, the Busch family, of Budweiser fame, maintains local residence. The Cooperstown Brewing Company (see point of interest 36) has been brewing beer in the English tradition since 1994. The Brewery Ommegang opened its doors more recently, in the fall of 1997. This is the first microbrewery in the United States to tap directly the world-renowned beer traditions of Belgium. The Brewery Ommegang is located on County Route 33, a few miles south of Cooperstown.
- **Call 607-547-8184 for tour information.**
- **www.belgianexperts.com**
- **Tours: 7, 8**

35

Brewery Ommegang

Beer is not new to Otsego County (read point of interest 35). On River Street, in Milford, is the Cooperstown Brewing Company, founded in 1994, to make beer in the English tradition. Tour the microbrewery and sample Old Slugger Pale Ale in the tasting room. Daily tours: 11am, 2pm, 3pm.
- **Call: 607-286-9330**
- **Tours: 8, 18AB & detour on Tours 5, 7, 17ABCD, 19, 20**

36

Cooperstown Brewing Company

Gilbert Lake State Park is located high in the hills above Laurens on County Route 12. The Park is open year round. Activities include swimming, fishing, hiking, picnicking, and camping. Vehicle day use fee is $5.00. There is no charge for bicyclists.
- **Call: 607-432-2114; Camping reservations: 1-800-456-CAMP**
- **Tour: 8**

37

Gilbert Lake State Park

38
Milford Depot
Railway Museum

The Leatherstocking Railway Historical Society maintains this totally restored 1869 train station. The Depot is situated along the tracks of the Cooperstown and Charlotte Valley Railroad on State Route 166 in Milford. See the Station Agent's office and the freight room, just as they were at the turn of the century. See the railroad artifacts and historic displays. Watch the videotaped history of the Delaware and Hudson Railroad. Ride the train. Visit the gift shop. Open Saturdays 11am-4pm and Sundays 1pm-4pm. No admission fee.
- **Milford Depot call: 607-286-7805**
- **Leatherstocking Railway Historical Society call: 607-432-2429**
- **Tours: 8, 18AB & detour on Tours 5, 7, 17ABCD, 19, 20**

39
Fly Creek
Cider Mill

The Fly Creek Cider Mill was built in 1856 and refurbished to its former glory in 1964. During the fall, watch water from the old millpond turn the cast iron turbine waterwheel. Watch the pulleys and belts set the apple press in motion, squeezing the cider for you to drink. Visit the Cider Mill Gift Shop located upstairs in the old grist mill. Sample the freshly made cider, old-fashioned cider mill donuts, cider floats, apple stix, apple pie, and sharp New York State cheddar cheese. Plan your trip to enjoy the "Applefest Weekend" in late September. The Fly Creek Cider Mill is located off County Route 26 in Fly Creek. It is open seven days a week from 9am-6pm mid-August through November.
- **Call: 607-547-9692**
- **Tours: 9CD, 11AB**

40
Cooperstown
Fun Park

The Cooperstown Fun Park boasts a miniature golf course, a driving range, paddle boats, bumper boats, a go-kart track, and a Tuesday night DJ. The Fun Park is located next to the Hamburger Hall Of Fame in Hyde Park, three miles south of Cooperstown on State Route 80. It is open 7 days a week from 11am-11pm June, July, and August; and weekends noon-9pm April, May and September.
- **Call: 607-547-2767**
- **Tours:11B & detour on Tours 8, 9ABCD**

41
Leatherstocking
Falls

Leatherstocking Falls, just north of Cooperstown, is easy to spot during the spring runoff, before the leaves sprout. In mid-summer its water volume diminishes, and it becomes more difficult to find through the trees. Look for the parking turnout on the right, a few yards after turning off State Route 80 onto the Pierstown Road (County Route 28).
- **Tour: 10**

42
Mount Otsego
Ski Area

This ski area was a source of community pride and comraderie before it was insuranced out of existence twenty years ago. In its heyday, it boasted the longest rope tow in the East. Legend has it, that on particularly inclement snowdays, the school bus would transport children to ski at Mount Otsego, since school had been closed for the day. All that remains are the overgrown slopes.
- **Tour: 10**

The Meadow Links Golf Course offers a natural grass tee driving range and a challenging, 18 hole, executive length golf course in a scenic country setting. Meadowlinks is located on the Allen's Lake Road (County Route 27), north of Cooperstown.
- **Call: 547-858-1646**
- **Tours: 11AB**

(43) Meadow Links Golf

During the fall, stop at Sharon Orchards for a tasty apple while biking any of the Sharon Springs Tours. Pick your own apples in September and October. Watch cider pressed year round. Open all year.
- **Call: 518-284-2510**
- **Tours: 12ABC**

(44) Sharon Orchards

The village of Sharon Springs lies in a ravine 900 feet above the Mohawk Valley. The village takes its name from the magnesia, sulphur and chalybeate mineral springs in the area. The curative powers of the springs were known to the Indians, and became world famous by the early 1800's. During its heyday as a health spa in the 1920's, Sharon Spring's 60 hotels and rooming houses accommodated more than 10,000 visitors who would come to "take the waters." Today it continues as a summer health resort on a much smaller scale. Visit the Sharon Historical Museum on Main Street (across from Imperial Baths). No admission. Open 2pm-4pm July and August. Open at other times by request.
- **Call: 518-284-2350**
- **Tours: 12ABC**

(45) Sharon Spa Bath Houses

The Iroquois Indian Museum, built to resemble an Iroquois longhouse, is a comprehensive museum highlighting all aspects of Iroquois culture, artworks and crafts. Archeological and historical exhibits are displayed. Enjoy the nature trails in this 45 acre park. The museum is located on Caverns Road in Howe's Cave near Cobleskill. It is open April through December from 10am-5pm daily. Admission: adult $5.50, children 13-17 $4.50, children 5-12 $2.50.
- **Call: 518-296-8949**
- **Tour: 12C**

(46) Iroquois Indian Museum

Relax by this water-powered flour mill, built in 1816. Take the tour. Enjoy the nature walk. Shop in the store. The Grist Mill is located on Caverns Road in Howe's Cave near Cobleskill. Open daily May 15-October 15, 11am-6:00pm. Admission: adult $3.00, Children $1.00.
- **Call: 518-296-8448**
- **Tour: 12C**

(47) Caverns Creek Grist Mill

Howe Caverns was formed millions of years ago by an underground river, after the great glaciers receded. Journey 156 feet beneath the earth on a 1 hour and 20 minute guided tour. The tour ends with a memorable quarter mile boat

(48) Howe Caverns

ride on the underground Lake of Venus. The cavern temperature is 52 degrees, so a jacket is recommended. Howe Caverns is located in Howe's Cave, near Cobleskill. It is open year-round 9am-6pm. Admission: adult $11.50, children age 7-12 $6.00.

- **Call: 518-296-8900**
- **www.howecaverns.com**
- **Tour: 12C**

49

Secret Caverns

Secret Caverns was also formed millions of years ago. It is advertised as "New York's largest commercial cavern…also New York's best kept secret," apparently referring to the ever-popular Howe Caverns, just down the road. This is a no-frills enterprise, "renowned for its naturalness…a caver's cavern." The 45 minute tour leaves every 20 minutes and visits a 100 foot underground waterfall. The cavern temperature is 50 degrees, so a jacket is recommended. Even if you don't visit the cavern, stop by the lake for a picnic. Open 9am-5pm May and October, and 9am-7pm June, July, August, and September. Admission: adult $8.00, children 6-11 $4.50.

- **Call: 518-296-8558**
- **Tour: 12C**

50

Canajoharie Gorge

Wintergreen Park

Wintergreen Park is located high above the village of Canajoharie on the Old Sharon Road (County Route 94). Within the 72-acre park flows the Canajoharie Creek, which over the years has eroded an impressive gorge. Upon entering the park, and *before* dropping down to water level, look for a hiking trail on your right, at the edge of the field. This hiking trail along the top of the gorge provides impressive views down to the water and leads to an overlook deck above 60-foot-high Canajoharie Falls. Return to the park road, and plummet down to water level for a relaxing picnic lunch. Swimming is not allowed. Wintergreen Park offers a concession stand (open predominantly on weekends), drinking water, and restrooms. It is open 9am-9pm daily from Memorial Day to Labor Day. There is no admission charge. The Canajoharie Gorge is one of the best kept secrets in the area. Don't miss this natural wonder.

- **Call: 518-673-5508**
- **Tours: 15ABCD**

51

Mohawk
River Valley

During the glacial era, the Great Lakes extended to modern-day Little Falls. There, the icy waters of glacial Lake Iroquois plummeted over a waterfall grander than Niagara. At the base of the falls, on modern-day Moss Island, the torrential water eroded huge potholes. Then it gouged its way east, towards the sea, carving the deep Mohawk River channel along the way. Later, when the alternate St. Lawrence River channel was freed of ice, the Great Lakes' outlet to the sea was diverted northward. The mighty Mohawk River was reduced to a trickle. Now, it meanders leisurely at the bottom of its own deep and sharply-eroded valley. Today, with the assistance of a parallel, man-made canal system, the Mohawk River has once again found an outlet to the sea. The Erie Canal connects Lake Erie at the Niagara River with the Hudson River at Albany. When it was built between 1817 and 1835, the original canal was 40 feet wide and 4 feet deep. Between 1835 and 1862, it was widened to 70 feet and deepened to 7 feet. Eventually, it was abandoned and replaced when the New York State Barge Canal was constructed between 1910 and 1917. All three stages of this canal system development can be observed at the Schoharie Crossing Historic Site near Tribes Hill (see Point of Interest # 54).

The Erie Canal

• Moss Island is located between the Mohawk River and the New York State Barge Canal, at Lock 17, in Little Falls. Its numerous large potholes, formed by the glacial Lake Iroquois waterfall, are recognized as a National Historic Landmark by the National Park Service. From the trail-head, walk straight ahead to the river side of the island. Then turn left, keeping the river on your right. Cautiously and patiently explore the steep periphery of the island until you discover the potholes.
  • **Tour: 16C**

Moss Island Potholes

• Lock 17, on the New York State Barge Canal, in Little Falls, is one of the highest lift locks in the world. Watch the lock lift boats up the 40 feet from the Mohawk River to the Barge Canal.
  • **Tour: 16C**

Barge Canal Lock 17

Read Point of Interest # 51. Lock 16 is near St. Johnsville.
• **Tours: 16BC**

52
Barge Canal Lock 16

Read Point of Interest # 51. Lock 15 is in Fort Plain.
• **Tour: 2D**

53
Barge Canal Lock 15

Read Point of Interest # 51. At the Schoharie Crossing Historic Site you can see all three stages of the Erie Canal's development. Schoharie Crossing and Barge Canal Lock 12 are near Tribes Hill.
• **Tour: 15D**

54
Barge Canal Lock 12. Schoharie Crossing

Isaac Jogues and René Goupil were Jesuit missionaries tortured and martyred by the Mohawk Indians at this site in 1646.
• **Tour: 15D**

55
Auriesville Martyrs' Shrine

In 1777, the British planned to defeat New York and bring a swift end to the colonial revolution. General John Burgoyne descended to Fort Albany from Montreal via the Lake Champlain Valley. General Sir William Howe ascended to Fort Albany via the Hudson River Valley. Colonel Barry St. Leger marched east to Fort Albany from Oswego via the Mohawk River Valley. St. Leger's forces seized Fort Stanwix at the entrance to the Mohawk Valley near

56
Herkimer Home Historic Site

Utica. The colonial militia, under the leadership of General Nicholas Herkimer, marched to protect the Fort. En route, the militia was ambushed at Oriskany. General Herkimer was mortally injured and returned home to die. Though Herkimer lost the battle, he prevented St. Leger from uniting with Burgoyne at Fort Albany. As a result, the British were forced to surrender at Saratoga. Herkimer Home is open May through September. Hours of operation: Wednesday through Saturday, 10am-5pm; Sundays 1pm-5pm. Admission to the grounds and Visitor's Center is free. Admission to the mansion: adult $3.00, NYS senior $2.00, child $1.00.
- **Call: 315-823-0398**
- **Tour: 16C**

ONC BOCES Occupational Center (ONC BOCES)

All Milford "remote start" bicycle tours leave from, and return to, the ONC Boces Occupational Center on County Route 35 in Milford. Directions from the Clark Sports Center in Cooperstown to ONC BOCES are provided in **Part 5: How to Get Here**. Otsego Northern Catskill BOCES (Board of Cooperative Educational Services) offers 2 year, occupational programs to juniors and seniors in high school who desire training in automobile servicing, business data processing, building trades, cosmetology, criminal justice, culinary arts, health occupations, natural resource occupations, office technology and welding. The staff at ONC BOCES welcomes bicyclists to park (as unobtrusively as possible if school is in session), use restrooms, fill water bottles, use the phone, leave messages, request emergency assistance, and even use tools and local expertise for bicycle repair if necessary.
- **Call: 607-286-7715**
- **Tours: 5, 17ABCD, 18AB, 19, 20 & detour on Tours 7, 8**

Michael A. LaCava Nature Center

The LaCava Nature Center, on the grounds of the Cooperstown Middle/High School, boasts beautiful nature trails, which wander through the woods and marshes of the Susquehanna River. After you enter the school grounds, find the entrance to the Nature Center at the bottom of the hill, to the right of, and behind, the fenced track. A trail guide, with a map and a plant/animal sight list, can be obtained at the principal's office.
- **Call: 607-547-8181 or 5512**
- **Tours: 9ABCD, 11A**

Corvette Hall of Fame

Americana Museum

As stated in the brochure, the Chevrolet Corvette grew up hand in hand with American pop culture, during the years following World War II. This unique museum honors America's own sports car in exhibits which chronicle United States history over the past 40 years. Thirty rooms recreate the sights, sounds, and memorabilia of thirty post-war years, with a vintage Corvette from each year as the centerpiece. Let the soundtrack, slide shows, and video clips set the mood. Happy days are here again! The Corvette Hall of Fame is located 5 miles south of Cooperstown, on State Route 28. Hours of operation: 9:30am-8pm (last ticket sold at 6:30pm) seven days a week. Admission: adults $9.95, children 5-13 $6.95.

- Call: 607-547-4135
- www.corvette-americana.com.
- **Detour on Tours: 8, 9ABCD, 11B**

60

The Town of Middlefield Historical Association preserves this one-room schoolhouse built in 1875 and closed in 1954. The Schoolhouse is listed on the National Register of historic places. The museum is open Saturdays in July and August from 12pm-4pm. Call for other open times.
- **Call: 607-547-5376**
- **Tours: 4, 17C & detour on Tours 5, 17D, 19**

Old Middlefield Schoolhouse Museum

61

Soccer's history is enshrined at the National Soccer Hall of Fame in Oneonta, NY, Soccertown USA. Exhibits feature memorabilia from soccer's greatest moments, players, and teams. At present, the Soccer Hall of Fame is located at 5-11 Ford Avenue in downtown Oneonta. Soccer tournaments are played at the Wright Campus on State Route 205. Eventually, the Wright Campus will include a 54,000 foot museum, playing fields, an outdoor stadium for 10,000 fans, an indoor stadium, a sports medicine clinic, and soccer training facilities. The Ford Avenue facility is open 10am-5pm Monday-Friday, and 10am-6pm Saturday-Sunday. Admission: $8.00 adults, $4.00 children to age 12.
- **Call: 607-432-3351. 800-KIK-GOAL**
- www.wpe.com/~nshof/
- **Detour on Tour: 21C**

National Soccer Hall of Fame

Wright National Soccer Campus

62

The charming, historic village of Gilbertsville, in the beautiful Butternut Valley, is surrounded by hills and horse farms. Not far from the center of town is the site of the polo fields, which are currently inactive.
- **Tours: 21BC, 22C**

Gilbertsville Polo Fields

63

Gilbertsville was a thriving commercial and educational center in the 1800's. Between 1860 and 1900 it was devastated repetitively by a series of suspicious fires. Gilbertsville wisely rebuilt itself with beautiful, and less incendiary, brick and stone buildings. After the fire of 1895, in which the Gilbert Homestead burned, Major James T. Gilbert III began construction of an inn which was completed in 1917. The Major's Inn is the most impressive of the English Tudor buildings that line Main Street in Gilbertsville. Tour the Inn and visit the gift shop. The entire village of Gilbertsville is on the National Historic Register.
- **Call: 607-783-2967**
- **Tours: 21BC, 22C**

The Major's Inn

64

This is not a formal point of interest. It is, however, a place where locals seem to be wading or swimming whenever I bike this route. Stop for a few minutes to cool off at this intersection of the Butternut, Dunderberg and Cahoon Creeks.
- **Tours: 21BC, 22C**

Gilbertsville Swimming Hole

65

Holy Trinity Russian Orthodox Monastery

In 1928, two Russian monks made a $25 down-payment to establish a Russian Orthodox monastery on 300 acres near Jordanville, NY. The Holy Trinity Monastery has become the largest monastery of the Russian Orthodox Church Abroad. Since 1948, it has offered a 5 year Bachelor of Theology degree, conferred by SUNY. It's always exciting to discover the onion-shaped domes, typical of Russian architecture, peering unexpectedly through the trees of the rural, New York landscape. **Respect the monastery's request that men wear long pants, and that women wear a dress. No shorts are allowed on the premises.**
• **Tours: 25ABCDE**

66

Millers Mills Ice Harvest

Andrew Miller and his 6 sons built a sawmill and grist mill around 1709 and thus founded Millers Mills. To paraphrase Charles Kuralt from his television show *On the Road*: The residents, all 150 of them within a 3 mile radius, have been cutting the ice on Little Unadilla Lake and storing it for use in the summertime, every year since 1790. Initially the ice cutting was performed out of necessity, to keep the farmers' milk cool; but in later years, when refrigeration came in, the tradition continued "out of stubborn recognition that, refrigerators or no refrigerators, some old things are worth keeping." Today, the ice is harvested in February using antique tools to notch out the ice. The blocks of ice are carried on horse-drawn wagons and stored in the old icehouse behind the church. In July, the ice is used to chill ice cream for the annual Homemade Ice Cream Social.
• **Call: 315-822-5281 or 315-822-5215**
• **Tours: 25CDE**

67

Cherry Valley Gorge

This beautiful gorge is on private property. Enjoy the view from the roadway. Take Lancaster Street (CR 50) up East Hill in Cherry Valley. Turn right onto O'Neil Road (gravel) for 0.1 miles to the guardrail.
•**Tours: 5, 14, 19**

68

Rainbow Trout Fish Hatchery

The NYS Dept. of Environmental Conservation maintains this rainbow trout fish hatchery on Chyle Rd. just south of Van Hornesville. Watch thousands of fledgling fish in their circular pools. When mature, these trout are released into local waters.
• **Tours: 2CD, 3C, 25ABCDE**

69

Cherry Valley Massacre: Wormuth Marker

From behind this rock, Lieutenant Matthew Wormuth was shot, then scalped, by his friend Chief Joseph Brant in 1778. (**Author's Note**: From what I can gather, the legendary Chief Joseph Brant was everywhere, killing everyone, in the late 1700's. He made killing and scalping a full time job. He seemed to enjoy lurking behind large rocks. He was definitely a fine lurking man. It must have been demeaning to be killed by someone other than him back then.) Read point of interest # 29, The Cherry Valley Museum, for more information about the Cherry Valley Massacre. The Wormuth Marker is located 2.5 miles north of Cherry Valley on Vanderwerker Road near its intersection with Salt Springville Road.
• **Tour: 13**

Tour Summary Charts

TOURS LEAVING FROM COOPERSTOWN

TOUR NUMBER	TOUR NAME	DIR.	DIST.	TOUR CLIMB			COMBINE WITH 🤝
				CLIMB RATING	CLIMB FT/MI	FEET CLIMBED	
1	Cooperstown Village	N	7	Easy	44	300	
2A	Glimmerglass A Outback	N	16	Moderate	60	1000	
2B	Glimmerglass B	N	31	Moderate	45	1400	Opera: 25ABCDE
2C	Glimmerglass C	N	43	Moderate	51	2200	Opera: 25ABCDE
2D	Glimmerglass D	N	62	Moderate	52	3200	Opera: 25ABCDE
3A	Red Creek Valley A	NE	31	Moderate	55	1700	CV: 12ABC, 13, 14
3B	Red Creek Valley B	NE	44	Difficult	62	2700	SB: 15ABCD, 16ABC
3C	Red Creek Valley C	NE	62	Difficult	61	3800	SB: 15ABCD, 16ABC
4	Elk Creek Valley	E	35	Difficult	86	3000	
5	Cherry Valley Mountaineer	E	61	Difficult	85	5200	CV: 12ABC, 13 MIL: 18AB
6	Beaver Meadow	E	7	Easy	43	300	
7	Susquehanna River Outback	S	33	Easy	36	1200	Mil: 17ABCD, 18AB, 19, 20
8	Gilbert Lake	SW	49	Difficult	72	3500	Laur: 21ABC SL: 22BC Mil: 17ABCD,18AB, 19, 20
9A	Oaks Creek A	W	9	Easy	44	400	
9B	Oaks Creek B	W	12	Easy	41	500	
9C	Oaks Creek C	W	16	Easy	37	600	
9D	Oaks Creek D	W	18	Easy	39	700	
10	Mount Otsego	W	19	Difficult	78	1500	
11A	Fly Creek Valley A	NW	30	Moderate	57	1700	Opera: 25ABCDE
11B	Fly Creek Valley B	NW	40	Difficult	67	2700	Opera: 25ABCDE

Climb Rating in feet per mile climbed: 0-45 = Easy, 45-60 = Moderate, 60+ = Difficult

KEY TO TOUR SUMMARY CHARTS

DIR = *direction explored from Cooperstown*
DIST = *length of tour in miles*
FT/MI = *feet climbed per mile during the tour*
FEET CLIMBED = *total feet climbed (elevation) during the tour*
COMBINE WITH = *tours which combine with other tours to lengthen the ride and explore additional areas. These tours leave from "remote starts" (see chart on the next page).*
Opera = *tours which leave from the Glimmerglass Opera in Springfield*
CV = *tours which leave from Cherry Valley*
SB = *tours which leave from Sprout Brook*
Mil = *tours which leave from Milford*
Laur = *tours which leave from Laurens*
SL = *tours which leave from Schuyler Lake*
Coop = *tours which leave from Cooperstown*

This Tour Summary Chart compares all the tours which leave from the Clark Sports Center in Cooperstown.

To choose a tour, tear out this page and the Overview Map on the next page. Consult them as you read the Tour Descriptions and Points of Interest sections.

This Tour Summary Chart compares **all the tours which leave from "remote starts"** in villages within a 10-20 mile radius of Cooperstown.

You can choose to **bike or drive** to any remote start.

See the **Map** of the Remote Starts on page 92.

See the **Directions** to the Remote Starts on page 96.

TOURS LEAVING FROM REMOTE STARTS

TOUR NUMBER	TOUR NAME	DIR.	DIST.	CLIMB RATING	CLIMB FT/MI	FEET CLIMBED	COMBINE WITH
TOURS LEAVING FROM CHERRY VALLEY (CV)							
12A	Sharon Springs A	NE	22	Difficult	71	1600	Coop: 3A SB: 16ABC
12B	Sharon Springs B	NE	54	Difficult	74	4000	Coop: 3A SB: 16ABC
12C	Sharon Springs C	NE	70	Difficult	71	5000	Coop: 3A SB: 16ABC
13	Judd Falls	NE	14	Difficult	100	1400	Coop: 3A SB: 15ABCD, 16ABC
14	Belvedere Lake	NE	18	Difficult	106	1900	Coop: 3A
TOURS LEAVING FROM SPROUT BROOK (SB)							
15A	Canajoharie Gorge A	NE	19	Moderate	58	1100	Coop: 3BC
15B	Canajoharie Gorge B	NE	41	Moderate	56	2300	Coop: 3BC
15C	Canajoharie Gorge C	NE	58	Difficult	65	3800	Coop: 3BC
15D	Canajoharie Gorge D	NE	78	Difficult	64	5000	Coop: 3BC
16A	Otsquago Creek A	NE	19	Difficult	77	1500	Coop: 3BC CV: 12ABC
16B	Otsquago Creek B	NE	44	Difficult	80	3500	Coop: 3BC CV: 12ABC
16C	Otsquago Creek C	NE	56	Difficult	71	4000	Coop: 3BC CV: 12ABC
TOURS LEAVING FROM MILFORD (MIL)							
17A	Cherry Valley Flats A	E	9	Easy	34	300	Coop: 8
17B	Cherry Valley Flats B	E	12	Easy	35	400	Coop: 8
17C	Cherry Valley Flats C	E	18	Easy	33	600	Coop: 8
17D	Cherry Valley Flats D	E	29	Easy	34	1000	Coop: 8
18A	Spring Brook A	E	14	Moderate	45	600	
18B	Spring Brook B	E	20	Difficult	67	1300	
19	Cherry Valley Mountaineer	E	60	Difficult	87	5200	CV: 12ABC, 13
20	Crumhorn Mountain	E	14	Difficult	100	1400	
TOURS LEAVING FROM LAURENS (LAUR)							
21A	SW Hills & Valleys A	SW	23	Difficult	87	2000	Coop: 8
21B	SW Hills & Valleys B	SW	50	Difficult	73	3700	Coop: 8 SL: 22C
21C	SW Hills & Valleys C	SW	57	Moderate	47	2700	Coop: 8 SL: 22C
TOURS LEAVING FROM SCHUYLER LAKE (SL)							
22A	Butternut Valley A	W	31	Moderate	58	1800	
22B	Butternut Valley B	W	53	Moderate	58	3100	Coop: 8
22C	Butternut Valley C	W	68	Moderate	57	3900	Laur: 21BC Coop: 8
23A	Unadilla River Valley A	W	31	Difficult	87	2700	
23B	Unadilla River Valley B	W	49	Difficult	75	3700	
24	Canadarago Lake	W	16	Difficult	68	1100	
TOURS LEAVING FROM SPRINGFIELD (OPERA)							
25A	Monastery Meander A	NW	25	Moderate	52	1300	Coop: 2BCD, 11AB
25B	Monastery Meander B	NW	50	Difficult	69	3500	Coop: 2BCD, 11AB
25C	Monastery Meander C	NW	62	Difficult	69	4300	Coop: 2BCD, 11AB
25D	Monastery Meander D	NW	75	Difficult	68	5100	Coop: 2BCD, 11AB
25E	Monastery Meander E	NW	100	Difficult	65	6500	Coop: 2BCD, 11AB

Climb Rating in feet per mile climbed: 0-45 = Easy, 45-60 = Moderate, 60+ = Difficult

Part 5: How to Get Here

Cranks from Cooperstown Tour Area

Part 5 provides directions to:
- *Cooperstown*
- *The Clark Sports Center*
- *and to all the Remote Starts*

Refer to the maps of New York State and Cooperstown Village on the next pages.

DIRECTIONS TO COOPERSTOWN, NY BY CAR

Refer to the
New York State
Map below.

- **From Albany:**
  - NYS Thruway ⑨⓪ W toward Buffalo, take Exit 25A ⑧⑧
  - On ⑧⑧ take Duanesburg Exit ⓶⓪ W to ⑧⓪ W
  - Follow ⑧⓪ W to Cooperstown

- **From Utica and Syracuse:**
  - NYS Thruway ⑨⓪ E toward Albany, take Exit 30 ⓶⑧ S
  - Follow ⓶⑧ S to Cooperstown

- **From Binghamton:**
  - Interstate ⑧⑧ E, take Exit 17 ⓶⑧ N
  - Follow ⓶⑧ N to Cooperstown

- **From Kingston:**
  - NYS Thruway ⑧⑦, take Exit 19 ⓶⑧ N to Oneonta
  - In Oneonta take ⑧⑧ E to EXIT 17 ⓶⑧ N
  - Follow ⓶⑧ N to Cooperstown

- **From Catskill:**
  - NYS Thruway ⑧⑦, take EXIT 21 ⓶③ W to Oneonta
  - In Oneonta take ⑧⑧ E to EXIT 17 ⓶⑧ N
  - Follow ⓶⑧ N to Cooperstown

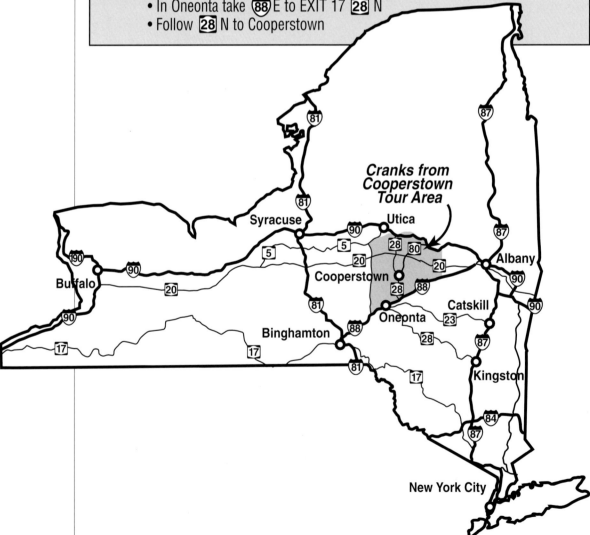

Cranks from Cooperstown Tour Area

DIRECTIONS TO THE CLARK SPORTS CENTER (CSC)

From 80 W (Albany):

0.0	R		CHESTNUT ST	0.1
0.1	S	SL	TRO CHESTNUT	0.2
0.3	L		SUSQUEHANNA AVE	0.9
1.1	R		CSC	

From 28 S (Utica & Syracuse):

0.0	L	SS	CHESTNUT ST	0.2
0.2	R		SUSQUEHANNA AVE	0.9
1.1	R		CSC	

From 28 N (Binghamton, Kingston, Catskill):

0.0	R		WALNUT ST	0.4
0.4	R	SS	SUSQUEHANNA AVE	0.3
0.7	R		CSC	

*This section is written in the "Cranks" Cue Sheet Format explained in Part 3. Refer to the **Cooperstown Village Map** below.*

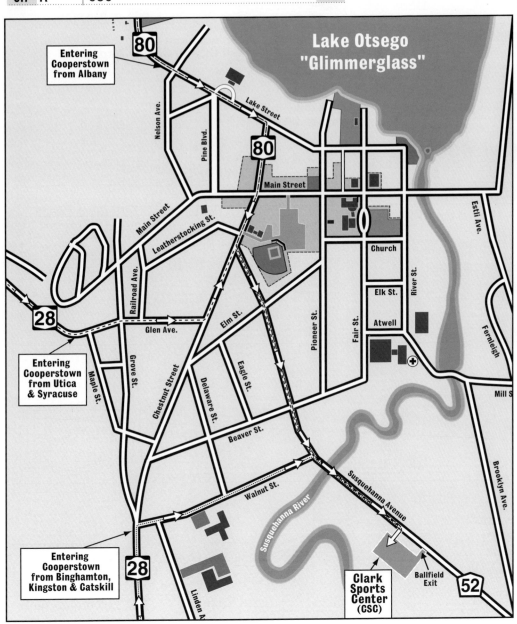

DIRECTIONS TO THE REMOTE STARTS FROM CSC

From CSC to Cherry Valley

0.0	R		UM 52	0.2
0.2	L		33 Before Bridge	0.3
0.5	BR		TRO 33	11.3
11.8	L	YS	166	2.2
14.1	R	SL	to Parking Lot @ Bank on R FOOD	

From CSC to Sprout Brook

0.0	R		UM 52	0.2
0.2	L		33 Before Bridge	0.3
0.5	BR		TRO 33	11.3
11.8	L	YS	166	2.2
14.0	R	SL	TRO 166 ⊘ Lancaster FOOD	0.7
14.7	BL		TRO 166 ⊘ 54	4.9
19.6	S		Sprout Brook General Store FOOD	0.1
19.7	L	SS	Park Near Barn @ Vivian Hawkins Beauty Shop On 163	

From CSC to Milford (ONC BOCES)

0.0	R		UM 52	0.2
0.2	BR		X Bridge Then BR 33	7.7
7.9	L	SS	166 ☞ R 0.8 FOOD	0.2
8.1	R		UM 35 X Bridge	0.3
8.3	BL		TRO 35 North ⊘ 35 South	0.2
8.5	R		ONC BOCES Occupational Center	

From CSC to Laurens, NY

0.0	R		UM 52	0.2
0.2	BR		X Bridge Then BR 33	2.5
2.7	R		11C	0.7
3.4	R	SS	28 ⚠ ☞ L 0.1 FOOD	0.2
3.6	L		11 Use Left Turn Lane ⚠	5.9
9.5	L	SS	205	9.3
18.8	R	SL	UM 11A (Water St) FOOD	0.3
19.1	L	SS	Maple (Becomes Main St)	0.4
19.5	R		@ intersection Gilbert Lake Rd 12 Park @ American Legion	

From CSC to Springfield (Opera)

0.0	R		UM 52	0.1
0.1	L		UM Brooklyn Ave	0.4
0.5	L	SS	Mill St	0.2
0.7	R	SS	River St	0.3
1.0	S	SS	TRO River X Main ☞ L 0.1 FOOD	0.1
1.1	L		Lake St (UM 80) ⚠ Summer	8.5
9.6	L		Glimmerglass Opera Parking Lot	

From CSC to Schuyler Lake

• By Car: Shorter, but more traffic

0.0	L		UM 52	0.8
0.8	L		At Third SS Onto Chestnut St ⚠	0.1
0.9	R		Glen Ave (28) ⚠	7.7
8.6	L		12 @ Post Office. Park @ Polly's House	

• By Bike: Longer, but more backroads. Consult Otsego County Map.

0.0	L		UM 52	0.4
0.4	L		Walnut St	0.4
0.8	L		Linden Ave	0.2
1.0	BR		TRO UM Linden ⊘ Dead End	0.3
1.3	L	SS	UM 28 ⚠	1.1
2.4	R		26	1.0
3.4	L		59 X Bridge	0.7
4.1	R		UM Bissell Rd	1.7
5.6	S	SS	TRO UM Bissell ⊘ R Cross Bridge	1.4
7.2	L	SS	UM 28 / 80	0.2
7.4	BL		Jones Rd ⚠	1.0
8.4	S	SS	UM SR 205 / 80	1.2
9.6	R		Fish Rd	1.7
11.3	S	SS	UM Robinson Rd	0.4
11.7	R	SS	UM 16	0.4
12.1	L	YS	28	1.3
13.4	L		12 @ Post Office. Park @ Polly's House	

Note:
See Directions to the
Remote Starts Map
on page 92.

R	Right	**S**	Straight	**SS** Stop Sign	**UM** Unmarked Road	⊘ Do Not Take
L	Left	**TRO**	To Remain On	**SL** Stop Light	26 County Route	☞ Detour Off
BR	Bear Right	**X**	Cross	**YS** Yield Sign	28 State Route	🤝 Combine With
BL	Bear Left	⚠	Caution			

Part 6: Where to Bike

Part 6 provides
***Cue Sheets and Maps
for 50 Cranks from
Cooperstown.***

Tear one out and....

Let's Get Cranking!➤

Gone Biking. Be Back Soon!

While on a tour, cyclists using this *Cranks from Cooperstown* book have permission to park at:

- **The Clark Sports Center** in Cooperstown
- **The Village Parking Lot** in Cherry Valley
- **The Vivian Hawkins Beauty Shop** in Sprout Brook
- **The ONC Boces Occupational Center** in Milford
- **The American Legion Post** in Laurens
- **The Exeter Historical Society's "Polly's House"** in Schuyler Lake
- **The Glimmerglass Opera** in Springfield

Tear out this page and leave it in your car window while you're cycling.

Please park courteously and have a wonderful tour!

Cooperstown Village Pathfinder

Start: Clark Sports Center. Ballfield Exit.

Miles	7
Rating	Easy
Climb	300' @ 44 ft/mi

Tour 1

•	0.0	R		UM 52	0.1
•	0.1	L		UM Brooklyn Ave	0.4
•	0.5	L	SS	Mill St	0.2
••	0.7	R	SS	River St	0.3
	1.0	S	SS	TRO River X Main	0.1
•	1.1	L		Lake St	0.1
•	1.2	L	SS	Fair St	0.0
••	1.2	S	SS	Thru Iron Gate TRO Fair X Main	0.1
	1.3	S		Thru Iron Gate TRO Fair X Church	0.3
	1.6	R		Beaver St	0.1
•	1.7	R		Pioneer St	0.4
	2.1	S		@ Flagpole TRO Pioneer X Main	0.1
••	2.2	L	SS	Lake St	1.1
•	3.3	R		Fenimore House Museum Entrance	0.1
	3.4	BL		@ Fire Hydrant to Exit	0.1
	3.5	L		UM 80 (Lake St) ⚠	0.1
•	3.6	S		TRO UM 80 @ Farmers' Museum R	0.7
	4.3	R		Nelson Ave @ Blue/White "H" Sign	0.3
	4.6	L	SS	Main St	0.0
	4.6	L		Pine Blvd @ Granite Marker	0.3
	4.9	R		Lake St (80)	0.1
	5.0	R		Chestnut St (80)	0.1
	5.1	S	SL	TRO Chestnut X Main	0.1
•	5.2	L		Between C of C & Global Traders	0.1
•	5.3	L		In Parking Lot @ Doubleday Field	0.1
•	5.4	R		Main St @ Statue Sandlot Kid	0.4
•	5.8	R		Estli Ave ⊘ Woodside Hall	0.3
	6.1	BR		TRO Estli ⊘ 33 North to L	0.6
	6.7	R	SS	UM 52	0.3
	7.0	L		Clark Sports Center	

NOTE
Caution in summer tourist season.

NOTE
Do not follow blue/white bike route signs.

R	Right	S	Straight	SS Stop Sign
L	Left	TRO	To Remain On	SL Stop Light
BR	Bear Right	X	Cross	YS Yield Sign
BL	Bear Left	⚠	Caution	

UM	Unmarked Road	⊘	Do Not Take
26	County Route	☞	Detour Off
28	State Route	🤝	Combine With

Mile	•POINTS OF INTEREST	#
0.0	Clark Sports Center	1
0.4	Deer Park (fenced enclosure @ fire hydrant) on L	2
0.7	Bassett Healthcare /Emergency Rm @ Atwell/River	3
0.8	Christ Church Historic Cemetery on L	4
1.1	Susquehanna Headwaters ☞ S downstairs	5
1.2	Chief Uncas Tour Boat ☞ R SS 0.1 Fair St.	6
1.2	Village Library& Police on L @ Fair/ Main	7
1.2	Baseball Hall of Fame to R @ Fair/Main	8
1.2	Cooper Park S @ Fair/Main	9
2.0	The Smithy on R just beyond Church St	10
2.2	Lakefront Park/ Restrm ☞ S 0.1 @Pioneer/Lake	11
2.4	Otesaga Resort Hotel & Golf Course on R	12
3.3	Fenimore House Museum	13
3.6	The Farmers' Museum	14
5.2	Chamber of Commerce Information/Restroom	15
5.3	Doubleday Field & The Sandlot Kid Statue	16
5.4	Cooperstown Main Street Commercial District	17
5.8	Indian Grave @ Main/Estli	18

COUNTY

Otsego

TOUR DESCRIPTION

The Cooperstown Village Pathfinder is a short and leisurely exploration of Cooperstown's quaint and historic streets. The Pathfinder can serve as a brief introductory ride or as a day trip to the local points of interest.

Plan time to visit the Baseball Hall of Fame. Enjoy the Fenimore House Museum's American Folk Art collection and its American Indian wing. Stroll though the 19th century streets of The Farmers' Museum. Shop on Cooperstown's Main Street. Picnic at Lakefront Park. Enjoy the views of Lake Otsego from the deck of the Chief Uncas Tour Boat.

Take a trip back in time to the days of James Fenimore Cooper and his *Leatherstocking Tales*. Enjoy this remnant of unspoiled Americana.

BIKE SHOP

@ 0.0 ☞ L 1.0 Cooperstown Bicycle. See map.

Let us know what you think of this tour! Email: crankmail@usa.net

©1998 Tourmaster Publications, Inc.

Climb Rating in feet per mile climbed: 0-45 = Easy, 45-60 = Moderate, 60+ = Difficult

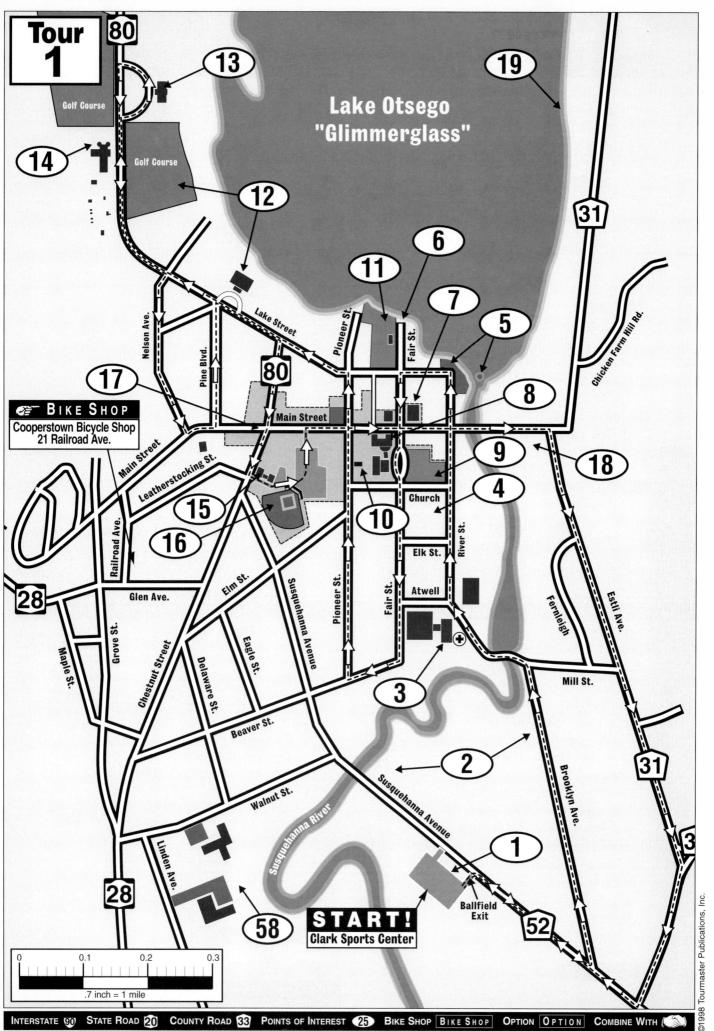

Glimmerglass "A" Outback

Start: Clark Sports Center. Ballfield Exit.

	Miles	16
	Rating	Moderate
	Climb	1000' @ 60 ft/mi

Tour 2A

OUT

•	0.0	R	UM (52)	0.2
	0.2	L	Before Bridge (33)	0.3
•	0.5	BL	UM Estli Ave ⊘ (33)	0.6
••	1.1	R SS	Main St (UM (31)) ☞ L 0.2 FOOD	0.2
•	1.3	BL	TRO (31) ⊘ Chicken Farm Hill	4.6
•	5.9	S	Steel Deck Bridge ⚠	2.3
•	8.2	L	Glimmerglass Park Summer FOOD	

BACK

•	0.0	R	Leave Glimmerglass State Park	2.3
••	2.3	S	Steel Deck Bridge ⚠	4.7
••	7.0	L	Estli Ave. ☞ S 0.2 FOOD	0.7
	7.7	BR	TRO UM Estli ⊘ (33) North to L	0.2
•	7.9	R SS	UM (52)	0.3
•	8.2	L	Clark Sports Center	

R Right	**S** Straight	**SS** Stop Sign	**UM** Unmarked Road	⊘ Do Not Take
L Left	**TRO** To Remain On	**SL** Stop Light	(26) County Route	☞ Detour Off
BR Bear Right	**X** Cross	**YS** Yield Sign	(28) State Route	🤝 Combine With
BL Bear Left	⚠ Caution			

•POINTS OF INTEREST

Mile		#
OUT		
0.0	Clark Sports Center	(1)
1.1	Indian Grave @ Main/Estli	(18)
1.1	Cooperstown Main St ☞ L 0.2	(17)
1.9	Fairy Springs Swim	(19)
5.9	East Lake Road Hiking Trail (on R before bridge)	(20)
8.2	Glimmerglass State Park & Hyde Hall Landmark	(21)
BACK		
0.0	Glimmerglass State Park & Hyde Hall Landmark	(21)
2.3	East Lake Road Hiking Trail (on L after bridge)	(20)
6.3	Fairy Springs Swim	(19)
7.0	Cooperstown Main St ☞ S 0.2	(17)
7.0	Indian Grave @ Main/Estli	(18)
8.2	Clark Sports Center	(1)

COUNTIES
Otsego

BIKE SHOP
@ 0.0 ☞ L 1.0 Cooperstown Bicycle. See map.

TOUR DESCRIPTION

The Glimmerglass Series explores the perimeter of beautiful Lake Otsego, the tranquil headwaters of the mighty Susquehanna River, and the famed "Glimmerglass" in James Fenimore Cooper's *Leatherstocking Tales*.

Glimmerglass "A" is an outback tour which explores the eastern shore of Lake Otsego. It provides the most direct route for a day swimming and picnicking at Glimmerglass State Park. Meet at the park with friends biking the longer Glimmerglass tours. Since this is an outback route, turn around anytime for a shorter ride. Plan time to visit the village of Cooperstown.

Let us know what you think of this tour! Email: crankmail@usa.net

©1998 Tourmaster Publications, Inc.

Climb Rating in feet per mile climbed: 0-45 = Easy, 45-60 = Moderate, 60+ = Difficult

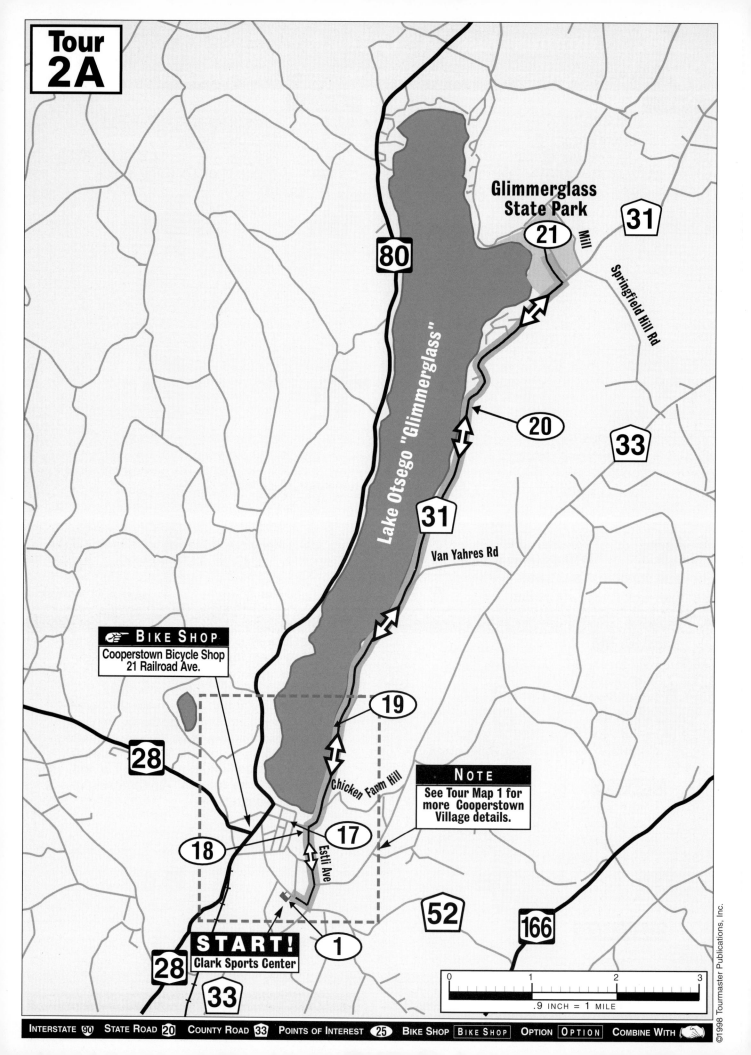

Tour 2A

Glimmerglass State Park

Mill

Springfield Hill Rd

31

21

80

20

33

Lake Otsego "Glimmerglass"

31

Van Yahres Rd

☞ BIKE SHOP
Cooperstown Bicycle Shop
21 Railroad Ave.

19

28

Chicken Farm Hill

NOTE
See Tour Map 1 for
more Cooperstown
Village details.

18

17

Estli Ave

52

166

1

START!
Clark Sports Center

28

33

| 0 | 1 | 2 | 3 |

.9 INCH = 1 MILE

INTERSTATE 90   STATE ROAD 20   COUNTY ROAD 33   POINTS OF INTEREST 25   BIKE SHOP BIKE SHOP   OPTION OPTION   COMBINE WITH 🤝

Glimmerglass "B"

Start: Clark Sports Center. Ballfield Exit.

Miles	31 🤝
Rating	Moderate
Climb	1400' @ 45 ft/mi

Tour 2B

•	0.0	R		UM 52	0.1
•	0.1	L		UM Brooklyn Ave	0.4
	0.5	L	SS	Mill St	0.2
••	0.7	R	SS	River St	0.3
•	1.0	S	SS	TRO River **X** Main ☞ L 0.1 FOOD	0.1
••	1.1	L		Lake St (UM 80) ⚠ Summer	8.5
••	9.6	S		TRO UM 80 @ Opera 🤝	1.9
	11.5	R		Public Landing ☞ L 0.7 80 FOOD	0.7
	12.2	L	SS	UM 53	1.7
	13.9	L		Continental ⊘ Dean Rathbun	1.8
	15.7	S	SS	Fassett Rd **X** 20 ⚠	1.3
	17.0	R	YS	UM 30	0.4
	17.4	R	YS	UM 31	1.1
	18.5	S	SS	TRO 31 **X** 20 ⚠ FOOD	4.1
•	22.6	S		TRO 31 ☞ R Glimmerglass Park	2.4
••	25.0	S		Steel Deck Bridge ⚠	4.9
	29.9	L		River St ☞ S 0.1 FOOD	0.3
	30.2	L	SS	Atwell	0.1
	30.3	R		Brooklyn Ave	0.5
	30.8	R	SS	UM 52	0.1
	30.9	L		Clark Sports Center	

🤝 **Opera: 25A,B,C,D,E**
@ 9.6 (Opera crosswalk) join
Tours 25A,B,C,D,E @ cue 0.0

R	Right	**S**	Straight	**SS**	Stop Sign	**UM** Unmarked Road	⊘ Do Not Take
L	Left	**TRO**	To Remain On	**SL**	Stop Light	26 County Route	☞ Detour Off
BR	Bear Right	**X**	Cross	**YS**	Yield Sign	28 State Route	🤝 Combine With
BL	Bear Left	⚠	Caution				

Mile	•POINTS OF INTEREST	#
0.0	Clark Sports Center	1
0.4	Deer Park (fenced enclosure @ fire hydrant) on L	2
0.7	Bassett Healthcare/Emergency Rm @ Atwell/River	3
0.8	Christ Church Historic Cemetery L	4
1.0	Cooperstown Main St ☞ L (or S @ 29.9)	17
1.1	Susquehanna Headwaters ☞ S downstairs	5
1.2	Chief Uncas Tour Boat ☞ R SS 0.1 Fair St	6
1.3	Lakefront Park/Restroom ☞ R SS 0.1 Pioneer	11
1.5	Otesaga Resort Hotel & Golf Course on R	12
2.3	Farmers' Museum L	14
2.3	Fenimore House Museum R	13
4.6	Three Mile Point Swim	22
9.6	Glimmerglass Opera & Goodyear Nature Trail	23
20.7	Diamond Tee Sport Center. Mini-golf	25
22.6	Glimmerglass State Park & Hyde Hall Landmark	21
25.0	East Lake Road Hiking Trail (on L after bridge)	20
29.0	Fairy Springs Swim	19
29.7	Indian Grave @ Estli/ Main	18

COUNTIES

Otsego

TOUR DESCRIPTION

The Glimmerglass Series explores the perimeter of beautiful Lake Otsego, the tranquil headwaters of the mighty Susquehanna River, and the famed "Glimmerglass" in James Fenimore Cooper's *Leatherstocking Tales*. An early morning departure is recommended to avoid traffic during the summer tourist season.

Glimmerglass "B" explores the lake's entire circumference. The route travels north following the lake's western shore on more heavily traveled State Route 80. After climbing east over "The Sleeping Lion," Mount Wellington, the tour returns to Cooperstown following the rolling and lightly traveled East Lake Road.

Plan time to visit the many points of interest along the way. Swim and picnic at Glimmerglass State Park.

BIKE SHOP
@ 0.0 ☞ L 1.0 Cooperstown Bicycle. See map.

Climb Rating in feet per mile climbed: 0-45 = Easy, 45-60 = Moderate, 60+ = Difficult

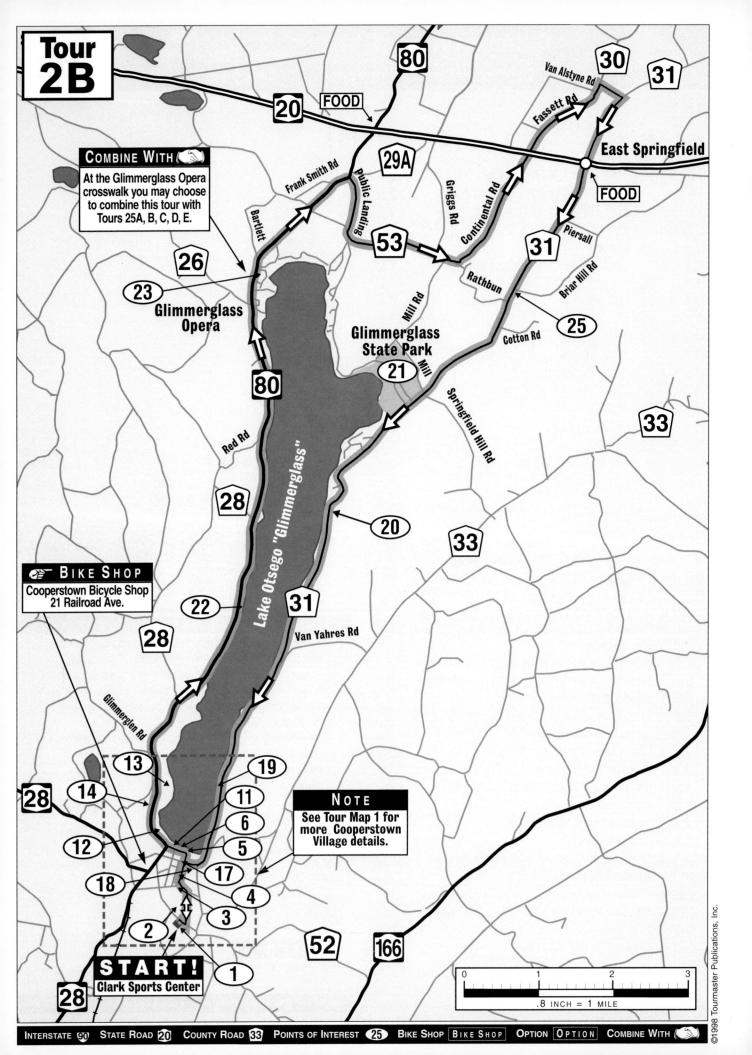

Glimmerglass "C"

Start: Clark Sports Center. Ballfield Exit.

Miles	43 🤝	**Tour**
Rating	Moderate	**2C**
Climb	2200' @ 51 ft/mi	

•	0.0	R	UM 52	0.1
•	0.1	L	UM Brooklyn Ave	0.4
	0.5	L	SS	Mill St	0.2
••	0.7	R	SS	River St	0.3
•	1.0	S	SS	TRO River X Main ☞ L 0.1 FOOD	0.1
••	1.1	L	Lake St (UM 80) ⚠ Summer	8.5
•	9.6	S	TRO UM 80 @ Opera 🤝	1.9
	11.5	R	Public Landing ☞ L 0.7 80 FOOD	0.7
	12.2	L	SS	UM 53	1.7
	13.9	L	Continental ⊘ Dean Rathbun	1.8
	15.7	S	SS	Fassett Rd X 20 ⚠	1.3
	17.0	S	YS	UM 30	0.7
	17.7	BR	TRO UM 30 ⊘ Willsey Hill Rd	5.6
•	23.3	L	SS	80 FOOD	0.6
•	23.9	BL	TRO 80 ⊘ Chyle Rd	1.4
	25.3	L	Willsey Hill Rd	0.7
	26.0	R	Hinds Rd	1.2
	27.2	BL	TRO UM Hinds Rd ⊘ Domion Rd	1.4
	28.6	L	SS	20 ⚠	2.0
•	30.6	R	31 FOOD	4.1
•	34.7	S	TRO 31 ☞ R Glimmerglass Park	2.4
••	37.1	S	Steel Deck Bridge ⚠	4.9
	42.0	L	River St ☞ S 0.1 FOOD	0.3
	42.3	L	SS	Atwell	0.1

42.4	R	Brooklyn Ave	0.5
42.9	R	SS	UM 52	0.1
43.0	L	Clark Sports Center	

🤝 **Opera: Tours 25A,B,C,D,E**
@ 9.6 (Opera crosswalk) join
Tours 25A,B,C,D,E @ cue 0.0

R	Right	**S**	Straight	**SS** Stop Sign
L	Left	**TRO**	To Remain On	**SL** Stop Light
BR	Bear Right	**X**	Cross	**YS** Yield Sign
BL	Bear Left	**⚠**	Caution	

UM Unmarked Road	**⊘** Do Not Take
26 County Route	**☞** Detour Off
28 State Route	**🤝** Combine With

Points of Interest

Tour Description

The Glimmerglass Series explores the perimeter of beautiful Lake Otsego, the tranquil headwaters of the mighty Susquehanna River, and the famed "Glimmerglass" in James Fenimore Cooper's *Leatherstocking Tales*. An early morning departure is recommended to avoid traffic during the summer tourist season.

Glimmerglass "C" explores the lake's entire circumference. It adds 12 miles and an 800 foot climb to the Glimmerglass "B" tour. The extension skirts the edge of the highlands overlooking the Mohawk Valley. From this vantage point, excellent views of the Valley and the Adirondacks can be enjoyed.

Visit the charming village of Van Hornesville. Picnic and hike at the Woodruff Nature Trail. Swim at Glimmerglass State Park. Plan time to visit the many points of interest along the way.

COUNTIES
Otsego, Herkimer

BIKE SHOP
@ 0.0 ☞ L 1.0 Cooperstown Bicycle. See map.

Let us know what you think of this tour! Email: crankmail@usa.net

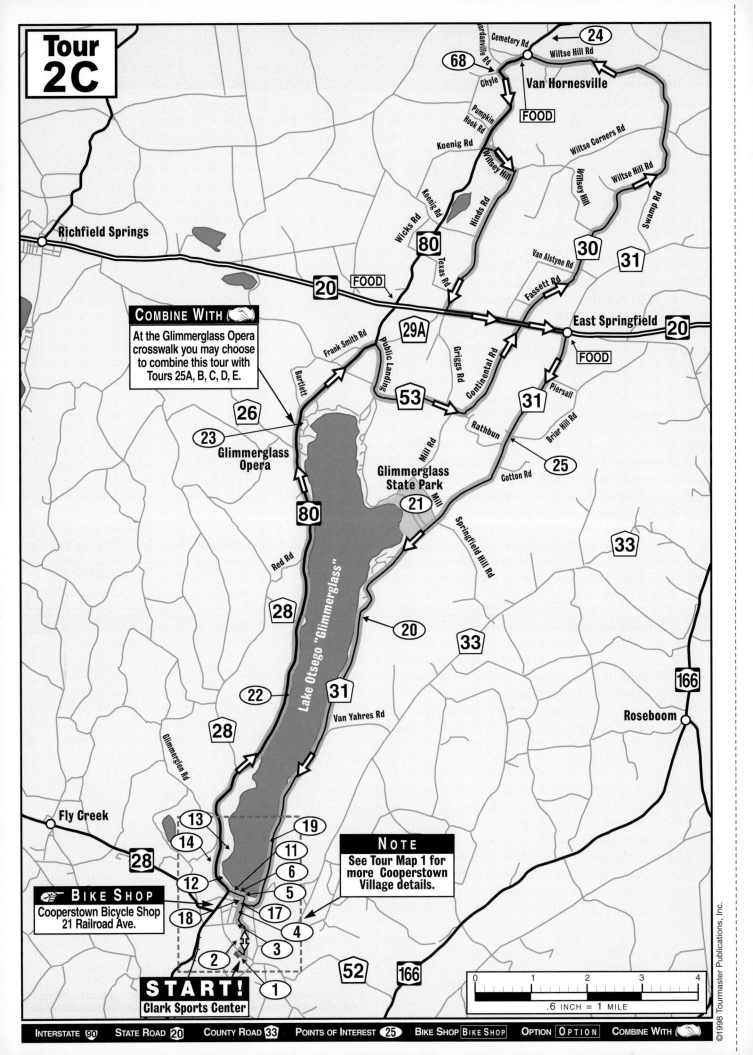

Glimmerglass "D"

Start: Clark Sports Center. Ballfield Exit.

Miles	62
Rating	Moderate
Climb	3200' @ 52 ft/mi

Tour 2D

• 0.0	R		UM 52	0.1
• 0.1	L		UM Brooklyn Ave	0.4
0.5	L	SS	Mill St	0.2
•• 0.7	R	SS	River St	0.3
• 1.0	S	SS	TRO River **X** Main 👉L 0.1 FOOD	0.1
•• 1.1	L		Lake St (UM 80) ⚠ Summer	8.5
• 9.6	S		TRO UM 80 @ Opera 🤝	1.9
11.5	R		Public Landing 👉L 0.7 80 FOOD	0.7
12.2	L	SS	UM 53	1.7
13.9	L		Continental ⊘Dean Rathbun	1.8
15.7	S	SS	Fassett Rd **X** 20 ⚠	1.3
17.0	S	YS	UM 30	0.7
17.7	BR		TRO UM 30 ⊘ Willsey Hill Rd	5.6
•• 23.3	R	SS	80 👉L 0.1 FOOD	11.7
• 35.0	R		163 FOOD	0.1
35.1	L		Clinton Ave	0.2
35.3	R		Waddell Ave	0.3
35.6	L	SS	Garfield St	0.5
36.1	BR		TRO Garfield ⊘Fisk Hill Rd	0.2
36.3	L	SS	163	1.5
37.8	BR		Freysbush ⊘ 163	0.3
38.1	L		Walts Rd after Cemetery	1.3
39.4	R	SS	UM Hessville Rd	0.2
39.6	L		Goulds Rd	1.1

40.7	L		Bauder	1.1
41.8	R	SS	UM 163	0.8
42.6	R		Indian Trail Rd	3.1
• 45.7	S		Clinton St ⊘Ripple/Salt Springville	4.5
• 50.2	S	SS	31 **X** 20 ⚠ FOOD	4.1
• 54.3	S		TRO 31 👉R Glimmerglass Park	2.4
•• 56.7	S		Steel Deck Bridge ⚠	4.9
61.6	L		River St 👉S 0.1 FOOD	0.3
61.9	L	SS	Atwell	0.2
62.1	R		Brooklyn Ave	0.4
62.5	R	SS	UM 52	0.1
62.6	L		Clark Sports Center	

🤝 **Opera: 25A,B,C,D,E**
@ 9.6 (Opera crosswalk) join
Tours 25A,B,C,D,E @ cue 0.0

BIKE SHOP
a) @ 0.0 👉 L 1.0 Cooperstown Bicycle. See map
b) @ 35.0 👉 S 80 0.3 True Value Hardware

R	Right	**S**	Straight	**SS**	Stop Sign	**UM** Unmarked Road ⊘ Do Not Take
L	Left	**TRO**	To Remain On	**SL**	Stop Light	26 County Route 👉 Detour Off
BR	Bear Right	**X**	Cross	**YS**	Yield Sign	28 State Route 🤝 Combine With
BL	Bear Left	⚠	Caution			

Mile	•POINTS OF INTEREST	#
0.0	Clark Sports Center	1
0.4	Deer Park (fenced enclosure @ fire hydrant) on L	2
0.7	Bassett Healthcare/Emergency Rm @Atwell/River	3
0.8	Christ Church Historic Cemetery L	4
1.0	Cooperstown Main St 👉 L (or S @ 59.8)	17
1.1	Susquehanna Headwaters 👉 S downstairs	5
1.2	Chief Uncas Tour Boat 👉 R SS 0.1 Fair St	6
1.3	Lakefront Park/Restroom 👉 R SS 0.1 Pioneer	11
1.5	Otesaga Resort Hotel & Golf Course on R	12
2.3	Farmers' Museum L	14
2.3	Fenimore House Museum R	13
4.6	Three Mile Point Swim	22
9.6	Glimmerglass Opera & Goodyear Nature Trail	23
23.3	Rainbow Fish Hatchery 👉 L0.5 then BR Chyle	68
23.4	Owen D. Young Marker & Nature Trail	24
35.0	Barge Canal Lock 15 👉 S 80 0.9 follow signs	53
45.7	Windfall Dutch Barn	26
52.4	Diamond Tee Sport Center. Mini-golf	25
54.3	Glimmerglass State Park & Hyde Hall Landmark	21
56.7	East Lake Road Hiking Trail (on L after bridge)	20
60.7	Fairy Springs Swim	19

TOUR DESCRIPTION

| 61.4 | Indian Grave @ Estli/ Main | 18 |

The Glimmerglass Series explores the perimeter of beautiful Lake Otsego, the tranquil headwaters of the mighty Susquehanna River, and the famed "Glimmerglass" in James Fenimore Cooper's *Leatherstocking Tales*. An early morning departure is recommended to avoid traffic during the summer tourist season

Glimmerglass "D" explores the lake's entire circumference. It adds 19 miles and a 1000 foot climb to the Glimmerglass "C" tour. The extension follows the Otsquago Creek from Van Hornesville down to the Mohawk Valley at Fort Plain. Then it climbs back to Lake Otsego. Though the climb rating for the entire tour is moderate at 52 feet per mile, an eleven mile segment is difficult, climbing 145 feet per mile!

While in Fort Plain, visit Lock 15 of the New York State Barge Canal. Swim and picnic at Glimmerglass State Park. Plan time to visit the many other points of interest along the way.

COUNTIES
Otsego, Herkimer, Montgomery

Let us know what you think of this tour! Email: crankmail@usa.net

©1998 Tourmaster Publications, Inc.

Climb Rating in feet per mile climbed: 0-45 = Easy, 45-60 = Moderate, 60+ = Difficult

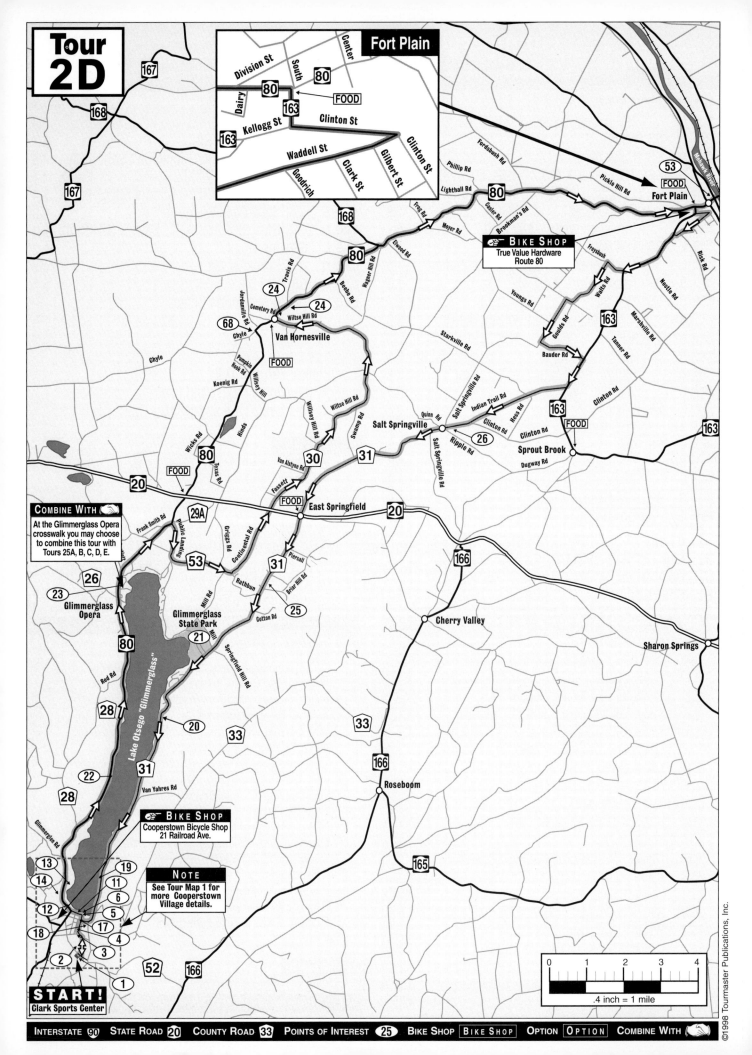

Tour 2D

167
168
167

Fort Plain

Division St
Center
South
80
80
FOOD
163
Kellogg St
Clinton St
Dairy
163
Waddell St
Goodrich
Clark St
Gilbert St
Clinton St

53 FOOD
Fort Plain

Fordsbush Rd
Phillip Rd
Pickle Hill Rd
Lighthall Rd
80
Casler Rd
Brookman's Rd
Risk Rd
Frog Rd
Moyer Rd
Freysbush
Nestle Rd
168
Elwood Rd
80

BIKE SHOP
True Value Hardware
Route 80

Youngs Rd
Walts Rd
Marshville Rd
Travis Rd
24
Beebe Rd
Wagner Hill Rd
163
Tanner Rd
Cemetery Rd
24
Goulds Rd
Jordanville Rd
Wiltse Hill Rd
Starkville Rd
Bauder Rd
68
Chyle
Van Hornesville
FOOD
Clinton Rd
Pumpkin Hook Rd
Wiltsey Hill
Wiltse Hill Rd
163
Chyle
Koenig Rd
Salt Springville Rd
Indian Trail Rd
FOOD
Clinton Rd
163
Hinds
Swamp Rd
Quinn Rd
Hess Rd
Clinton Rd
Sprout Brook
Wicks Rd
80
Van Alstyne Rd
30
Salt Springville
26
Clinton Rd
Texas Rd
31
Ripple Rd
Salt Springville Rd
Dugway Rd
FOOD
Fassett
20
FOOD
East Springfield
20

COMBINE WITH
At the Glimmerglass Opera crosswalk you may choose to combine this tour with Tours 25A, B, C, D, E.

Frank Smith Rd
Public Landing
29A
Griggs Rd
Continental Rd
Piersall
166
53
Rathbun
31
Brier Hill Rd
26
Mill Rd
25
23
Glimmerglass Opera
Glimmerglass State Park
Cotton Rd
Cherry Valley
Sharon Springs
80
21
Mill
Springfield Hill Rd
Red Rd
33
28
20
33
166
Lake Otsego "Glimmerglass"
22
31
Roseboom
28
Van Yahres Rd

BIKE SHOP
Cooperstown Bicycle Shop
21 Railroad Ave.

Glimmerglen Rd
13
19
14
11
165
12
6

NOTE
See Tour Map 1 for more Cooperstown Village details.

5
18
17
4
2
3
52
1
166

START!
Clark Sports Center

0 1 2 3 4
.4 inch = 1 mile

INTERSTATE **90**   STATE ROAD **20**   COUNTY ROAD **33**   POINTS OF INTEREST **25**   BIKE SHOP **BIKE SHOP**   OPTION **OPTION**   COMBINE WITH

©1998 Tourmaster Publications, Inc.

Red Creek Valley "A"

Start: Clark Sports Center, Ballfield Exit

Miles	31
Rating	Moderate
Climb	1700' @ 55 ft/mi

Tour 3A

•	0.0 R		UM 52		0.2
	0.2 L		33 Before Bridge		0.3
	0.5 BR		TRO 33		11.3
••	11.8 L	YS	166		2.2
•	14.0 L	SL	Genesee St	🤝 FOOD	4.2
	18.2 L	SS	UM 20 ⚠	FOOD	0.5
•	18.7 L		31	FOOD	4.1
•	22.8 S		TRO 31 👉 R Glimmerglass Park		2.4
••	25.2 S		Steel Deck Bridge ⚠		4.9
••	30.1 L		River St 👉 S 0.1 FOOD		0.2
•	30.3 L	SS	Atwell		0.2
•	30.5 R		Brooklyn Ave		0.5
	31.0 R		UM 52		0.1
	31.1 L		Clark Sports Center		

🤝 **Cherry Valley: 12A,B,C; 13,14**
@ 14.0 R SL then BL ⊘ Lancaster to parking lot
@ bank on R to join Tours 12A,B,C; 13,14
@ cue 0.0

R Right	**S** Straight	**SS** Stop Sign	**UM** Unmarked Road	⊘ Do Not Take
L Left	**TRO** To Remain On	**SL** Stop Light	26 County Route	👉 Detour Off
BR Bear Right	**X** Cross	**YS** Yield Sign	28 State Route	🤝 Combine With
BL Bear Left	⚠ Caution			

Mile	•POINTS OF INTEREST	#
0.0	Clark Sports Center	1
13.6	Cherry Valley Massacre: Alden Monument	27
13.8	Cherry Valley Massacre: Historic Cemetery	28
14.0	Cherry Valley Museum 👉 R/BL @ SL 0.2 on 166	29
20.6	Diamond Tee Sport Center. Mini-golf.	25
22.8	Glimmerglass State Park & Hyde Hall Landmark	21
25.2	East Lake Road Hiking Trail (on L after bridge)	20
29.1	Fairy Springs Swim	19
29.8	Indian Grave @ Estli/ Main	18
30.1	Cooperstown Main Street 👉 S 0.1	17
30.1	Susquehanna Headwaters 👉 R 0.1(go downstairs)	5
30.2	Christ Church Historic Cemetery on R	4
30.3	Bassett Healthcare/Emergency Rm @Atwell/River	3
30.6	Deer Park (fenced enclosure @ fire hydrant on R)	2

COUNTIES
Otsego

BIKE SHOP
a) 0.0 👉 L 1.0 Cooperstown Bicycle. See map.
b) @ 11.8 Hawk Mountain Sports

TOUR DESCRIPTION

The Red Creek Valley Series explores the first valley east of Lake Otsego.

Red Creek Valley "A" descends into the historic village of Cherry Valley before returning to Cooperstown following the eastern shore of Lake Otsego.

Plan time to visit the Cherry Valley Museum. Learn about the Cherry Valley Massacre. Swim and picnic at Glimmerglass State Park.

©1998 Tourmaster Publications, Inc.

Let us know what you think of this tour! Email: crankmail@usa.net

Climb Rating in feet per mile climbed: 0-45 = Easy, 45-60 = Moderate, 60+ = Difficult

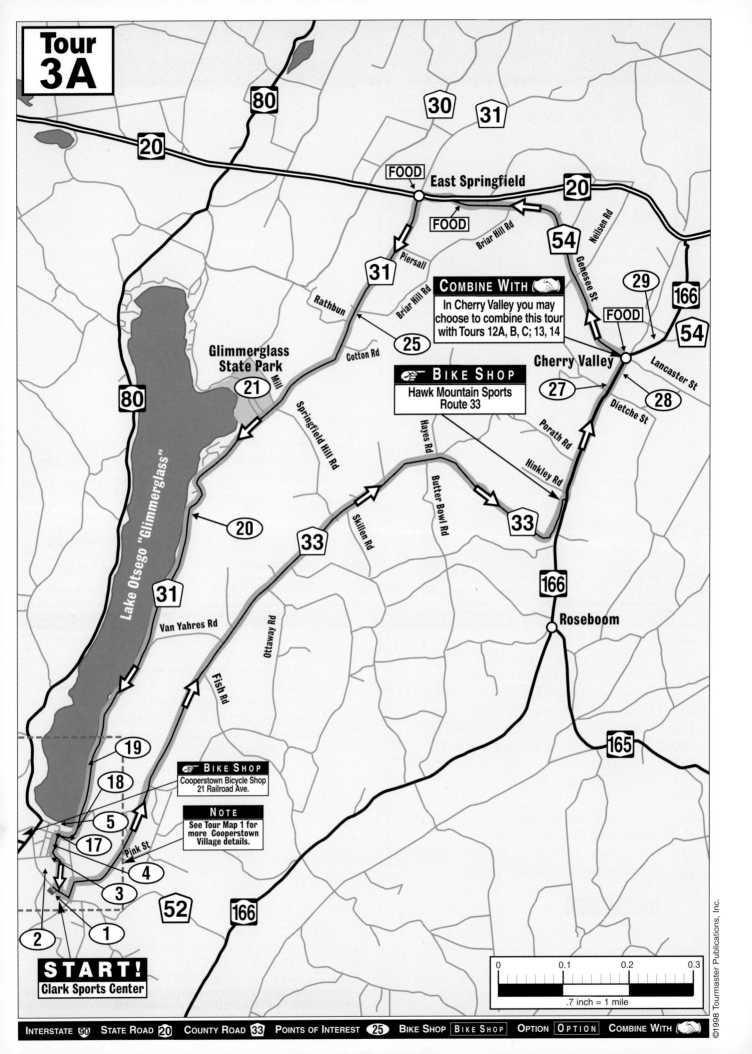

Tour 3A

80

20

80

30 **31**

FOOD East Springfield **20**

FOOD ← Briar Hill Rd **54** Neilsen Rd

Piersall

Rathbun Briar Hill Rd **29** FOOD **166**

Glimmerglass State Park Cotton Rd **25** **54**

21 Genesee St

COMBINE WITH 🤝
In Cherry Valley you may choose to combine this tour with Tours 12A, B, C; 13, 14

Springfield Hill Rd **BIKE SHOP**
Hawk Mountain Sports
Route 33

Cherry Valley Lancaster St

Lake Otsego "Glimmerglass" **20** **27** **28**

Hayes Rd Dietche St

80 Skillen Rd Porath Rd

31 **33** Butter Bowl Rd Hinkley Rd

Van Yahres Rd **33**

Ottaway Rd

166

Fish Rd Roseboom

19

18 **BIKE SHOP**
Cooperstown Bicycle Shop
21 Railroad Ave.

165

5 **NOTE**
See Tour Map 1 for more Cooperstown Village details.

17 Pink St

4

3

2 **1** **52** **166**

START!
Clark Sports Center

0   0.1   0.2   0.3

.7 inch = 1 mile

INTERSTATE 90   **STATE ROAD** 20   **COUNTY ROAD** 33   **POINTS OF INTEREST** 25   **BIKE SHOP** BIKE SHOP   **OPTION** OPTION   **COMBINE WITH** 🤝

©1998 Tourmaster Publications, Inc.

Red Creek Valley "B"

Start: Clark Sports Center. Ballfield Exit.

Miles	44 🤝
Rating	Difficult
Climb	2700' @ 62 ft/mi

Tour 3B

	Mile	Turn	Sign	Directions	Next
•	0.0	R		UM 52	0.2
	0.2	L		33 Before Bridge	0.3
	0.5	BR		TRO 33	11.3
••	11.8	L	YS	166	2.3
•	14.1	R	SL	BL TRO 166 ⊘ Lancaster FOOD	0.6
•	14.7	BR		54 ⊘ 166	2.8
	17.5	L		⊘ 34A Then L SS 20 ⚠	2.4
	19.9	BR		Cherry Valley Exit	0.1
•	20.0	R	SS	32 ☞ S X Field to Judd Falls	3.3
•	23.3	L		Dugway @ Gen. Store 🤝 FOOD	1.5
	24.8	BR		TRO UM Dugway ⊘ Vanderwerker	2.1
•	26.9	L	SS	Clinton (UM 31)	4.4
•	31.3	S	SS	TRO 31 X 20 ⚠ FOOD	4.2
•	35.5	S		TRO 31 ☞ R Glimmerglass Park	2.4
••	37.9	S		Steel Deck Bridge ⚠	4.9
••	42.8	L		River St ☞ S 0.1 FOOD	0.3
•	43.1	L	SS	Atwell	0.1
•	43.2	R		Brooklyn Ave	0.5
	43.7	R		UM 52	0.1
	43.8	L		Clark Sports Center	

🤝 **Sprout Brook: 15A,B,C,D; 16A,B,C**
@ 23.3 Sprout Brook General Store join Tours 15 A,B,C,D; 16A,B,C @ Cue 0.0

R	Right	S	Straight	SS	Stop Sign	UM	Unmarked Road	⊘	Do Not Take
L	Left	TRO	To Remain On	SL	Stop Light	26	County Route	☞	Detour Off
BR	Bear Right	X	Cross	YS	Yield Sign	28	State Route	🤝	Combine With
BL	Bear Left	⚠	Caution						

Mile	•Points of Interest	#
0.0	Clark Sports Center	1
13.6	Cherry Valley Massacre: Alden Monument	27
13.8	Cherry Valley Massacre: Historic Cemetery	28
14.3	Cherry Valley Museum	29
16.8	The Pleasantview Breakfast House	30
20.0	Judd Falls ☞ S across the field	31
23.3	Birthplace Henry J. Kaiser	32
26.9	Windfall Dutch Barn ☞ R 0.1	26
33.3	Diamond Tee Sport Center. Mini-golf	25
35.5	Glimmerglass State Park & Hyde Hall Landmark	21
37.9	East Lake Road Hiking Trail (on L after bridge)	20
41.8	Fairy Springs Swim	19
42.6	Indian Grave @ Estli/ Main	18
42.8	Cooperstown Main St ☞ S 0.1	17
42.8	Susquehanna Headwaters ☞ R 0.1 (downstairs)	5
42.9	Christ Church Historic Cemetery on R	4
43.1	Bassett Healthcare/Emergency Rm @Atwell/River	3
43.4	Deer Park (fenced enclosure @ fire hydrant on R)	2

Counties

Otsego, Montgomery

Tour Description

The Red Creek Valley Series explores the first valley east of Lake Otsego.

Red Creek Valley "B" adds 13 miles and a 1000 foot climb to the Red Creek Valley "A" tour. The extension visits the highlands overlooking the Mohawk Valley, descends briskly to Sprout Brook and Salt Springville, then climbs up to Springfield before returning home via the eastern shore of Lake Otsego.

Visit the Cherry Valley Museum. Learn about the Cherry Valley Massacre. Plan time for a leisurely homecooked breakfast at the Breakfast House. Explore Judd Falls. Swim and picnic at Glimmerglass State Park.

Bike Shop

a) @ 0.0 ☞ L 1.0 Cooperstown Bicycle. See map.

b) @ 11.8 Hawk Mountain Sports

Let us know what you think of this tour! Email: crankmail@usa.net

Climb Rating in feet per mile climbed: 0-45 = Easy, 45-60 = Moderate, 60+ = Difficult

©1998 Tourmaster Publications, Inc.

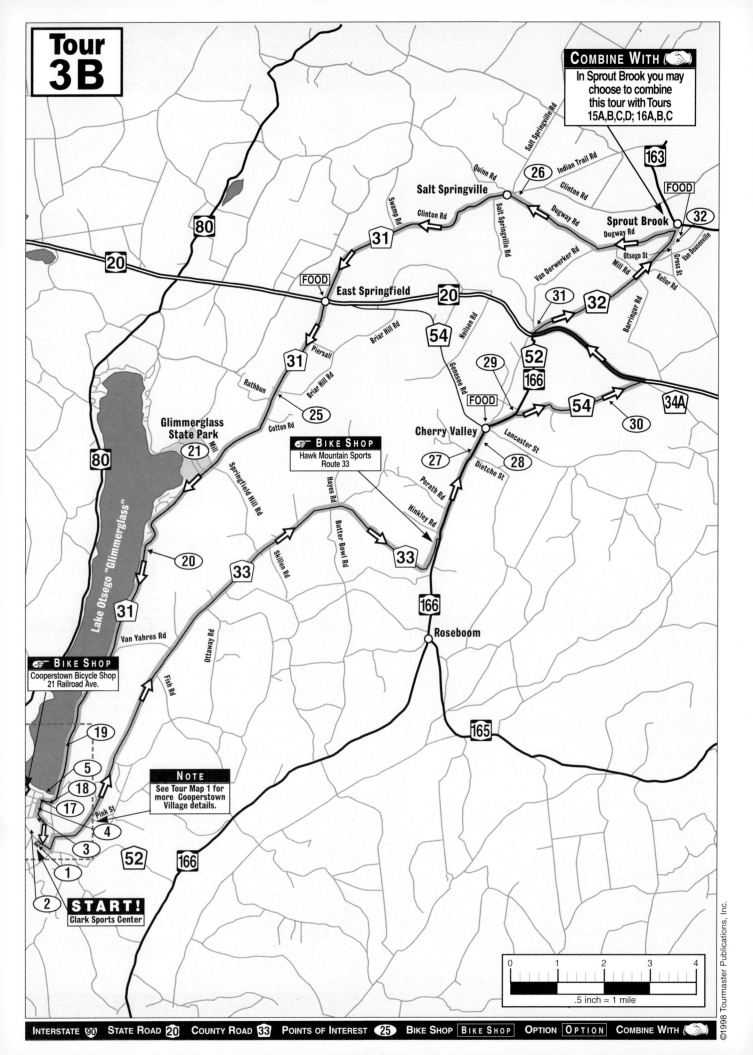

Red Creek Valley "C"

Start: Clark Sports Center. Ballfield Exit.

Miles	62
Rating	Difficult
Climb	3800' @ 61 ft/mi

Tour 3C

Mile	Turn		Description			Dist
• 0.0	R		UM 52			0.2
0.2	L		33 Before Bridge			0.3
0.5	BR		TRO 33			11.3
•• 11.8	L	YS	166			2.3
• 14.1	R	SL	BL TRO 166 ⊘ Lancaster	FOOD		0.6
• 14.7	BR		54 ⊘ 166			2.8
17.5	L		⊘ 34A Then L SS 20 ⚠			2.4
19.9	BR		Cherry Valley Exit			0.1
• 20.0	R	SS	32 ☞ S X Field to Judd Falls			3.3
• 23.3	L		Dugway @ Gen. Store 🤝 FOOD			1.5
24.8	BR		TRO UM Dugway ⊘ Vanderwerker			2.1
• 26.9	L	SS	Clinton (UM 31)			3.4
30.3	R		30			0.3
30.6	BR		TRO UM 30 ⊘ Fassett Rd			0.7
31.3	BR		TRO UM 30 ⊘ Willsey Hill Rd			5.6
• 36.9	L	SS	80	FOOD		0.6
• 37.5	BL		TRO 80 ⊘ Chyle Rd			4.4
41.9	S	SL	TRO 80 X 20 ⚠	FOOD		0.7
42.6	S		Public Landing ⊘ 80			0.8
43.4	L	SS	UM 53			1.6
45.0	L		Continental Rd ⊘ Dean Rathbun			1.9
46.9	S	SS	Fassett Rd X 20 ⚠			1.3
48.2	R	YS	UM 30			0.4
48.6	R	YS	UM 31			1.0
• 49.6	S	SS	TRO 31 X 20 ⚠	FOOD		4.2
• 53.8	S		TRO 31 ☞ R Glimmerglass Park			2.4
•• 56.2	S		Steel Deck Bridge ⚠			4.9
•• 61.1	L		River St ☞ S 0.1 FOOD			0.3
• 61.4	L	SS	Atwell			0.1
• 61.5	R		Brooklyn Ave			0.5
62.0	R		UM 52			0.1
62.1	L		Clark Sports Center			

🤝 **Sprout Brook: 15A,B,C,D; 16A,B,C**
@ 23.3 Sprout Brook General Store join
Tours 15 A,B,C,D; 16A,B,C @ cue 0.0

Legend

R Right	**S** Straight	**SS** Stop Sign	**UM** Unmarked Road	⊘ Do Not Take
L Left	**TRO** To Remain On	**SL** Stop Light	26 County Route	☞ Detour Off
BR Bear Right	**X** Cross	**YS** Yield Sign	28 State Route	🤝 Combine With
BL Bear Left	⚠ Caution			

Points of Interest

Mile	• POINTS OF INTEREST	#
0.0	Clark Sports Center	1
13.6	Cherry Valley Massacre: Alden Monument	27
13.8	Cherry Valley Massacre: Historic Cemetery	28
14.3	Cherry Valley Museum	29
16.8	Pleasantview Breakfast House	30
20.0	Judd Falls ☞ S across the field	31
23.3	Birthplace Henry J. Kaiser	32
26.9	Windfall Dutch Barn ☞ R 0.1	26
36.9	Owen D. Young Marker & Nature Trail ☞ R 0.1	24
37.5	Rainbow Trout Fish Hatchery ☞ BR 0.1	68
51.6	Diamond Tee Sport Center. Mini-golf	25
53.8	Glimmerglass State Park & Hyde Hall Landmark	21
56.2	East Lake Road Hiking Trail (on L after bridge)	20
60.1	Fairy Springs Swim	19
60.8	Indian Grave @ Estli/ Main	18
61.1	Cooperstown Main St ☞ S 0.1	17
61.1	Susquehanna Headwaters ☞ R0.1 (go down stairs)	5
61.2	Christ Church Historic Cemetery on R	4
61.4	Bassett Healthcare/Emergency Rm @Atwell/River	3
61.7	Deer Park (fenced enclosure @ fire hydrant on R)	2

TOUR DESCRIPTION

The Red Creek Valley Series explores the first valley east of Lake Otsego.

Red Creek Valley "C" adds 18 miles and an 1100 foot climb to the Red Creek Valley "B" tour. The extension visits additional highlands overlooking the Mohawk Valley and descends to the charming village of Van Hornesville before returning home via the eastern shore of Lake Otsego.

Visit the Cherry Valley Museum. Learn about the Cherry Valley Massacre. Plan time for a leisurely homecooked breakfast at the Breakfast House. Explore Judd Falls. Picnic and hike at the Woodruff Nature Trail. Swim and picnic at Glimmerglass State Park.

COUNTIES

Otsego, Montgomery, Herkimer

BIKE SHOP

a) @ 0.0 ☞ L 1.0 Cooperstown Bicycle. See map.
b) @ 11.8 Hawk Mountain Sports

©1998 Tourmaster Publications, Inc.

Climb Rating in feet per mile climbed: 0-45 = Easy, 45-60 = Moderate, 60+ = Difficult

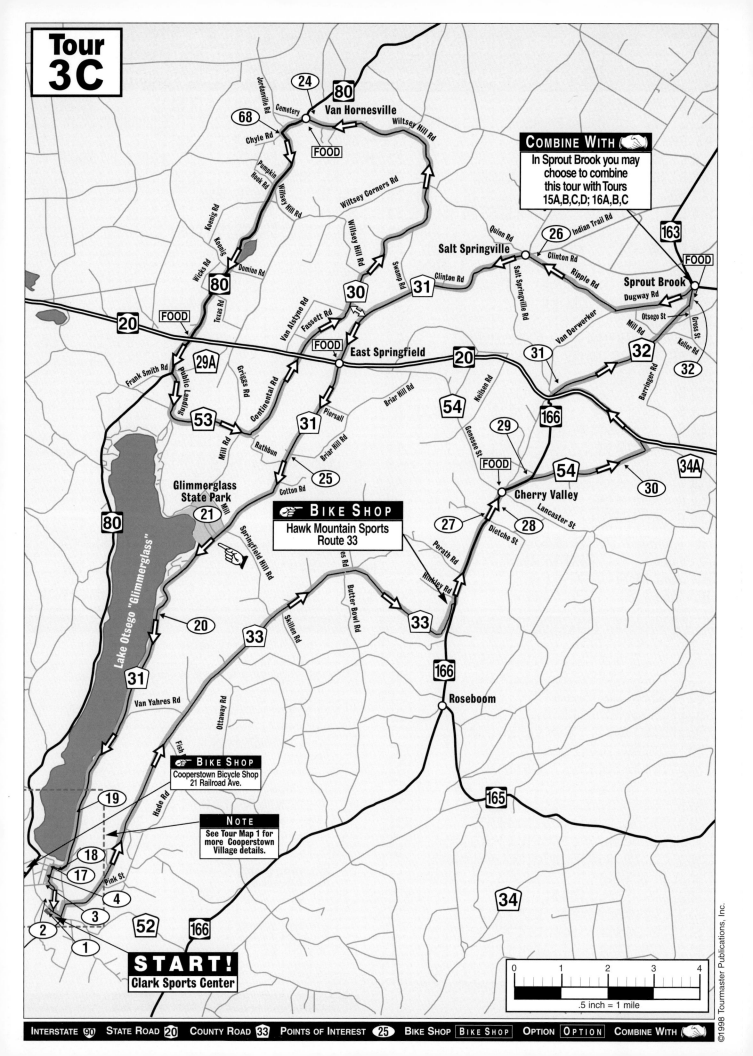

Tour 3C

Van Hornesville

(24) (80)
(68)
Jordanville Rd
Cemetery
Chyle Rd
FOOD
Pumpkin Hook Rd
Koenig Rd
Wiltsey Hill Rd
Wiltsey Hill Rd
Wiltsey Corners Rd
Wiltsey Hill Rd
Swamp Rd

Koenig
Wicks Rd
Domion Rd
(80)
Texas Rd

COMBINE WITH 🤝
In Sprout Brook you may choose to combine this tour with Tours 15A,B,C,D; 16A,B,C

Quinn Rd
(26) Indian Trail Rd
(163)
Salt Springville
Clinton Rd
Ripple Rd
Clinton Rd
Salt Springville Rd
Sprout Brook
FOOD
Dugway Rd
Otsego St
Gross St
Keller Rd
(32)
(32)
Van Derwerker
(31)

(30)
Van Alstyne Rd
Fassett Rd
FOOD
East Springfield
(20)
(20)
FOOD
(29A)
Frank Smith Rd
Public Landing
Griggs Rd
Continental Rd
(53)
Mill Rd
Rathbun
Piersall
Briar Hill Rd
(31)
(25)
Briar Hill Rd
Cotton Rd

(54)
Neilsen Rd
(166)
(31)
Genesee St
(29)
FOOD
(54)
(34A)
Cherry Valley
Lancaster St
(30)

BIKE SHOP
Hawk Mountain Sports
Route 33

Glimmerglass State Park
(21)
Mill
Springfield Hill Rd

(27)
(28)
Porath Rd
Dietche St
Hinkley Rd
(33)

(80)
Lake Otsego "Glimmerglass"
(20)
(31)
Van Yahres Rd
(33)
Skillan Rd
Butter Bowl Rd
es Rd
(33)

(166)
Roseboom

Fish
BIKE SHOP
Cooperstown Bicycle Shop
21 Railroad Ave.
Ottaway Rd
Hade Rd

NOTE
See Tour Map 1 for more Cooperstown Village details.

(19)
(18)
(17)
Pink St
(4)
(3)
(2)
(1)
(52)
(166)
(165)
(34)

START!
Clark Sports Center

0 1 2 3 4
.5 inch = 1 mile

INTERSTATE (90)   STATE ROAD (20)   COUNTY ROAD (33)   POINTS OF INTEREST (25)   BIKE SHOP [BIKE SHOP]   OPTION [OPTION]   COMBINE WITH 🤝

©1998 Tourmaster Publications, Inc.

Elk Creek Valley

Start: Clark Sports Center. Ballfield Exit.

Miles	35
Rating	Difficult
Climb	3000' @ 86 ft/mi

Tour 4

• 0.0	R		UM 52		0.2
0.2	L		33 Before Bridge		0.3
0.5	BR		TRO 33		0.8
1.3	R		Pink St		1.5
2.8	R	SS	Hade Hollow Rd		1.2
4.0	R	YS	Pete Hendricks Rd		2.4
• 6.4	S	SS	35 X 166		0.7
7.1	L		Rezen Rd		0.7
7.8	BR		TRO Pavement		3.8
11.6	S	SS	165		3.0
• 14.6	R		34 Then BR	⊘ Krishman Hill	6.2
20.8	L		36	☞ S 0.1 FOOD	0.6
21.4	BR		TRO UM 36	⊘ Skellie Rd	0.7
22.1	BR		UM Greenbush	⊘ UM 36 To L	2.2
24.3	R	SS	UM 34		1.4
25.7	L		Darling Hill Rd		0.7
26.4	BR		TRO Pavement	⊘ Ed Herman Rd	1.0
27.4	BR		TRO Pavement	⊘ Rabbit Run Rd	1.8
29.2	S	SS	Norton Cross Rd X UM 35		1.0
30.2	R	SS	UM 166		1.8
32.0	L		52		3.0
35.0	BR		X Bridge Then BL TRO UM 52	⊘ 33	0.3
35.3	L		Clark Sports Center		

R	Right	S	Straight	SS Stop Sign	UM Unmarked Road	⊘ Do Not Take
L	Left	TRO	To Remain On	SL Stop Light	26 County Route	☞ Detour Off
BR	Bear Right	X	Cross	YS Yield Sign	28 State Route	🤝 Combine With
BL	Bear Left	⚠	Caution			

Mile	•POINTS OF INTEREST	#
0.0	Clark Sports Center	1
6.9	Middlefield Schoolhouse Museum	60
16.0	English Fallow Deer Farm (look L 16.0-16.3)	33

TOUR DESCRIPTION

This beautiful and challenging tour explores Elk Creek Valley, the third valley east of Lake Otsego. Leave the Susquehanna River Valley to visit the Red Creek Valley, the Cherry Valley and the Elk Creek Valley with four major climbs along the way. This is a relatively short, but sweet, climber's delight.

COUNTIES

Otsego

BIKE SHOP

@ 0.0 ☞ L 1.0 Cooperstown Bicycle. See map.

Let us know what you think of this tour! Email: crankmail@usa.net

Climb Rating in feet per mile climbed: 0-45 = Easy, 45-60 = Moderate, 60+ = Difficult

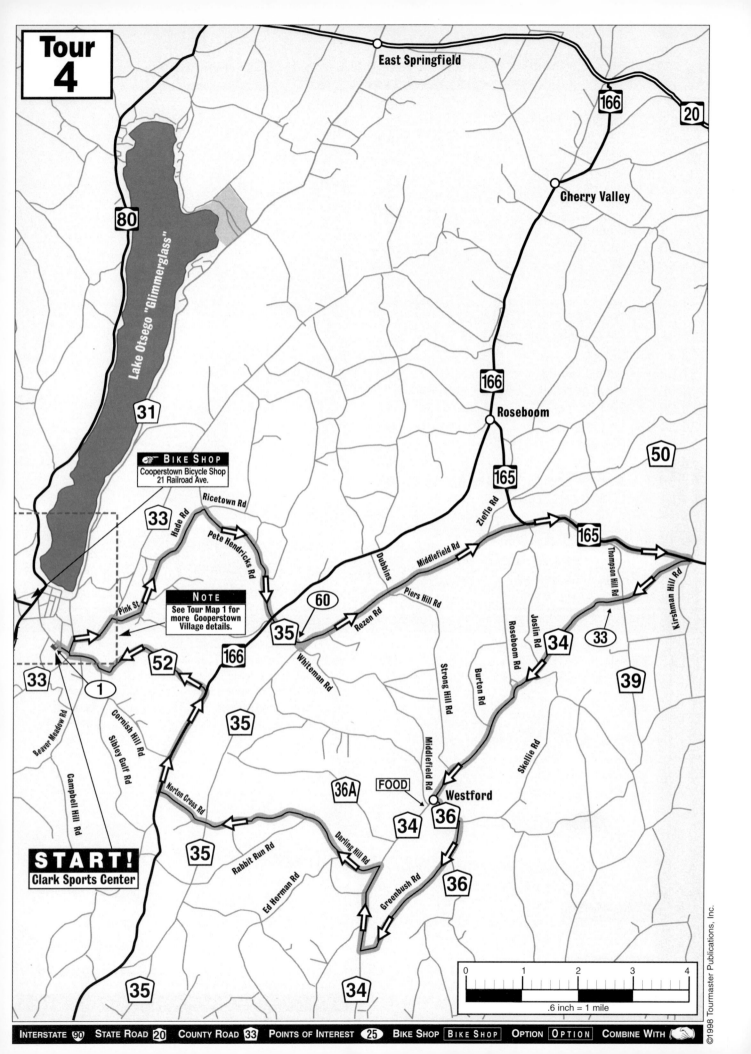

Tour 4

East Springfield

166

20

Cherry Valley

80

Lake Otsego "Glimmerglass"

31

Roseboom

50

166

165

🚲 **BIKE SHOP**
Cooperstown Bicycle Shop
21 Railroad Ave.

Ricetown Rd

Hade Rd

33

Ziefle Rd

165

Pete Hendricks Rd

Middlefield Rd

Thompson Hill Rd

Kirshman Hill Rd

NOTE
See Tour Map 1 for more Cooperstown Village details.

Pink St

Dubbins

Piers Hill Rd

60

Rezen Rd

Joslin Rd

34

33

33

35

Whiteman Rd

166

52

39

1

Cornish Hill Rd

Sibley Gulf Rd

Beaver Meadow Rd

35

Strong Hill Rd

Burton Rd

Roseboom Rd

Skellie Rd

Campbell Hill Rd

Norton Cross Rd

36A

FOOD

Middlefield Rd

Westford

34

36

START!
Clark Sports Center

35

Rabbit Run Rd

Darling Hill Rd

Ed Herman Rd

Greenbush Rd

36

35

34

0 1 2 3 4

.6 inch = 1 mile

Cherry Valley Mountaineer

Start: Clark Sports Center. Ballfield Exit.

Miles	61	OPTION
Rating	Difficult	
Climb	5200' @ 85 ft/mi	

Tour 5

• 0.0	R		UM 52		0.2
0.2	BR		X Bridge Then BL TRO UM 52 ⊘ 33		3.0
• 3.2	L	SS	166		7.1
10.3	S		TRO 166 ⊘ 165	FOOD	4.1
•• 14.4	R	SL	Then BR Lancaster 🤝-CV	FOOD	10.8
25.2	R	SS	165		0.7
25.9	BL		Middlefield Rd @ Pleasant Brook Hotel		4.4
• 30.3	L	SS	Whiteman Rd OPTION-1		4.3
34.6	R	SS	UM 34	FOOD	0.9
35.5	R		36A		3.5
39.0	L	SS	35		1.3
40.3	S		TRO UM 35 X Norton		1.1
41.4	S		TRO UM 35 ⊘ 43 To R		0.6
42.0	L		UM 42 OPTION-2		4.9
46.9	BR		TRO UM 42 ⊘ Kenyon		1.1
48.0	S		TRO UM 42 ⊘Crumhorn Mntn. Rd		0.2
48.2	R		Crumhorn Lake Rd		3.4
51.6	R	YS	UM 35		0.9
• 52.5	L	YS	35 🤝-Mil		0.3
• 52.8	R	SS	166 ☞ L 1.0 FOOD		5.6
58.4	L		Cornish Hill Rd		2.1
60.5	L	SS	UM 52		0.6
61.1	BR		X Bridge Then BL ⊘ 33		0.3
61.4	L		Clark Sports Center		

OPTION -1

To eliminate 6.5 miles and an 1100 foot climb:
@ 30.3 S SS 35 for 2.2 then resume @ cue 40.3

OPTION -2

To eliminate 7.1 miles and a 1300 foot climb:
@ 42.0 S TRO 35 ⊘ 42 for 3.7 then resume @ cue 52.8

🤝 **Cherry Valley: 12A,B,C; 13**
@ 14.4 R SL then BL ⊘ Lancaster to parking lot @ bank on R to join Tours 12A,B,C; 13 @ cue 0.0

🤝 **Milford: 18A,B**
@ 52.5 R YS 0.2 to ONC to join Tours 18A,B @ cue 0.0

R Right	**S** Straight	**SS** Stop Sign	**UM** Unmarked Road	⊘ Do Not Take
L Left	**TRO** To Remain On	**SL** Stop Light	26 County Route	☞ Detour Off
BR Bear Right	**X** Cross	**YS** Yield Sign	28 State Route	🤝 Combine With
BL Bear Left	⚠ Caution			

POINTS OF INTEREST

Mile	•POINTS OF INTEREST	#
0.0	Clark Sports Center	1
5.0	Middlefield Schoolhouse Museum ☞ R 0.5 35	60
14.0	Cherry Valley Massacre: Alden Monument	27
14.2	Cherry Valley Massacre: Historic Cemetery	28
14.4	Cherry Valley Museum R SL then ☞ BL 0.2	29
16.2	Cherry Valley Gorge ☞ R 0.1 O'Neil Rd (gravel)	67
30.3	Middlefield Schoolhouse Museum ☞ R 0.2 35	60
52.5	ONC Boces Occupational Center ☞ R 0.2	57
52.8	Cooperstown Brewing Company ☞ L 0.7	36
52.8	Milford Depot Railway Museum ☞ L 0.8	38

TOUR DESCRIPTION

The Cherry Valley Mountaineer climbs the scenic ridges surrounding the Cherry Valley Flats series (Tours 17ABCD). The seven major climbs are thankfully separated by miles of relatively flat terrain, but this remains a very challenging ride. Climbers, enjoy! Flatlanders, beware! Tour options are available to eliminate some of the climbs if your legs tire out.

The Cherry Valley Mountaineer is also offered as a remote start from ONC Boces Occupational Center in Milford (Tour 19).

COUNTIES

Otsego

BIKE SHOP

a) @ 0.0 ☞ L 1.0 Cooperstown Bicycle. See map.
b) @ 11.9 ☞ L 0.1 33 Hawk Mountain Sports

Let us know what you think of this tour! Email: crankmail@usa.net

Climb Rating in feet per mile climbed: 0-45 = Easy, 45-60 = Moderate, 60+ = Difficult

©1998 Tourmaster Publications, Inc.

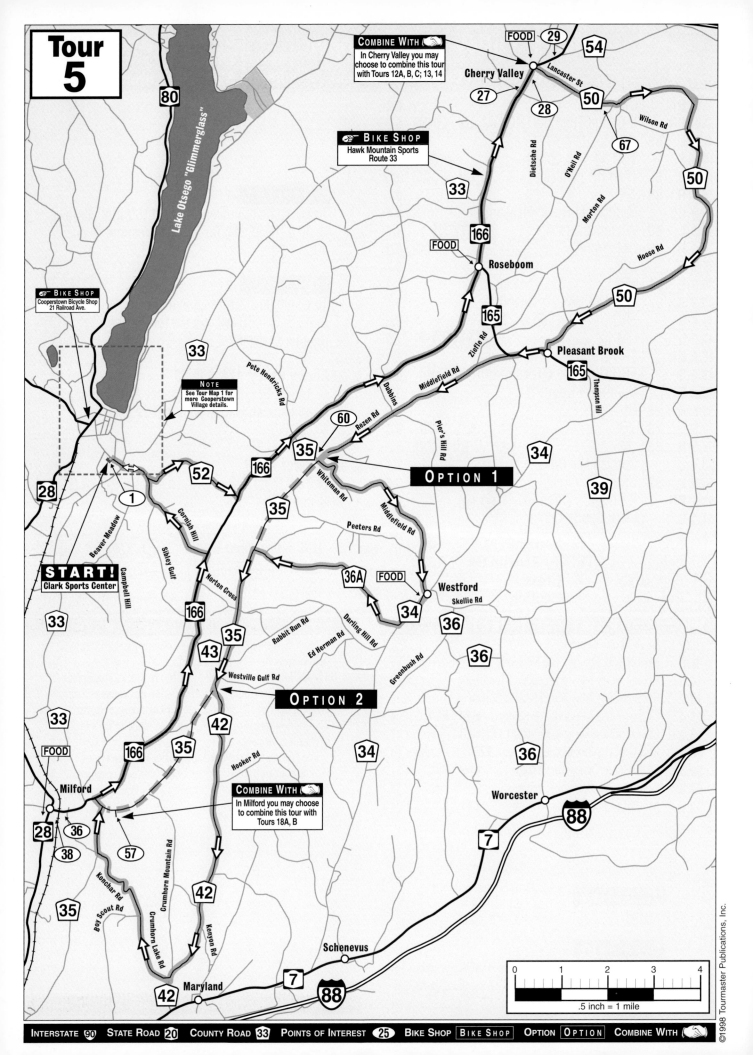

Tour 5

COMBINE WITH 🤝
In Cherry Valley you may choose to combine this tour with Tours 12A, B, C; 13, 14

BIKE SHOP 🚲
Hawk Mountain Sports
Route 33

BIKE SHOP 🚲
Cooperstown Bicycle Shop
21 Railroad Ave.

NOTE
See Tour Map 1 for more Cooperstown Village details.

START!
Clark Sports Center

Lake Otsego "Glimmerglass"

FOOD

FOOD

FOOD

FOOD

FOOD

OPTION 1

OPTION 2

COMBINE WITH 🤝
In Milford you may choose to combine this tour with Tours 18A, B

Cherry Valley
Lancaster St
Wilson Rd
Roseboom
Pleasant Brook
Dietsche Rd
O'Neill Rd
Morton Rd
Hoose Rd
Thompson Hill
Ziefle Rd
Middlefield Rd
Dubbins
Rezen Rd
Pier's Hill Rd
Pete Hendricks Rd
Whiteman Rd
Peeters Rd
Middlefield Rd
Westford
Skellie Rd
Cornish Hill
Sibley Gulf
Beaver Meadow
Campbell Hill
Norton Cross
Rabbit Run Rd
Ed Herman Rd
Darling Hill Rd
Greenbush Rd
Westville Gulf Rd
Hooker Rd
Milford
Konchar Rd
Boy Scout Rd
Crumhorn Mountain Rd
Crumhorn Lake Rd
Kenyon Rd
Maryland
Schenevus
Worcester

Roads/Route markers: 80, 33, 166, 165, 67, 50, 54, 29, 50, 50, 28, 27, 34, 39, 60, 35, 35, 52, 166, 35, 36A, 34, 36, 36, 36, 36, 34, 43, 35, 166, 42, 35, 42, 33, 33, 33, 35, 166, 28, 36, 38, 57, 42, 1, 7, 88, 7, 88

Beaver Meadow

Start: Clark Sports Center. Ballfield Exit.

• 0.0 R		UM 52	0.2
0.2 BR		**X** Bridge Then BL TRO UM 52 ⊘ 33	0.3
0.5 R		Beaver Meadow Rd	3.0
3.5 R	SS	UM 33	2.7
6.2 L	SS	**X** Bridge Then BL UM 52 ⊘ 33	0.3
6.5 L		Clark Sports Center	

R Right	**S** Straight	**SS** Stop Sign	**UM** Unmarked Road	⊘ Do Not Take
L Left	**TRO** To Remain On	**SL** Stop Light	26 County Route	☞ Detour Off
BR Bear Right	**X** Cross	**YS** Yield Sign	28 State Route	🤝 Combine With
BL Bear Left	⚠ Caution			

Mile	•POINTS OF INTEREST	#
0.0	Clark Sports Center	①

TOUR DESCRIPTION

The Beaver Meadow Tour is a short and easy loop on lightly traveled, relatively flat backroads. This ride is a good choice for beginning cyclists. It is a great warm-up ride which can be combined with the Cooperstown Village Pathfinder for an excellent introduction to Leatherstocking Country. Keep an eye out for the beaver pond!

COUNTIES

Otsego

BIKE SHOP

@ 0.0 ☞ L 1.0 Cooperstown Bicycle. See map.

Let us know what you think of this tour! Email: crankmail@usa.net

Climb Rating in feet per mile climbed: 0-45 = Easy, 45-60 = Moderate, 60+ = Difficult

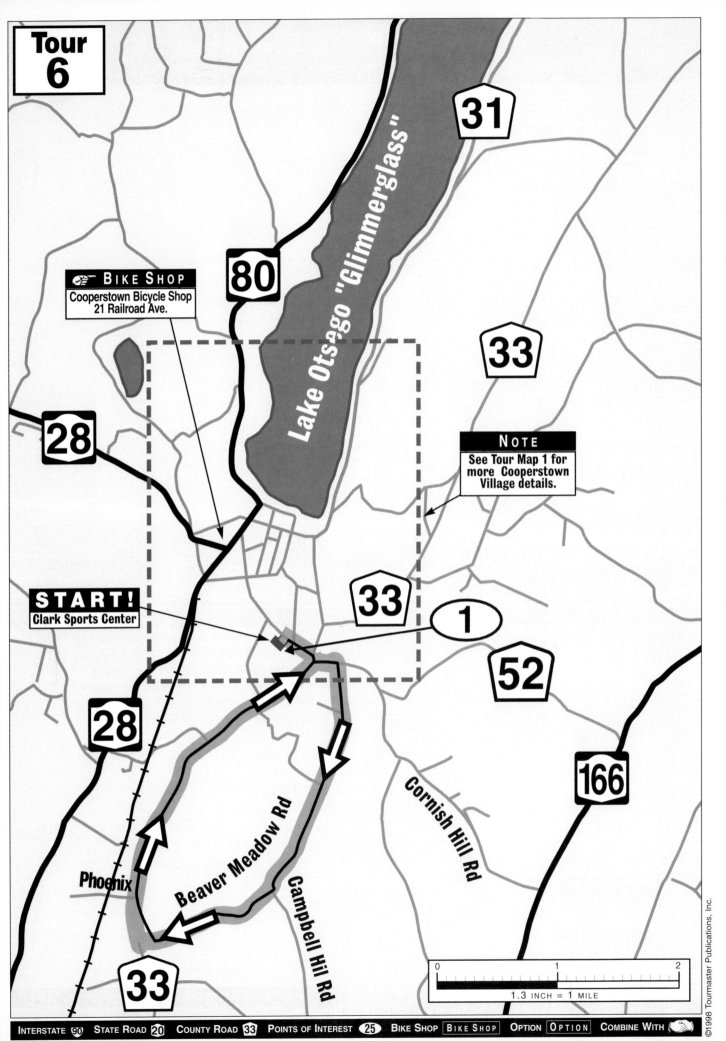

Tour 6

31

Lake Otsago "Glimmerglass"

80

33

BIKE SHOP
Cooperstown Bicycle Shop
21 Railroad Ave.

28

NOTE
See Tour Map 1 for more Cooperstown Village details.

33

START!
Clark Sports Center

33

1

52

28

166

Beaver Meadow Rd

Campbell Hill Rd

Cornish Hill Rd

Phoenix

33

0   1   2
1.3 INCH = 1 MILE

INTERSTATE 90   STATE ROAD 20   COUNTY ROAD 33   POINTS OF INTEREST 25   BIKE SHOP BIKE SHOP   OPTION OPTION   COMBINE WITH

©1998 Tourmaster Publications, Inc.

Susquehanna River Valley Outback

Start: Clark Sports Center. Ballfield Exit.

Miles	33 🤝 OPTION	**Tour**
Rating	Easy	**7**
Climb	1200' @ 36 ft/mi	

OUT

•	0.0	R	UM 52	0.2
•	0.2	R	**X** Bridge Then BR 33	7.7
••	7.9	L	SS	166	☞ R 0.8 FOOD	0.2
	8.1	R	UM 35 South **X** Bridge	0.2
	8.3	R	TRO 35 South 🤝-Out	5.4
	13.7	L	SS	TRO UM 35 South	3.1
	16.8		SS	Stop **OPTION** ☞ R 1.3 FOOD	

BACK   **Turn Around**

	0.0	S	Retrace 35 North Towards CSC	3.1
	3.1	R	TRO 35 North	5.4
	8.5	L	YS	TRO 35 🤝-Back	0.2
	8.7	L	SS	166	0.2
••	8.9	R	33 ☞ S 0.8 FOOD	0.2
•	9.1	BL	TRO UM 33 ⊘ Eggleston Rd	7.4
	16.5	L	SS	**X** Bridge Then BL UM 52 ⊘ 33	0.3
•	16.8	L	Clark Sports Center	

OPTION

@ 16.8 (Out) L SS SR 7 East to extend this tour up the Schenevus Creek Valley towards Maryland, Schenevus, and Worcester (food in each community). Turn around at any point to return to the main route.

🤝 **-Out**
Milford: 17A,B,C,D; 18A,B; 19; 20
@ 8.3 S 0.2 to ONC to join Tours 17A,B,C,D; 18A,B; 19; 20 @ cue 0.0

🤝 **-Back**
Milford: 17A,B,C,D; 18A,B; 19; 20
@ 8.5 R YS 0.2 to ONC to join Tours 17A,B,C,D; 18A,B; 19; 20 @ cue 0.0

R	Right	**S**	Straight	**SS**	Stop Sign	**UM**	Unmarked Road	⊘	Do Not Take
L	Left	**TRO**	To Remain On	**SL**	Stop Light	26	County Route	☞	Detour Off
BR	Bear Right	**X**	Cross	**YS**	Yield Sign	28	State Route	🤝	Combine With
BL	Bear Left	⚠	Caution						

Mile   •POINTS OF INTEREST

OUT

0.0	Clark Sports Center	①
5.1	Brewery Ommegang on L	35
7.9	Cooperstown Brewing Co. ☞ R 0.5 then L River	36
7.9	Milford Depot Railway Museum ☞ R 0.5	38
8.3	ONC BOCES Occupational Center ☞ S 0.2	57

BACK

8.5	ONC BOCES Occupational Center ☞ R YS 0.2	57
8.9	Milford Depot Railway Museum ☞ S 0.5	38
8.9	Cooperstown Brewing Co. ☞ S 0.5 then L River	36
11.7	Brewery Ommegang on R	35
16.8	Clark Sports Center	①

COUNTIES

Otsego

BIKE SHOP

@ 0.0 ☞ L 1.0 Cooperstown Bicycle. See map.

TOUR DESCRIPTION

The Susquehanna River Valley Outback Tour explores the eastern bank of the Susquehanna River from Cooperstown to Cooperstown Junction.

This flat and scenic tour is an excellent training ride for beginning cyclists. Since this is an outback route, turn around anytime for a shorter ride. Alternatively, extend the tour by adding the Schenevus Creek Valley option, or by combining with any of the Milford remote start tours.

Let us know what you think of this tour! Email: crankmail@usa.net

Climb Rating in feet per mile climbed: 0-45 = Easy, 45-60 = Moderate, 60+ = Difficult

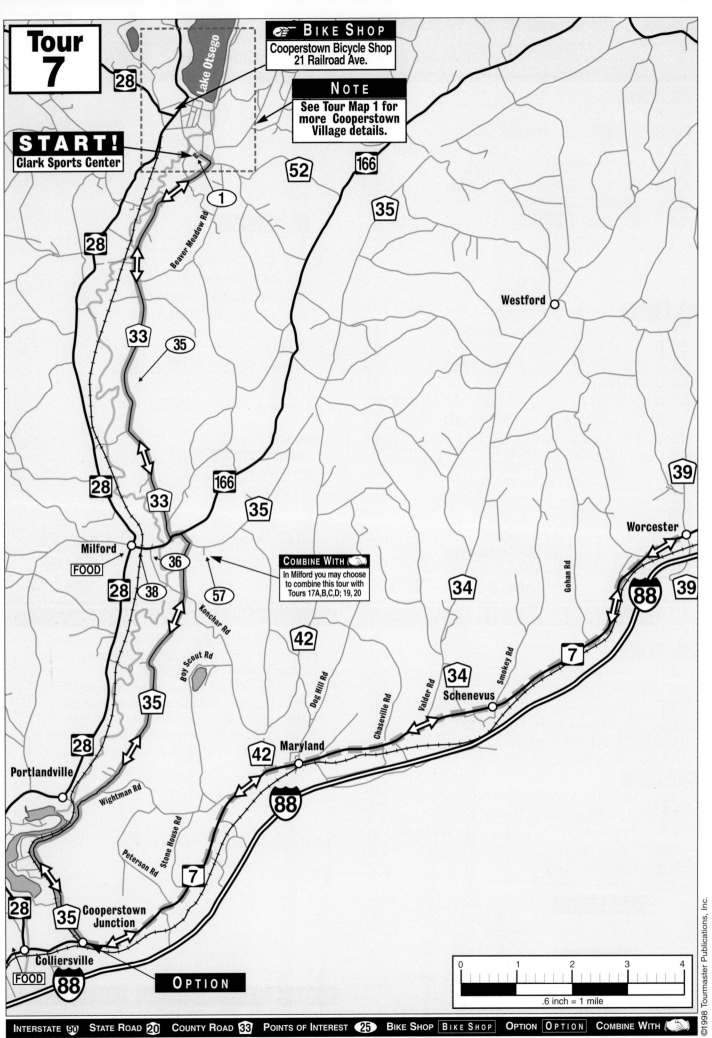

Tour 7

BIKE SHOP
Cooperstown Bicycle Shop
21 Railroad Ave.

NOTE
See Tour Map 1 for
more Cooperstown
Village details.

28

Lake Otsego

START!
Clark Sports Center

1

52

166

35

28

33

35

Westford

28

33

166

35

39

Worcester

Milford
FOOD

36

COMBINE WITH
In Milford you may choose
to combine this tour with
Tours 17A,B,C,D; 19, 20

34

88

39

28

38

57

Konchar Rd

42

Gohan Rd

7

Boy Scout Rd

Dog Hill Rd

Chaseville Rd

Valder Rd

34
Schenevus

Smokey Rd

35

28

42
Maryland

Portlandville

Wightman Rd

88

Stone House Rd

Peterson Rd

7

28

35
Cooperstown
Junction

Colliersville
FOOD

88

OPTION

| 0 | 1 | 2 | 3 | 4 |
.6 inch = 1 mile

INTERSTATE 90   STATE ROAD 20   COUNTY ROAD 33   POINTS OF INTEREST 25   BIKE SHOP BIKE SHOP   OPTION OPTION   COMBINE WITH

©1998 Tourmaster Publications, Inc.

Gilbert Lake

Start: Clark Sports Center. Ballfield Exit.

Miles	49
Rating	**Difficult**
Climb	**3500' @ 72 ft/mi**

Tour 8

Mile	Dir		Route		Dist
• 0.0	R		UM 52		0.2
0.2	BR		**X** Bridge Then BR 33		2.5
2.7	R		11C		0.7
•• 3.4	R	SS	28 ⚠	☞ L 0.1 FOOD	0.2
3.6	L		11 Use Left Turn Lane ⚠		5.9
9.5	S	SS	TRO 11 **X** 205	☞ S Or L 0.1 FOOD	0.4
9.9	L		TRO UM 11	⊘ Weeks Rd	1.2
11.1	R		14		1.1
12.2	BL		TRO Paved UM 14	⊘ Harrington	3.7
15.9	BL		TRO 14	⊘ 16	3.6
19.5	L	SS	12	🤝-SL	2.7
22.2	BL		Towards Gilbert Lake	⊘ Morse	0.7
• 22.9	S		TRO UM 12	☞ L Gilbert Lake	3.8
26.7	L	SS	Main St (UM 11)	🤝-Laur FOOD	0.4
27.1	S		**X** Bridge TRO UM 11	☞ R 0.2 FOOD	0.8
27.9	BR		TRO UM 11	⊘ Pool Brook Rd	2.7
30.6	R		11B		0.5
31.1	R	SS	205	☞ L 0.3 FOOD	0.6
31.7	L		46		2.2
33.9	BL		TRO UM 46	⊘ Hoose	3.6
37.5	L	SS	UM 44		2.0
•• 39.5	S	SL	166	FOOD	0.8
40.3	L		33	🤝-Mil	0.2
• 40.5	BL		TRO UM 33	⊘ Eggleston	4.7
45.2	R		Beaver Meadow Rd		3.0
48.2	L	SS	UM 52		0.2
48.4	BR		**X** Bridge Then BL TRO UM 52 ⊘ 33		0.3
48.7	L		Clark Sports Center		

🤝 **Schuyler Lake: 22B,C**
a) 22B: @ 19.5 join Tour 22B
  @ cue 30.6 R SS 12
b) 22C: @ 19.5 join Tour 22C
  @ cue 45.2 R SS 12

🤝 **Laurens: 21A,B,C**
@ 26.7 American Legion parking lot join
Tours 21A,B,C @ cue 0.0

🤝 **Milford: 17A,B,C,D; 18A,B; 19, 20**
@ 40.3 S 0.2, then R UM 35 0.5 to ONC to
join Tours 17A,B,C,D; 18A,B; 19, 20 @ cue 0.0

R	Right	S	Straight	SS	Stop Sign	UM	Unmarked Road	⊘	Do Not Take
L	Left	TRO	To Remain On	SL	Stop Light	26	County Route	☞	Detour Off
BR	Bear Right	X	Cross	YS	Yield Sign	28	State Route	🤝	Combine With
BL	Bear Left	⚠	Caution						

Mile	•POINTS OF INTEREST		#
0.0	Clark Sports Center		1
3.4	Cooperstown Fun Park	☞ L 0.1	40
3.4	Corvette Hall of Fame	☞ L 1.5	59
22.9	Gilbert Lake State Park		37
39.7	Milford Depot Railway Museum		38
39.8	Cooperstown Brewing Co.	☞ R 0.1 River St	36
40.3	ONC Occupational Center	☞ See 🤝 Milford	57
43.0	Brewery Ommegang on R		35

TOUR DESCRIPTION

The Gilbert Lake Tour climbs west out of the Susquehanna River valley and descends into the Otego Creek Valley. It then climbs out of the Otego Creek Valley and descends into the Butternut Valley. The return trip traverses the same ridges via a more southerly route.

Visit the villages of Hartwick, Laurens and Milford. Swim and picnic at Gilbert Lake State Park. Extend the ride by combining with any of the Laurens, Milford, or Schuyler Lake remote starts.

COUNTIES
Otsego

BIKE SHOP
@ 0.0 ☞ L 1.0 Cooperstown Bicycle. See map.

Let us know what you think of this tour! Email: crankmail@usa.net

Climb Rating in feet per mile climbed: 0-45 = Easy, 45-60 = Moderate, 60+ = Difficult

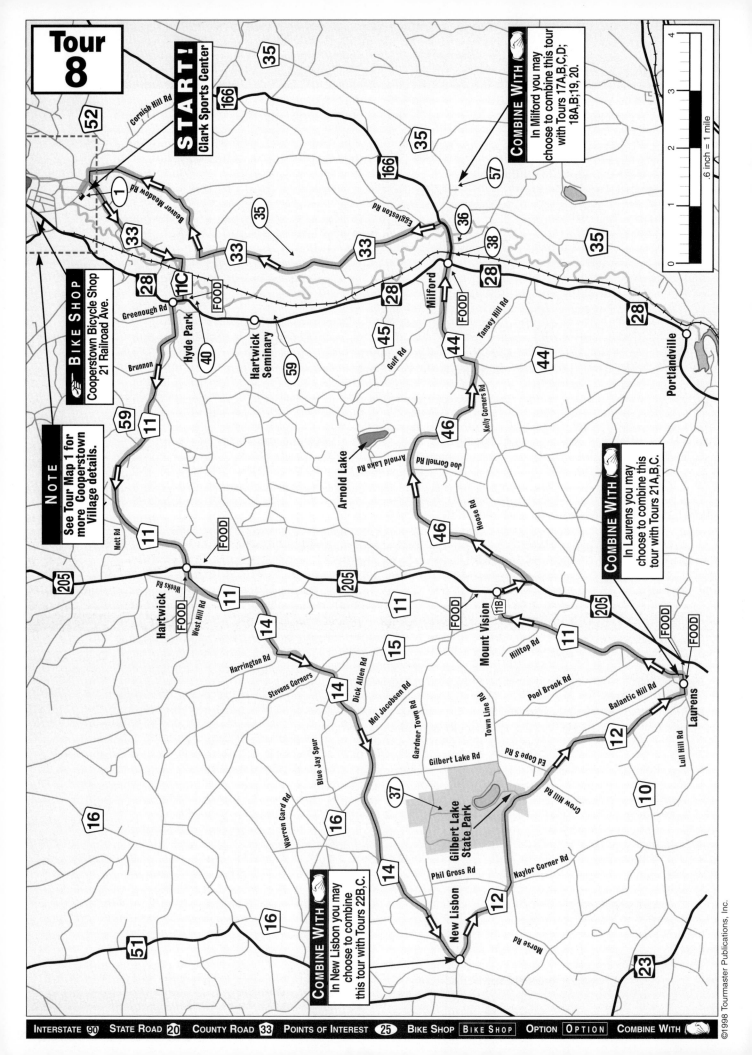

Tour
8

START!
Clark Sports Center

Cornish Hill Rd

Beaver Meadow Rd

35
166
52
1
166
35
35
57

COMBINE WITH
In Milford you may choose to combine this tour with Tours 17A,B,C,D; 18A,B; 19, 20.

33
33
33
35
35
35
33
Eggleston Rd
36
38
28

28
28
FOOD
FOOD
Milford
28
Portlandville
BIKE SHOP
Cooperstown Bicycle Shop
21 Railroad Ave.

Greenough Rd
11C
Hyde Park
40
Brunnon
Hartwick Seminary
59
45
Gulf Rd
44
Tansey Hill Rd
44

NOTE
See Tour Map 1 for more Cooperstown Village details.

59
11
46
Arnold Lake Rd
Joe Cornell Rd
Kelly Corners Rd

Mott Rd
11
46

Arnold Lake
46
Hoose Rd

205
FOOD
11
205
11
205

COMBINE WITH
In Laurens you may choose to combine this tour with Tours 21A,B,C.

Hartwick
FOOD
West Hill Rd
Weeks Rd
11
11
Mount Vision
11B
Hilltop Rd
FOOD
11
205
FOOD
FOOD

14
15
Dick Allen Rd
Pool Brook Rd
Balantic Hill Rd
Laurens

Harrington Rd
Stevens Corners
14
Mel Jacobsen Rd
Gardner Town Rd
Town Line Rd
Gilbert Lake Rd
Lull Hill Rd
12

16
Warren Gard Rd
Blue Jay Spur
16
37
Gilbert Lake State Park
Ed Cope S Rd
Crow Hill Rd
10

16
COMBINE WITH
In New Lisbon you may choose to combine this tour with Tours 22B,C.

14
New Lisbon
Phil Gross Rd
Naylor Corner Rd
12

16
51
Morse Rd
23

INTERSTATE 90   STATE ROAD 20   COUNTY ROAD 33   POINTS OF INTEREST 25   BIKE SHOP BIKE SHOP   OPTION OPTION   COMBINE WITH

©1998 Tourmaster Publications, Inc.

Oaks Creek "A"

Start: Clark Sports Center. Ballfield Exit.

Miles	9
Rating	Easy
Climb	400' @ 44 ft/mi

Tour 9A

•	0.0 R	UM 52	0.2
	0.2 BR	**X** Bridge Then BR 33	2.5
	2.7 R	11C	0.7
••	3.4 R SS	28 ⚠ ☞ L 0.1 FOOD	0.2
	3.6 L	11 Use Left Turn Lane ⚠	0.2
	3.8 R	Greenough Rd	1.6
	5.4 BL	TRO UM Greenough ⊘ Road Closed	0.3
	5.7 R SS	UM 59 **X** Bridge	0.1
	5.8 R SS	UM 26	1.0
	6.8 L SS	28 ⚠	1.0
	7.8 R	@ Cooperstown Optical/ Wilber Bank	0.1
	7.9 L	TRO Pavement	0.2
•	8.1 L SS	UM Linden Ave	0.3
	8.4 R SS	Walnut Ave ☞ S 0.1 FOOD	0.3
•	8.7 R SS	Susquehanna Ave (UM 52)	0.3
	9.0 R	Clark Sports Center	

R	Right	**S**	Straight	**SS**	Stop Sign	**UM**	Unmarked Road	⊘ Do Not Take
L	Left	**TRO**	To Remain On	**SL**	Stop Light	26	County Route	☞ Detour Off
BR	Bear Right	**X**	Cross	**YS**	Yield Sign	28	State Route	🤝 Combine With
BL	Bear Left	⚠	Caution					

Mile	•POINTS OF INTEREST		#
0.0	Clark Sports Center		1
3.4	Cooperstown Fun Park	☞ L 0.1	40
3.4	Corvette Hall of Fame	☞ L 1.5	59
8.2	LaCava Nature Tr. ☞ R @ Coop. Midd./High Sch.		58
8.9	Deer Park on L		2

TOUR DESCRIPTION

Oaks Creek is an easy practice series for beginning and casual cyclists. The distances are short and slowly progressive. The routes are flat to rolling with an occasional short "practice" hill. The tours provide traffic experience by crossing and riding a short distance on State Route 28. The "D" option even provides practice riding a short distance on gravel.

The Oaks Creek "A" tour rides to the first bridge crossing Oaks Creek at Toddsville.

COUNTIES
Otsego

BIKE SHOP
@ 0.0 ☞ L 1.0 Cooperstown Bicycle. See map.

©1998 Tourmaster Publications, Inc.

Climb Rating in feet per mile climbed: 0-45 = Easy, 45-60 = Moderate, 60+ = Difficult

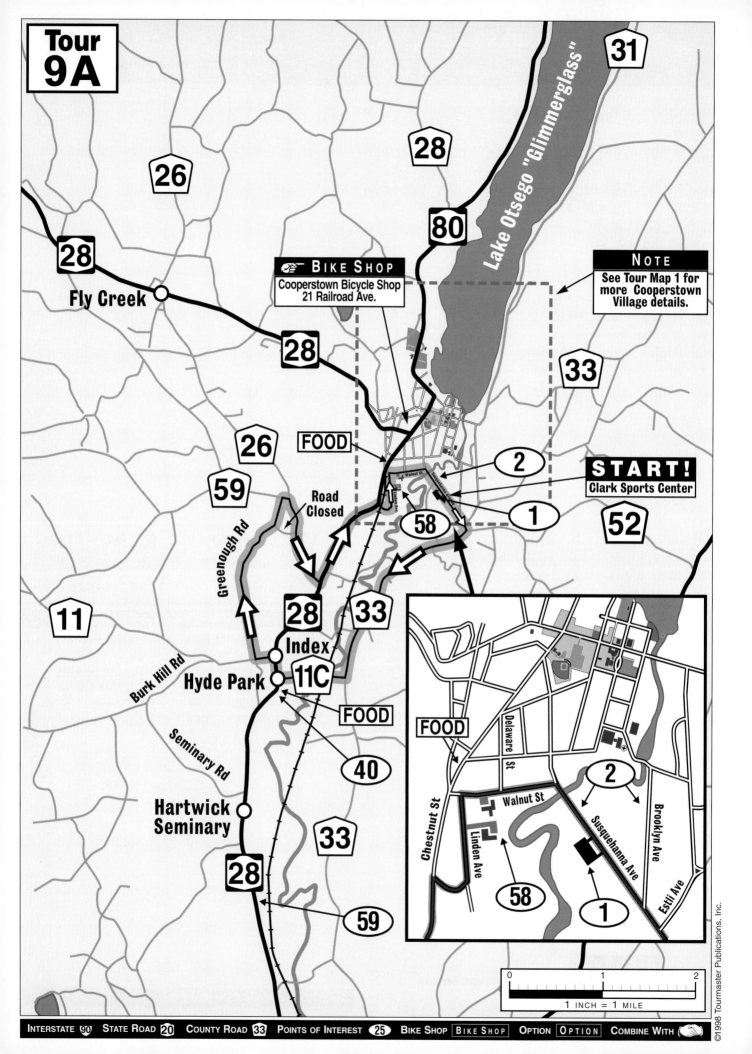

Oaks Creek "B"

Start: Clark Sports Center. Ballfield Exit.

Miles	12
Rating	Easy
Climb	500' @ 41 ft/mi

Tour 9B

•	0.0	R	UM ⑤②	0.2
	0.2	BR	**X** Bridge Then BR ㉝	2.5
	2.7	R	⑪⒞	0.7
••	3.4	R SS	㉘ ⚠ ☞ L 0.1 [FOOD]	0.2
	3.6	L	⑪ Use Left Turn Lane ⚠	0.2
	3.8	R	Greenough Rd	1.6
	5.4	BL	TRO UM Greenough ∅ Road Closed	0.3
	5.7	L SS	UM ㊾	0.6
	6.3	R	UM Stone House Rd	0.9
	7.2	R	Fork Shop Rd **X** Bridge	0.3
	7.5	R SS	UM ㉖	2.3
	9.8	L SS	㉘ ⚠	1.1
	10.9	R	@ Cooperstown Optical/ Wilber Bank	0.1
	11.0	L	TRO Pavement	0.2
•	11.2	L SS	UM Linden Ave	0.3
	11.5	R SS	Walnut Ave ☞ S 0.1 [FOOD]	0.3
•	11.8	R SS	Susquehanna Ave (UM ⑤②)	0.3
	12.1	R	Clark Sports Center	

R	Right	**S**	Straight	**SS**	Stop Sign	**UM**	Unmarked Road	∅	Do Not Take
L	Left	**TRO**	To Remain On	**SL**	Stop Light	㉖	County Route	☞	Detour Off
BR	Bear Right	**X**	Cross	**YS**	Yield Sign	㉘	State Route	🤝	Combine With
BL	Bear Left	⚠	Caution						

Mile	•POINTS OF INTEREST	#
0.0	Clark Sports Center	①
3.4	Cooperstown Fun Park ☞ L 0.1	㊵
3.4	Corvette Hall of Fame ☞ L 1.5	㊾
11.3	LaCava Nature Tr. ☞ R @ Coop. Midd./High Sch.	㊳
12.0	Deer Park on L	②

TOUR DESCRIPTION

Oaks Creek is an easy practice series for beginning and casual cyclists. The distances are short and slowly progressive. The routes are flat to rolling with an occasional short "practice" hill. The tours provide traffic experience by crossing and riding a short distance on State Route 28. The "D" option even provides practice riding a short distance on gravel.

Oaks Creek "B" adds 3 miles and a 100 foot climb to the Oaks Creek "A" tour. The extension rides to the second bridge crossing Oaks Creek at Fork Shop Road.

COUNTIES

Otsego

BIKE SHOP

@ 0.0 ☞ L 1.0 Cooperstown Bicycle. See map.

Let us know what you think of this tour! Email: crankmail@usa.net

Climb Rating in feet per mile climbed: 0-45 = Easy, 45-60 = Moderate, 60+ = Difficult

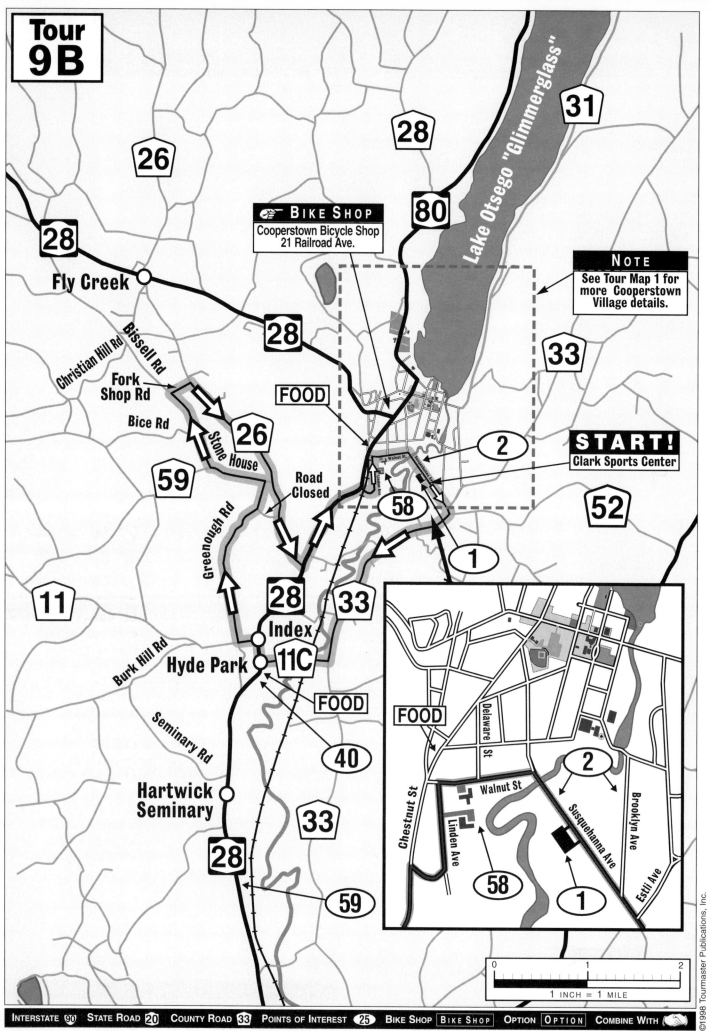

Tour 9B

28 26 31

28

28 Fly Creek 80

BIKE SHOP
Cooperstown Bicycle Shop
21 Railroad Ave.

Lake Otsego "Glimmerglass"

NOTE
See Tour Map 1 for more Cooperstown Village details.

33

Christian Hill Rd
Bissell Rd
Fork Shop Rd
Bice Rd
Stone House

28

FOOD

26

59

Road Closed

58

2

START!
Clark Sports Center

52

Greenough Rd

1

11

28

33

Index

11C

FOOD

Burk Hill Rd

Hyde Park

40

Seminary Rd

Hartwick Seminary

33

28

59

FOOD

Chestnut St

Delaware St

Walnut St

Linden Ave

2

Susquehanna Ave

Brooklyn Ave

Estli Ave

58

1

0   1   2
1 INCH = 1 MILE

INTERSTATE 90 STATE ROAD 20 COUNTY ROAD 33 POINTS OF INTEREST 25 BIKE SHOP BIKE SHOP OPTION OPTION COMBINE WITH

Cranks

Oaks Creek "C"

Start: Clark Sports Center. Ballfield Exit.

Miles	16
Rating	Easy
Climb	600' @ 37 ft/mi

Tour 9C

Mile	Turn	Directions	Dist
• 0.0	R	UM ⑤②	0.2
0.2	BR	**X** Bridge Then BR ㉝	2.5
2.7	R	⑪Ⓒ	0.7
•• 3.4	R SS	㉘ ⚠ ☞ L 0.1 FOOD	0.2
3.6	L	⑪ Use Left Turn Lane ⚠	0.2
3.8	R	Greenough Rd	1.6
5.4	BL	TRO UM Greenough ⊘ Road Closed	0.3
5.7	L SS	UM ㊾	0.6
6.3	R	UM Stone House Rd	1.7
8.0	S SS	Then R **X** Bridge UM Allison Rd	0.2
8.2	L	UM Cemetery Rd ⊘ S Allison	0.4
8.6	BL	TRO UM Cemetery ⊘ Feed Store	0.2
8.8	S SL	㉖ **X** ㉘ ⚠ FOOD	0.5
• 9.3	R	Goose St Then L Into Cider Mill	0.0
9.3	R	Goose St Leaving Cider Mill	0.1
9.4	L SS	UM ㉖	0.4
9.8	S SL	**X** ㉘ ⚠ Then BL TRO ㉖ FOOD	3.7
13.5	L SS	㉘ ⚠	1.1
14.6	R	@ Cooperstown Optical/Wilber Bank	0.1
14.7	L	TRO Pavement	0.2
• 14.9	L SS	UM Linden Ave	0.2
15.1	R SS	Walnut Ave ☞ S 0.1 FOOD	0.4
• 15.5	R SS	Susquehanna Ave (UM ⑤②)	0.3
15.8	R	Clark Sports Center	

R	Right	**S**	Straight	**SS**	Stop Sign
L	Left	**TRO**	To Remain On	**SL**	Stop Light
BR	Bear Right	**X**	Cross	**YS**	Yield Sign
BL	Bear Left	⚠	Caution		

UM	Unmarked Road	⊘	Do Not Take
㉖	County Route	☞	Detour Off
㉘	State Route	🤝	Combine With

Mile	•POINTS OF INTEREST	#
0.0	Clark Sports Center	①
3.4	Cooperstown Fun Park ☞ L 0.1	㊵
3.4	Corvette Hall of Fame ☞ L 1.5	㊾
9.3	Fly Creek Cider Mill	㊴
15.0	LaCava Nature Trail ☞ R @ Coop. Mid/High Sch.	㊽
15.7	Deer Park on L	②

TOUR DESCRIPTION

Oaks Creek is an easy practice series for beginning and casual cyclists. The distances are short and slowly progressive. The routes are flat to rolling with an occasional short "practice" hill. The tours provide traffic experience by crossing and riding a short distance on State Route 28. The "D" option even provides practice riding a short distance on gravel.

Oaks Creek "C" adds 4 miles and a 100 foot climb to the Oaks Creek "B" tour. The extension rides to the third bridge crossing Oaks Creek at Allison Road and then proceeds to the Fly Creek Cider Mill.

At the Cider Mill you can drink fresh cider as you watch it being made. You can snack on apples, cheeses, and homemade goodies. You can browse in the craft shop, picnic by the mill pond, and, if your timing is right, polka at the Applefest Weekend in late September.

COUNTIES

Otsego

BIKE SHOP

@ 0.0 ☞ L 1.0 Cooperstown Bicycle. See map.

©1998 Tourmaster Publications, Inc.

Climb Rating in feet per mile climbed: 0-45 = Easy, 45-60 = Moderate, 60+ = Difficult

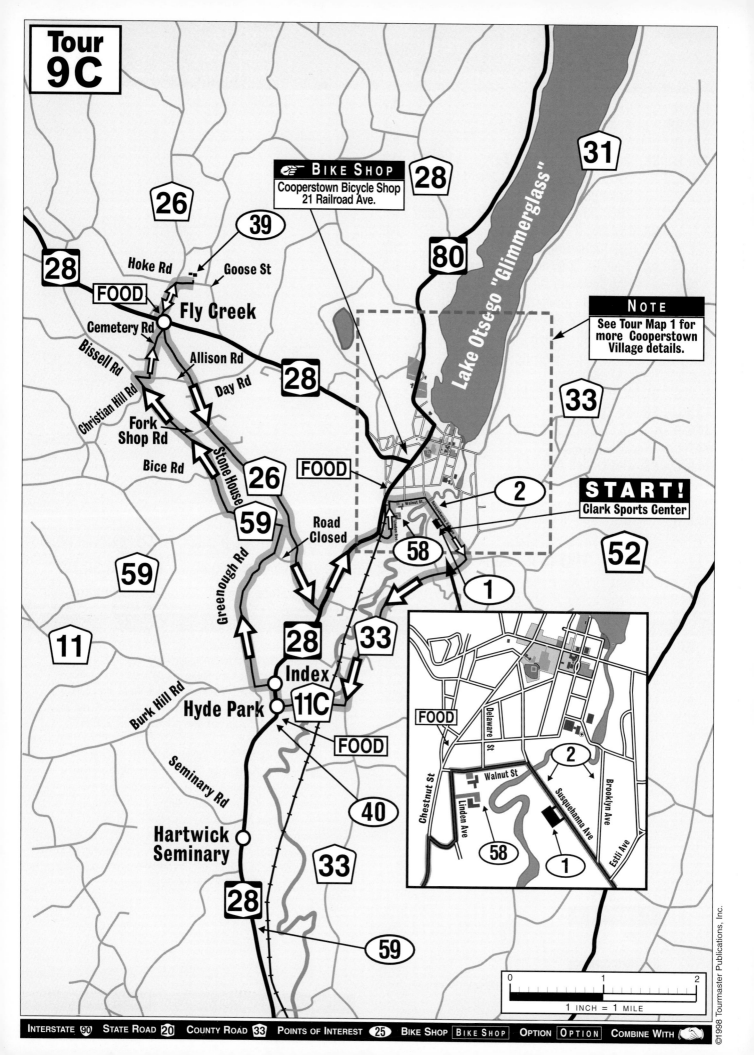

Tour 9C

BIKE SHOP
Cooperstown Bicycle Shop
21 Railroad Ave.

26

28

31

39

Hoke Rd Goose St

28

FOOD

Fly Creek

Cemetery Rd

Bissell Rd

Allison Rd

28

Day Rd

Christian Hill Rd

Fork Shop Rd

Bice Rd

Stone House

26

59

Road Closed

Greenough Rd

59

11

Burk Hill Rd

Seminary Rd

Hartwick Seminary

28

80

Lake Otsego "Glimmerglass"

NOTE
See Tour Map 1 for more Cooperstown Village details.

33

FOOD

2

START!
Clark Sports Center

52

Walnut St

Linden Ave

Susquehanna Ave

58

1

28

Index

11C

Hyde Park

FOOD

40

33

59

FOOD

Chestnut St

Delaware St

Walnut St

Linden Ave

2

Brooklyn Ave

Susquehanna Ave

Estli Ave

58

1

0   1   2
1 INCH = 1 MILE

©1998 Tourmaster Publications, Inc.

INTERSTATE **90**   STATE ROAD **20**   COUNTY ROAD **33**   POINTS OF INTEREST **25**   BIKE SHOP BIKE SHOP   OPTION OPTION   COMBINE WITH

Oaks Creek "D"

Start: Clark Sports Center. Ballfield Exit.

Miles	18
Rating	Easy
Climb	700' @ 39 ft/mi

Tour 9D

Mile	Dir		Instruction		Dist
• 0.0	R		UM 52		0.2
0.2	BR		X Bridge Then BR 33		2.5
2.7	R		11C		0.7
•• 3.4	R	SS	28 ⚠	☞ L 0.1 FOOD	0.2
3.6	L		11 Use Left Turn Lane ⚠		0.2
3.8	R		Greenough Rd		1.6
5.4	BL		TRO UM Greenough ⊘ Road Closed		0.3
5.7	L	SS	UM 59		0.6
6.3	R		UM Stone House Rd		1.7
8.0	S	SS	UM Bissell S ⊘ BR Bridge		0.7
8.7	BR		UM Bissell ⊘ Wileytown Rd		0.7
9.4	S	SS	UM Cat Town Rd X UM 28 ⚠		0.4
9.8	R		UM Hoke X Bridge ⊘ Parslow		0.1
9.9	BR		TRO UM Hoke ⊘ Keating		0.2
10.1	BR		TRO UM Hoke (**Gravel**) ⊘ Bed Bug		1.2
• 11.3	S	SS	Goose St Then L Into Cider Mill		0.1
11.4	R		Goose St Leaving Cider Mill		0.0
11.4	L	SS	UM 26		0.5
11.9	S	SL	X 28 ⚠ Then BL TRO 26 FOOD		3.6
15.5	L	SS	28 ⚠		1.1
16.6	R		@ Cooperstown Optical/Wilber Bank		0.1
16.7	L		TRO Pavement		0.2
• 16.9	L	SS	UM Linden Ave		0.2
17.1	R	SS	Walnut Ave ☞ S 0.1 FOOD		0.4
• 17.5	R	SS	Susquehanna Ave (UM 52)		0.4
17.9	R		Clark Sports Center		

NOTE
This Tour Includes 1.0 Miles On Gravel @ Mile 10.1 Hoke Rd.

R	Right	S	Straight	SS	Stop Sign
L	Left	TRO	To Remain On	SL	Stop Light
BR	Bear Right	X	Cross	YS	Yield Sign
BL	Bear Left	⚠	Caution		

UM	Unmarked Road	⊘	Do Not Take
26	County Route	☞	Detour Off
28	State Route	🤝	Combine With

POINTS OF INTEREST

Mile	• POINTS OF INTEREST	#
0.0	Clark Sports Center	1
3.4	Cooperstown Fun Park ☞ L 0.1	40
3.4	Corvette Hall of Fame ☞ L 1.5	59
11.3	Fly Creek Cider Mill	39
17.0	LaCava Nature Trail ☞ R @ Coop. Mid/High Sch.	58
17.7	Deer Park on L	2

COUNTIES
Otsego

BIKE SHOP
@ 0.0   ☞ L 1.0 Cooperstown Bicycle. See map.

TOUR DESCRIPTION

Oaks Creek is an easy practice series for beginning and casual cyclists. The distances are short and slowly progressive. The routes are flat to rolling with an occasional short "practice" hill. The tours provide traffic experience by crossing and riding a short distance on State Route 28.

Oaks Creek "D" adds 2 miles and a 100 foot climb to the Oaks Creek "C" tour. It rides to the fourth bridge crossing Oaks Creek at Hoke Road, provides practice riding a short distance on gravel, and then proceeds to the Fly Creek Cider Mill.

At the Cider Mill you can drink fresh cider as you watch it being made. You can snack on apples, cheeses, and homemade goodies. You can browse in the craft shop, picnic by the mill pond, and, if your timing is right, polka at the Applefest Weekend in late September.

Let us know what you think of this tour! Email: crankmail@usa.net

Climb Rating in feet per mile climbed: 0-45 = Easy, 45-60 = Moderate, 60+ = Difficult

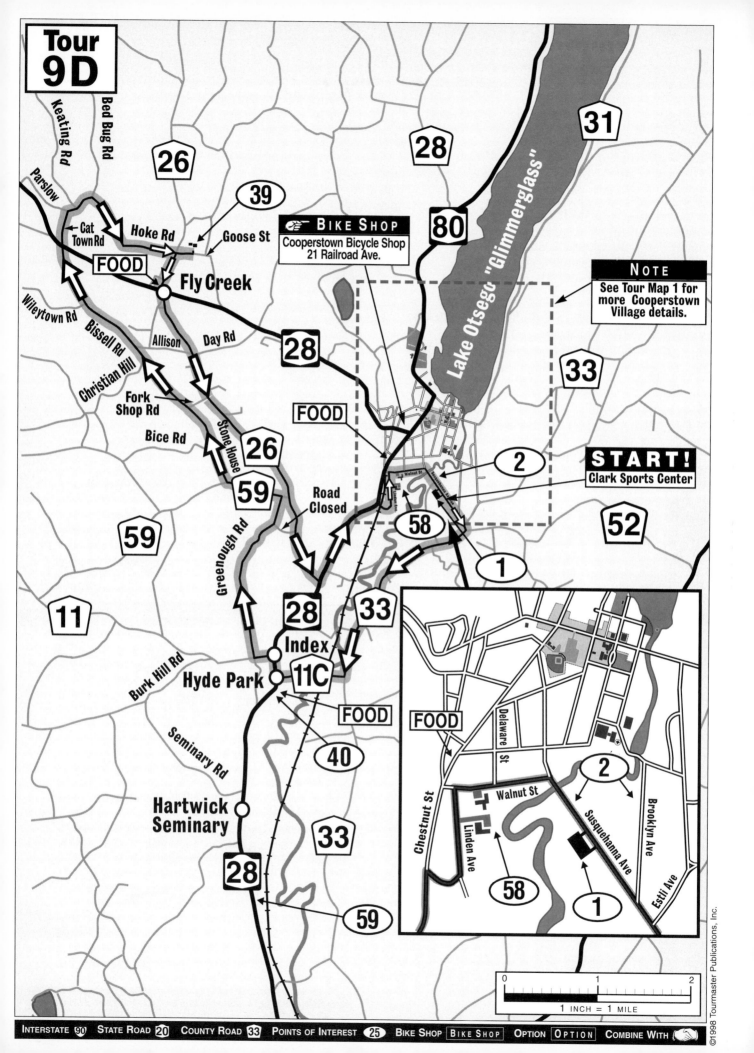

Tour 9D

Keating Rd

Bed Bug Rd

26

Parslow

Cat Town Rd

Hoke Rd

39

Goose St

FOOD

Fly Creek

Wileytown Rd

Bissell Rd

Christian Hill

Allison

Day Rd

28

Fork Shop Rd

Bice Rd

Stone House

26

59

Greenough Rd

Road Closed

59

11

28

33

Index

Hyde Park

11C

FOOD

40

Burk Hill Rd

Seminary Rd

Hartwick Seminary

28

59

33

👉 **BIKE SHOP**
Cooperstown Bicycle Shop
21 Railroad Ave.

28

80

Lake Otsego "Glimmerglass"

28

31

NOTE
See Tour Map 1 for more Cooperstown Village details.

33

FOOD

2

58

1

START!
Clark Sports Center

52

Inset map

FOOD

Delaware St

2

Chestnut St

Walnut St

Linden Ave

Brooklyn Ave

Susquehanna Ave

Estli Ave

58

1

0   1   2
1 INCH = 1 MILE

INTERSTATE 90   STATE ROAD 20   COUNTY ROAD 33   POINTS OF INTEREST 25   BIKE SHOP BIKE SHOP   OPTION OPTION   COMBINE WITH 🤝

Mount Otsego

Start: Clark Sports Center. Ballfield Exit.

Miles	19
Rating	Difficult
Climb	1500' @ 78 ft/mi

Tour 10

• 0.0	R		UM 52	0.1
• 0.1	L		UM Brooklyn Ave	0.4
0.5	L	SS	Mill St	0.2
•• 0.7	R	SS	River St	0.3
• 1.0	S	SS	TRO River **X** Main ☞ L 0.1 FOOD	0.1
•• 1.1	L		Lake St (UM 80)	2.4
• 3.5	BL		28 (Pierstown Rd) ⊘ 80	3.3
6.8	S		Wedderspoon Hollow Rd ⊘ 28 R	0.2
• 7.0	L		TRO Pavement ⊘ Red House Hill Rd	2.3
9.3	L		Keyes Rd	0.8
10.1	BR		UM Huff @ Danger Sign ⊘ S UM Keyes	1.1
11.2	BL		TRO Huff ⊘ Smith Cross Road	1.9
13.1	R	SS	UM 28	0.2
13.3	R		Armstrong Rd	0.4
13.7	L		Glimmerglen Rd	0.8
14.5	BL		TRO Pavement ⊘ Tripp Hill Spur	2.0
16.5	R	SS	UM 80 ⚠	1.5
18.0	R		River St	0.1
18.1	S	SS	TRO River **X** Main ☞ R 0.1 FOOD	0.3
18.4	L	SS	Atwell Rd	0.2
18.6	R		Brooklyn Ave	0.4
19.0	R	SS	UM 52	0.2
19.2	L		Clark Sports Center	

NOTE

This Tour Includes 2.8 Miles On Gravel. A 2.5 Mile Section Begins Just Beyond Mount Otsego (Mile 8.0) On Wedderspoon Hollow Rd. A Second 0.3 Mile Section Is Found On Glimmerglen Rd.

R	Right	**S**	Straight	**SS** Stop Sign
L	Left	**TRO**	To Remain On	**SL** Stop Light
BR	Bear Right	**X**	Cross	**YS** Yield Sign
BL	Bear Left	⚠	Caution	

UM Unmarked Road	⊘ Do Not Take	
26 County Route	☞ Detour Off	
28 State Route	🤝 Combine With	

• POINTS OF INTEREST

Mile		#
0.0	Clark Sports Center	1
0.4	Deer Park (fenced enclosure @ fire hydrant) on L	2
0.7	Bassett Healthcare/Emergency Rm @ Atwell/River	3
0.8	Christ Church Historic Cemetery on L	4
1.0	Cooperstown Main St ☞ L	17
1.1	Susquehanna Headwaters ☞ S downstairs	5
1.2	Chief Uncas Tour Boat ☞ R SS 0.1 Fair St	6
1.3	Lakefront Park/Restroom ☞ R SS 0.1 Pioneer	11
1.5	Otesaga Resort Hotel & Golf Course on R	12
2.3	Farmers' Museum L	14
2.3	Fenimore House Museum R	13
3.6	Leatherstocking Falls R	41
8.0	Site of Mount Otsego Ski Area L	42

COUNTIES

Otsego

BIKE SHOP

@ 0.0 ☞ L 1.0 Cooperstown Bicycle. See map.

TOUR DESCRIPTION

This hilly route explores the ridges west of Lake Otsego with visits to Leatherstocking Falls and to the old Mount Otsego ski area.

The Mount Otsego ski area was a source of community pride and comraderie before it was insuranced out of existence twenty years ago. In its heyday it boasted the longest rope tow in the East. Legend has it that on particularly inclement snowdays, the school bus would transport children to ski at Mount Otsego since school had been closed for the day.

Though this tour is short, the climbs and the uphill gravel sections make it very challenging. The vistas and descents are your rewards.

Let us know what you think of this tour! Email: crankmail@usa.net

©1998 Tourmaster Publications, Inc.

Climb Rating in feet per mile climbed: 0-45 = Easy, 45-60 = Moderate, 60+ = Difficult

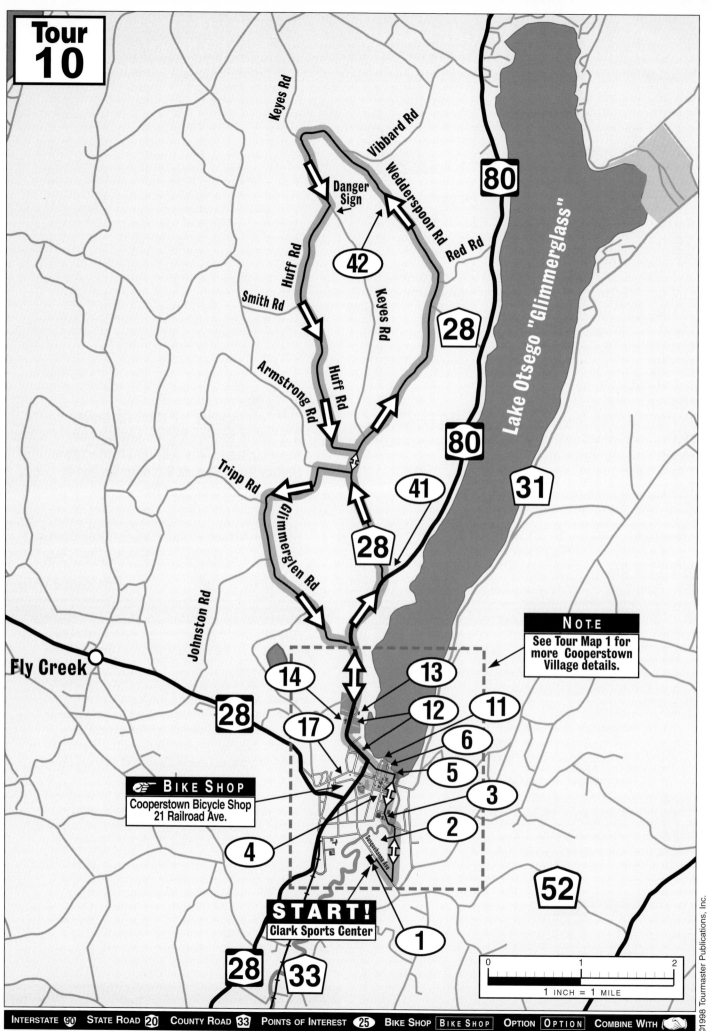

Tour 10

Keyes Rd

Vibbard Rd

Wedderspoon Rd

Red Rd

80

Lake Otsego "Glimmerglass"

Danger Sign

42

Huff Rd

Smith Rd

Keyes Rd

28

Armstrong Rd

Huff Rd

80

Tripp Rd

31

41

Glimmerglen Rd

28

Johnston Rd

NOTE
See Tour Map 1 for more Cooperstown Village details.

Fly Creek

14

13

28

17

12

11

6

5

🖐 BIKE SHOP
Cooperstown Bicycle Shop
21 Railroad Ave.

3

Susquehanna Ave

2

4

52

START!
Clark Sports Center

1

28 **33**

0   1   2

1 INCH = 1 MILE

INTERSTATE 90 STATE ROAD 20 COUNTY ROAD 33 POINTS OF INTEREST 25 BIKE SHOP BIKE SHOP OPTION OPTION COMBINE WITH 🤝

©1998 Tourmaster Publications, Inc.

Cranks

Fly Creek Valley "A"

Start: Clark Sports Center. Ballfield Exit.

Miles	30
Rating	Moderate
Climb	1700' @ 57 ft/mi

Tour 11A

•	0.0	R		UM ㊱	0.1
•	0.1	L		UM Brooklyn Ave	0.4
	0.5	L	SS	Mill St	0.2
••	0.7	R	SS	River St	0.3
•	1.0	S	SS	TRO River X Main ☞ L 0.1 FOOD	0.1
••	1.1	L		Lake St (UM ㊿) ⚠ In Summer	8.1
••	9.2	L		Allen Lake Rd (㉗) 🤝	2.2
	11.4	L		TRO UM ㉗ ⊘ Frank Patterson	0.9
	12.3	S		㉖ ⊘ Buddle/UM ㉗ To ⑳	1.3
	13.6	BL		TRO UM ㉖ ⊘ Walnut Grove	1.3
	14.9	S		TRO UM ㉖ ⊘UM Brickhouse/Ainslie	3.6
	18.5	L		TRO UM ㉖ ⊘ Pope Rd	2.3
	20.8	L		Stone House Rd	0.3
	21.1	BR		TRO UM Stone House ⊘ Buck Rd	0.5
	21.6	BR		TRO UM Stonehouse ⊘ Tripp To L	0.6
	22.2	BL		Bailey Rd	0.5
	22.7	R	SS	UM Goose St	0.3
•	23.0	L	SS	UM ㉖	0.4
	23.4	S	SL	X ㉘ ⚠ Then BR Cemetery Rd FOOD	0.7
	24.1	R	SS	Allison Rd	0.1
	24.2	L	SS	Then BL UM Bissell ⊘ Christian Hill	1.8
	26.0	L	SS	UM ㊾	0.7
	26.7	R	SS	UM ㉖	1.0
	27.7	L	SS	㉘ ⚠	1.0

	28.7	R		@ Cooperstown Optical/Wilber Bank	0.2
	28.9	L		TRO Pavement	0.1
•	29.0	L	SS	UM Linden Ave	0.3
	29.3	R	SS	Walnut Ave ☞ S 0.1 FOOD	0.3
•	29.6	R	SS	Susquehnna Ave (UM ㊱)	0.4
	30.0	R		Clark Sports Center	

🤝 **Opera: 25A,B,C,D,E**
@ 9.2 S 0.4 to Opera crosswalk to join
Tours 25A,B,C,D,E @ cue 0.0

R	Right	**S**	Straight	**SS**	Stop Sign
L	Left	**TRO**	To Remain On	**SL**	Stop Light
BR	Bear Right	**X**	Cross	**YS**	Yield Sign
BL	Bear Left	⚠	Caution		

UM	Unmarked Road	⊘	Do Not Take
㉖	County Route	☞	Detour Off
㉘	State Route	🤝	Combine With

• POINTS OF INTEREST

Mile	Point	#
0.0	Clark Sports Center	1
0.4	Deer Park (fenced enclosure @ fire hydrant) on L	2
0.7	Bassett Healthcare/Emergency Rm @ Atwell/River	3
0.8	Christ Church Historic Cemetery L	4
1.0	Cooperstown Main St Commercial District ☞ L	17
1.1	Susquehanna Headwaters ☞ S downstairs	5
1.2	Chief Uncas Tour Boat ☞ R SS 0.1 Fair St	6
1.3	Lakefront Park/Restroom ☞ R SS 0.1 Pioneer	11
1.5	Otesaga Resort Hotel & Golf Course on R	12
2.3	Farmers' Museum L	14
2.3	Fenimore House Museum R	13
4.6	Three Mile Point Swim	22
9.2	Glimmerglass Opera & Nature Trail ☞ S 0.4	23
11.0	Meadowlinks Golf	43
23.0	Fly Creek Cider Mill	39
29.1	LaCava Nature Tr. ☞ R @ Coop. Midd./High Sch.	58
29.8	Deer Park on L	2

COUNTIES
Otsego

BIKE SHOP
@ 0.0 ☞ L 1.0 Cooperstown Bicycle. See map.

TOUR DESCRIPTION

The Fly Creek Valley Series follows the western shore of Lake Otsego and then climbs to explore the definitely rolling terrain of the beautiful Fly Creek Valley. An early morning departure is recommended to avoid traffic during the summer tourist season.

Take time to explore the Fly Creek Cider Mill. At the Cider Mill you can drink fresh cider as you watch it being made. You can snack on apples, cheeses, and homemade goodies. You can browse in the craft shop, picnic by the mill pond, and, if your timing is right, polka at the Applefest Weekend in late September.

Enjoy the many other attractions along the way.

©1998 Tourmaster Publications, Inc.

Climb Rating in feet per mile climbed: 0-45 = Easy, 45-60 = Moderate, 60+ = Difficult

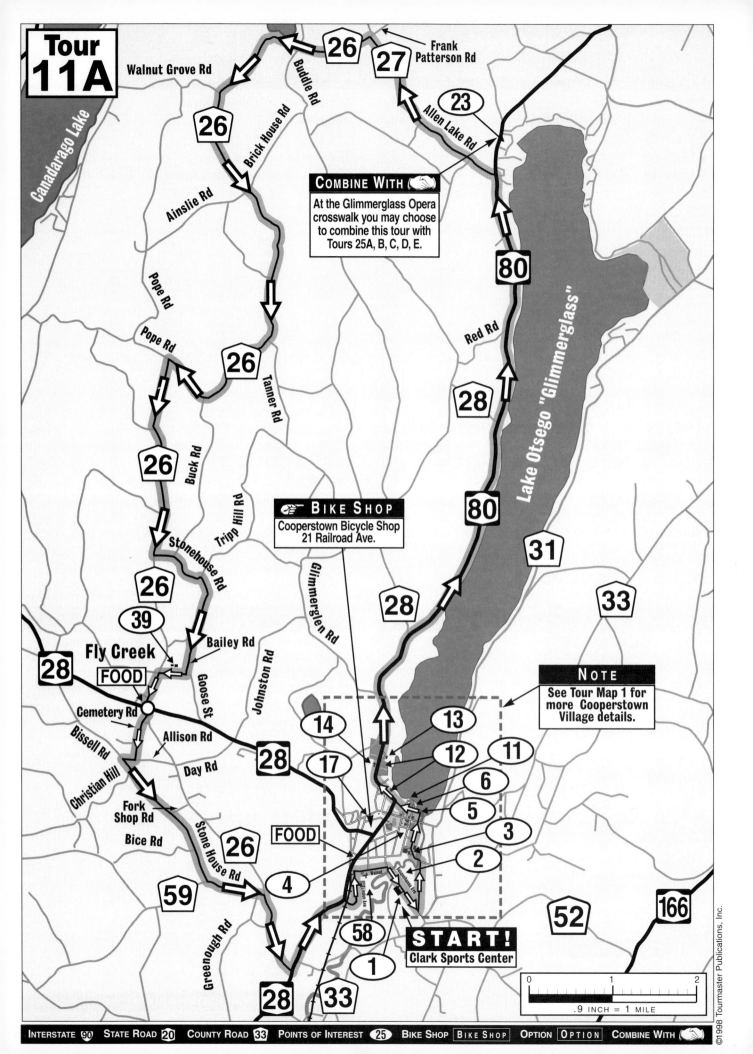

Tour 11A

Canadarago Lake

Walnut Grove Rd

Buddle Rd

26 **26** **27** Frank Patterson Rd

Brick House Rd

26 **23** Allen Lake Rd

Ainslie Rd

COMBINE WITH 🤝
At the Glimmerglass Opera crosswalk you may choose to combine this tour with Tours 25A, B, C, D, E.

Pope Rd

Pope Rd

26

Tanner Rd

80

Red Rd

26 Buck Rd

Tripp Hill Rd

28

Lake Otsego "Glimmerglass"

Stonehouse Rd

26

80

BIKE SHOP
Cooperstown Bicycle Shop
21 Railroad Ave.

31

39 Bailey Rd

Fly Creek Goose St

33

28 FOOD

Johnston Rd

28

28

Cemetery Rd

Bissell Rd Allison Rd

Day Rd

Christian Hill

NOTE
See Tour Map 1 for more Cooperstown Village details.

Glimmerglen Rd

14 **13**

17 **12** **11**

6

Fork Shop Rd **5**

Bice Rd **3**

Stone House Rd **26** FOOD

2

59 **4** Walnut

52 **166**

58

1

START!
Clark Sports Center

28 **33**

0 1 2
.9 INCH = 1 MILE

INTERSTATE 90 STATE ROAD 20 COUNTY ROAD 33 POINTS OF INTEREST 25 BIKE SHOP BIKE SHOP OPTION OPTION COMBINE WITH 🤝

©1998 Tourmaster Publications, Inc.

Fly Creek Valley "B"

Start: Clark Sports Center. Ballfield Exit.

Miles	40
Rating	Difficult
Climb	2700' @ 67 ft/mi

Tour 11B

0.0	R		UM 52	0.1
0.1	L		UM Brooklyn Ave	0.4
0.5	L	SS	Mill St	0.2
0.7	R	SS	River St	0.3
1.0	S	SS	TRO River **X** Main ☞ L 0.1 FOOD	0.1
1.1	L		Lake St (UM 80) ⚠ In Summer	8.1
9.2	L		Allen Lake Rd (27) 🤝	2.2
11.4	L		TRO UM 27 ⊘ Frank Patterson	0.9
12.3	S		26 ⊘ Buddle/UM 27 To 20	1.3
13.6	BL		TRO UM 26 ⊘ Walnut Grove	1.3
14.9	S		TRO UM 26 ⊘ UM Brickhouse/Ainslie	3.6
18.5	L		TRO UM 26 ⊘ Pope Rd	2.3
20.8	L		Stone House Rd	0.3
21.1	BR		TRO UM Stone House ⊘ Buck Rd	0.5
21.6	BR		TRO UM Stonehouse ⊘ Tripp To L	0.6
22.2	BL		Bailey Rd	0.5
22.7	R	SS	UM Goose St	0.3
23.0	L	SS	UM 26	0.4
23.4	S	SL	**X** 28 ⚠ Then BR Cemetery Rd FOOD	0.7
24.1	R	SS	Allison Rd	0.1
24.2	L	SS	Then BL UM Bissell ⊘ Christian Hill	1.8
26.0	R	SS	UM 59	0.8
26.8	R		Bush Rd	0.8
27.6	BL		TRO UM Bush Rd ⊘ Jarvis Rd	1.0

28.6	L	SS	Petkewec Rd	1.3
29.9	L	SS	UM 11	1.2
31.1	L		59	1.8
32.9	BL		TRO UM 59 ⊘ Brunner	1.3
34.2	R		UM Greenough Rd (Before Bridge)	0.3
34.5	BR		TRO UM Greenough ⊘ Closed Road	1.5
36.0	S	SS	TRO Greenough @ 1819 House	0.6
36.6	L	SS	UM 28 ⚠ FOOD	0.4
37.0	R		11C	0.7
37.7	L		33	2.4
40.1	L	SS	**X** Bridge Then BL UM 52 ⊘ 33	0.3
40.4	L		Clark Sports Center	

🤝 **Opera: 25A,B,C,D,E**
@ 9.2 S 0.4 to Opera crosswalk to join
Tours 25A,B,C,D,E @ cue 0.0

R	Right	**S**	Straight	**SS**	Stop Sign
L	Left	**TRO**	To Remain On	**SL**	Stop Light
BR	Bear Right	**X**	Cross	**YS**	Yield Sign
BL	Bear Left	⚠	Caution		

UM	Unmarked Road	⊘	Do Not Take	
26	County Route	☞	Detour Off	
28	State Route	🤝	Combine With	

POINTS OF INTEREST

Mile	•POINTS OF INTEREST	#
0.0	Clark Sports Center	1
0.4	Deer Park (fenced enclosure @ fire hydrant) on L	2
0.7	Bassett Healthcare/Emergency Rm @ Atwell/River	3
0.8	Christ Church Historic Cemetery L	4
1.0	Cooperstown Main St Commercial District ☞ L	17
1.1	Susquehanna Headwaters ☞ S downstairs	5
1.2	Chief Uncas Tour Boat ☞ R SS 0.1 Fair St	6
1.3	Lakefront Park/Restroom ☞ R SS 0.1 Pioneer	11
1.5	Otesaga Resort Hotel & Golf Course on R	12
2.3	Farmers' Museum L	14
2.3	Fenimore House Museum R	13
4.6	Three Mile Point Swim	22
9.2	Glimmerglass Opera & Nature Trail ☞ S 0.4	23
11.0	Meadowlinks Golf	43
23.0	Fly Creek Cider Mill	39
36.6	Corvette Hall of Fame ☞ R 1.1	59
36.7	Cooperstown Fun Park	40

COUNTIES
Otsego

BIKE SHOP
@ 0.0 ☞ L 1.0 Cooperstown Bicycle. See map.

TOUR DESCRIPTION

The Fly Creek Valley Series follows the western shore of Lake Otsego and then climbs to explore the definitely rolling terrain of the beautiful Fly Creek Valley. An early morning departure is recommended to avoid traffic during the summer tourist season.

Fly Creek Valley "B" adds 10 miles and a 1000 foot climb to the Fly Creek Valley "A" tour. The extension climbs to explore the rolling backroads of Christian Hill.

Take time to explore the Fly Creek Cider Mill. At the Cider Mill you can drink fresh cider as you watch it being made. You can snack on apples, cheeses, and homemade goodies. You can browse in the craft shop, picnic by the mill pond, and, if your timing is right, polka at the Applefest Weekend in late September.

Enjoy the many other attractions along the way.

Let us know what you think of this tour! Email: crankmail@usa.net

©1998 Tourmaster Publications, Inc.

Climb Rating in feet per mile climbed: 0-45 = Easy, 45-60 = Moderate, 60+ = Difficult

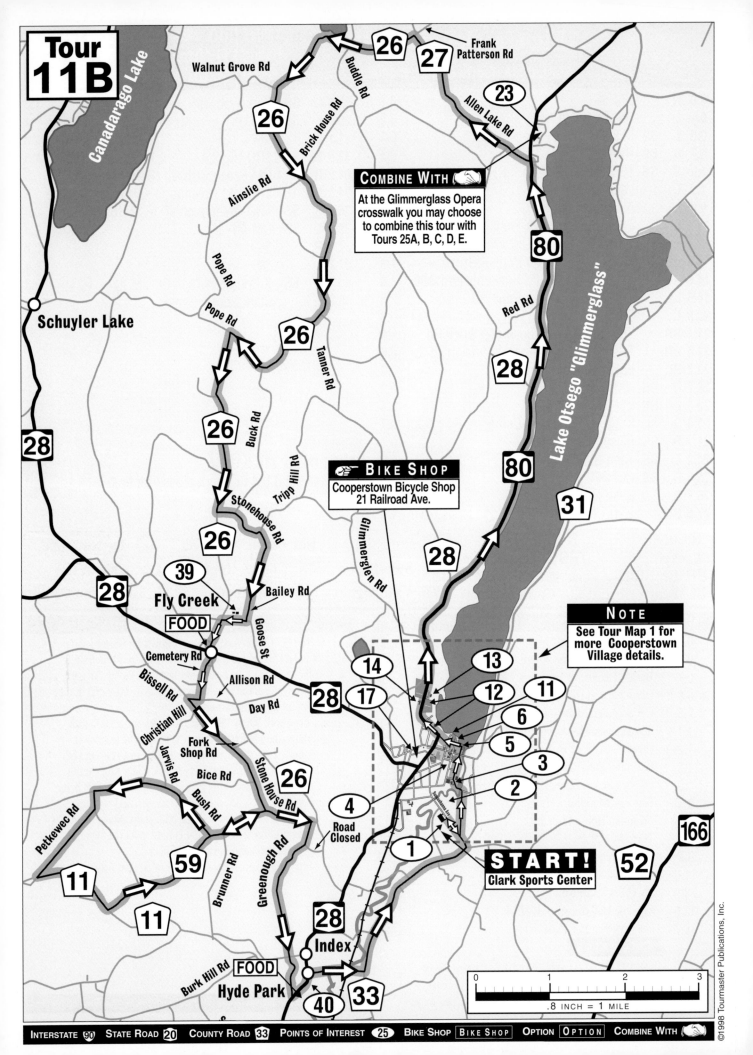

Tour 11B

Canadarago Lake

Walnut Grove Rd

Frank Patterson Rd

26
27
23
Allen Lake Rd

26
Brick House Rd
Buddle Rd

Ainslie Rd

COMBINE WITH
At the Glimmerglass Opera crosswalk you may choose to combine this tour with Tours 25A, B, C, D, E.

80

Schuyler Lake

Pope Rd
Pope Rd

26

Tanner Rd

Red Rd

28

28

Lake Otsego "Glimmerglass"

Buck Rd

26

Tripp Hill Rd

BIKE SHOP
Cooperstown Bicycle Shop
21 Railroad Ave.

80

26
Stonehouse Rd

31

26

39
Fly Creek
FOOD

Bailey Rd

Goose St

Glimmerglen Rd

NOTE
See Tour Map 1 for more Cooperstown Village details.

28

Cemetery Rd

Allison Rd

Day Rd

28

14

13

17

12

11

6

5

Bissell Rd

Christian Hill

Fork Shop Rd

Jarvis Rd

Bice Rd

Stone House Rd

26

3

2

Bush Rd

Brunner Rd

Greenough Rd

Road Closed

4

Petkewec Rd

11

59

1

START!
Clark Sports Center

52

166

11

28
Index

Burk Hill Rd

FOOD

Hyde Park

40

33

0   1   2   3
.8 INCH = 1 MILE

©1998 Tourmaster Publications, Inc.

INTERSTATE 90   STATE ROAD 20   COUNTY ROAD 33   POINTS OF INTEREST 25   BIKE SHOP   OPTION   COMBINE WITH

Sharon Springs "A"

Start: Cherry Valley. Parking Lot @ C.N. Bank.

Miles	22
Rating	**Difficult**
Climb	**1600'** @ 71 ft/mi

Tour 12A

• 0.0	R	UM 166	🤝-Coop	0.4
• 0.4	BR	54 ⊘ 166		2.9
• 3.3	BR	34A ⊘ 20	(34A Becomes 55)	3.0
6.3	BL	TRO UM 55 ⊘ UM Luenburgh		0.3
6.6	L SS	UM 40		0.9
7.5	R SS	20 ⚠		0.1
• 7.6	L SL	10	FOOD	3.0
10.6	R	Old Sharon Rd		0.9
11.5	L SS	Latimer Hill Rd		0.8
12.3	S SS	W. Ames Rd **X** 10	FOOD	2.6
14.9	S SS	163		2.0
16.9	L	Cherry Valley Rd ⊘ 163		0.1
• 17.0	BL	@ Store ⊘ Dugway 🤝-SB	FOOD	0.2
17.2	BR	TRO UM C.V. Rd ⊘ Otsego Rd		3.2
• 20.4	S	166 ⊘ Vander. ☞ R **X** Field To Falls		2.1
22.5	L	Parking Lot @ C. N. Bank		

🤝 **Cooperstown: 3A**
@ 0.0 L 0.1 to SL to join Tour 3A
@ cue 14.0 S SL Genesee St

🤝 **Sprout Brook: 16A,B,C**
@ 17.0 Sprout Brook General Store join Tours
16A,B,C @ cue 0.0

R	Right	**S**	Straight	**SS**	Stop Sign	**UM**	Unmarked Road
L	Left	**TRO**	To Remain On	**SL**	Stop Light	26	County Route
BR	Bear Right	**X**	Cross	**YS**	Yield Sign	28	State Route
BL	Bear Left	⚠	Caution				

⊘	Do Not Take	
☞	Detour Off	
🤝	Combine With	

POINTS OF INTEREST

Mile	•POINTS OF INTEREST	#
0.1	Cherry Valley Museum	29
2.6	Pleasantview Breakfast House	30
5.6	Sharon Orchards	44
8.3	Sharon Spa Bath Houses	45
17.1	Henry J. Kaiser Birthplace	32
20.4	Judd Falls ☞ R across the field	31

TOUR DESCRIPTION

The Sharon Springs Series explores northwestern Schoharie County.

The Sharon Springs "A" Tour climbs to the highlands overlooking the Mohawk Valley, travels east to Sharon Springs' historic bath houses, plummets to the village of Ames, travels west over flat valley roads to Sprout Brook, and then climbs back to Cherry Valley.

Plan time to visit the museums in Cherry Valley and Sharon Springs. Explore Judd Falls.

COUNTIES

Otsego, Schoharie, Montgomery

BIKE SHOP

@ 0.0 ☞ L 2.2 166 to Hawk Mountain Sports
@ 33

©1998 Tourmaster Publications, Inc.

Climb Rating in feet per mile climbed: 0-45 = Easy, 45-60 = Moderate, 60+ = Difficult

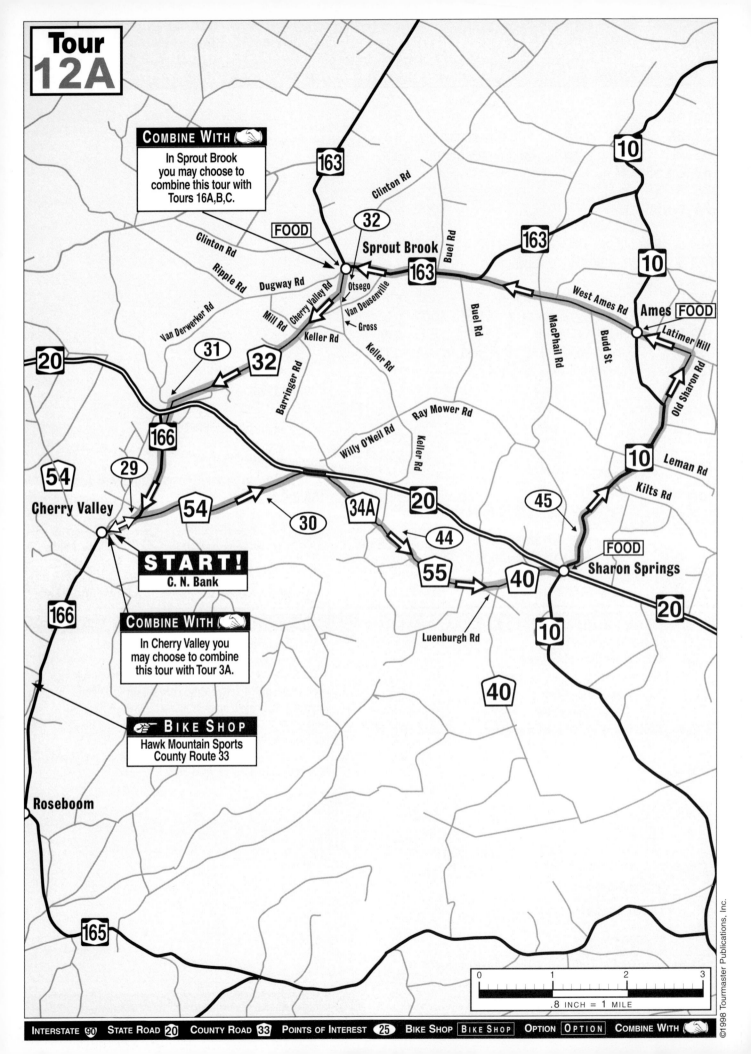

Tour 12A

COMBINE WITH 🤝
In Sprout Brook you may choose to combine this tour with Tours 16A,B,C.

163

Clinton Rd

10

FOOD

32
Sprout Brook

Clinton Rd

163

163

Buel Rd

West Ames Rd

10

10

Ames FOOD

Ripple Rd

Dugway Rd

Otsego

Van Deusenville

Latimer Hill

Cherry Valley Rd

Van Derwerker Rd

Mill Rd

Keller Rd

Gross

Buel Rd

Budd St

Old Sharon Rd

31

32

Barringer Rd

Keller Rd

MacPhail Rd

20

Keller Rd

Ray Mower Rd

10

Leman Rd

166

Willy O'Neil Rd

Keller Rd

Kilts Rd

54

29

10

45

Cherry Valley

54

30

34A

20

44

FOOD

Sharon Springs

55

40

START!
C. N. Bank

40

20

166

COMBINE WITH 🤝
In Cherry Valley you may choose to combine this tour with Tour 3A.

Luenburgh Rd

10

40

👉 BIKE SHOP
Hawk Mountain Sports
County Route 33

Roseboom

165

| 0 | 1 | 2 | 3 |

.8 INCH = 1 MILE

INTERSTATE 90   STATE ROAD 20   COUNTY ROAD 33   POINTS OF INTEREST 25   BIKE SHOP BIKE SHOP   OPTION OPTION   COMBINE WITH 🤝

Sharon Springs "B"

Start: Cherry Valley. Parking Lot @ C.N. Bank.

	Miles	54 [handshake]
	Rating	Difficult
	Climb	4000' @ 74 ft/mi

Tour 12B

Mile	Turn	Description	Dist
• 0.0	R	UM [166] [handshake]-Coop	0.4
• 0.4	BR	[54] Ø [166]	2.9
• 3.3	BR	[34A] Ø [20] ([34A] Becomes [55])	3.0
6.3	BR	UM Luenburgh Tnpk #3 Ø UM [55]	0.3
6.6	R SS	UM [40]	2.2
8.8	BL	TRO UM [40] Ø Engelville Pond	0.8
9.6	BL	TRO Paved UM [40]	1.7
11.3	R YS	[5] (Slate Hill Rd)	0.4
11.7	BL	TRO Paved UM [5] Ø Guernsey Rd	0.6
12.3	L SS	[165] FOOD	0.4
12.7	L	UM [30] Ø Seward Lane To R	1.0
13.7	S SS	TRO [30] X [10]	1.2
14.9	S	TRO UM [30] X Loonenburg Tnpk	1.8
16.7	R SS	[145]	2.1
18.8	L	[11] (Little York Rd)	0.9
19.7	S	TRO UM [11] X [37] (Hubb Stutts)	1.6
21.3	BL	TRO UM [11] Ø [72] (Becker)	1.3
22.6	R SS	[20] ⚠ **Get In Left Lane**	0.2
22.8	L	Little York Rd ⚠	0.6
23.4	R YS	Bear Swamp Rd	1.6
25.0	L YS	Cemetery Rd (Becomes Helmire)	1.0
26.0	L SS	Crosby Rd (Becomes [5B])	2.8
28.8	L	UM [5A]	0.3
29.1	BR	UM Onderdunk Rd	1.7
30.8	R SS	Sharon Rd Then BL TRO Pavement	1.7
32.5	BL	TRO Paved UM [34] Ø UM Kilts S	1.0
33.5	R SS	[20] ⚠	0.7
34.2	L	[32] (Parsons Rd) @ Do Not Enter ⚠	2.2
36.4	R SS	[10]	2.9
• 39.3	S SL	TRO [10] X [20] FOOD	3.0
42.3	R	Old Sharon Rd	0.9
43.2	L SS	Latimer Hill Rd	0.9
44.1	S SS	W. Ames Rd X [10] FOOD	2.5
46.6	S SS	[163]	2.0
48.6	L	Cherry Valley Rd Ø [163]	0.1
• 48.7	BL	@ Store Ø Dugway [handshake]-SB FOOD	0.2
48.9	BR	TRO C.V. Rd Ø Otsego Rd	3.2
• 52.1	S	[166] Ø Vander. 👉 R X Field To Falls	2.1
54.2	L	Parking Lot @ C. N. Bank	

[handshake] **Cooperstown: 3A**
@ 0.0 L 0.1 to SL to join Tour 3A
@ cue 14.0 S SL Genesee St

[handshake] **Sprout Brook: 16A,B,C**
@ 17.0 Sprout Brook General Store join
Tours 16A,B,C @ cue 0.0

R	Right	S	Straight	SS	Stop Sign	UM	Unmarked Road	Ø	Do Not Take
L	Left	TRO	To Remain On	SL	Stop Light	[26]	County Route	👉	Detour Off
BR	Bear Right	X	Cross			[28]	State Route	[handshake]	Combine With
BL	Bear Left	⚠	Caution	YS	Yield Sign				

Mile	•POINTS OF INTEREST	#
0.1	Cherry Valley Museum	(29)
2.6	Pleasantview Breakfast House	(30)
5.6	Sharon Orchards	(44)
40.0	Sharon Spa Bath Houses	(45)
48.8	Henry J. Kaiser Birthplace	(32)
52.1	Judd Falls 👉 R across the field	(31)

TOUR DESCRIPTION

The Sharon Springs Series explores northwestern Schoharie County.

Sharon Springs "B" adds 32 miles and a 2400 foot climb to the Sharon Springs "A" tour. The extension follows scenic backroads to Little York, Bear Swamp and Onderdunk.

Plan time to visit the museums in Cherry Valley and Sharon Springs. Explore Judd Falls.

COUNTIES

Otsego, Schoharie, Montgomery

BIKE SHOP

@ 0.0 👉 L 2.2 [166] to Hawk Mountain Sports
@ (33)

Let us know what you think of this tour! Email: crankmail@usa.net

©1998 Tourmaster Publications, Inc.

Climb Rating in feet per mile climbed: 0-45 = Easy, 45-60 = Moderate, 60+ = Difficult

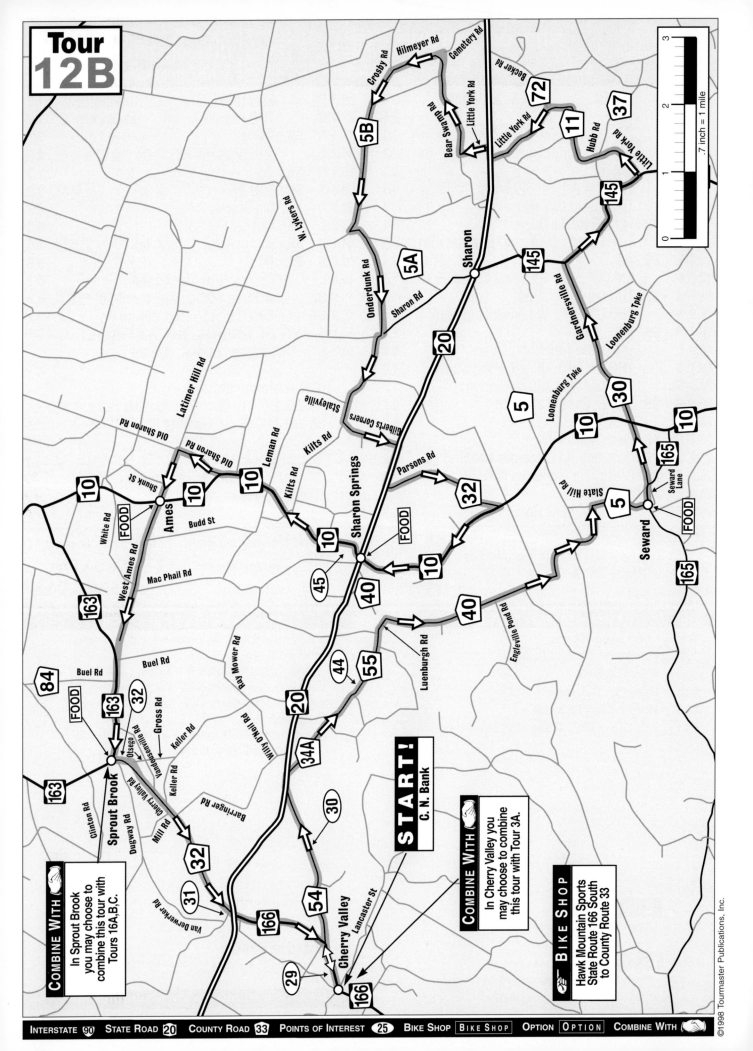

Tour 12B

3
2
1
0
.7 inch = 1 mile

Hilmeyer Rd
Crosby Rd
Cemetery Rd
Becker Rd
72
37
11
Little York Rd
Little York Rd
Bear Swamp Rd
Hubb Rd
5B
Little York Rd
145
W. Lykers Rd
145
Sharon
145
Gardnersville Rd
Loonenburg Tpke
Onderdunk Rd
5A
Sharon Rd
20
5
Loonenburg Tpke
30
10
10
Latimer Hill Rd
Staleyville
Gilberts Corners
Leman Rd
165
Old Sharon Rd
Kilts Rd
Parsons Rd
State Hill Rd
Seward Lane
Old Sharon Rd
10
Kilts Rd
Sharon Springs
32
FOOD
Shunk St
10
FOOD
10
10
165
10
Ames
10
Budd St
45
40
10
5
Seward
White Rd
FOOD
West Ames Rd
Mac Phail Rd
40
40
165
Engleville Pond Rd
163
Luenburgh Rd
Buel Rd
Buel Rd
84
Ray Mower Rd
44
55
FOOD
163
32
Gross Rd
20
Willy O'Neil Rd
Otsego Rd
Keller Rd
34A
Vandersenville Rd
163
Keller Rd
30
Clinton Rd
Sprout Brook
Barringer Rd
Cherry Valley Rd
Dugway Rd
Mill Rd
32
START!
C. N. Bank
31
54
Van Derwerker Rd
166
Lancaster St
Cherry Valley
29
166

COMBINE WITH 🤝
In Sprout Brook you may choose to combine this tour with Tours 16A,B,C.

COMBINE WITH 🤝
In Cherry Valley you may choose to combine this tour with Tour 3A.

BIKE SHOP 🚲
Hawk Mountain Sports
State Route 166 South
to County Route 33

INTERSTATE 90 STATE ROAD 20 COUNTY ROAD 33 POINTS OF INTEREST 25 BIKE SHOP BIKE SHOP OPTION OPTION COMBINE WITH 🤝

©1998 Tourmaster Publications, Inc.

Cranks

Sharon Springs "C"

Start: Cherry Valley. Parking Lot @ C.N. Bank.

Miles	70 🤝
Rating	Difficult
Climb	5000' @ 71 ft/mi

Tour 12C

Mile	Turn		Description	Dist
• 0.0	R		UM 166 🤝 -Coop	0.4
• 0.4	BR		54 Ø 166	2.9
• 3.3	BR		34A Ø 20 (34A Becomes 55)	3.0
6.3	BR		UM Luenburgh Tnpk #3 Ø UM 55	0.3
6.6	R	SS	UM 40	2.2
8.8	BL		TRO UM 40 Ø Engelville P.D.	0.8
9.6	BL		TRO Paved UM 40	1.7
11.3	R	YS	5 (Slate Hill Rd)	0.4
11.7	BL		TRO Paved UM 5 Ø Guernsey Rd	0.6
12.3	L	SS	165 FOOD	0.4
12.7	L		UM 30 Ø Seward Lane To R	1.0
13.7	S	SS	TRO 30 X 10	1.2
14.9	S		TRO UM 30 X Loonenburg Tnpk	1.8
16.7	R	SS	145	2.1
18.8	L		11 (Little York Rd)	0.9
19.7	R		37 (Hubb Stutts Rd)	1.2
20.9	S		TRO UM 37 Ø Snyder/Lake	0.5
21.4	BR		TRO UM 37 Ø Wetsel Rd	1.6
23.0	S	SS	UM 7 Toward 7 / 145	0.6
23.6	L	SS	UM 8 (UM Barnerville Rd)	0.2
23.8	BR		TRO UM 8 Ø Myers Rd	1.5
25.3	BL		Barnerville (UM 8) Ø Sign To 7	0.9
•• 26.2	S		8 Becomes 9 FOOD	0.3
• 26.5	S		TRO 9 ☞R Howe Caverns & FOOD	0.9
27.4	S		TRO UM 9 X Sagendorf Corners	0.5
• 27.9	S		TRO UM 9 @ Secret Caverns	0.8
28.7	L		UM 10 Ø Voege Road To R	1.4
30.1	BL		TRO UM 10 Ø UM 38 To R	0.3
30.4	BR		TRO UM 10 Ø Lawton Rd	2.8
33.2	R		UM 7 (UM Crommie Rd) Ø (C.Crapser)	1.3
34.5	L		Snyder Rd	0.9
35.4			Crapser Rd	1.1
36.5	L	YS	UM 72 (UM Becker Rd)	0.6
37.1	R	SS	UM 11 (UM Little York Rd)	1.3
38.4	S	SS	20 ! Get In Left Lane	0.2
38.6	L		Little York Rd !	0.6
39.2	R	YS	Bear Swamp Rd	1.6
40.8	L	YS	Cemetery Rd (Becomes Helmire)	1.0
41.8	L	SS	Crosby Rd (Becomes 5B)	2.8
44.6	L		UM 5A	0.3
44.9	BR		UM Onderdunk Rd	1.7
46.6	R	SS	Sharon Rd Then BL TRO Pavement	1.7
48.3	BL		TRO Paved UM 34 Ø UM Kilts S	1.0
49.3	R	SS	20 !	0.7
50.0	L		32 (Parsons Rd) @ Do Not Enter !	2.2
52.2	R	SS	10	2.9
• 55.1	S	SL	TRO 10 X 20 FOOD	3.0
58.1	R		Old Sharon Rd	0.9

Legend

R	Right	S	Straight	SS	Stop Sign
L	Left	TRO	To Remain On	SL	Stop Light
BR	Bear Right	X	Cross	YS	Yield Sign
BL	Bear Left	!	Caution		

UM	Unmarked Road	Ø	Do Not Take
26	County Route	☞	Detour Off
28	State Route	🤝	Combine With

...Tour Cues Continued

Mile	Turn		Description	Dist
59.0	L	SS	Latimer Hill Rd	0.9
59.9	S	SS	W. Ames Rd X 10 FOOD	2.5
62.4	S	SS	163	2.0
64.4	L		Cherry Valley Rd Ø 163	0.1
• 64.5	BL		@ Store Ø Dugway 🤝-SB FOOD	0.2
64.7	BR		TRO UM C.V. Rd Ø Otsego Rd	3.2
• 67.9	S		166 Ø Vander. ☞R X Field To Falls	2.1
70.0	L		Parking Lot @ C.N. Bank	

Tour Description

The Sharon Springs Series explores northwestern Schoharie County.

Sharon Springs "C" adds 16 miles and a 1000 foot climb to the Sharon Springs "B" Tour. The extension visits Howe Caverns, Secret Caverns, the Iroquios Indian Museum and the Caverns Creek Grist Mill Museum. You can also explore Judd Falls and visit the museums in Cherry Valley and Sprout Brook. Plan a full day for this excellent adventure.

🤝 **Cooperstown: 3A**
@ 0.0 L 0.1 to SL to join Tour 3A
@ cue 14.0 S SL Genesee St

🤝 **Sprout Brook: 16A,B,C**
@ 64.5 Sprout Brook General Store join Tours 16A,B,C @ cue 0.0

COUNTIES
Otsego, Schoharie, Montgomery

BIKE SHOP
@ 0.0 ☞ L 2.2 166 to Hawk Mountain Sports
@ 33

Let us know what you think of this tour! Email: crankmail@usa.net

• Points of Interest

Mile		#
0.1	Cherry Valley Museum	29
2.6	Pleasantview Breakfast House	30
5.5	Sharon Orchards	44
26.2	Iroquois Indian Museum ☞ R 0.1 8	46
26.2	Caverns Creek Grist Mill Museum ☞ R 0.4 8	47
26.5	Howe Caverns ☞ R 0.8	48
27.9	Secret Caverns	49
55.8	Sharon Spa Bath Houses	45
64.6	Henry J Kaiser Birthplace	32
67.9	Judd Falls ☞ R across the field	31

Climb Rating in feet per mile climbed: 0-45 = Easy, 45-60 = Moderate, 60+ = Difficult

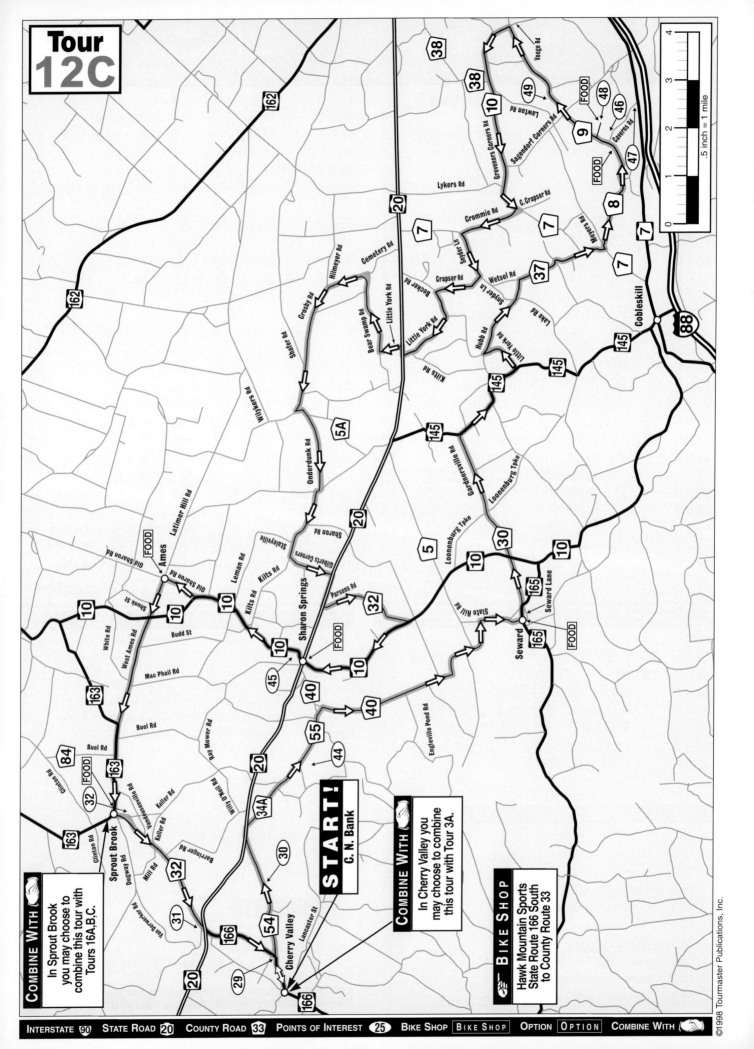

Tour 12C

Lykers Rd

Vroege Rd

FOOD

Groveners Corners Rd

Lawton Rd

Sagendorf Corners Rd

Caverns Rd

FOOD

C. Crapser Rd

Crommie Rd

Snyder Ln

Crapser Rd

Wetsel Rd

Myers Rd

Becker Rd

Little York Rd

Bear Swamp Rd

Little York Rd

Snyder Ln

Lake Rd

Little York Rd

Hubb Rd

Kitts Rd

Cobleskill

Cemetery Rd

Hilmeyer Rd

Crosby Rd

Shafer Rd

Willykers Rd

Latimer Hill Rd

Onderdunk Rd

Sharon Rd

Staleyville

Gilbert's Corners

Gardnersville Rd

Loonenburg Tpke

Loonenburg Tpke

Old Sharon Rd

FOOD

Ames

Old Sharon Rd

Shunk St

White Rd

West Ames Rd

Leman Rd

Kilts Rd

Kilts Rd

Budd St

Mac Phail Rd

Sharon Springs

Parsons Rd

FOOD

State Hill Rd

Seward Lane

Seward

FOOD

Buel Rd

Buel Rd

Roy Mower Rd

Engleville Pond Rd

Clinton Rd

FOOD

Sprout Brook

Vandessensville Rd

Keller Rd

Keller Rd

Willy O'Neil Rd

Barringer Rd

Dugway Rd

Mill Rd

Van Derwerker Rd

Cherry Valley

Lancaster St

START!
C. N. Bank

COMBINE WITH

In Sprout Brook you may choose to combine this tour with Tours 16A,B,C.

COMBINE WITH

In Cherry Valley you may choose to combine this tour with Tour 3A.

BIKE SHOP

Hawk Mountain Sports State Route 166 South to County Route 33

Scale: .5 inch = 1 mile

0 1 2 3 4

INTERSTATE 90   STATE ROAD 20   COUNTY ROAD 33   POINTS OF INTEREST 25   BIKE SHOP [BIKE SHOP]   OPTION [OPTION]   COMBINE WITH

©1998 Tourmaster Publications, Inc.

Judd Falls

Start: Cherry Valley. Parking Lot @ C.N. Bank.

Miles	14
Rating	**Difficult**
Climb	**1400'** @ 100 ft/mi

Tour 13

• 0.0	R	UM 166	[🤝]-Coop	0.4
• 0.4	BR	54	⊘ 166	2.9
3.3	L	⊘ 34A	Then R SS 20 ⚠	1.0
4.3	L	Keller Rd ⚠		1.2
5.5	S	TRO UM Keller **X** O'Neill/ Mower		1.6
7.1	BR	UM Gross (Becomes Otsego) ⊘UM Mill		0.4
7.5	S SS	TRO Otsego **X** Vandeusenville		0.2
7.7	S SS	UM 82 / 32		0.2
• 7.9	L	Dugway @ Gen. Store [🤝]-SB FOOD		1.5
• 9.4	BL	Vanderwerker Rd		2.6
• 12.0	R SS	166 ☞ L **X** Field To Judd Falls		2.1
14.1	L	Parking Lot @ C.N. Bank		

[🤝] **Cooperstown: 3A**
  @ 0.0 L 0.1 to SL to join Tour 3A
  @ cue 14.0 S SL Genesee St
[🤝] **Sprout Brook: 15A,B,C,D; 16A,B,C**
  @ 7.9 join Tours 15A,B,C,D; 16A,B,C
  @ cue 0.0 S Dugway Rd

R	Right	**S**	Straight	**SS**	Stop Sign	**UM** Unmarked Road	⊘ Do Not Take
L	Left	**TRO**	To Remain On	**SL**	Stop Light	26 County Route	☞ Detour Off
BR	Bear Right	**X**	Cross	**YS**	Yield Sign	28 State Route	[🤝] Combine With
BL	Bear Left	⚠	Caution				

Mile	•POINTS OF INTEREST	#
0.1	Cherry Valley Museum	29
2.6	Pleasantview Breakfast House	30
7.9	Henry J. Kaiser Birthplace	32
11.5	Cherry Valley Massacre: Wormuth Marker	69
12.0	Judd Falls ☞ L across the field	31

TOUR DESCRIPTION

  The Judd Falls Tour is short, but it claims to deliver more scenic vistas per mile than any other tour in this book.

  Climb from Cherry Valley to the highlands overlooking the Mohawk Valley. Then enjoy a 5 mile descent to Sprout Brook before climbing back to Cherry Valley following the western edge of the Judd Falls Gorge.

COUNTIES
Otsego, Montgomery

BIKE SHOP
  @ 0.0   ☞ L 2.2 166 to Hawk Mountain Sports
  @ 33

Let us know what you think of this tour! Email: crankmail@usa.net

Climb Rating in feet per mile climbed: 0-45 = Easy, 45-60 = Moderate, 60+ = Difficult

©1998 Tourmaster Publications, Inc.

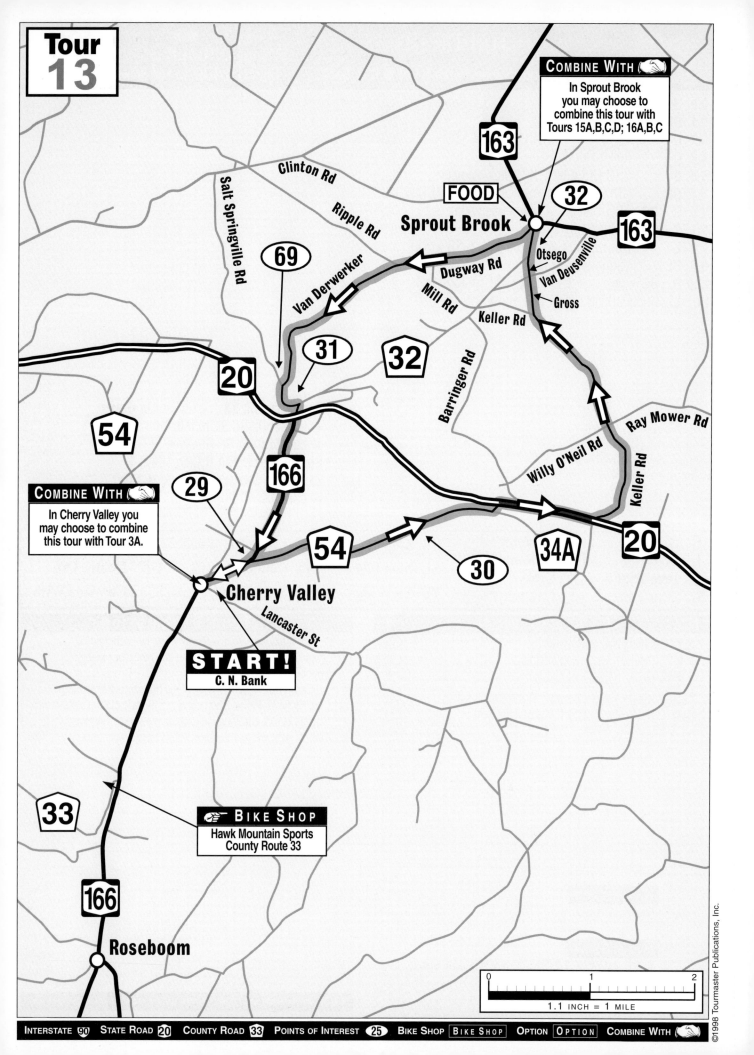

Tour 13

Combine With 🤝
In Sprout Brook you may choose to combine this tour with Tours 15A,B,C,D; 16A,B,C

163

FOOD

32

163

Sprout Brook

Otsego

Van Deusenville

Gross

Clinton Rd

Ripple Rd

Salt Springville Rd

69

Van Derwerker

Dugway Rd

Mill Rd

Keller Rd

31

32

20

Barringer Rd

54

166

Willy O'Neil Rd

Ray Mower Rd

Keller Rd

Combine With 🤝
In Cherry Valley you may choose to combine this tour with Tour 3A.

29

54

30

34A

20

Cherry Valley

Lancaster St

START!
C. N. Bank

👉 **Bike Shop**
Hawk Mountain Sports
County Route 33

33

166

Roseboom

0   1   2
1.1 INCH = 1 MILE

Interstate 90 **State Road** 20 **County Road** 33 **Points of Interest** 25 **Bike Shop** BIKE SHOP **Option** OPTION **Combine With** 🤝

©1998 Tourmaster Publications, Inc.

Belvedere Lake

Start: Cherry Valley. Parking Lot @ C.N. Bank.

Miles	18
Rating	**Difficult**
Climb	1900'@ 106 ft/mi

Tour 14

•	0.0	L		UM 166	0.0
•	0.0	L		Lancaster St (50)	9.9
	9.9	R		UM Crounch Rd	0.4
	10.3	L	SS	UM Hoose Rd	1.5
	11.8	R	SS	UM 165	0.2
	12.0	R		UM Snyder Rd ☞ S 1.3 FOOD	0.8
	12.8	R		Gage Rd	0.3
	13.1	BL		TRO UM Gage ⊘ Stannard Hill	0.5
•	13.6	S		@ Belvedere Lake FOOD	1.4
	15.0	L	SS	UM Doc Ahlers (Becomes Dietchie)	2.6
••	17.6	R	YS	166	0.5
	18.1	R	SL	TRO 166	0.1
	18.2	BL		To Parking Lot @ C.N. Bank	

NOTE

This Tour Includes 1.4 Miles On Gravel @ Mile 15.5 Doc Ahlers Rd.

Cooperstown: 3A
@ 0.0 L 0.1 to SL to join Tour 3A
@ cue 14.0 S SL Genesee St

R	Right	**S**	Straight	**SS**	Stop Sign	**UM** Unmarked Road	⊘ Do Not Take
L	Left	**TRO**	To Remain On	**SL**	Stop Light	26 County Route	☞ Detour Off
BR	Bear Right	**X**	Cross	**YS**	Yield Sign	28 State Route	Combine With
BL	Bear Left	⚠	Caution				

Mile	• POINTS OF INTEREST	#
0.0	Cherry Valley Museum ☞ R 0.1	29
1.8	Cherry Valley Gorge ☞ R 0.1 O'Neil Rd (gravel)	67
13.6	Belvedere Lake	34
17.8	Cherry Valley Massacre: Alden Monument	27
18.0	Cherry Valley Massacre: Historic Cemetery	28

COUNTIES

Otsego

BIKE SHOP

@ 0.0 ☞ L 2.2 166 to Hawk Mountain Sports
@17.6 ☞ L 1.6 166 to Hawk Mountain Sports

TOUR DESCRIPTION

The Belvedere Lake Tour is a climber's delight. Climb to the Cherry Valley Gorge and to spectacular views at the summit of East Hill. Descend to Pleasant Brook and then climb to the heights above Belvedere Lake before descending on gravel back to Cherry Valley. Look for ostriches along the way.

©1998 Tourmaster Publications, Inc.

Climb Rating in feet per mile climbed: 0-45 = Easy, 45-60 = Moderate, 60+ = Difficult

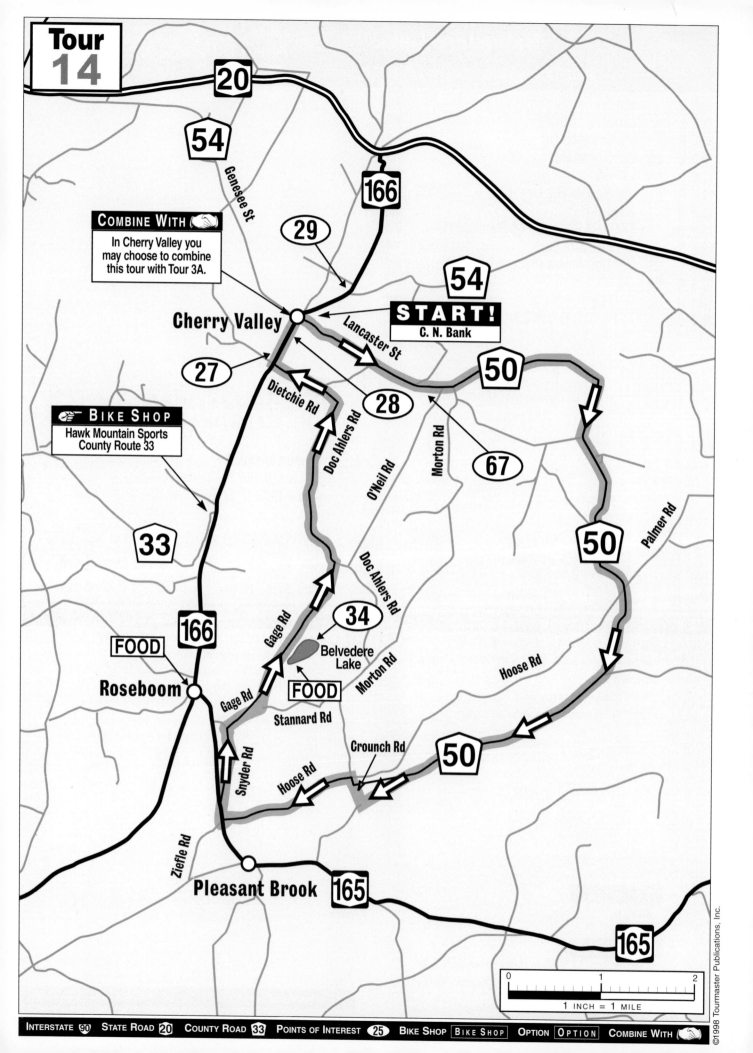

Tour 14

20

54

166

29

COMBINE WITH 👬
In Cherry Valley you may choose to combine this tour with Tour 3A.

54

START!
C. N. Bank

Cherry Valley

Lancaster St

27

50

Dietchie Rd

28

👉 **BIKE SHOP**
Hawk Mountain Sports
County Route 33

Morton Rd

O'Neil Rd

Doc Ahlers Rd

67

33

50

Palmer Rd

Doc Ahlers Rd

166

FOOD

34

Gage Rd

Belvedere Lake

FOOD

Morton Rd

Hoose Rd

Roseboom

Gage Rd

Stannard Rd

Snyder Rd

Crounch Rd

50

Hoose Rd

Hoose Rd

50

Ziefle Rd

Pleasant Brook

165

165

0   1   2
1 INCH = 1 MILE

INTERSTATE 90   **STATE ROAD** 20   **COUNTY ROAD** 33   **POINTS OF INTEREST** 25   **BIKE SHOP** BIKE SHOP   **OPTION** OPTION   **COMBINE WITH** 👬

©1998 Tourmaster Publications, Inc.

Canajoharie Gorge "A"

Start: Sprout Brook. General Store.

Miles	19 
Rating	Moderate
Climb	1100' @ 58 ft/mi

Tour 15A

• 0.0	R		Leaving The General Store 🤝		0.0
0.0	L	SS	[163]		0.5
0.5	R		Clinton Rd		6.9
7.4	L		Shaper Ave	⊘ Highland Place	0.1
7.5	R	YS	Cliff St		0.4
7.9	L	SS	[10] ⚠		0.0
7.9	R	SL	Montgomery	☞ S/L @ SL [FOOD]	0.1
8.0	R		Moyer		0.7
8.7	BR		Carlisle		0.6
9.3	BR		TRO UM Carlisle	⊘ Cunningham	0.3
9.6	S		Old Orchard	⊘ BL Carlisle	0.1
• 9.7	S		TRO UM Old Orchard	☞ R **Gorge**	2.6
12.3	S		TRO UM Old Orchard	⊘ Maple Hill	0.6
12.9	R		Maple Town Rd		0.6
13.5	L		Shunk Rd		0.8
14.3	R	SS	UM Latimer Hill Rd		0.3
14.6	S	SS	W. Ames Rd	X [10] [FOOD]	2.3
16.9	S	SS	[163]		2.1
19.0	L		Cherry Valley Rd To General Store		

🤝 **Cooperstown: 3B,C**
@ 0.0 join Tours 3B,C
@ cue 23.3 S Dugway Rd

NOTE
Park @ Hawkins Beauty Shop L @ SS [163]

NOTE
For planning purposes, groups with members simultaneously biking different Canajoharie Gorge tours should note that Tour "A" is the only ride in the series that circles clockwise.

R	Right	**S**	Straight	**SS**	Stop Sign	**UM**	Unmarked Road	⊘ Do Not Take
L	Left	**TRO**	To Remain On	**SL**	Stop Light	[26]	County Route	☞ Detour Off
BR	Bear Right	**X**	Cross	**YS**	Yield Sign	[28]	State Route	🤝 Combine With
BL	Bear Left	⚠	Caution					

Mile	•POINTS OF INTEREST	#
0.0	Henry J. Kaiser Birthplace ☞ L 0.1	(32)
9.7	Canajoharie Gorge & Wintergreen Park	(50)

TOUR DESCRIPTION

The Canajoharie Gorge Series explores the hills and valleys east of Sprout Brook.

Canajoharie Gorge "A" is the shortest and most direct route to Canajoharie Gorge in Wintergreen Park.

After entering Wintergreen Park, notice a parking area on the right *before* the road descends. Walk the footpath to the right beyond the parking area for excellent views down to the Gorge.

Continue on the gravel trail beyond a wooden bridge until the footpath becomes paved. The paved section leads to a deck overlooking Canajoharie Falls.

After returning to the parking area, turn right and bike downhill to water level where you can picnic before completing your tour.

COUNTIES
Montgomery

©1998 Tourmaster Publications, Inc.

Climb Rating in feet per mile climbed: 0-45 = Easy, 45-60 = Moderate, 60+ = Difficult

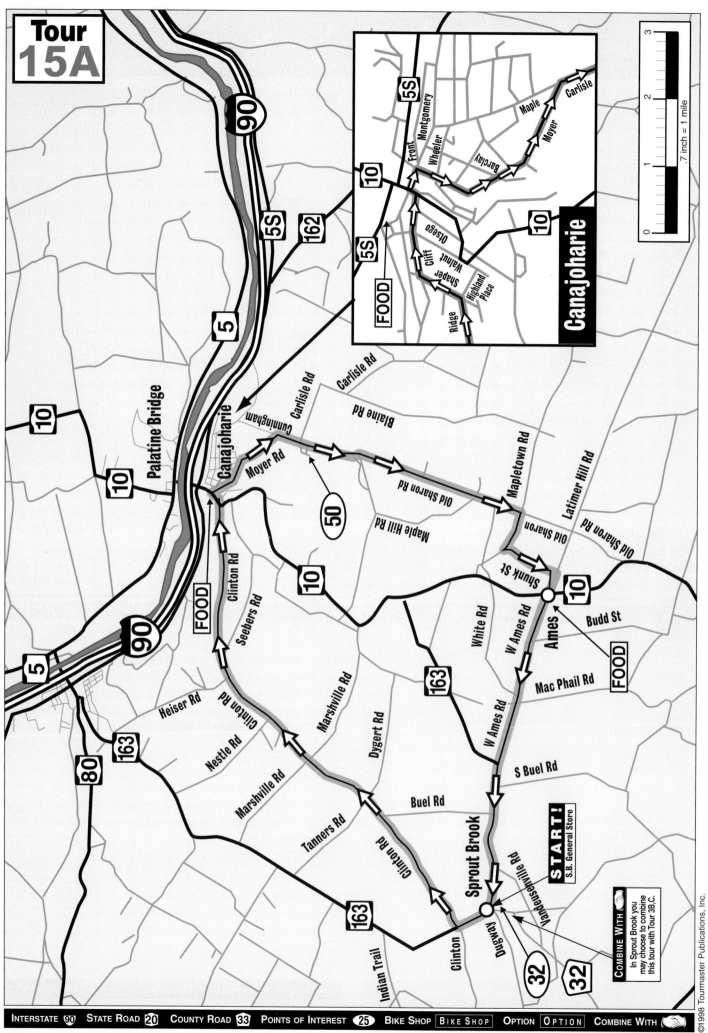

Tour 15A

Canajoharie

.7 inch = 1 mile

FOOD

Canajoharie

Palatine Bridge

Carlisle Rd
Carlisle Rd
Blaine Rd
Cunningham
Moyer Rd
Clinton Rd
FOOD
Seebers Rd
Old Sharon Rd
Maple Hill Rd
50
Mapletown Rd
Latimer Hill Rd
Old Sharon Rd
Old Sharon
Shunk St
Ames
Budd St
FOOD
White Rd
W Ames Rd
Mac Phail Rd
163
Marshville Rd
Dygert Rd
W Ames Rd
Heiser Rd
Clinton Rd
Nestle Rd
S Buel Rd
163
Marshville Rd
Buel Rd
Tanners Rd
Clinton Rd
Sprout Brook
START!
S.B. General Store
163
Indian Trail
Clinton
Dugway
Vandeusenville Rd
32
32
COMBINE WITH
In Sprout Brook you may choose to combine this tour with Tour 3B,C.

Canajoharie inset
5S
Montgomery
Maple
Carlisle
Front
Wheeler
Moyer
Barclay
10
5S
Otsego
Cliff
Walnut
Shaper
Highland Place
10
FOOD
Ridge

INTERSTATE 90   STATE ROAD 20   COUNTY ROAD 33   POINTS OF INTEREST 25   BIKE SHOP BIKE SHOP   OPTION OPTION   COMBINE WITH

©1998 Tourmaster Publications, Inc.

Canajoharie Gorge "B"

Start: Sprout Brook. General Store.

Miles	41 
Rating	Moderate
Climb	2300' @ 56 ft/mi

Tour 15B

• 0.0	R		Leaving The General Store		0.0
0.0	R	SS	163		2.0
2.0	S		UM W. Ames Rd ⊘ 163		2.5
4.5	S	SS	Latimer Hill Rd **X** 10	FOOD	5.8
10.3	L	SS	W. Lykers Rd		1.4
11.7	S	SS	E. Lykers Rd **X** Carlisle Rd		3.8
15.5	R	SS	**X** 162 Then **L** Corbin Hill	FOOD	1.7
17.2	L		Brand		4.0
21.2	S		UM Rural Grove Rd		0.3
21.5	R	YS	162		1.7
23.2	L		Flat Creek Rd		2.0
25.2	R	SS	Carlisle Rd		0.8
26.0	L		Conway Rd		2.2
28.2	R	SS	Blaine Rd		1.9
30.1	S	SS	Carlisle Rd		1.2
• 31.3	BR	Y	TRO UM Carlisle ☞ L 0.1 **Gorge**		0.3
31.6	BL		TRO UM Carlisle ⊘ Cunningham		0.5
32.1	BL		Moyer St ⊘ Carlisle		0.8
32.9	L	SS	Montgomery St		0.1
33.0	L	SL	Then R Cliff ☞ R/L @ SL 0.1 FOOD		0.4
33.4	L		Shaper Ave		0.1
33.5	R		Ridge Rd (Becomes Clinton Rd)		5.0
38.5	BR		TRO Clinton ⊘ Buel		1.9
40.4	L	SS	163		0.5
40.9	BR		Cherry Valley Rd. To General Store		

 **Cooperstown: 3B,C**
@ 0.0 join Tours 3B,C
@ cue 23.3 S Dugway Rd

NOTE
Park @ Hawkins Beauty Shop L @ SS 163

R Right	**S** Straight	**SS** Stop Sign	**UM** Unmarked Road	⊘ Do Not Take
L Left	**TRO** To Remain On	**SL** Stop Light	26 County Route	☞ Detour Off
BR Bear Right	**X** Cross	**YS** Yield Sign	28 State Route	 Combine With
BL Bear Left	⚠ Caution			

Mile	•POINTS OF INTEREST	#
0.0	Henry J. Kaiser Birthplace ☞ L 0.1	32
31.3	Canajoharie Gorge & Wintergreen Park	50

COUNTIES
Montgomery

TOUR DESCRIPTION

The Canajoharie Gorge Series explores the hills and valleys east of Sprout Brook.

Canajoharie Gorge "B" adds 22 miles and a 1200 foot climb to the Canajoharie Gorge "A" tour. The extension climbs Latimer Hill and Corbin Hill for views of the Mohawk Valley before joining the other tours at Canajoharie Gorge in Wintergreen Park.

A visit to spectacular Canajoharie Gorge is the highlight of this tour. After entering Wintergreen Park, notice a parking area on the right *before* the road descends. Walk the footpath to the right beyond the parking area for excellent views down to the Gorge. Continue on the gravel trail beyond a wooden bridge until the footpath becomes paved. The paved section leads to a deck overlooking Canajoharie Falls.

After returning to the parking area, turn right and bike downhill to water level where you can picnic before completing your tour.

©1998 Tourmaster Publications, Inc.

Climb Rating in feet per mile climbed: 0-45 = Easy, 45-60 = Moderate, 60+ = Difficult

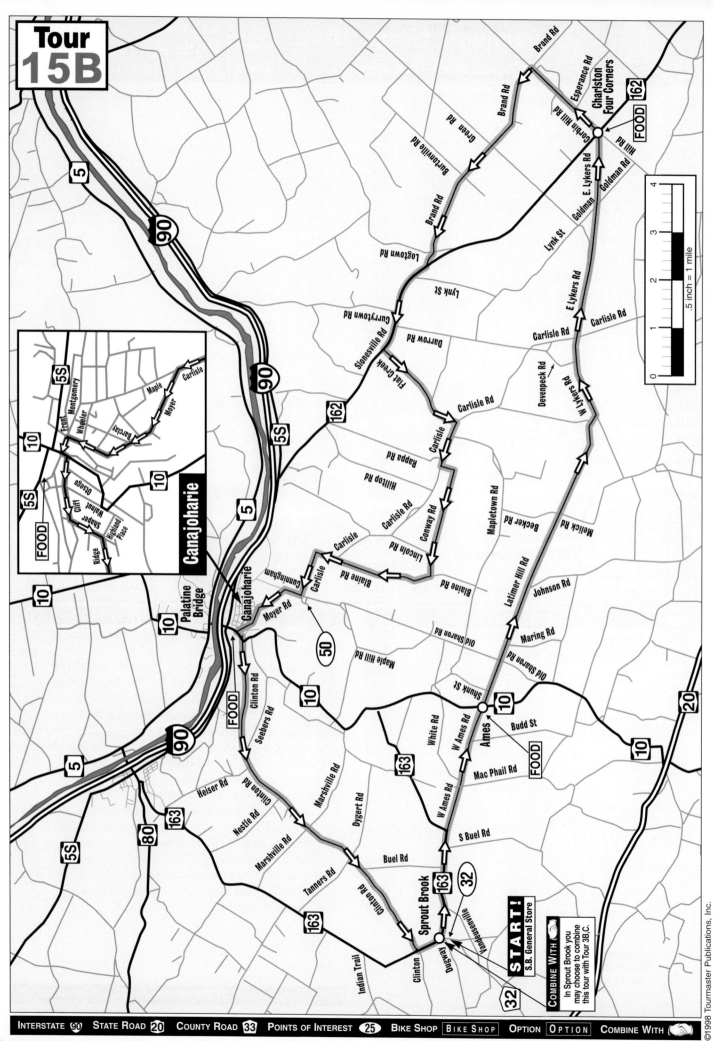

Tour 15B

Canajoharie

Charlston Four Corners

FOOD

START! S.B. General Store

COMBINE WITH In Sprout Brook you may choose to combine this tour with Tour 3B.C.

.5 inch = 1 mile

INTERSTATE 90 STATE ROAD 20 COUNTY ROAD 33 POINTS OF INTEREST 25 BIKE SHOP BIKE SHOP OPTION OPTION COMBINE WITH

©1998 Tourmaster Publications, Inc.

Canajoharie Gorge "C"

Start: Sprout Brook. General Store.

Miles	58 🤝
Rating	**Difficult**
Climb	3800' @ 65 ft/mi

Tour 15C

0.0	R		Leaving The General Store 🤝		0.0
0.0	R	SS	163		2.0
2.0	S		UM W. Ames Rd ⊘ 163		2.5
4.5	S	SS	Latimer Hill Rd **X** 10	FOOD	5.8
10.3	L	SS	W. Lykers Rd		1.4
11.7	S	SS	E. Lykers Rd **X** Carlisle Rd		3.8
15.5	R	SS	**X** 162 Then L Corbin Hill	FOOD	3.2
18.7	S	YS	30A		1.3
20.0	BR		Hughes Rd ⊘ 30A		0.5
20.5	BR		TRO Hughes Rd ⊘ Hughes Spur		5.5
26.0	L	SS	UM 161		3.7
29.7	R	SS	30A		0.1
29.8	BL		Fisher Rd ⊘ 30A		2.0
31.8	BR		TRO Fisher ⊘ Hall Rd		0.2
32.0	L		Lansing Rd		1.5
33.5	L		TRO UM Lansing ⊘ Brumley		1.5
35.0	R	SS	Logtown Rd		1.0
36.0	BL		TRO Logtown ⊘ Anderson		1.8
37.8	R	SS	UM 125		0.3
38.1	R	YS	162		1.7
39.8	L		Flat Creek Rd		2.0
41.8	R	SS	Carlisle Rd		0.8
42.6	L		Conway Rd		2.2
44.8	R	SS	Blaine Rd		1.9

46.7	S	SS	Carlisle Rd		1.2
47.9	BR		TRO UM Carlisle ☞ L 0.1 **Gorge**		0.3
48.2	BL		TRO UM Carlisle ⊘ Cunningham		0.5
48.7	BL		Moyer St ⊘ Carlisle		0.8
49.5	L	SS	Montgomery St		0.1
49.6	L	SL	Then R Cliff ☞ R /L @ SL 0.1 FOOD		0.4
50.0	L		Shaper Ave		0.1
50.1	R		Ridge Rd (Becomes Clinton Rd)		5.0
55.1	BR		TRO Clinton ⊘ Buel		1.9
57.0	L	SS	163		0.5
57.5	BR		Cherry Valley Rd To General Store	

🤝 **Cooperstown: 3B,C**
@ 0.0 join Tours 3B,C
@ cue 23.3 S Dugway Rd

NOTE
Park @ Hawkins Beauty Shop L @ SS 163

R	Right	**S**	Straight	**SS** Stop Sign
L	Left	**TRO**	To Remain On	**SL** Stop Light
BR	Bear Right	**X**	Cross	**YS** Yield Sign
BL	Bear Left	**!**	Caution	
				UM Unmarked Road
				26 County Route
				28 State Route
				⊘ Do Not Take
				☞ Detour Off
				🤝 Combine With

Mile °	•POINTS OF INTEREST	#
0.0	Henry J. Kaiser Birthplace ☞ L 0.1	32
47.9	Canajoharie Gorge & Wintergreen Park	50

COUNTIES
Montgomery

TOUR DESCRIPTION

The Canajoharie Gorge Series explores the hills and valleys east of Sprout Brook.

Canajoharie Gorge "C" adds 17 miles and a 1500 foot climb to the Canajoharie Gorge "B" tour. The extension provides an exhilarating 5 mile descent to the Schoharie Creek then climbs to impressive views of the Mohawk Valley before joining the other tours at Canajoharie Gorge in Wintergreen Park.

A visit to spectacular Canajoharie Gorge is the highlight of this tour. After entering Wintergreen Park, notice a parking area on the right *before* the road descends. Walk the footpath to the right beyond the parking area for excellent views down to the Gorge. Continue on the gravel trail beyond a wooden bridge until the footpath becomes paved. The paved section leads to a deck overlooking Canajoharie Falls.

After returning to the parking area, turn right and bike downhill to water level where you can picnic before completing your tour.

Let us know what you think of this tour! Email: crankmail@usa.net

Climb Rating in feet per mile climbed: 0-45 = Easy, 45-60 = Moderate, 60+ = Difficult

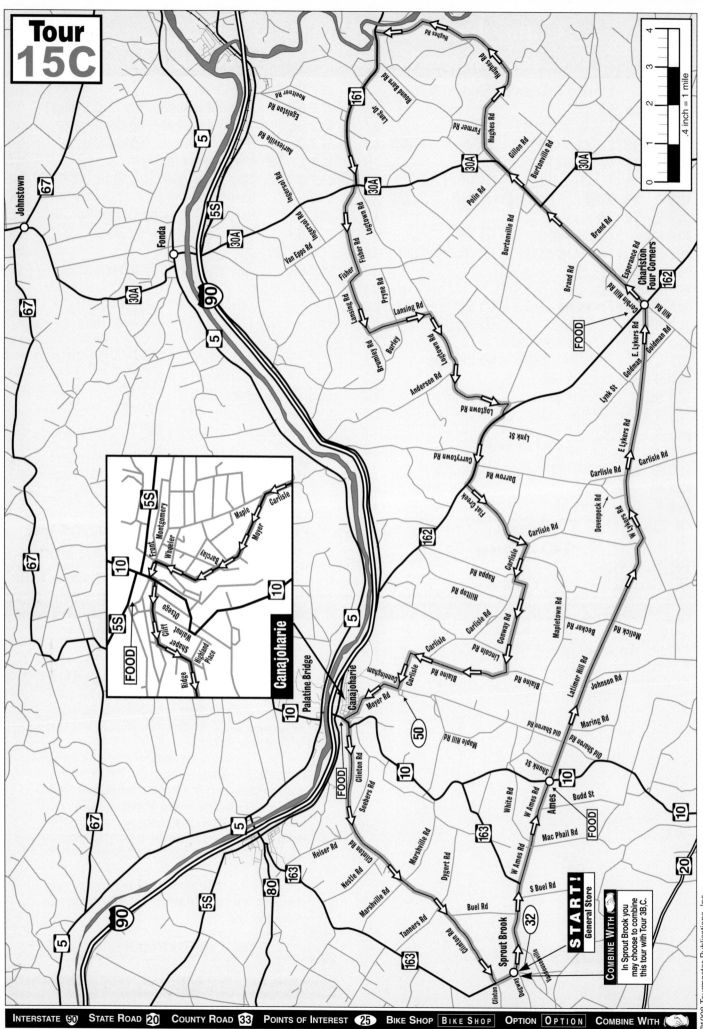

Tour
15C

Johnstown

Fonda

Palatine Bridge

Canajoharie

Sprout Brook

START! General Store

COMBINE WITH In Sprout Brook you may choose to combine this tour with Tour 3B,C.

Charliston Four Corners

Ames

FOOD

Canajoharie

Montgomery
Wheeler
Front
5S
Maple
Carlisle
Moyer
Barclay
10
10
5S
Otsego
Cliff
Walnut
Shaper
Highland
Place
Ridge
FOOD

INTERSTATE **90**   STATE ROAD **20**   COUNTY ROAD **33**   POINTS OF INTEREST **25**   BIKE SHOP **BIKE SHOP**   OPTION **OPTION**   COMBINE WITH

©1998 Tourmaster Publications, Inc.

Canajoharie Gorge "D"
Start: Sprout Brook. General Store.

Miles	78 🤝
Rating	Difficult
Climb	5000' @ 64 ft/mi

Tour 15D

0.0	R		Leaving The General Store 🤝		0.0
• 0.0	R	SS	163		2.0
2.0	S		UM W. Ames Rd ⊘ 163		2.5
4.5	S	SS	Latimer Hill Rd **X** 10 FOOD		5.8
10.3	L	SS	W. Lykers Rd		1.4
11.7	S	SS	E. Lykers Rd **X** Carlisle Rd		3.8
15.5	R	SS	**X** 162 Then L Corbin Hill FOOD		3.2
18.7	S	YS	30A		1.3
20.0	BR		Hughes Rd ⊘ 30A		0.5
20.5	BR		TRO Hughes Rd ⊘ Hughes Spur		5.5
26.0	S	SS	UM 161 **X** Bridge		0.1
26.1	R		Youngs Corners Rd		1.4
27.5	BL		TRO UM Youngs ⊘ Power House		0.7
28.2	BL		TRO UM Youngs ⊘ Millers Corners		0.9
29.1	BR		Dunlap ⊘ Youngs Corners Rd		1.1
30.2	R	SS	Fort Hunter Rd		0.3
30.5	R	SS	30		0.1
30.6	BL		Langley ☞ BR 30 0.1 FOOD		1.6
32.2	BL		TRO UM Langley ⊘ Schuyler		0.8
33.0	L		Belldons Rd		1.5
34.5	BL		TRO Belldons ⊘ Abraham Rd		0.5
35.0	BR		TRO UM Belldons ⊘ Fuller Rd		0.8
35.8	R	SS	30 ⚠		0.5
36.3	BR		Exit To 5S ⚠		0.1
36.4	L	SS	5S ⚠	FOOD	0.5
36.9	L		Verbraska Ave		0.8
37.7	BL		Down To Bridge ⊘ SS 5S		0.1
37.8	R	SS	Under Bridge ☞ L 0.1 Waterfall		0.4
38.2	L		Broadway (To Infirmary)		0.3
38.5	R	SS	Queen Ann Rd		0.2
38.7	S	SS	TRO Queen Ann **X** Windswept/Sandy		1.8
• 40.5	S		TRO UM Queen Ann ⊘ Bike Path		2.3
42.8	R	SS	UM Main St		0.1
42.9	L		Railroad		0.4
43.3	S	SS	UM Main		0.2
43.5	L		Church St		0.1
43.5	L		Quackenbush		0.1
• 43.6	R	SS	Main ☞ S **X** Bridge 0.2 Lock 12		0.0
43.6	BR		TRO UM Main		0.3
43.9	L		@ P.O. TRO UM Main ⊘ Schoharie		0.3
44.2	R		TRO Main ⊘ E. Church St		0.2
44.4	R		Onto Bike Path Before Queen Ann		0.6
45.0	L		@ End Of Bike Path (Dufel Rd)		0.0
45.0	S	SS	UM 5S	FOOD	0.7
• 45.7	BL		Entrance Martyrs' Shrine		0.4
46.1	BR		After Church		0.2
46.3	R		@ Rest Room Sign		0.1
46.4	S	SS	Then BL Egelston ☞ BR FOOD		2.3

R	Right	**S** Straight
L	Left	**TRO** To Remain On
BR	Bear Right	**X** Cross
BL	Bear Left	⚠ Caution

SS	Stop Sign	**UM** Unmarked Road	⊘ Do Not Take
SL	Stop Light	26 County Route	☞ Detour Off
YS	Yield Sign	28 State Route	🤝 Combine With

...Tour Cues Continued

48.7	R	SS	UM 161		1.0
49.7	R	SS	30A		0.1
49.8	BL		Fisher Rd ⊘ 30A		2.0
51.8	BR		TRO Fisher ⊘ Hall Rd		0.2
52.0	L		Lansing Rd		1.5
53.5	L		TRO UM Lansing ⊘ Brumley		1.5
55.0	S	SS	Logtown Rd		1.0
56.0	BL		TRO Logtown ⊘ Anderson		1.8
57.8	R	SS	UM 125		0.3
58.1	R	YS	162		1.7
59.8	L		Flat Creek Rd		2.0
61.8	R	SS	Carlisle Rd		0.8
62.6	L		Conway Rd		2.2
64.8	R	SS	Blaine Rd		1.9
66.7	S	SS	Carlisle Rd		1.2
• 67.9	BR		TRO UM Carlisle ☞ L 0.1 **Gorge**		0.3
68.2	BL		TRO UM Carlisle ⊘ Cunningham		0.5
68.7	BL		Moyer St ⊘ Carlisle		0.8
69.5	L	SS	Montgomery St		0.1
69.6	L	SL	Then R Cliff ☞ R/L @ SL 0.1 FOOD		0.4
70.0	L		Shaper Ave		0.1

...Tour Cues Continued

70.1	R		Ridge Rd (Becomes Clinton Rd)	5.0
75.1	BR		TRO Clinton ⊘ Buel	1.9
77.0	L	SS	163	0.5
77.5	BR		Cherry Valley Rd To General Store	

🤝 **Cooperstown: 3B,C**
@ 0.0 join Tours 3B,C @ cue 23.3 S Dugway Rd

COUNTIES
Montgomery

BIKE SHOP
Dan's Bike Shop, ☞ to 203 W. Main St, Amsterdam

NOTE
Park @ Hawkins Beauty Shop L @ SS 163

Mile	• POINTS OF INTEREST	#
0.0	Henry J. Kaiser Birthplace ☞ L 0.1	32
40.5	Schoharie Crossing (also 43.1)	54
43.6	Erie Canal & NYS Barge Canal, Lock 12	54
45.7	Auriesville Martyrs' Shrine	55
67.9	Canajoharie Gorge & Wintergreen Park	50

TOUR DESCRIPTION
Due to space limitations, see Tour Description on reverse Side...

Let us know what you think of this tour! Email: crankmail@usa.net

---

Climb Rating in feet per mile climbed: 0-45 = Easy, 45-60 = Moderate, 60+ = Difficult

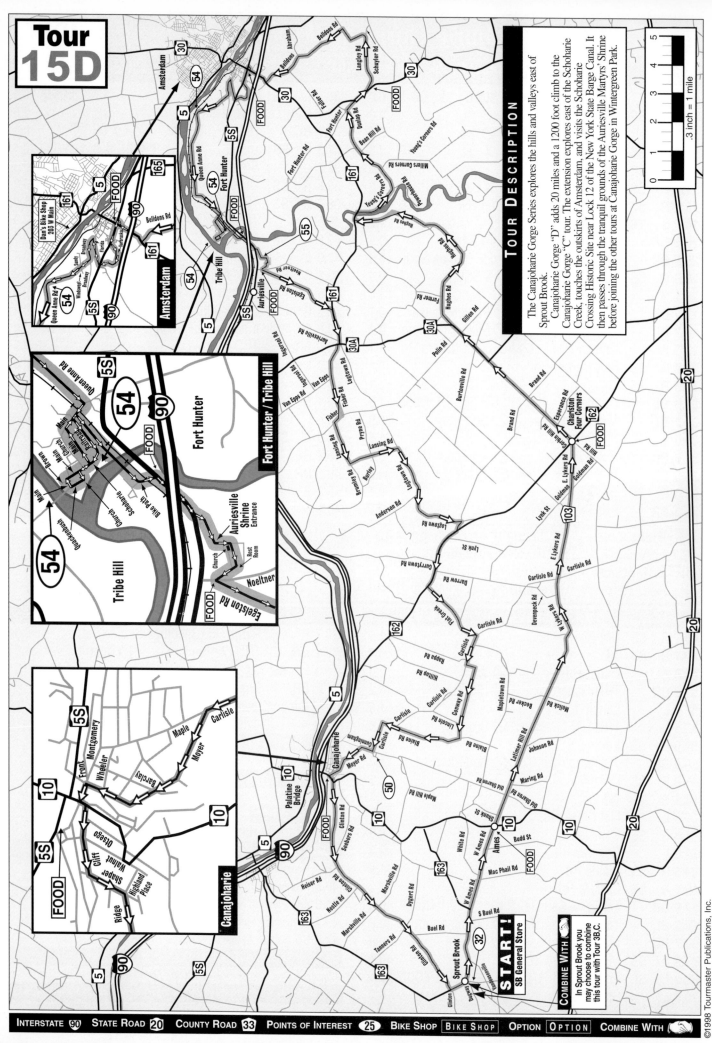

Tour 15D

Tour Description

The Canajoharie Gorge Series explores the hills and valleys east of Sprout Brook.

Canajoharie Gorge "D" adds 20 miles and a 1200 foot climb to the Canajoharie Gorge "C" tour. The extension explores east of Amsterdam, and visits the Schoharie Creek, touches the outskirts of Amsterdam, and visits the Schoharie Crossing Historic Site near Lock 12 of the New York State Barge Canal. It then passes through the tranquil grounds of the Auriesville Martyrs' Shrine before joining the other tours at Canajoharie Gorge in Wintergreen Park.

.3 inch = 1 mile

0 1 2 3 4 5

Amsterdam

Dan's Bike Shop
203 W Main

Fort Hunter / Tribe Hill

Auriesville Shrine Entrance
Rest Room

Canajoharie

COMBINE WITH In Sprout Brook you may choose to combine this tour with Tour 3B,C.

START! SB General Store

INTERSTATE 90 STATE ROAD 20 COUNTY ROAD 33 POINTS OF INTEREST 25 BIKE SHOP OPTION COMBINE WITH

©1998 Tourmaster Publications, Inc.

Cranks

Otsquago Creek "A"

Start: Sprout Brook. General Store.

Miles	19 
Rating	**Difficult**
Climb	**1500' @ 77 ft/mi**

Tour 16A

• 0.0	R		Leaving The General Store 🤝	0.0
0.0	L	SS	163	0.5
0.5	L		Clinton Rd	2.4
2.9	L	SS	TRO UM Clinton ⊘ UM Indian Trail To R	0.6
• 3.5	R		Salt Springville Rd	1.7
5.2	L		Starkville Rd	1.6
6.8	R		Brookmans Corners Rd	2.3
9.1	L	SS	TRO UM Brookmans ⊘ Salt Springville	1.7
10.8	R		Freysbush Rd	1.7
12.5	S		TRO UM Freysbush ⊘ Spring/Keesler	0.7
13.2	R		Walts Rd @ Cemetery	1.3
14.5	R	SS	UM Hessville Rd	0.2
14.7	L		Goulds Rd	1.1
15.8	L		Bauder	1.1
16.9	R	SS	UM 163	2.4
19.3	BR		Cherry Valley Rd ⊘ 163	0.1
19.4			Sprout Brook General Store	

🤝 **Cooperstown: 3B,C**
@ 0.0 join Tours 3B,C @ cue 23.3 S Dugway

🤝 **Cherry Valley: 12A**
@ 0.0 join Tour 12A @ cue 17.0 S Dugway

🤝 **Cherry Valley: 12B**
@ 0.0 join Tour 12B @ cue 48.7 S Dugway

🤝 **Cherry Valley: 12C**
@ 0.0 join Tour 12C @ cue 64.5 S Dugway

NOTE
Park @ Hawkins Beauty Shop L @ SS 163

R	Right	**S**	Straight	**SS** Stop Sign	**UM** Unmarked Road
L	Left	**TRO** To Remain On	**SL** Stop Light	26 County Route
BR	Bear Right	**X** Cross	**YS** Yield Sign	28 State Route
BL	Bear Left	⚠ Caution		

⊘ Do Not Take   ☞ Detour Off   🤝 Combine With

POINTS OF INTEREST

Mile	• POINTS OF INTEREST	#
0.0	Henry J. Kaiser Birthplace ☞ L 0.1	32
3.5	Windfall Dutch Barn	26

TOUR DESCRIPTION

The Otsquago Creek Series explores the hills and valleys west of Sprout Brook.

Otsquago Creek "A" explores the hilly backroads of southwestern Montgomery County. This tour is short and scenic.

COUNTIES
Montgomery

Let us know what you think of this tour! Email: crankmail@usa.net

Climb Rating in feet per mile climbed: 0-45 = Easy, 45-60 = Moderate, 60+ = Difficult

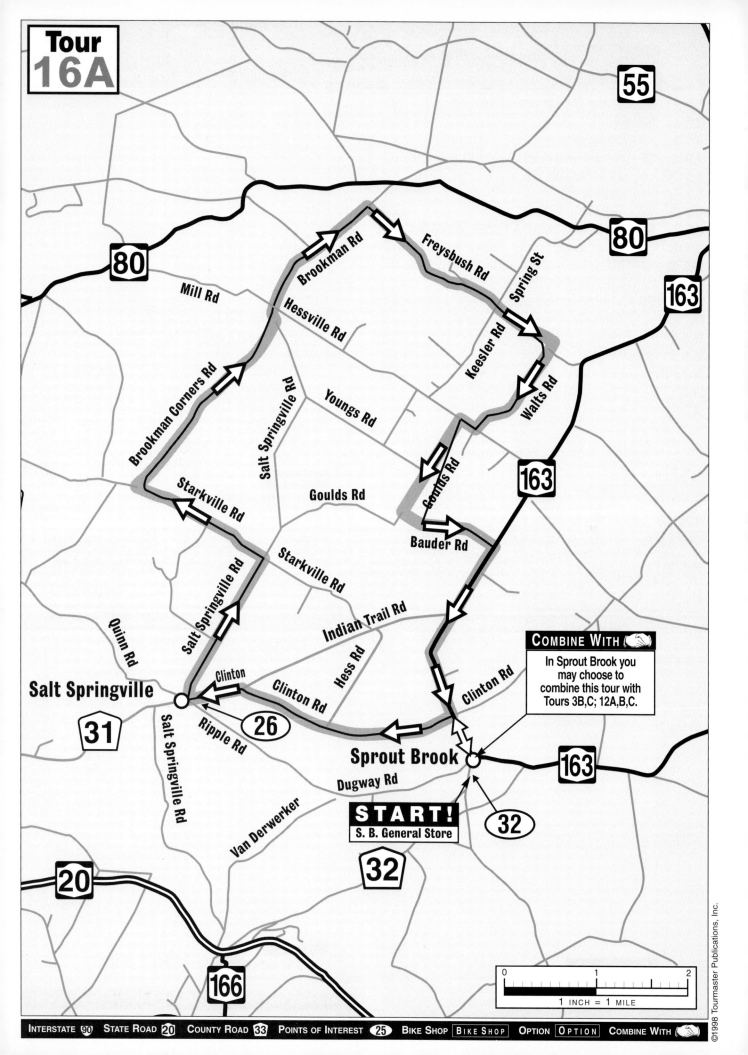

Tour
16A

55

80

80

163

Mill Rd

Brookman Rd

Freysbush Rd

Spring St

Hessville Rd

Keesler Rd

Brookman Corners Rd

Salt Springville Rd

Youngs Rd

Walts Rd

Starkville Rd

Goulds Rd

Goulds Rd

163

Salt Springville Rd

Starkville Rd

Bauder Rd

Quinn Rd

Indian Trail Rd

Salt Springville

Hess Rd

Clinton

Clinton Rd

COMBINE WITH

In Sprout Brook you
may choose to
combine this tour with
Tours 3B,C; 12A,B,C.

31

26

Ripple Rd

Clinton Rd

Sprout Brook

163

Salt Springville Rd

Dugway Rd

32

Van Derwerker

START!
S. B. General Store

32

20

166

0   1   2
1 INCH = 1 MILE

INTERSTATE 90 STATE ROAD 20 COUNTY ROAD 33 POINTS OF INTEREST 25 BIKE SHOP BIKE SHOP OPTION OPTION COMBINE WITH

©1998 Tourmaster Publications, Inc.

Otsquago Creek "B"

Start: Sprout Brook. General Store.

Miles	44
Rating	Difficult
Climb	3500' @ 80 ft/mi

Tour 16B

0.0	R		Leaving The General Store		0.0
0.0	L	SS	163		0.5
0.5	L		Clinton Rd		2.4
2.9	L	SS	TRO UM Clinton ⊘ UM Indian Trail To R		0.6
3.5	R		Salt Springville Rd		1.7
5.2	L		Starkville Rd		1.6
6.8	R		Brookmans Corners Rd		2.3
9.1	L	SS	TRO UM Brookmans ⊘ Salt Springville		2.1
11.2	L	SS	80		0.2
11.4	R		Fordsbush Rd		2.5
13.9	BL		Clark (Later Klock) ⊘ Fordsbush		2.2
16.1	R	SS	Fiery Hill Rd		0.9
17.0	L	SS	Fordsbush Rd		2.2
19.2	BR		TRO Pavement ⊘ W. Fiery Hill Rd		0.2
19.4	R		Creek Rd (Before Bridge)		0.5
19.9	L		TRO Creek ⊘ Bellinger		3.2
23.1	R	SS	5S ☞ L 0.5 FOOD		0.1
23.2	R		Dillenbeck Rd		1.7
24.9	L	SS	Bellinger		1.2
26.1	R	SS	5S		1.6
27.7	L		Mindenville Rd		0.7
28.4	R	SS	UM River Rd ☞ L 0.2, R 0.3 Lock 16		1.7
30.1	BR		TRO River ⊘ Bridge ☞ L 0.6 FOOD		0.8
30.9	R		Sanders Rd		1.6

32.5	S	SS	TRO Sanders	X 5S		0.8
33.3	S		TRO Sanders	X Paris		1.3
34.6	BR		Pickle Hill Rd			0.2
34.8	R	SS	80			0.4
35.2	L		Brookmans Corners Rd			0.4
35.6	L		Freysbush Rd			1.7
37.3	S		TRO UM Freysbush ⊘ Spring/Keesler			0.7
38.0	R		Walts Rd @ Cemetery			1.3
39.3	R	SS	UM Hessville Rd			0.2
39.5	L		Goulds Rd			1.1
40.6	L		Bauder			1.1
41.7	R	SS	UM 163			2.4
44.1	BR		Cherry Valley Rd ⊘ 163			0.1
44.2			Sprout Brook General Store			

🤝 **Cooperstown: 3B,C**
@ 0.0 join Tours 3B,C @ cue 23.3 S Dugway

🤝 **Cherry Valley: 12A**
@ 0.0 join Tour 12A @ cue 17.0 S Dugway

🤝 **Cherry Valley: 12B**
@ 0.0 join Tour 12B @ cue 48.7 S Dugway

🤝 **Cherry Valley: 12C**
@ 0.0 join Tour 12C @ cue 64.5 S Dugway

R Right	**S** Straight	**SS** Stop Sign	**UM** Unmarked Road	⊘ Do Not Take
L Left	**TRO** To Remain On	**SL** Stop Light	26 County Route	☞ Detour Off
BR Bear Right	**X** Cross	**YS** Yield Sign	28 State Route	🤝 Combine With
BL Bear Left	! Caution			

POINTS OF INTEREST

Mile	•Points of Interest	#
0.0	Henry J. Kaiser Birthplace ☞ L 0.1	32
3.5	Windfall Dutch Barn	26
28.4	NYS Barge Canal, Lock 16 ☞ L 0.2, then R 0.3	52

TOUR DESCRIPTION

The Otsquago Creek Series explores the hills and valleys west of Sprout Brook.

Otsquago Creek "B" adds 25 miles and a 2000 foot climb to the Otsquago Creek "A" tour. The extension provides incredible panoramas of the Mohawk Valley before descending to the Mohawk River via beautiful Nowadaga Creek. Plan time to visit New York State Barge Canal Lock 16.

Save some energy for climbing back to Sprout Brook.

COUNTIES
Montgomery, Herkimer

NOTE
Park @ Hawkins Beauty Shop L @ SS

Let us know what you think of this tour! Email: crankmail@usa.net

Climb Rating in feet per mile climbed: 0-45 = Easy, 45-60 = Moderate, 60+ = Difficult

©1998 Tourmaster Publications, Inc.

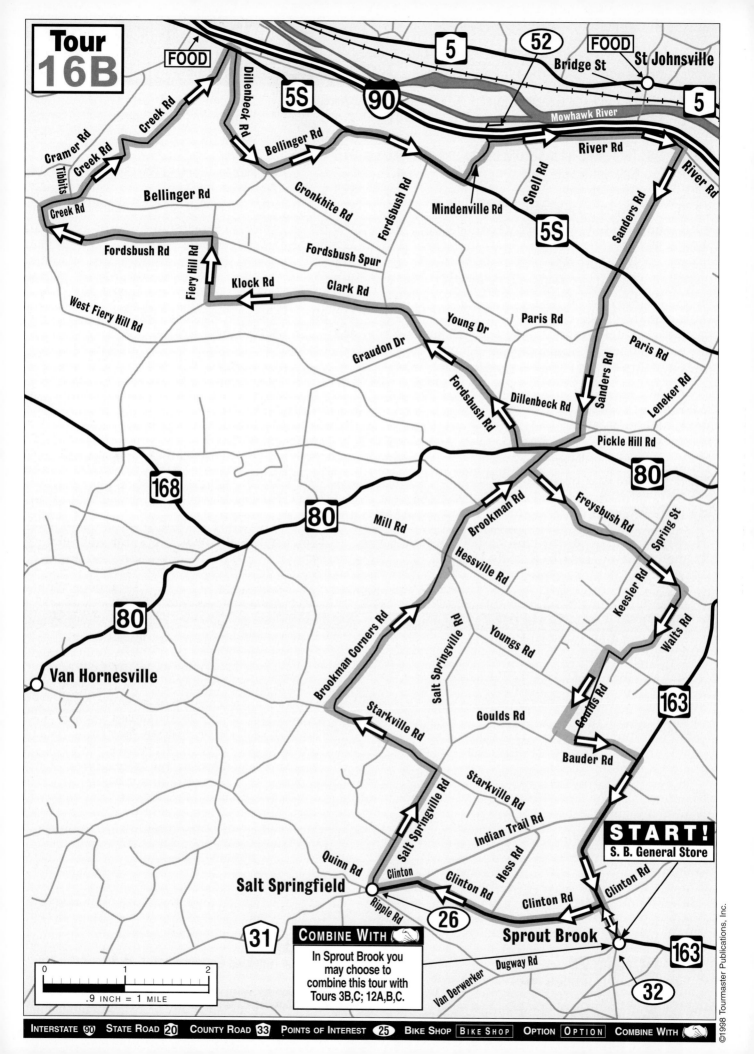

Tour 16B

FOOD

Cramer Rd
Tibbits
Creek Rd
Creek Rd
Creek Rd
Creek Rd
Dillenbeck Rd
5S
90
5
52
Bridge St
FOOD
St Johnsville
5
Mowhawk River
Bellinger Rd
Bellinger Rd
Cronkhite Rd
Fordsbush Rd
Mindenville Rd
Snell Rd
River Rd
Sanders Rd
River Rd
5S
Fordsbush Rd
Fordsbush Spur
Fiery Hill Rd
Klock Rd
Clark Rd
Young Dr
Paris Rd
West Fiery Hill Rd
Graudon Dr
Fordsbush Rd
Dillenbeck Rd
Sanders Rd
Paris Rd
Leneker Rd
Pickle Hill Rd
168
80
Mill Rd
Brookman Rd
Freysbush Rd
80
Spring St
80
Hessville Rd
Keesler Rd
Van Hornesville
Brookman Corners Rd
Salt Springville Rd
Youngs Rd
Walts Rd
Goulds Rd
Goulds Rd
163
Starkville Rd
Bauder Rd
Starkville Rd
Salt Springville Rd
Indian Trail Rd
START!
S. B. General Store
Quinn Rd
Clinton
Hess Rd
Clinton Rd
Clinton Rd
Clinton Rd
Salt Springfield
Ripple Rd
26
Clinton Rd
Sprout Brook
163
31
32
Van Derwerker
Dugway Rd

COMBINE WITH 🤝

In Sprout Brook you may choose to combine this tour with Tours 3B,C; 12A,B,C.

0 1 2
.9 INCH = 1 MILE

INTERSTATE 90 **STATE ROAD** 20 **COUNTY ROAD** 33 **POINTS OF INTEREST** 25 **BIKE SHOP** BIKE SHOP **OPTION** OPTION **COMBINE WITH** 🤝

Cranks

Otsquago Creek "C"

Start: Sprout Brook. General Store.

Miles	56
Rating	Difficult
Climb	4000' @ 71 ft/mi

Tour 16C

•	0.0	R	Leaving The General Store 🤝	0.0
	0.0	L SS	163	0.5
	0.5	L	Clinton Rd	2.4
	2.9	L SS	TRO UM Clinton ⊘ UM Indian Trail To R	0.6
•	3.5	R	Salt Springville Rd	1.7
	5.2	L	Starkville Rd	1.6
	6.8	R	Brookmans Corners Rd	2.3
	9.1	L SS	TRO UM Brookmans ⊘ Salt Springville	2.1
	11.2	L SS	80	0.2
	11.4	R	Fordsbush Rd	2.5
	13.9	BL	Clark (Later Klock) ⊘ Fordsbush	2.2
	16.1	R SS	Fiery Hill Rd	0.9
	17.0	L SS	Fordsbush Rd	2.2
	19.2	BR	TRO Pavement ⊘ W. Fiery Hill Rd	0.2
	19.4	BL	X Bridge Newville RD	0.3
	19.7	BR	TRO Newville ⊘ Johnnycake	0.4
	20.1	S	Paradise Rd ⊘ Newville/Cramer	1.2
	21.3	L	TRO Paradise ⊘ Lower Paradise	2.5
	23.8	S SS	TRO Paradise X 5S	0.3
	24.1	R SS	UM Flint Ave	0.5
	24.6	S YS	TRO UM Flint	0.7
	25.3	L	Casler St Then R SS 167 ⚠	0.3
	25.6	R SS	UM Canal Place ☞ S 0.1 FOOD	0.1
	25.7	R YS	S. Ann St	0.1
	25.8	BL	Hydroelectric Access Road	0.3
	26.1	BR	Thru Fenced Pedestrian Access	0.4
••	26.5	R	Walk R, Downstairs, Then Left	0.1
	26.6	R	UM 169	1.6
•	28.2	R	TRO 169 ⊘ Thruway	0.4
	28.6	L SS	5S	1.8
	30.4	S	TRO UM 5S FOOD	0.5
	30.9	R	Creek Rd	3.1
	34.0	L	Bellinger	3.7
	37.7	R SS	5S	1.6
	39.3	L	Mindenville Rd	0.7
•	40.0	R SS	UM River Rd ☞ L 0.2, R 0.3 Lock 16	1.7
	41.7	BR	TRO River ⊘ Bridge ☞ L 0.6 FOOD	0.8
	42.5	R	Sanders Rd	1.6
	44.1	S SS	TRO Sanders X 5S	0.8
	44.9	S	TRO Sanders X Paris	1.3
	46.2	BR	Pickle Hill Rd	0.2
	46.4	R SS	80	0.4
	46.8	L	Brookmans Corners Rd	0.4
	47.2	L	Freysbush Rd	1.7
	48.9	S	TRO UM Freysbush ⊘ Spring/Keesler	0.7
	49.6	R	Walts Rd @ Cemetery	1.3
	50.9	R SS	UM Hessville Rd	0.2
	51.1	L	Goulds Rd	1.1

R	Right	**S**	Straight	**SS** Stop Sign
L	Left	**TRO**	To Remain On	**SL** Stop Light
BR	Bear Right	**X**	Cross	**YS** Yield Sign
BL	Bear Left	⚠	Caution	

UM Unmarked Road	⊘ Do Not Take	
26 County Route	☞ Detour Off	
28 State Route	🤝 Combine With	

...TOUR CUES CONTINUED

	52.2	L	Bauder Rd	1.1
	53.3	R SS	UM 163	2.4
	55.7	BR	Cherry Valley Rd ⊘ 163	0.1
	55.8		Sprout Brook General Store	

🤝 **Cooperstown: 3B,C**
@ 0.0 join Tours 3B,C @ cue 23.3 S Dugway

🤝 **Cherry Valley: 12A**
@ 0.0 join Tour 12A @ cue 17.0 S Dugway

🤝 **Cherry Valley: 12B**
@ 0.0 join Tour 12B @ cue 48.7 S Dugway

🤝 **Cherry Valley: 12C**
@ 0.0 join Tour 12C @ cue 64.5 S Dugway

Mile	•POINTS OF INTEREST	#
0.0	Henry J. Kaiser Birthplace ☞ L 0.1	32
3.5	Windfall Dutch Barn	26
26.5	Moss Island	51
26.5	NYS Barge Canal, Lock 17	51
28.2	Herkimer Home Historic Site	56
40.0	NYS Barge Canal, Lock 16 ☞ L 0.2, then R 0.3	52

TOUR DESCRIPTION

The Otsquago Creek Series explores the hills and valleys west of Sprout Brook.

Otsquago Creek "C" adds 12 miles and a 500 foot climb to the Otsquago Creek "B" tour. The extension visits Little Falls, Moss Island's impressive glacial potholes, New York State Barge Canal Lock 17 (the world's highest canal lift lock), the historic home of Revolutionary War hero General Nicholas Herkimer, beautiful Nowadaga Creek, and New York State Barge Canal Lock 16.

Plan a full day to enjoy this excellent adventure. To save time and energy, consider abbreviating the tour by asking a non-biking driver to pick you up at mile 28.2, the Herkimer Home Historic Site on State Route 169.

COUNTIES

Montgomery, Herkimer

NOTE

Park @ Hawkins Beauty Shop L @ SS 163

©1998 Tourmaster Publications, Inc.

Climb Rating in feet per mile climbed: 0-45 = Easy, 45-60 = Moderate, 60+ = Difficult

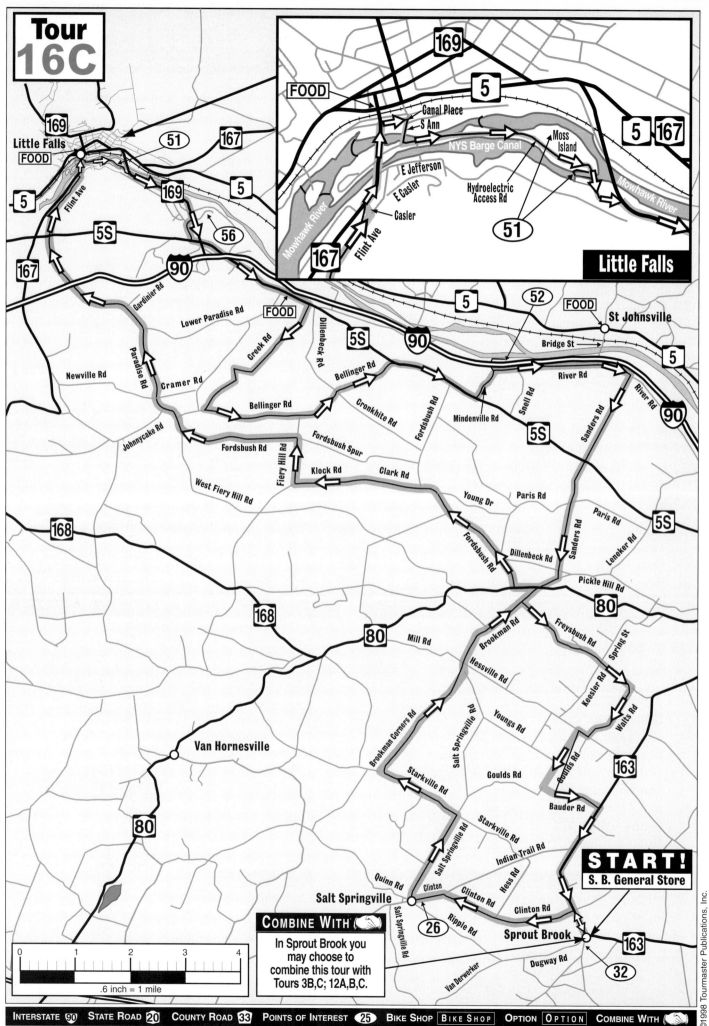

Tour 16C

Little Falls FOOD

169 · 51 · 167 · 5 · 5S · 167 · 90

Flint Ave · Gardinier Rd · 56 · Lower Paradise Rd · Creek Rd · Dillenbeck Rd · 5S · FOOD · 90 · 5 · 52 · FOOD · St Johnsville · Bridge St · River Rd · 5

Paradise Rd · Cramer Rd · Newville Rd · Bellinger Rd · Bellinger Rd · Cronkhite Rd · Fordsbush Rd · Mindenville Rd · Snell Rd · Sanders Rd · River Rd · 90 · 5S

Johnnycake Rd · Fordsbush Rd · Fordsbush Spur · Klock Rd · Clark Rd · Young Dr · Paris Rd · Paris Rd · 5S

West Fiery Hill Rd · Fiery Hill Rd · Fordsbush Rd · Dillenbeck Rd · Sanders Rd · Leneker Rd

168 · Pickle Hill Rd · 80

168 · 80 · Mill Rd · Brookman Rd · Freysbush Rd · Spring St · Keesler Rd · Hessville Rd · Walts Rd

Van Hornesville · Brookman Corners Rd · Salt Springville Rd · Youngs Rd · Goulds Rd · 163

80 · Starkville Rd · Goulds Rd · Bauder Rd

Salt Springville Rd · Starkville Rd · Indian Trail Rd

Quinn Rd · Clinton · Hess Rd · **START!** S. B. General Store

Salt Springville · Salt Springville Rd · 26 · Clinton Rd · Ripple Rd · Clinton Rd · Sprout Brook · 163 · 32 · Van Derwerker · Dugway Rd

Little Falls (inset)

169 · 5 · FOOD · Canal Place · S Ann · Moss Island · 5 · 167 · E Jefferson · E Casler · NYS Barge Canal · Mowhawk River · Hydroelectric Access Rd · Casler · 51 · 167 · Flint Ave · Mowhawk River

COMBINE WITH 🤝
In Sprout Brook you may choose to combine this tour with Tours 3B,C; 12A,B,C.

Scale: 0 1 2 3 4 — .6 inch = 1 mile

INTERSTATE 90 **STATE ROAD** 20 **COUNTY ROAD** 33 **POINTS OF INTEREST** 25 **BIKE SHOP** BIKE SHOP **OPTION** OPTION **COMBINE WITH** 🤝

The Cherry Valley Flats "ABCD"

Start: Milford. ONC Occupational Center.

Miles	9-29
Rating	Easy
Climb	300-1000' @ 33-35 ft/mi

Tour 17A-D

Tour 17A: 9 MILES / 300 FT. CLIMB / EASY: 34 FT/MI

•	0.0	L	SS	Leaving ONC UM ⟨35⟩		0.4
••	0.4	R	SS	⟨166⟩ 🤝 ☞ L 1.0 FOOD		4.0
	4.4	R		⟨43⟩		0.7
	5.1	R	SS	⟨35⟩		3.8
	8.9	L		ONC Parking Lot		

🤝 **Cooperstown: 8**

@ 0.4 L 0.2 to join Tour 8 @ cue 40.3 R ⟨33⟩

Mile	•POINTS OF INTEREST	#
0.0	ONC BOCES Occupational Center	⟨57⟩
0.4	Cooperstown Brewing Co. ☞ L 0.7, then L River	⟨36⟩
0.4	Milford Depot Railway Museum ☞ L 0.8	⟨38⟩

COUNTIES

Otsego

TOUR DESCRIPTION

The Cherry Valley Flats Series explores the periphery of the flat and fertile Cherry Valley, the second valley east of Lake Otsego.

The "A" tour explores north to Westville.

Tour 17B: 12 MILES / 400 FT. CLIMB / EASY: 35 FT/MI

•	0.0	L	SS	Leaving ONC UM ⟨35⟩		0.4
••	0.4	R	SS	⟨166⟩ 🤝 ☞ L 1.0 FOOD		5.2
	5.6	R		Norton Cross Rd		1.0
	6.6	R	YS	UM ⟨35⟩		4.9
	11.5	L		ONC Parking Lot		

🤝 **Cooperstown: 8**

@ 0.4 L 0.2 to join Tour 8 @ cue 40.3 R ⟨33⟩

Mile	•POINTS OF INTEREST	#
0.0	ONC BOCES Occupational Center	⟨57⟩
0.4	Cooperstown Brewing Co. ☞ L 0.7, then L River	⟨36⟩
0.4	Milford Depot Railway Museum ☞ L 0.8	⟨38⟩

COUNTIES

Otsego

TOUR DESCRIPTION

The Cherry Valley Flats Series explores the periphery of the flat and fertile Cherry Valley, the second valley east of Lake Otsego.

The "B" tour explores north to Norton Cross Road.

R	Right	**S**	Straight	**SS** Stop Sign	**UM** Unmarked Road	🚫 **Do Not Take**
L	Left	**TRO**	To Remain On	**SL** Stop Light	⟨26⟩ County Route	☞ **Detour Off**
BR	Bear Right	**X**	Cross	**YS** Yield Sign	⟨28⟩ State Route	🤝 **Combine With**
BL	Bear Left	**⚠**	Caution			

Tour 17C: 18 MILES / 600 FT. CLIMB / EASY: 33 FT/MI

•	0.0	L	SS	Leaving ONC UM ⟨35⟩		0.4
••	0.4	R	SS	⟨166⟩ 🤝 ☞ L 1.0 FOOD		8.7
•	9.1	R		⟨35⟩		0.7
	9.8	R		Rezen Rd (UM ⟨35⟩)		4.5
	14.3	S		⟨35⟩ 🚫 ⟨43⟩ To R		3.9
	18.2	L		ONC Parking Lot		

🤝 **Cooperstown: 8**

@ 0.4 L 0.2 to join Tour 8 @ cue 40.3 R ⟨33⟩

Mile	•POINTS OF INTEREST	#
0.0	ONC BOCES Occupational Center	⟨57⟩
0.4	Cooperstown Brewing Co. ☞ L 0.7, then L River	⟨36⟩
0.4	Milford Depot Railway Museum ☞ L 0.8	⟨38⟩
9.6	Middlefield Schoolhouse Museum on L	⟨60⟩

COUNTIES

Otsego

TOUR DESCRIPTION

The Cherry Valley Flats Series explores the periphery of the flat and fertile Cherry Valley.

The "C" tour explores north to Middlefield.

Tour 17D: 29 MILES / 1000 FT. CLIMB / EASY: 34 FT/MI

•	0.0	L	SS	Leaving ONC UM ⟨35⟩		0.4
••	0.4	R	SS	⟨166⟩ 🤝 ☞ L 1.0 FOOD		14.0
	14.4			⟨165⟩ FOOD		2.0
	16.4	R		Middlefield Rd @ Pleasant Brook Hotel		4.5
•	20.9	S	SS	Rezen Rd (UM ⟨35⟩)		4.5
	25.4	S		⟨35⟩ 🚫 ⟨43⟩ To R		3.9
	29.3	L		ONC Parking Lot		

🤝 **Cooperstown: 8**

@ 0.4 L 0.2 to join Tour 8 @ cue 40.3 R ⟨33⟩

Mile	•POINTS OF INTEREST	#
0.0	ONC BOCES Occupational Center	⟨57⟩
0.4	Cooperstown Brewing Co. ☞ L 0.7, then L River	⟨36⟩
0.4	Milford Depot Railway Museum ☞ L 0.8	⟨38⟩
9.1	Middlefield Schoolhouse Museum ☞ R 0.5 ⟨35⟩	⟨60⟩
20.9	Middlefield Schoolhouse Museum ☞ L 0.2 ⟨35⟩	⟨60⟩

COUNTIES Otsego

BIKE SHOP 14.4 ☞ S 1.6 Hawk Mountain Sports

TOUR DESCRIPTION

The Cherry Valley Flats Series explores the periphery of the flat and fertile Cherry Valley. The "D" tour explores north to Roseboom and Pleasant Brook.

Climb Rating in feet per mile climbed: 0-45 = Easy, 45-60 = Moderate, 60+ = Difficult

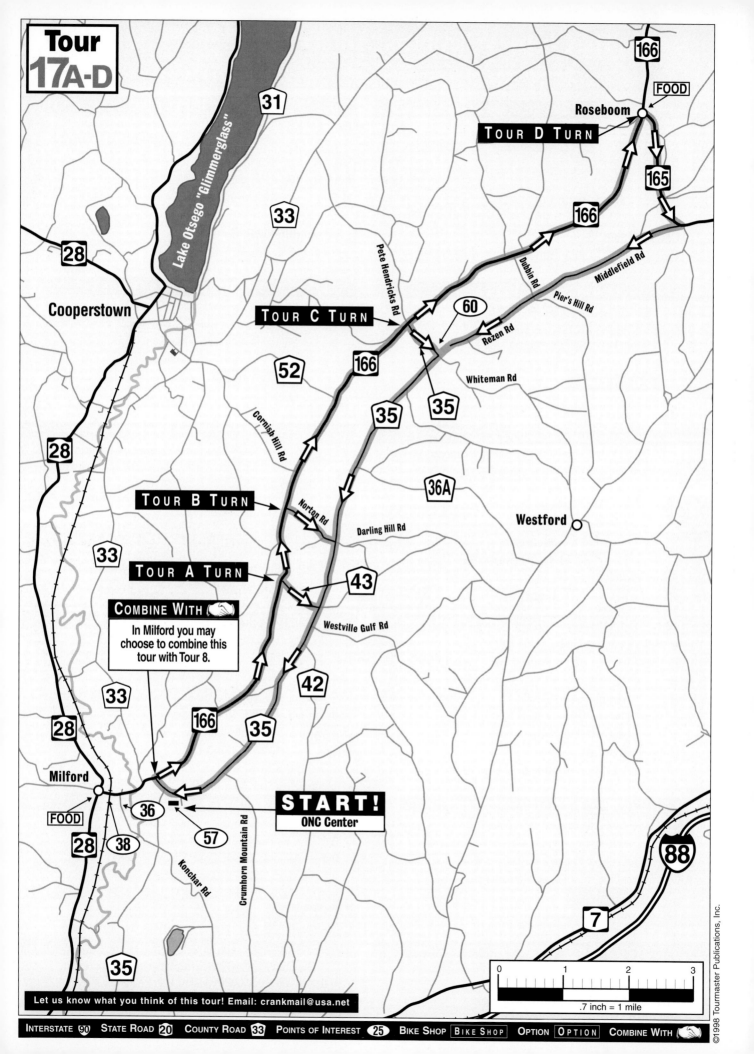

Spring Brook "A"

Start: Milford. ONC Occupational Center.

Miles	14
Rating	Moderate
Climb	600' @ 45 ft/mi

Tour 18A

Mile	Turn		Description		Next
• 0.0	L	SS	Leaving ONC UM ㉟		0.2
0.2	L		㉟		5.3
5.5	R	SS	UM Cliffside Rd		0.3
5.8	L	SS	㉘ ⚠		0.6
6.4	R		㊸ @ Upstate Home		0.7
7.1	BR		TRO UM ㊸ ⊘ Upper Dutch Hill		0.2
7.3	BR		TRO UM ㊸ ⊘ Lougheed Rd		3.0
10.3	S		TRO UM ㊸ ⊘ ㊽ / Tansey Hill		2.0
•• 12.3	S	SL	⒗⒍ X ㉘ ⚠ FOOD		1.0
13.3	R		UM ㉟ X Bridge		0.2
13.5	BL		TRO ㉟ North		0.2
13.7	R		ONC Parking Lot		

R	Right	**S**	Straight	**SS**	Stop Sign	**UM** Unmarked Road ⊘ Do Not Take
L	Left	**TRO**	To Remain On	**SL**	Stop Light	㉖ County Route ☞ Detour Off
BR	Bear Right	**X**	Cross	**YS**	Yield Sign	㉘ State Route 🤝 Combine With
BL	Bear Left	⚠	Caution			

POINTS OF INTEREST

Mile	•POINTS OF INTEREST	#
0.0	ONC BOCES Occupational Center	�57
12.5	Milford Depot Railway Museum	㊳
12.6	Cooperstown Brewing Co. ☞ R 0.1 River St	㊱

TOUR DESCRIPTION

The Spring Brook Series explores the hills and valleys south and west of Milford.

Spring Brook "A" follows the Susquehanna River Valley south, then gradually climbs west up the Spring Brook Valley before descending briskly back to Milford.

Plan time to tour the Milford Depot Railway Museum and the Cooperstown Brewery.

COUNTIES
Otsego

Let us know what you think of this tour! Email: crankmail@usa.net

Climb Rating in feet per mile climbed: 0-45 = Easy, 45-60 = Moderate, 60+ = Difficult

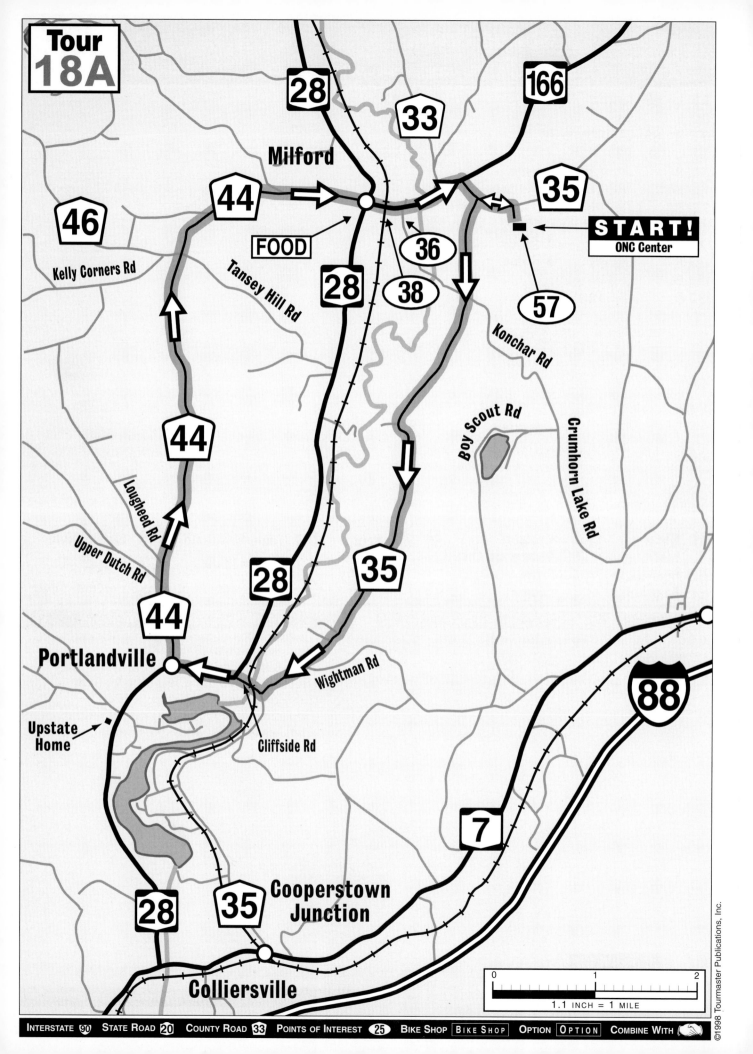

Spring Brook "B"

Start: Milford. ONC Occupational Center.

Miles	20
Rating	Difficult
Climb	1300' @ 67 ft/mi

Tour 18B

•	0.0	L	SS	Leaving ONC UM 35		0.2
	0.2	L		35		5.3
	5.5	R	SS	UM Cliffside Rd		0.3
	5.8	L	SS	28 ⚠		0.6
	6.4	R		44 @ Upstate Home		0.7
	7.1	BR		TRO UM 44 ⊘ Upper Dutch Hill		0.2
	7.3	BR		TRO UM 44 ⊘ Lougheed Rd		3.0
	10.3	L		46 ⊘ Tansey Hill		0.2
	10.5	BR		TRO UM 46 ⊘ Kelley Corners		2.1
	12.6	R		UM Arnold Lake Rd		0.9
	13.5	BL		TRO UM Arnold Lake Rd		1.3
	14.8	R	SS	UM 45		0.3
	15.1	BL		TRO Pavement ⊘ Chlorinator		2.0
	17.1	R	SS	28 ⚠		1.4
••	18.5	L	SL	166 ⚠	FOOD	1.0
	19.5	R		UM 35 **X** Bridge		0.2
	19.7	BL		TRO 35 North		0.2
	19.9	R		ONC Parking Lot		

R	Right	**S**	Straight	**SS**	Stop Sign	**UM**	Unmarked Road	⊘	Do Not Take
L	Left	**TRO**	To Remain On	**SL**	Stop Light	26	County Route	☞	Detour Off
BR	Bear Right	**X**	Cross	**YS**	Yield Sign	28	State Route	🤝	Combine With
BL	Bear Left	⚠	Caution						

Mile	•POINTS OF INTEREST	#
0.0	ONC BOCES Occupational Center	57
18.7	Milford Depot Railway Museum	38
18.8	Cooperstown Brewing Co. ☞ R 0.1 River St	36

TOUR DESCRIPTION

The Spring Brook Series explores the hills and valleys south and west of Milford.

Spring Brook "B" adds 6 miles and a 700 foot climb to the Spring Brook "A" tour. The extension climbs to secluded Arnold's Lake and then visits impressive wetlands before descending to Milford.

Plan time to tour the Milford Depot Railway Museum and the Cooperstown Brewery.

COUNTIES

Otsego

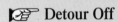

Let us know what you think of this tour! Email: crankmail@usa.net

Climb Rating in feet per mile climbed: 0-45 = Easy, 45-60 = Moderate, 60+ = Difficult

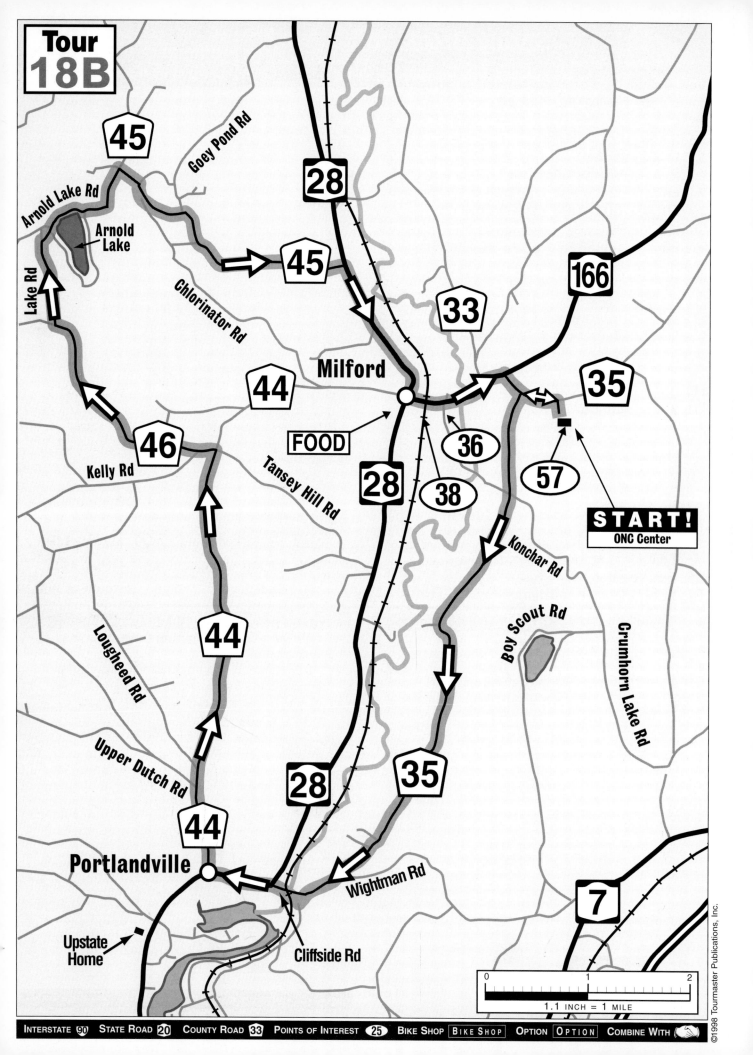

Tour 18B

Goey Pond Rd

45

Arnold Lake Rd

Arnold Lake

Lake Rd

45

28

166

Chlorinator Rd

33

35

44

Milford

FOOD

36

46

57

Kelly Rd

38

START!
ONC Center

Tansey Hill Rd

28

44

Konchar Rd

Lougheed Rd

Boy Scout Rd

Crumhorn Lake Rd

Upper Dutch Rd

28

35

44

Portlandville

7

Wightman Rd

Upstate Home

Cliffside Rd

0   1   2

1.1 INCH = 1 MILE

INTERSTATE 90   STATE ROAD 20   COUNTY ROAD 33   POINTS OF INTEREST 25   BIKE SHOP BIKE SHOP   OPTION OPTION   COMBINE WITH

The Cherry Valley Mountaineer

Start: Milford. ONC Occupational Center.

Miles	60 🤝 OPTION
Rating	Difficult
Climb	5200' @ 87 ft/mi

Tour 19

	Mile	Dir	Sign	Instruction		Dist
•	0.0	L	SS	Leaving ONC	UM ㉟	0.4
••	0.4	R	SS	⑯⑥	☞ L 1.0 FOOD	5.7
	6.1	L		Cornish Hill Rd	OPTION-1	2.0
	8.1	R	SS	UM ㊾		2.3
•	10.4	L	SS	⑯⑥		7.0
••	17.4	S		TRO ⑯⑥	⊘ ⑯⑤ FOOD	4.2
••	21.6	R	SL	Then BR Lancaster 🤝	FOOD	10.8
	32.4	R	SS	⑯⑤		0.6
	33.0	BL		Middlefield Rd @ Pleasant Brook Hotel		4.5
•	37.5	L	SS	Whiteman Rd	OPTION-2	4.3
	41.8	R	SS	UM ㉞	FOOD	0.9
	42.7	R		㊱Ⓐ		3.5
	46.2	L	SS	㉟		1.3
	47.5	S		TRO UM ㉟	X Norton	1.1
	48.6	S		TRO UM ㉟	⊘ ㊸ To R	0.6
	49.2	L		UM ㊷	OPTION-3	4.9
	54.1	BR		TRO UM ㊷	⊘ Kenyon	1.1
	55.2	S		TRO UM ㊷	⊘ Crumhorn Mtn Rd	0.2
	55.4	R		Crumhorn Lake Rd		3.4
	58.8	R	YS	UM ㉟		0.9
	59.7	R	YS	㉟		0.2
	59.9	R		ONC Parking Lot		

🤝 **Cherry Valley: 12A,B,C; 13**
@ 21.6 R SL then BL ⊘ Lancaster to parking lot
@ C.N. Bank on R to join Tours 12A,B,C; 13
@ cue 0.0

OPTION -1:
To eliminate 3.1 miles and an 800 foot climb:
@ 6.1 S TRO ⑯⑥ for 12.4 then resume @ cue 21.6

OPTION -2:
To eliminate 6.5 miles and an 1100 foot climb:
@ 37.5 S SS ㉟ for 2.2 then resume @ cue 47.5

OPTION -3:
To eliminate 7.4 miles and a 1300 foot climb:
@ 49.2 S TRO ㉟ for 3.3 to ONC parking lot

R	Right	S	Straight	SS	Stop Sign	UM Unmarked Road	⊘ Do Not Take
L	Left	TRO	To Remain On	SL	Stop Light	㉖ County Route	☞ Detour Off
BR	Bear Right	X	Cross	YS	Yield Sign	㉘ State Route	🤝 Combine With
BL	Bear Left	⚠	Caution				

• POINTS OF INTEREST

Mile			#
0.0	ONC Boces Occupational Center		㊲
0.4	Cooperstown Brewing Company	☞ L 0.7	㊱
0.4	Milford Depot Railway Museum	☞ L 0.8	㊳
12.1	Middlefield Schoolhouse Museum	☞ R 0.5 ㉟	㉖⓪
21.1	Cherry Valley Massacre: Alden Monument		㉗
21.3	Cherry Valley Massacre: Historic Cemetery		㉘
21.6	Cherry Valley Museum R SL then ☞ BL 0.2		㉙
23.4	Cherry Valley Gorge ☞ R 0.1 O'Neil Rd (gravel)		㉖⑦
37.5	Middlefield Schoolhouse Museum ☞ R 0.2 ㉟		㉖⓪

COUNTIES

Otsego

BIKE SHOP

@ 19.3 ☞ L 0.1 ㉝ Hawk Mountain Sports

TOUR DESCRIPTION

The Cherry Valley Mountaineer climbs the scenic ridges surrounding the Cherry Valley Flats series (Tours 17ABCD). The seven major climbs are thankfully separated by miles of relatively flat terrain, but this remains a very challenging ride. Climbers, enjoy! Flatlanders, beware! Tour options are available to eliminate some of the climbs if your legs tire out.

The Cherry Valley Mountaineer is also offered as a Cooperstown start from the Clark Sports Center (Tour 5).

Let us know what you think of this tour! Email: crankmail@usa.net

Climb Rating in feet per mile climbed: 0-45 = Easy, 45-60 = Moderate, 60+ = Difficult

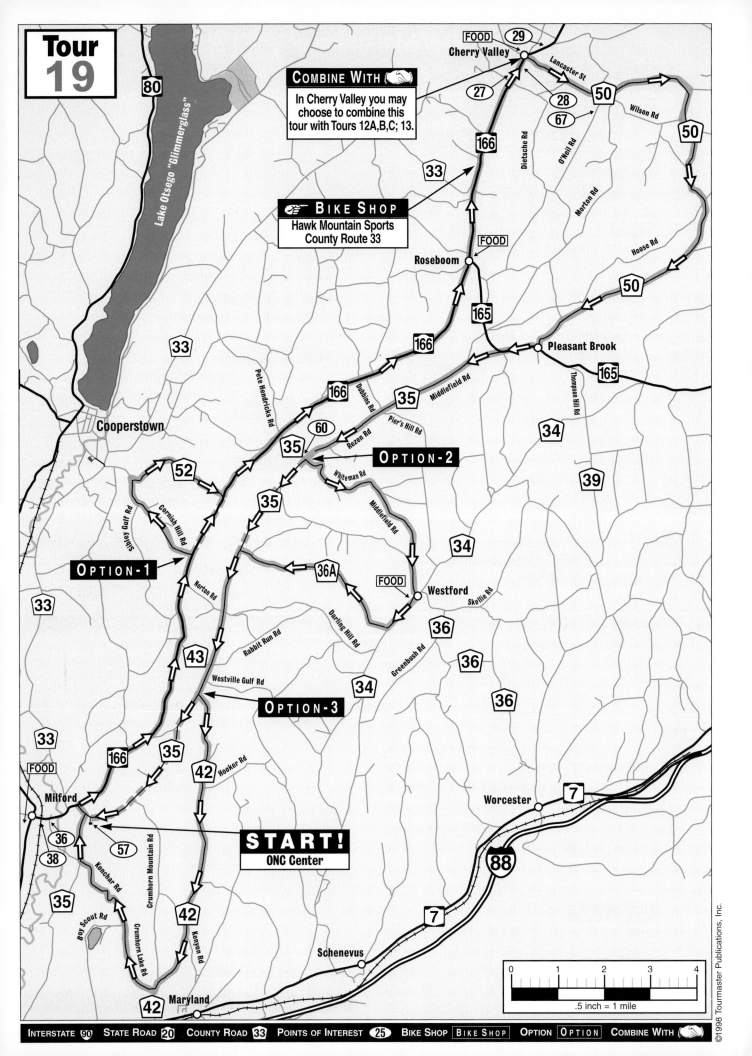

Tour 19

80

Lake Otsego "Glimmerglass"

COMBINE WITH 🤝
In Cherry Valley you may choose to combine this tour with Tours 12A,B,C; 13.

FOOD ⟨29⟩
Cherry Valley

⟨27⟩ Lancaster St ⟨28⟩ 50
Dietsche Rd O'Neil Rd ⟨67⟩ Wilson Rd 50
166 Morton Rd
33 Hoose Rd 50

🖚 BIKE SHOP
Hawk Mountain Sports
County Route 33

FOOD
Roseboom

33 165
166 Pleasant Brook
Pete Hendricks Rd 166 Dubbins Rd 35 Middlefield Rd 165
Cooperstown 166 60 Pier's Hill Rd 34
35 Rezen Rd
35 Whiteman Rd OPTION-2 39
52 Cornish Hill Rd 35 Middlefield Rd
OPTION-1 34
Sibley Gulf Rd 36A FOOD
Norton Rd Westford Skellie Rd
33 Darling Hill Rd 36
43 Rabbit Run Rd 36
33 Westville Gulf Rd 34 Greenbush Rd 36
166 OPTION-3
35 42 Hooker Rd Worcester 7
FOOD 57
Milford 36 Konchar Rd Crumhorn Mountain Rd 88
38 START! 7
35 ONC Center
Boy Scout Rd 42 Kenyon Rd
Crumhorn Lake Rd Schenevus
42 Maryland

Scale: .5 inch = 1 mile 0 1 2 3 4

INTERSTATE ⟨90⟩ STATE ROAD ⟨20⟩ COUNTY ROAD ⟨33⟩ POINTS OF INTEREST ⟨25⟩ BIKE SHOP [BIKE SHOP] OPTION [OPTION] COMBINE WITH 🤝

©1998 Tourmaster Publications, Inc.

Cranks

Crumhorn Mountain

Start: Milford. ONC Occupational Center.

Miles	14
Rating	Difficult
Climb	1400' @ 100 ft/mi

Tour 20

• 0.0	R	SS	Leaving ONC UM ㉟		3.2
3.2	R		UM ㊷		4.9
8.1	BR		TRO UM ㊷ ⊘ Kenyon		1.1
9.2	S		TRO UM ㊷ ⊘ Crumhorn Mtn Rd		0.2
9.4	R		Crumhorn Lake Rd		3.4
12.8	R	YS	UM ㉟		0.9
•• 13.7	R	YS	㉟ ☞ L YS 0.2 Then L ⑯⑥ 1.0 **FOOD**		0.2
13.9	R		ONC Parking Lot		

R	Right	**S**	Straight	**SS**	Stop Sign	**UM**	Unmarked Road	⊘	Do Not Take
L	Left	**TRO**	To Remain On	**SL**	Stop Light	㉖	County Route	☞	Detour Off
BR	Bear Right	**X**	Cross	**YS**	Yield Sign	㉘	State Route	🤝	Combine With
BL	Bear Left	⚠	Caution						

•POINTS OF INTEREST

Mile	•POINTS OF INTEREST	#
0.0	ONC Boces Occupational Center	㉗
13.7	Cooperstown Brewing Co. ☞ L 0.1 then L SS 0.7	㊱
13.7	Milford Railway Museum ☞ L 0.1 then L SS 0.8	㊳

COUNTIES
Otsego

TOUR DESCRIPTION

The Crumhorn Mountain Tour is a climber's delight. Climb up Hooker Mountain, descend for a while, and then climb up Crumhorn Mountain before diving back to the Cherry Valley. Can you say, "switchback?" This short, demanding tour ascends two of the seven climbs in the Cherry Valley Mountaineer (Tours 5 and 19).

Let us know what you think of this tour! Email: crankmail@usa.net

Climb Rating in feet per mile climbed: 0-45 = Easy, 45-60 = Moderate, 60+ = Difficult

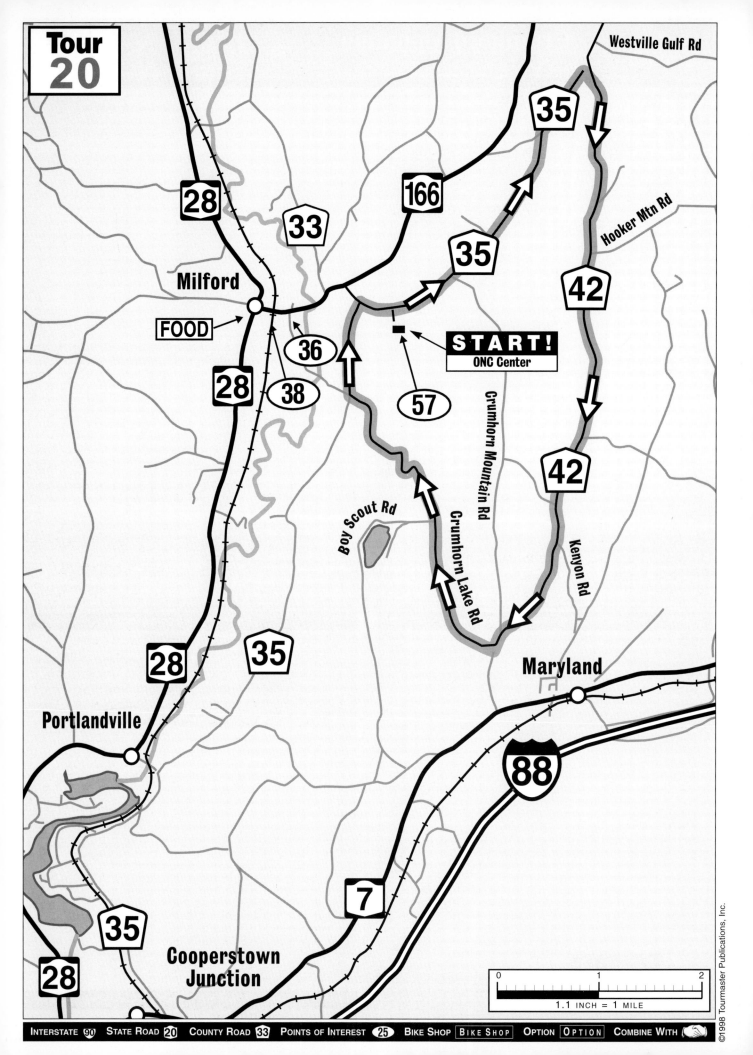

Tour 20

Westville Gulf Rd

35

Hooker Mtn Rd

28

33

166

35

42

Milford

FOOD

36

28

38

START!
ONC Center

57

Crumhorn Mountain Rd

42

Boy Scout Rd

Crumhorn Lake Rd

Kenyon Rd

35

Maryland

28

Portlandville

88

7

35

28

Cooperstown
Junction

0   1   2
1.1 INCH = 1 MILE

©1998 Tourmaster Publications, Inc.

INTERSTATE 90   STATE ROAD 20   COUNTY ROAD 33   POINTS OF INTEREST 25   BIKE SHOP BIKE SHOP   OPTION OPTION   COMBINE WITH

Southwest Hills & Valleys "A"

Start: Laurens. Main Street. American Legion.

Miles	23
Rating	Difficult
Climb	2000' @ 87 ft/mi

Tour 21A

Mile	Dir	Description		Dist
0.0	R	Leave American Legion 🤝		0.0
0.0	BL	UM ⑪ To Oneonta ⊘ ⑩		3.5
3.5	L SS	㉓		1.0
4.5	BR	Then R @ YS South St	FOOD	1.9
6.4	S	TRO ⑧ X Forest Way/ Spur		0.5
6.9	BL	TRO UM ⑧ ⊘ UM Smith		1.8
8.7	BR	TRO ⑧ ⊘ ⑦		2.0
10.7	BR	TRO ⑧ ⊘ ⑥		2.5
13.2	R	⑩		0.2
13.4	BR	TRO UM ⑩ ⊘ Sampson Rd		2.7
16.1	BR	TRO UM ⑩ ⊘ �51		2.2
18.3	R SS	㉓ Then Immediate L ⑩ ⚠		4.9
23.2	S SS	Main St Then L American Legion		

🤝 **Cooperstown: 8**
@ 0.0 join Tour 8 @ cue 26.7
L On Main St Leaving American Legion

R	Right	**S**	Straight	**SS**	Stop Sign	**UM**	Unmarked Road	⊘ Do Not Take
L	Left	**TRO**	To Remain On	**SL**	Stop Light	㉖	County Route	☞ Detour Off
BR	Bear Right	**X**	Cross	**YS**	Yield Sign	㉘	State Route	🤝 Combine With
BL	Bear Left	⚠	Caution					

Mile	•POINTS OF INTEREST	#

TOUR DESCRIPTION

The Southwest Hills and Valleys Series explores the southwestern corner of Otsego County.

Southwest Hills and Valleys "A" explores more hills than valleys. After a few warm-up miles along the flat Otego Creek Valley, the tour climbs up Mill Creek to Maple Grove and beyond before descending to Laurens.

COUNTIES
Otsego

©1998 Tourmaster Publications, Inc.

Climb Rating in feet per mile climbed: 0-45 = Easy, 45-60 = Moderate, 60+ = Difficult

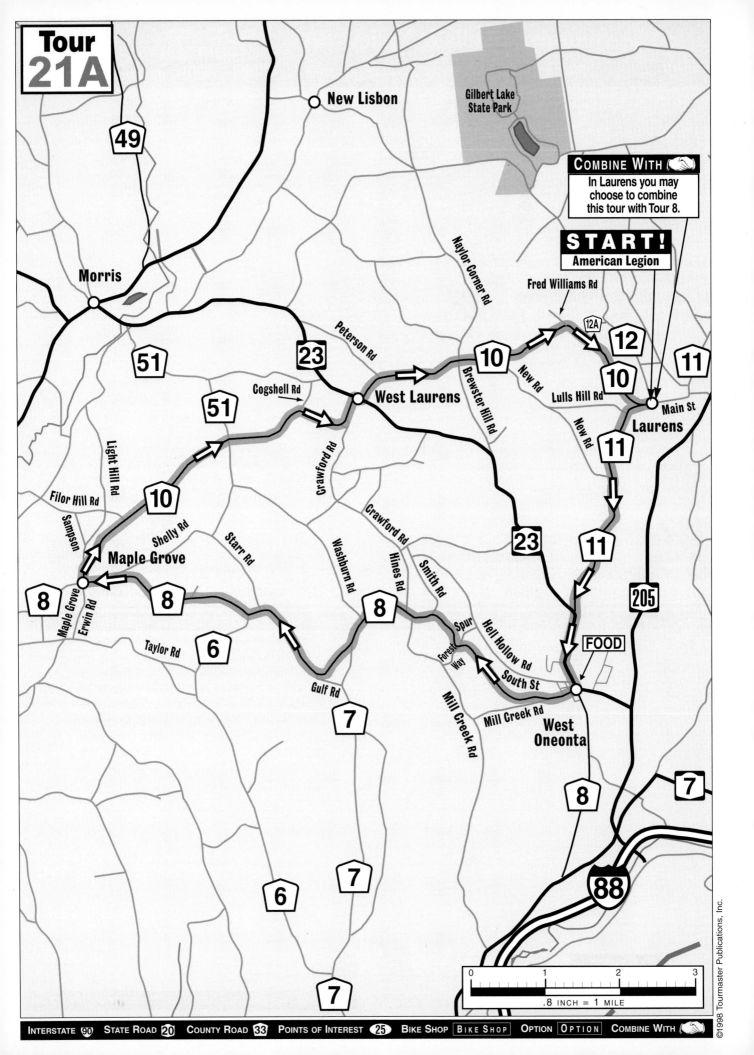

Tour
21A

49

New Lisbon

Gilbert Lake
State Park

COMBINE WITH
In Laurens you may
choose to combine
this tour with Tour 8.

START!
American Legion

Morris

Naylor Corner Rd

Fred Williams Rd

12A

51

23

Peterson Rd

10

12

11

Cogshell Rd

West Laurens

Brewster Hill Rd

New Rd

10

51

Crawford Rd

New Rd

Lulls Hill Rd

Main St

Laurens

Light Hill Rd

10

Crawford Rd

11

Filor Hill Rd

Shelly Rd

Starr Rd

Washburn Rd

Crawford Rd

Smith Rd

23

11

Sampson

Maple Grove

Hines Rd

8

8

Maple Grove
Erwin Rd

8

6

Taylor Rd

Gulf Rd

8

Spur

Forest
Way

Hell Hollow Rd

South St

11

205

FOOD

7

Mill Creek Rd

West
Oneonta

Mill Creek Rd

8

7

7

6

7

88

7

0   1   2   3

.8 INCH = 1 MILE

INTERSTATE 90   STATE ROAD 20   COUNTY ROAD 33   POINTS OF INTEREST 25   BIKE SHOP BIKE SHOP   OPTION OPTION   COMBINE WITH

©1998 Tourmaster Publications, Inc.

Southwest Hills & Valleys "B"

Start: Laurens. Main Street. American Legion.

Miles	50 [Combine With]
Rating	Difficult
Climb	3700' @ 73 ft/mi

Tour 21B

Mile	Turn	Sign	Cue	Next
0.0	R		Leave American Legion [Combine With]-COOP	0.0
0.0	BL		UM [11] To Oneonta ⊘ [10]	3.5
3.5	L	SS	[23]	1.0
4.5	BR		Then R @ YS South St FOOD	1.9
6.4	S		TRO UM [8] ⊘ Forest Way/ Spur	0.5
6.9	BL		TRO UM [8] ⊘ UM Smith	1.8
8.7	BR		TRO [8] ⊘ [7]	2.0
10.7	BL		[6] ⊘ [8]	1.2
11.9	BL		TRO UM [6] ⊘ UM Kent	4.7
16.6	R	YS	[7]	0.3
16.9	BR		TRO UM [7] ⊘ UM Secore	1.1
18.0	R	SS	Main St (UM [7]) Caution	0.2
18.2	S	SL	TRO Main St (UM [7])	1.2
19.4	L		Toward [88] FOOD	0.6
20.0	R	YS	UM [48]	3.8
23.8	R	SS	[44] X Bridge	0.1
23.9	L	YS	[7] Caution Then Immediate R [4]	7.0
30.9	BR		TRO UM [4] ⊘ Guy Beardsley	1.0
•• 31.9	BL		TRO UM [4] ⊘ Lobdell	3.4
35.3	BL		Spring St Before Statue	0.1
35.4	R		Maple St	0.1
35.5	R		Elm St	0.1
35.6	L	SS	Commercial St FOOD	0.1
• 35.7	R	SS	UM [51]	0.1
35.8	BR		Vale Then BL ⊘ Green	0.4
36.2	BR		X Bridge ⊘ Lovers Lane	0.8
37.0	S		X Clarence Musson [Combine With]-SL	1.4
38.4	BL		TRO UM [8] ⊘ Taylor Rd	2.0
40.4	L		[10]	0.3
40.7	BR		TRO UM [10] ⊘ Sampson Rd	2.6
43.3	BR		TRO UM [10] ⊘ [51]	2.3
45.6	R	SS	[23] Then Immediate L [10] Caution	4.8
50.4	S	SS	Main St Then L American Legion	

[Combine With] **Cooperstown: 8**
@ 0.0 join Tour 8 @ cue 26.7
L On Main St Leaving American Legion

[Combine With] **Schuyler Lake: 22C**
@ 37.0 join Tour 22C @ cue 34.6 L Mussen

R	Right	S	Straight	SS	Stop Sign	UM	Unmarked Road	⊘	Do Not Take
L	Left	TRO	To Remain On	SL	Stop Light	[26]	County Route	☞	Detour Off
BR	Bear Right	X	Cross	YS	Yield Sign	[28]	State Route	[Combine With]	Combine With
BL	Bear Left	⚠	Caution						

•Points of Interest

Mile	•Points of Interest	#
34.4	Gilbertsville Polo Fields	(62)
34.8	Gilbertsville Swimming Hole, on R before bridge	(64)
35.7	The Major's Inn	(63)

Counties

Otsego, Delaware

Tour Description

The Southwest Hills and Valleys Series explores the southwestern corner of Otsego County.

Southwest "C" has its ups and downs. It goes up Mill Creek, then down the west branch of the Otsdawa Creek to the Susquehanna River Valley. It climbs up Sand Hill Creek, then down Cahoon Creek to the Butternut Valley. Then it climbs up to Maple Grove, and beyond, before descending to the Otego Creek Valley in Laurens. The ups and downs are long, but gentle. Relax. Pace yourself. Persevere. Enjoy this beautiful tour.

Let us know what you think of this tour! Email: crankmail@usa.net

©1998 Tourmaster Publications, Inc.

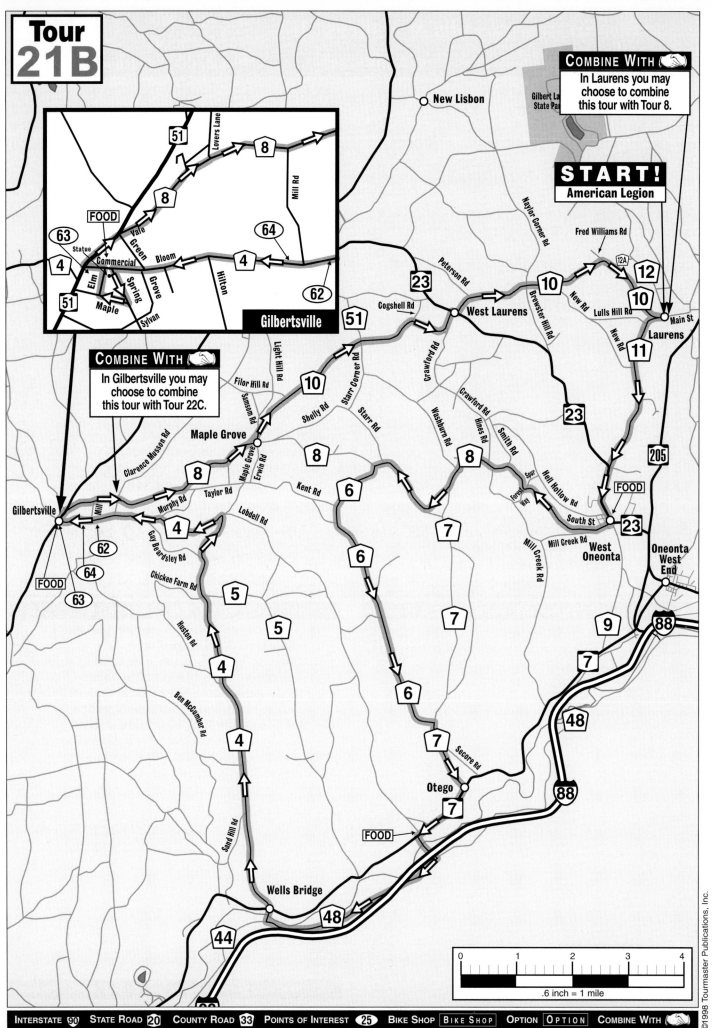

Tour 21B

COMBINE WITH 🤝
In Laurens you may choose to combine this tour with Tour 8.

START!
American Legion

COMBINE WITH 🤝
In Gilbertsville you may choose to combine this tour with Tour 22C.

Gilbertsville (inset)

FOOD
Statue
Lovers Lane
Mill Rd
51
8
8
63
4
4
51
Vale
Green
Grove
Bloom
Hilton
64
4
62
Commercial
Elm
Spring
Maple
Sylvan

Main map

New Lisbon
Gilbert La... State Par...
Naylor Corner Rd
Fred Williams Rd
12A
12
10
10
Peterson Rd
West Laurens
Brewster Hill Rd
New Rd
Lulls Hill Rd
Main St
Laurens
23
Cogshell Rd
Crawford Rd
11
51
Light Hill Rd
Filor Hill Rd
10
Starr Corner Rd
Crawford Rd
Hines Rd
Smith Rd
23
205
Samsom Rd
Shelly Rd
Starr Rd
Washburn Rd
8
FOOD
Maple Grove
Maple Grove
Erwin Rd
8
Spur
Hell Hollow Rd
Clarence Musson Rd
8
Taylor Rd
Kent Rd
6
Forest Way
South St
23
Gilbertsville
Mill
Murphy Rd
4
Lobdell Rd
7
Mill Creek Rd
West Oneonta
Oneonta West End
62
Guy Beardsley Rd
6
Mill Creek Rd
64
FOOD
Chicken Farm Rd
5
7
9
88
63
Huston Rd
5
7
4
Ben McCumber Rd
6
48
4
7
Secora Rd
Sand Hill Rd
7
Otego
7
FOOD
Wells Bridge
88
48
44

0 1 2 3 4
.6 inch = 1 mile

©1998 Tourmaster Publications, Inc.

INTERSTATE 90   **STATE ROAD** 20   **COUNTY ROAD** 33   **POINTS OF INTEREST** 25   **BIKE SHOP** BIKE SHOP   **OPTION** OPTION   **COMBINE WITH** 🤝

Southwest Hills & Valleys "C"
Start: Laurens. Main Street. American Legion.

Miles	57	OPTION
Rating	Moderate	
Climb	2700' @ 47 ft/mi	

Tour 21C

Mile	Turn		Instruction		Dist
0.0	R		Leave American Legion [Combine]-Coop		0.0
0.0	BL		UM (11) To Oneonta ⊘ (10)		3.5
3.5	L	SS	(23)		1.0
4.5	BR		Then S @ YS (8)	FOOD	1.0
5.5	BL		TRO (8) ⊘ (9)		0.5
6.0	R		Browne St		0.6
6.6	R	SS	UM (205) (!)		0.3
6.9	S	SL	X (7) (!) ☞ L 0.2	FOOD	0.1
7.0	S	SL	TRO (205) (!) OPTION-1		0.5
7.5	R	YS	(48)		7.0
14.5	S		TRO (48)	FOOD	3.6
18.1	L	SS	(44)		1.4
19.5	R		Covered Bridge Rd ⊘ Underpass		2.1
21.6	R	SS	UM (357)		0.5
22.1	L		UM River Rd (Before Bridge)		1.7
23.8	S	SS	UM (23)		3.9
27.7	S	SS	Main St Sidney	FOOD	0.2
27.9	S	SL	TRO Main St		0.2
28.1	L	YS	(7) (!)		0.7
28.8	R		Valley View Rd		0.4
29.2	BR		TRO UM Valley View Rd		1.4
30.6	L	SS	UM (1)		0.4
31.0	R	YS	TRO UM (1)		0.2
31.2	BL		TRO UM (1) ⊘ (2) OPTION-2		2.5

Mile	Turn		Instruction		Dist
33.7	S		River Rd X Lockwood Hill		4.8
38.5	L	SS	UM (3)		0.2
38.7	BL		TRO UM (3) ⊘ River Rd		0.5
39.2	R	SS	(51)		2.5
• 41.7	R		Commercial St ((4))	FOOD	0.1
41.8	R		Elm St		0.1
41.9	L	SS	Maple St		0.1
42.0	L	SS	Spring St		0.0
• 42.0	BR	YS	Bloom St Before Statue		0.7
• 42.7	L		After Bridge UM Mill St		0.4
43.1	S	SS	UM (8)		0.5
43.6	S		X Clarence Mussen [Combine]-SL		1.4
45.0	BL		TRO UM (8) ⊘ Taylor Rd		1.9
46.9	L		(10)		0.3
47.2	BR		TRO UM (10) ⊘ Sampson Rd		2.6
49.8	BR		TRO UM (10) ⊘ (51)		2.3
52.1	R	SS	(23) Then Immediate L (10) (!)		4.8
56.9	S	SS	Main St Then L American Legion		

[Combine] **Cooperstown: 8**
@ 0.0 join Tour 8 @ cue 26.7
L On Main St Leaving American Legion

[Combine] **Schuyler Lake: 22C**
@ 37.0 join Tour 22C @ cue 34.6 L Mussen

R Right	**S** Straight	**SS** Stop Sign	**UM** Unmarked Road	⊘ **Do Not Take**
L Left	**TRO** To Remain On	**SL** Stop Light	(26) **County Route**	☞ **Detour Off**
BR Bear Right	**X** Cross			
BL Bear Left	(!) **Caution**	**YS** Yield Sign	(28) **State Route**	[Combine] **Combine With**

Mile	•POINTS OF INTEREST	#
7.0	Soccer Hall of Fame ☞ 2.7 See Option-1	(61)
41.7	The Major's Inn	(63)
42.6	Gilbertsville Swimming Hole, on L after bridge	(64)
42.7	Gilbertsville Polo Fields ☞ S 0.4	(62)

COUNTIES
Otsego, Delaware

BIKE SHOP
a) Sport Tech. Take Option-1
b) Jim's: @ 22.1 ☞ S 0.1 SS then R 1.0 on SR 7
c) Dave's: @ 27.7 ☞ R 0.1 Cartwright

OPTION -1:
Add 5.4 Miles Round Trip To Visit Soccer Hall of Fame Or Sport Tech:

Mile	Turn		Instruction	Dist
7.0	L	SL	River St Access	1.1
8.1	R	SS	River St	1.2
9.3	L		At 2nd SL Main St	0.3
9.6	on R		At 3rd SL Sport Tech	0.1
9.7	L		Ford Ave Soccer Hall of Fame	

TOUR DESCRIPTION
The Southwest Hills and Valleys Series explores the southwestern corner of Otsego County.

Southwest Hills and Valleys "C" visits the four river valleys in this region. Follow the Otego Creek Valley to the Susquehanna River Valley to the Unadilla River Valley to the Butternut Creek Valley before climbing back to Laurens. Visit Oneonta, Sidney and Gilbertsville along the way. Consider a side trip to the Soccer Hall of Fame.

OPTION -2:
To Add 1.7 Miles And An 800 Foot Climb:

Mile	Turn	Instruction		Dist
31.2	BR	(2) Rogers Hollow ⊘ (1)		0.6
31.8	BR	TRO UM (2) ⊘ Hutchinson Hill		1.7
33.5	BR	TRO UM (2) ⊘ Lockwood Hill		0.9
34.4	S	X Ideuma / Alton		1.4
35.8	L SS	UM (3)		1.9
37.7	S	X Ideuma / (3A)		3.0
40.7	BR	TRO UM (3) ⊘ River Rd		0.2
40.9	BL	TRO UM (3) ⊘ River Rd		0.5
		Then Resume @ Cue 39.2 R SS (51)		

©1998 Tourmaster Publications, Inc.

Climb Rating in feet per mile climbed: 0-45 = Easy, 45-60 = Moderate, 60+ = Difficult

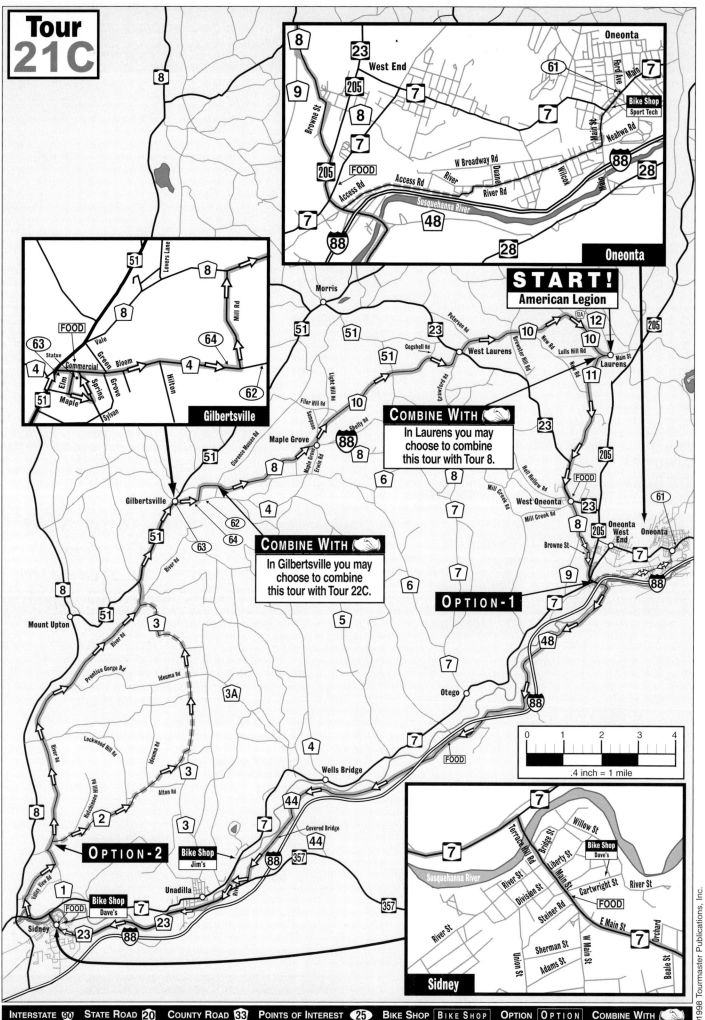

Tour 21C

Oneonta (inset map)
Oneonta, West End, 8, 23, 9, 205, 7, Browne St, 61, Ford Ave, Main, 7, Bike Shop Sport Tech, Main St, Neahwa Rd, 88, 28, W Broadway Rd, River, Duane, Wilcox, Access Rd, Access Rd, River Rd, 205, FOOD, 7, Susquehanna River, 48, 88, 28

Gilbertsville (inset map)
51, Lovers Lane, 8, 8, Mill Rd, FOOD, Vale, 63, Statue, Commercial, Green Grove, Bloom, 4, 64, 4, Hilton, 62, Elm, Maple, Spring, Sylvan, 51

START! American Legion

COMBINE WITH In Laurens you may choose to combine this tour with Tour 8.

COMBINE WITH In Gilbertsville you may choose to combine this tour with Tour 22C.

Morris, 51, 51, 23, Peterson Rd, 10, 12A, 12, 10, Cogshell Rd, West Laurens, Brewster Hill Rd, New Rd, Lulls Hill Rd, Laurens, 51, Main St, Crawford Rd, New Rd, 11, Light Hill Rd, Filor Hill Rd, Sampson, 10, 23, Maple Grove, Maple Grove Rd, Erwin Rd, 88, 8, Shelly Rd, Clarence Musson Rd, 8, 205, 6, Hell Hollow Rd, 51, 8, 4, 9, FOOD, 23, Mill Creek Rd, West Oneonta, Mill Creek Rd, 8, 205, Oneonta West End, Oneonta, 61, Browne St, 7, 6, 9, 9, **OPTION-1**, 7, 88, 5, 48, 7

Gilbertsville, 51, 62, 63, 64, River Rd, Mount Upton, 8, 51, 3, 3A, Prentice Gorge Rd, Ideuma Rd, Ideuma Rd, 4, Otego, 88, Lockwood Hill Rd, River Rd, Ideuma Rd, 3, Alton Rd, 2, 3, 8, Hutchinson Hill Rd, **OPTION-2**, Wells Bridge, 44, 7, Covered Bridge, 44, 357, Bike Shop Jim's, 88, 357, FOOD, 7, 7, Valley View Rd, 1, Bike Shop Dave's, 7, Unadilla, River, 23, FOOD, Sidney, 23, 88, 23, 357

Sidney (inset map)
7, 7, Terrace Hill Rd, Bridge St, Willow St, Liberty St, Bike Shop Dave's, River St, Susquehanna River, Main St, Cartwright St, River St, River St, Division St, FOOD, Steiner Rd, E Main St, River St, Union St, Sherman St, Adams St, W Main St, 7, Orchard, 7, Beale St

Scale: 0 1 2 3 4 .4 inch = 1 mile

©1998 Tourmaster Publications, Inc.

INTERSTATE 90 **STATE ROAD** 20 **COUNTY ROAD** 33 **POINTS OF INTEREST** 25 **BIKE SHOP** BIKE SHOP **OPTION** OPTION **COMBINE WITH**

Butternut Valley "A"

Start: Schuyler Lake. Post Office.

Miles	31
Rating	Moderate
Climb	1800' @ 58 ft/mi

Tour 22A

Mile	Dir		Instruction			Dist
0.0	R		Leave Post Office 80 ⚠			1.3
1.3	BR		16			0.8
2.1	BL		TRO UM 16	⊘ UM Angel Hill Rd		5.9
8.0	S	SS	TRO 16	X 80		0.9
8.9	BR		TRO UM 16	⊘ Patent Rd		3.5
12.4	BL		TRO UM 16	⊘ Gregory Rd		1.7
14.1	R		51		FOOD	0.8
18.6	R	SS	TRO 51 / 80		FOOD	1.1
19.7	L		TRO 51	⊘ 80		1.8
21.5	BR		UM South Rd @ Gazebo	⊘ UM 51		0.1
21.6	R		@ The Stone House UM Arnold Rd			0.1
21.7	L		UM Norton Rd @ Otsego Mutual			1.5
23.2	S	SS	UM 19			0.3
23.5	BR		TRO UM 19	⊘ UM Munson Rd		3.2
26.7	R	SS	UM 22			4.3
31.0	BL		TRO UM 22	⊘ Church St		0.2
31.2	R	SS	Post Office			

NOTE

Park @ Polly's House Behind Post Office On 22

R Right	**S** Straight	**SS** Stop Sign	**UM** Unmarked Road	⊘ Do Not Take
L Left	**TRO** To Remain On	**SL** Stop Light	26 County Route	☞ Detour Off
BR Bear Right	**X** Cross	**YS** Yield Sign	28 State Route	🤝 Combine With
BL Bear Left	⚠ Caution			

Mile	•POINTS OF INTEREST	#

COUNTIES
Otsego

TOUR DESCRIPTION

The Butternut Valley series explores the beautiful Butternut Valley region of southwestern Otsego County. Butternut Valley "A" explores the northern third of the Butternut Valley from Burlington to Garrettsville.

Let us know what you think of this tour! Email: crankmail@usa.net

©1998 Tourmaster Publications, Inc.

Climb Rating in feet per mile climbed: 0-45 = Easy, 45-60 = Moderate, 60+ = Difficult

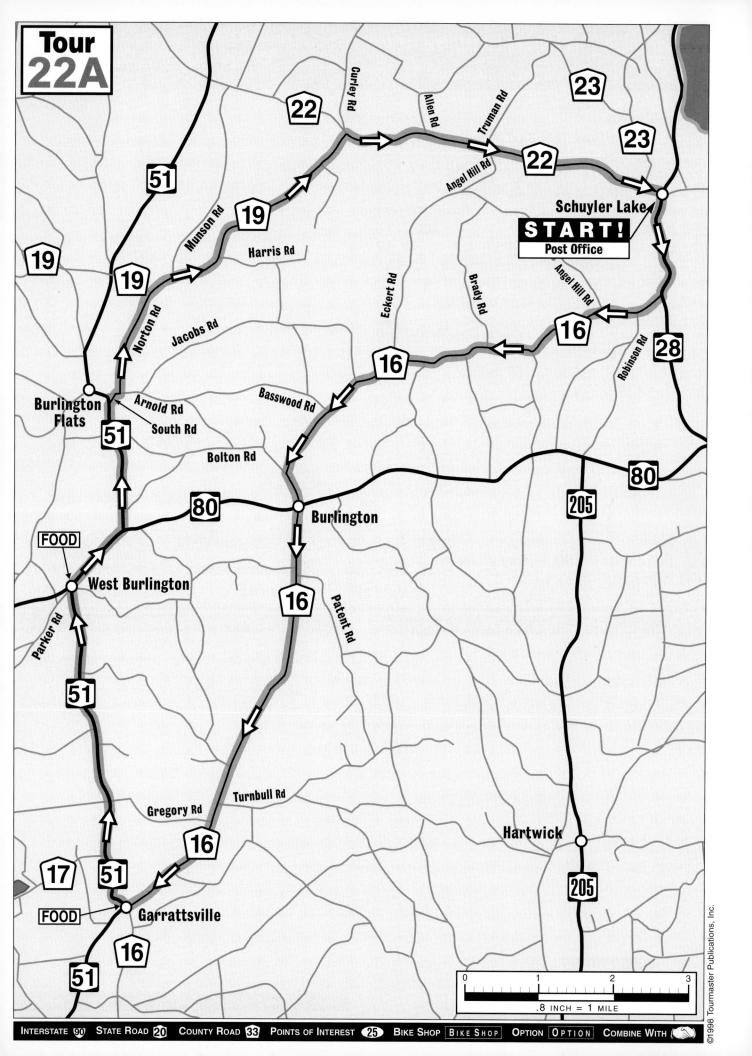

Butternut Valley "B"

Start: Schuyler Lake. Post Office.

Miles 53
Rating Moderate
Climb 3100' @ 58 ft/mi

Tour 22B

Mile	Turn		Directions		Next
0.0	R		Leave Post Office 80 !		1.3
1.3	BR		16		0.8
2.1	BL		TRO UM 16	⊘UM Angel Hill Rd	5.9
8.0	S	SS	TRO 16	X 80	0.9
8.9	BR		TRO UM 16	⊘Patent Rd	3.5
12.4	BL		TRO UM 16	⊘Gregory Rd	1.7
14.1	R		51	FOOD	0.8
14.9	L		17		1.1
16.0	BL		TRO UM 17	⊘East Side/Turtle	1.2
17.2	BR		TRO UM 17	⊘Miller Rd	1.1
18.3	L		UM 49		6.4
24.7	R	SS	UM 51		0.9
25.6	L	SL	23	⊘ 51 FOOD	1.3
26.9	L		Pegg Rd		0.7
27.6	BR		TRO UM Paved Pegg	⊘Bemis	0.7
28.3	BL		TRO UM Pegg	⊘Butternut Ridge	2.3
30.6	L	SS	UM 12	⊘ 14 🤝	0.7
31.3	R	SS	51		4.5
35.8	L		TRO 51	⊘S 16 FOOD	4.5
40.3	R	SS	TRO 51 / 80	FOOD	1.1
41.4	L		TRO 51	⊘ 80	1.8
43.2	BR		UM South Rd @ Gazebo	⊘UM 51	0.1
43.3	R		@ The Stone House UM Arnold Rd		0.1
43.4	L		UM Norton Rd @ Otsego Mutual		1.5
44.9	S	SS	UM 19		0.3
45.2	BR		TRO UM 19	⊘UM Munson Rd	3.2
48.4	R	SS	UM 22		4.3
52.7	BL		TRO UM 22	⊘Church St	0.2
52.9	R	SS	Post Office		

🤝 **Cooperstown: 8**
@ 30.6 join Tour 8 @ cue 19.5 R SS 12

NOTE
Park @ Polly's House Behind Post Office On 22

R	Right	**S**	Straight	**SS**	Stop Sign	**UM** Unmarked Road	⊘ Do Not Take
L	Left	**TRO**	To Remain On	**SL**	Stop Light	26 County Route	☞ Detour Off
BR	Bear Right	**X**	Cross			28 State Route	🤝 Combine With
BL	Bear Left	**!**	Caution	**YS**	Yield Sign		

Mile	•POINTS OF INTEREST	#

COUNTIES
Otsego

TOUR DESCRIPTION

The Butternut Valley series explores the beautiful Butternut Valley region of southwestern Otsego County.

Butternut Valley "B" adds 22 miles and a 1300 foot climb to the Butternut Valley "A" tour. The extension explores the middle third of the Butternut Valley from Garrattsville to Morris.

Let us know what you think of this tour! Email: crankmail@usa.net

Climb Rating in feet per mile climbed: 0-45 = Easy, 45-60 = Moderate, 60+ = Difficult

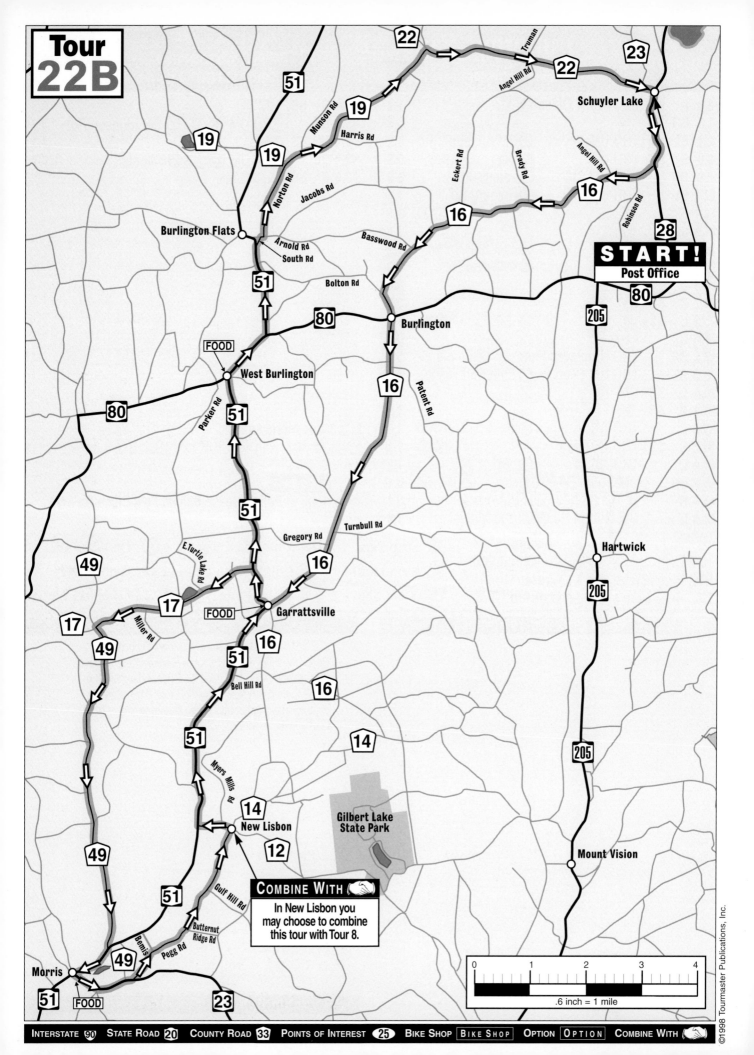

Tour 22B

19 **51** **19** **22** **22** **23**

Munson Rd
Truman
Angel Hill Rd

19 Harris Rd

19 Schuyler Lake

Norton Rd
Jacobs Rd
Eckert Rd
Brady Rd
Angel Hill Rd

Burlington Flats
Arnold Rd
South Rd
Basswood Rd
16
16
Robinson Rd

51
Bolton Rd
28

START!
Post Office

FOOD
80
Burlington
205
80

West Burlington
Parker Rd
51
16
Patent Rd

51
80

51
49
E. Turtle Lake Rd
Gregory Rd
Turnbull Rd
Hartwick

17
16
205

17
Miller Rd
FOOD
Garrattsville

49
51 **16**
16

Bell Hill Rd
16

51
14

51
Myers Mills Rd

14
Gilbert Lake
State Park
49
New Lisbon

12

Gulf Hill Rd

COMBINE WITH 🤝
In New Lisbon you
may choose to combine
this tour with Tour 8.
Mount Vision
205

51
Butternut
Ridge Rd

Bemis Rd
Pegg Rd

Morris
49
51
FOOD
23

0 1 2 3 4
.6 inch = 1 mile

INTERSTATE **90** STATE ROAD **20** COUNTY ROAD **33** POINTS OF INTEREST **25** BIKE SHOP BIKE SHOP OPTION OPTION COMBINE WITH 🤝

Butternut Valley "C"

Start: Schuyler Lake. Post Office.

Miles	68
Rating	Moderate
Climb	3900' @ 57 ft/mi

Tour 22C

Mile	Dir		Description				Dist
0.0	R		Leave Post Office 80 ⚠				1.3
1.3	BR		16				0.8
2.1	BL		TRO UM 16	⊘	UM Angel Hill Rd		5.9
8.0	S	SS	TRO 16	X	80		0.9
8.9	BR		TRO UM 16	⊘	Patent Rd		3.5
12.4	BL		TRO UM 16	⊘	Gregory Rd		1.7
14.1	R		51			FOOD	0.8
14.9	L		17				1.1
16.0	BL		TRO UM 17	⊘	East Side/Turtle		1.2
17.2	BR		TRO UM 17	⊘	Miller Rd		1.1
18.3	L		49				6.4
24.7	R	SS	UM 51				0.9
25.6	S	SL	TRO 51	☞	L 0.1	FOOD	0.4
26.0	S	SL	TRO 51	⊘	23		6.7
• 32.7	L		Commercial St (4)			FOOD	0.0
32.7	R		Elm St				0.1
32.8	L	SS	Maple St				0.1
32.9	L	SS	Spring St				0.1
• 33.0	R		Bloom St Before Statue				0.6
• 33.6	L		After Bridge UM Mill St				0.4
34.0	R	SS	UM 8				0.6
34.6	L		Musson (East Side Rd) 🤝-LAUR				3.3
37.9	BL		TRO East Side	⊘	Bailey/ Filor Hill		2.8
40.7	BR	YS	23	☞	L 0.3	FOOD	0.8
41.5	L		Pegg Rd				0.7
42.2	BR		TRO UM Paved Pegg	⊘	Bemis		0.7
42.9	BL		TRO UM Pegg	⊘	Butternut Ridge		2.3
45.2	L	SS	UM 12	⊘	14 🤝-COOP		0.7
45.9	R	SS	51				4.5
50.4	L		TRO 51	⊘	S 16	FOOD	4.5
54.9	R	SS	TRO 51 / 80			FOOD	1.1
56.0	L		TRO 51	⊘	80		1.8
57.8	BR		UM South Rd @ Gazebo	⊘	UM 51		0.1
57.9	R		@ The Stone House UM Arnold Rd				0.1
58.0	L		UM Norton Rd @ Otsego Mutual				1.5
59.5	S	SS	UM 19				0.3
59.8	BR		TRO UM 19	⊘	UM Munson Rd		3.2
63.0	R	SS	UM 22				4.3
67.3	BL		TRO UM 22	⊘	Church St		0.2
67.5	R	SS	Post Office				

NOTE
Park @ Polly's House Behind Post Office On 22

R	Right	S	Straight	SS	Stop Sign	UM	Unmarked Road	⊘	Do Not Take
L	Left	TRO	To Remain On	SL	Stop Light	26	County Route	☞	Detour Off
BR	Bear Right	X	Cross	YS	Yield Sign	28	State Route	🤝	Combine With
BL	Bear Left	⚠	Caution						

Mile	•POINTS OF INTEREST	#
32.7	The Major's Inn	63
33.5	Gilbertsville Swimming Hole, on L after bridge	64
33.6	Gilbertsville Polo Fields ☞ S 0.4	62

COUNTIES
Otsego

TOUR DESCRIPTION

The Butternut Valley series explores the beautiful Butternut Valley region of southwestern Otsego County.

Butternut Valley "C" adds 15 miles and an 800 foot climb to the Butternut Valley "B" tour. The extension explores the southern third of the Butternut Valley from Morris to Gilbertsville.

🤝 **Laurens:**
21B: @ 34.6 join Tour 21B @ cue 37.0
    S X Clarence Musson Rd
21C: @ 34.6 join Tour 21C @ cue 43.6
    S X Clarence Musson Rd

🤝 **Cooperstown: 8**
    @ 45.2 join Tour 8 @ cue 19.5 R SS 12

©1998 Tourmaster Publications, Inc.

Climb Rating in feet per mile climbed: 0-45 = Easy, 45-60 = Moderate, 60+ = Difficult

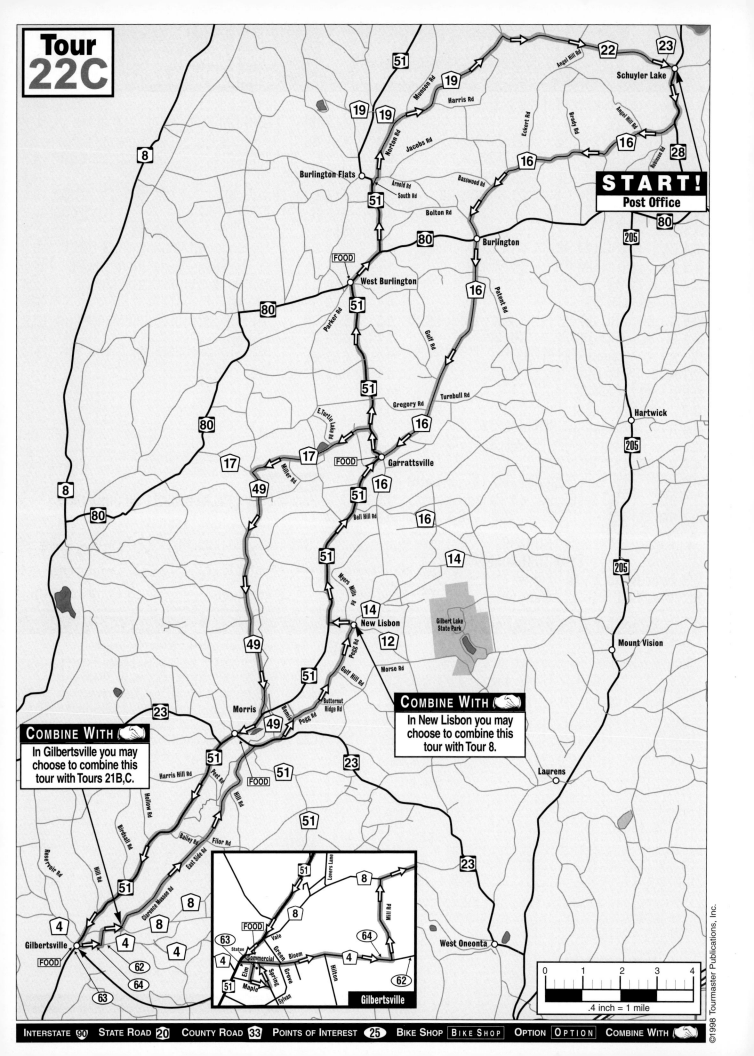

Tour 22C

8

51
19
19
19
19

Munson Rd
Harris Rd

22
23
Angel Hill Rd
Schuyler Lake

Norton Rd
Jacobs Rd
Eckert Rd
Brady Rd
Angel Hill Rd

16
16
Robinson Rd
28

Arnold Rd
South Rd
Basswood Rd

Burlington Flats
51

Bolton Rd

START!
Post Office

80
80
205

80
Burlington
51
Parker Rd

16
Patent Rd

West Burlington
FOOD
51

Gulf Rd

80

51

Gregory Rd
Turnbull Rd

Hartwick

8
E. Turtle Lake Rd
17
16

17
FOOD
Garrattsville
16

205

17
Miller Rd
49

16
51

Bell Hill Rd
16

51

14

Myers Mills Rd
14
New Lisbon

Gilbert Lake
State Park

49

12

Mount Vision

51
Pegg Rd
Morse Rd

COMBINE WITH 🤝
In New Lisbon you may
choose to combine this
tour with Tour 8.

23
Morris
Bemis
49
Pegg Rd
Butternut
Ridge Rd
Gulf Hill Rd

COMBINE WITH 🤝
In Gilbertsville you may
choose to combine this
tour with Tours 21B,C.

51
Harris Hill Rd
Peet Rd
Hill Rd
FOOD
51
23

51

Hollow Rd
Birdsall Rd
Bailey Rd
Filor Rd
East Side Rd

23

Reservoir Rd
Hill Rd

51

51
Clarence Musson Rd
8
8

8
51
8
Mill Rd
64

4
Gilbertsville
FOOD
4
4
4

FOOD
Vale
63
Statue
Commercial
Green
Bloom
Grove
Hilton

4
West Oneonta

62
64
63

51
Elm
Maple
Spring
Sylvan

4
62
Laurens

Gilbertsville

0 1 2 3 4
.4 inch = 1 mile

©1998 Tourmaster Publications, Inc.

INTERSTATE 90   **STATE ROAD** 20   **COUNTY ROAD** 33   **POINTS OF INTEREST** 25   **BIKE SHOP** BIKE SHOP   **OPTION** OPTION   **COMBINE WITH** 🤝

Unadilla River Valley "A"
Start: Schuyler Lake. Post Office.

Miles	31
Rating	**Difficult**
Climb	2700' @ 87 ft/mi

Tour 23A

0.0	S		Facing Post Office On ㉒	0.2
0.2	R		㉓	0.3
0.5	S		Steel Deck Bridge ⚠	0.6
1.1	BL		TRO Paved UM ㉒ ⊘ Van Court	2.2
3.3	S		Steel Deck Bridge ⚠	4.1
7.4	S		Steel Deck Bridge ⚠	0.4
7.8	R	SS	㊽ Then BL ⊘ South Rd	1.5
9.3	L		Skaneateles Turnpike	1.1
10.4	L	SS	UM ㉑	0.9
11.3	BR		TRO UM ㉑ ⊘ Armstrong	2.8
14.1	L	SS	UM ⑱	1.3
15.4	L		⑲	0.5
15.9	BR		TRO UM ⑲ ⊘ Bassett Rd	3.0
18.9	BL		TRO UM ⑲ ⊘ Summit Lake Rd	1.9
20.8	R	SS	Then L TRO UM ⑲ X ㊽	0.6
21.4	BL		TRO UM ⑲ ⊘ UM Norton	0.3
21.7	BL		UM Munson Rd ⊘UM ⑲	2.8
24.5	R	SS	UM ㉒	1.8
26.3	BL		TRO UM ㉒ ⊘ ⑲	4.3
30.6	BL		TRO UM ㉒ ⊘ Church St	0.3
30.9	R	SS	Post Office	

NOTE
Park @ Polly's House Behind Post Office On ㉒

R	Right	**S**	Straight	**SS**	Stop Sign	**UM** Unmarked Road ⊘ Do Not Take
L	Left	**TRO**	To Remain On	**SL**	Stop Light	26 County Route ☞ Detour Off
BR	Bear Right	**X**	Cross	**YS**	Yield Sign	28 State Route 🤝 Combine With
BL	Bear Left	⚠	Caution			

Mile	•POINTS OF INTEREST	#

COUNTIES
Otsego

TOUR DESCRIPTION

The meandering Unadilla River delineates the western border of Otsego County. The Unadilla River Valley Series explores the northern third of that western border. Be fore-warned that both rides in this series purposely seek out memorable climbs.

Unadilla River Valley "A" climbs from Canadarago Lake's Oak Creek Valley, drops down to the Wharton Creek Valley, then climbs up to Plainfield Center before descending to the Unadilla River Valley. The return trip starts with a memorable climb up to Summit Lake, dives back to the Wharton River Valley and then switchbacks up 800 feet in 3 miles before a final, exhilarating descent.

©1998 Tourmaster Publications, Inc.

Climb Rating in feet per mile climbed: 0-45 = Easy, 45-60 = Moderate, 60+ = Difficult

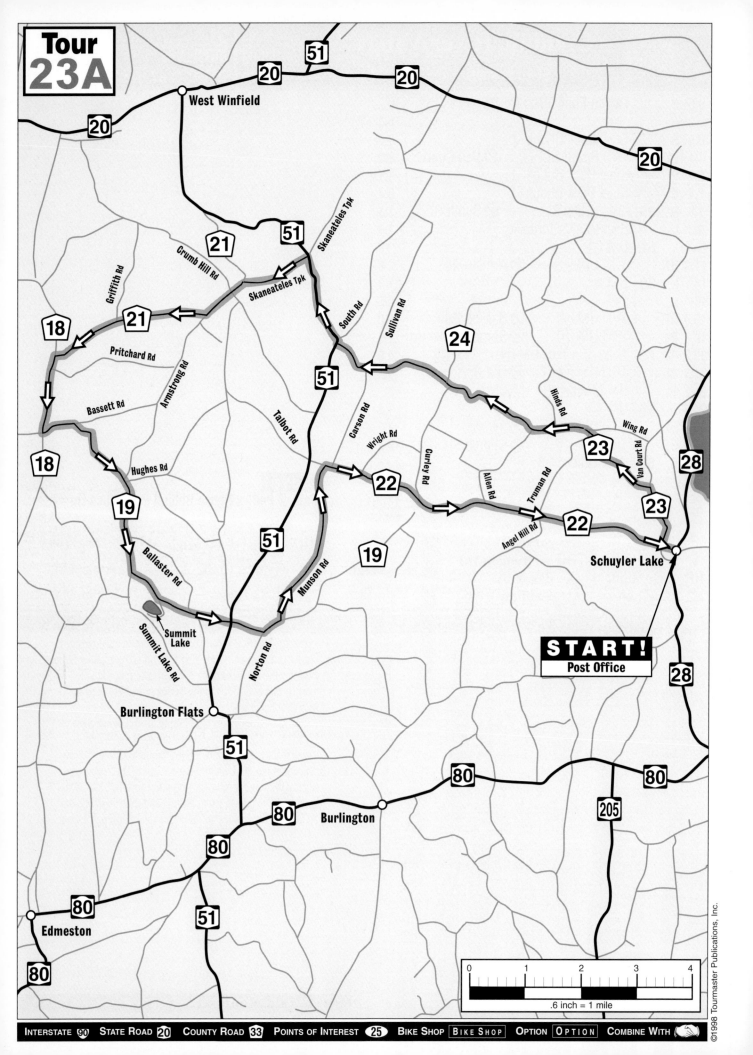

Tour 23A

West Winfield

51
20
20
20
20

Skaneateles Tpk
51
Crumb Hill Rd
21
Griffith Rd
21
18
Pritchard Rd
South Rd
Sullivan Rd
24
18
Bassett Rd
Armstrong Rd
51
Carson Rd
Wright Rd
Hinds Rd
Wing Rd
23
Van Court Rd
28
19
Hughes Rd
Talbot Rd
Curley Rd
Allen Rd
Truman Rd
23
22
22
Angel Hill Rd
Ballaster Rd
51
Munson Rd
19
Schuyler Lake
Summit Lake
Summit Lake Rd
Norton Rd
START!
Post Office
28

Burlington Flats
51
80
80
205
80
Burlington
80
80
51
80
Edmeston
80

0 1 2 3 4
.6 inch = 1 mile

Unadilla River Valley "B"

Start: Schuyler Lake. Post Office.

Cranks

Miles	49
Rating	Difficult
Climb	3700' @ 75 ft/mi

Tour 23B

0.0	S		Facing Post Office On (22)	0.2
0.2	R		(23)	0.3
0.5	S		Steel Deck Bridge (!)	0.6
1.1	BL		TRO Paved UM (22) ⊘ Van Court	2.2
3.3	S		Steel Deck Bridge (!)	4.1
7.4	S		Steel Deck Bridge (!)	0.4
7.8	R	SS	(51) Then BL ⊘ South Rd	1.5
9.3	L		Skaneateles Turnpike	1.1
10.4	L	SS	UM (21)	0.9
11.3	BR		TRO UM (21) ⊘ Armstrong	2.8
14.1	L	SS	UM (18)	11.2
25.3	L	SS	(20)	4.1
29.4	R	SS	(80) FOOD	0.8
30.2	BL		Borrow Pit Rd After Bridge	0.1
30.3	L	SS	Wharton Creek Rd	3.2
33.5	L	SS	(80) @ Roller Rink FOOD	0.8
34.3	R		Robinson Rd	3.3
37.6	R	SS	UM (51)	0.2
37.8	BL		UM Arnold Rd @ Gazebo ⊘ (51)	0.1
37.9	S	SS	TRO UM Arnold ⊘ South St	0.2
38.1	L		UM Norton Rd @ Otsego Mutual	1.5
39.6	S	SS	UM (19)	0.3
39.9	BL		UM Munson Rd ⊘ UM (19)	2.8
42.7	R	SS	UM (22)	1.8
44.5	S		TRO (22) ⊘ (19)	4.3
48.8	BL		TRO UM (22) ⊘ Church St	0.3
49.1	R	SS	Post Office	

Note

Park @ Polly's House Behind Post Office On (22)

R	Right	S	Straight	SS	Stop Sign	UM	Unmarked Road	⊘	Do Not Take
L	Left	TRO	To Remain On	SL	Stop Light	(26)	County Route	☞	Detour Off
BR	Bear Right	X	Cross	YS	Yield Sign	(28)	State Route	🤝	Combine With
BL	Bear Left	(!)	Caution						

Mile	•Points of Interest	#

Counties

Otsego

Tour Description

The meandering Unadilla River delineates the western border of Otsego County. The Unadilla River Valley Series explores the northern third of that western border. Be forewarned that both rides in this series purposely seek out memorable climbs.

Unadilla River Valley "B " adds 18 miles and a 1000 foot climb to the Unadilla River Valley "A" tour. The extension explores an additional ten miles of the relatively flat Unadilla River Valley before returning via a memorable climb from South Edmeston to Edmeston. As with the "A" tour, the grand finale includes an 800 foot switchback climb in 3 miles before a final, exhilarating descent.

Let us know what you think of this tour! Email: crankmail@usa.net

Climb Rating in feet per mile climbed: 0-45 = Easy, 45-60 = Moderate, 60+ = Difficult

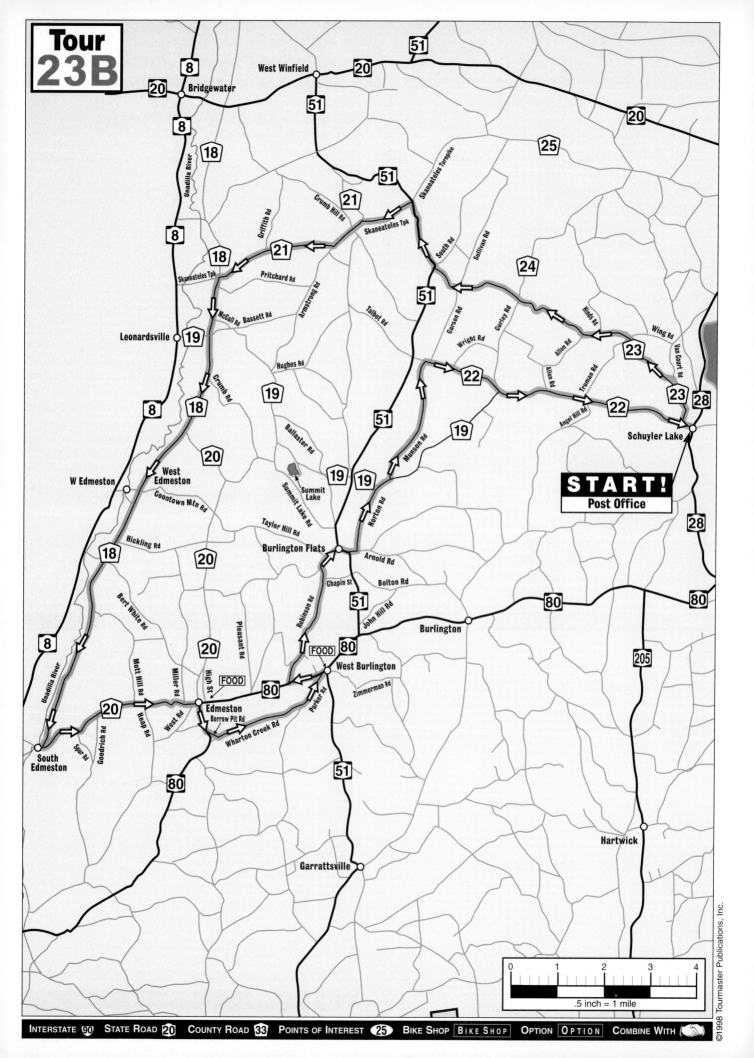

Tour
23B

8
20 Bridgewater
West Winfield
51
20
8
51
18
Unadilla River
51
8
21
Crumb Hill Rd
21
Skaneateles Turnpike
25
Griffith Rd
51
South Rd
Sullivan Rd
24
18
21
Skaneateles Tpk
51
Skaneateles Tpk
Pritchard Rd
McCall Rd
Bassett Rd
Armstrong Rd
Talbot Rd
Carson Rd
Curley Rd
Hinds Rd
Wing Rd
Leonardsville 19
Crumb Rd
Hughes Rd
Wright Rd
Allen Rd
23
Van Court Rd
8
18
19
Allen Rd
Truman Rd
23
28
19
Ballaster Rd
51
22
Angel Hill Rd
22
20
Summit Lake
19
Munson Rd
19
Schuyler Lake
W Edmeston
West Edmeston
Coontown Mtn Rd
Summit Lake Rd
19
19
STAR T!
Post Office
Taylor Hill Rd
Norton Rd
18
Hickling Rd
Burlington Flats
Arnold Rd
20
Chapin St
Bolton Rd
28
Bert White Rd
Pleasant Rd
Robinson Rd
51
John Hill Rd
Burlington
80
80
8
20
High St
FOOD
80
FOOD
80
West Burlington
205
Mott Hill Rd
Miller Rd
Parker Rd
Zimmerman Rd
20
Goodrich Rd
Neap Rd
West Rd
Edmeston
Borrow Pit Rd
Spur Rd
Wharton Creek Rd
South
Edmeston
80
Hartwick
51
Garrattsville

0 1 2 3 4

.5 inch = 1 mile

INTERSTATE 90 STATE ROAD 20 COUNTY ROAD 33 POINTS OF INTEREST 25 BIKE SHOP BIKE SHOP OPTION OPTION COMBINE WITH

Cranks

Canadarago Lake

Start: Schuyler Lake. Post Office.

Miles	16
Rating	Difficult
Climb	1100' @ 68 ft/mi

Tour 24

0.0	S		Leave Post Office ㉒ **X** ㉘ ⚠		4.8
4.8	BR		UM Butternut Rd		0.8
5.6	L		Cemetery Rd		0.6
6.2	R	SS	UM ㉒		0.3
6.5	L		Bronner St		0.3
6.8	S	SS	TRO Bronner	**X** Elm	0.3
7.1	R	YS	Prospect St (UM ㉘)		0.2
7.3	L	SS	Monticello ⊘ ⑳/㉘ ☞ R 0.1 **FOOD**		0.4
7.7	S	SS	㉕ **X** UM ㉕Ⓐ ⚠		2.5
10.2	L		Hyder Rd		0.9
11.1	BR		Gulf Rd	⊘ Hyder	0.6
11.7	BL		TRO UM Gulf	⊘ Filburn	0.8
12.5	BR		Henry Conklin Rd		1.4
13.9	S	SS	Taylor Rd **X** Wing Hill Rd		1.4
15.3	R	SS	UM ㉘ ⚠		0.1
15.4	BL		UM Tunnicliff Rd ⊘ ㉘ ⚠		0.4
15.8	S	SS	UM ㉒		0.3
16.1	S	SS	Post Office	**X** ㉘ ⚠	

NOTE
Park @ Polly's House Behind Post Office On ㉒

R	Right	**S**	Straight	**SS** Stop Sign	**UM** Unmarked Road	⊘ Do Not Take
L	Left	**TRO** To Remain On		**SL** Stop Light	㉖ County Route	☞ Detour Off
BR	Bear Right	**X**	Cross	**YS** Yield Sign	㉘ State Route	🤝 Combine With
BL	Bear Left	⚠	Caution			

Mile	•POINTS OF INTEREST	#

TOUR DESCRIPTION

This short, scenic tour explores the perimeter of Canadarago Lake. The first half warms up along the Lake's relatively flat eastern shore. The second half climbs to three summit vantage points far above the Lake's western shore. The incredible views are well worth the incredible climbs.

COUNTIES
Otsego

Let us know what you think of this tour! Email: crankmail@usa.net

Climb Rating in feet per mile climbed: 0-45 = Easy, 45-60 = Moderate, 60+ = Difficult

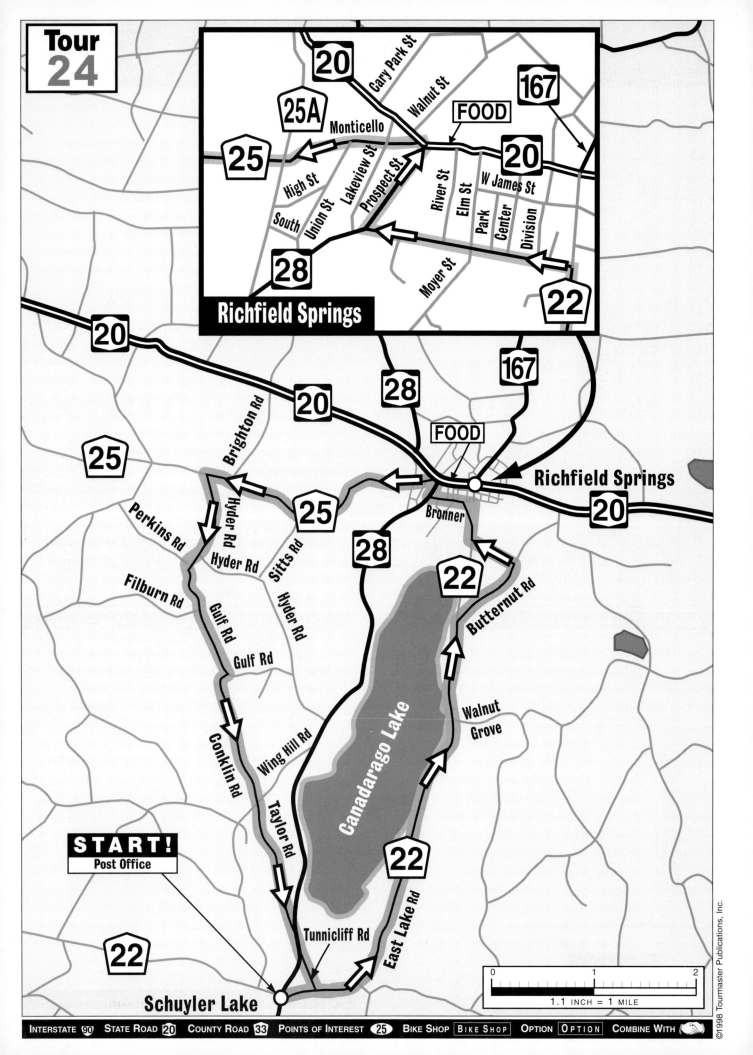

Tour 24

Richfield Springs (inset)

20 | 25A | 167
Cary Park St
Walnut St
Monticello
25
FOOD
20
High St
Lakeview St
Prospect St
River St
Elm St
W James St
Park
Center
Division
South
Union St
Moyer St
28
22
Richfield Springs

Main map

20
20
28
167
Brighton Rd
25
FOOD
28
Richfield Springs
20
Bronner
22
Perkins Rd
Hyder Rd
Hyder Rd
Sitts Rd
Butternut Rd
Filburn Rd
Hyder Rd
Gulf Rd
Walnut Grove
Gulf Rd
Canadarago Lake
Wing Hill Rd
Conklin Rd
22
Taylor Rd
START!
Post Office
22
East Lake Rd
Tunnicliff Rd
Schuyler Lake

0   1   2
1.1 INCH = 1 MILE

©1998 Tourmaster Publications, Inc.

INTERSTATE 90   STATE ROAD 20   COUNTY ROAD 33   POINTS OF INTEREST 25   BIKE SHOP [BIKE SHOP]   OPTION [OPTION]   COMBINE WITH

Monastery Meander "A"

Start: Springfield. Glimmerglass Opera.

Miles	25
Rating	Moderate
Climb	1300' @ 52 ft/mi

Tour 25A

• 0.0	L	@ Crosswalk Facing Opera 🤝	0.2
0.2	L	Bartlett Rd	1.2
1.4	L SS	UM Hoke Rd	2.2
3.6	L SS	⟨20⟩ ⚠	0.3
3.9	R	Little Lakes Rd	1.4
5.3	BL	TRO UM Little Lakes ⊘ Springer	3.0
8.3	BL	TRO Pavement (UM Little Lakes)	0.3
8.6	BR	TRO Pavement (UM Little Lakes)	0.7
9.3	S SS	Casler **X** Jordanville 👉 L 0.8 FOOD	0.3
9.6	S YS	⟨167⟩	0.5
10.1	BL	Robinson Rd ⊘ ⟨167⟩	0.2
• 10.3	R	Monastery Parking Lot	0.0
10.3	L	Leaving Monastery Parking Lot	0.2
10.5	S SS	⟨167⟩	0.3
10.8	L	Hicks Rd	0.6
11.4	BL	Then BR TRO UM Hicks	2.9
14.3	L SS	UM Jordanville Rd	1.9
16.2	R SS	TRO Jordanville ⊘ Puskarenko	1.2
• 17.4	R SS	⟨80⟩ 👉 L 0.4 FOOD	0.1
• 17.5	BL	TRO ⟨80⟩ ⊘ Chyle	4.4
21.9	S SL	TRO ⟨80⟩ **X** ⟨20⟩ ⚠ 👉 FOOD	0.8
22.7	BR	TRO ⟨80⟩ ⊘ Public Landing	0.2
22.9	BR	Frank Smith Rd	0.6
23.5	L SS	UM ⟨53⟩	0.2
23.7	R SS	UM ⟨80⟩	1.3
25.0	R	Opera Parking Lot	

🤝 **Cooperstown: 2B,C,D**
@ 0.0 join Tours 2B,C,D
@ cue 9.6 L @ Crosswalk Facing Opera

🤝 **Cooperstown: 11A,B**
@ 0.0 R 0.4 to join Tours 11A,B
@ cue 9.2 R ⟨27⟩

> **NOTE**
> **People Wearing Shorts Are Not Permitted On The Monastery Premises.**

> **NOTE**
> There Are Two Food Stops @ 9.3 in Jordanville. They Are Both Frequently Closed On Weekends.

R Right	**S** Straight	**SS** Stop Sign	**UM** Unmarked Road	⊘ Do Not Take
L Left	**TRO** To Remain On	**SL** Stop Light	⟨26⟩ County Route	👉 Detour Off
BR Bear Right	**X** Cross	**YS** Yield Sign	⟨28⟩ State Route	🤝 Combine With
BL Bear Left	⚠ Caution			

Mile	•POINTS OF INTEREST	#
0.0	Glimmerglass Opera & Goodyear Nature Trail	⟨23⟩
10.3	Holy Trinity Russian Orthodox Monastery	⟨65⟩
17.4	Owen D. Young Marker & Nature Trail 👉 L 0.5	⟨24⟩
17.5	Rainbow Trout Fish Hatchery 👉 BR 0.1	⟨68⟩

TOUR DESCRIPTION

The Monastery Meander Series explores the rolling hills and farmlands of southern Herkimer County. These tours purposely wander, so pay close attention to the cue sheet.

Monastery "A" is a leisurely quarter century ride to Jordanville. Discover a Russian Orthodox Monastery. Hike the Nature Trails behind the Glimmerglass Opera building and the Owen D. Young Central School. Enjoy the Rainbow Trout Fish Hatchery.

COUNTIES

Otsego, Herkimer

Let us know what you think of this tour! Email: crankmail@usa.net

Climb Rating in feet per mile climbed: 0-45 = Easy, 45-60 = Moderate, 60+ = Difficult

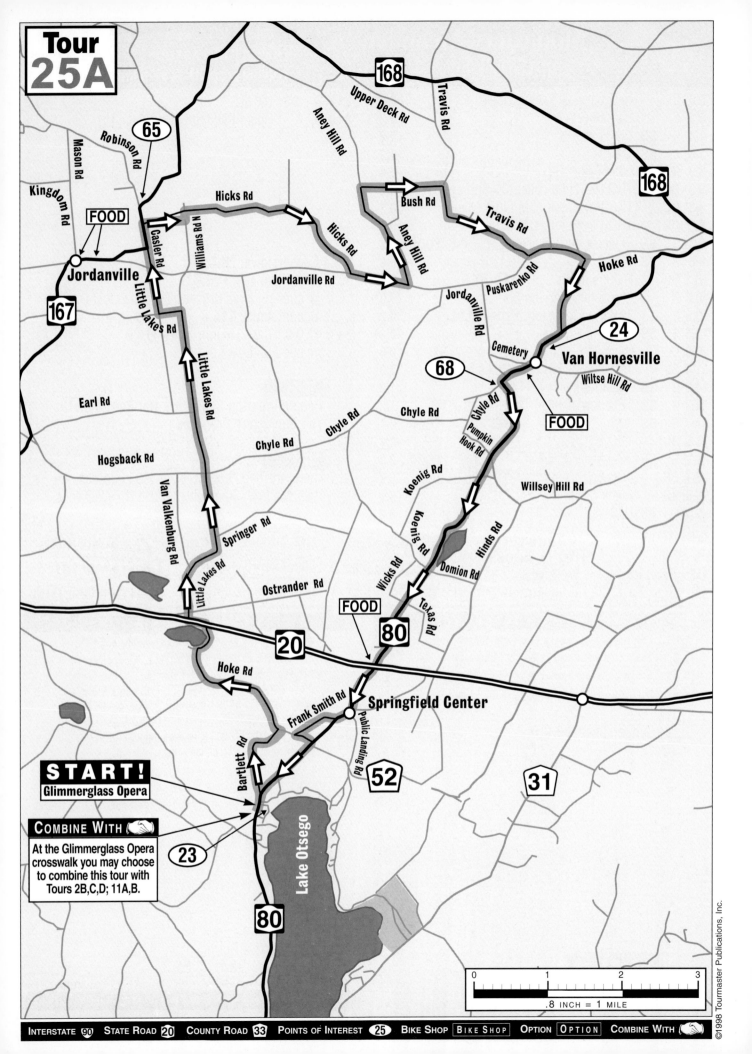

Tour 25A

65 Robinson Rd

Mason Rd

Kingdom Rd

FOOD

Jordanville

167

Casler Rd

Williams Rd N

Hicks Rd

Hicks Rd

Jordanville Rd

Little Lakes Rd

Earl Rd

Hogsback Rd

Van Valkenburg Rd

Little Lakes Rd

Springer Rd

Little Lakes Rd

Ostrander Rd

Chyle Rd

Chyle Rd

Chyle Rd

Chyle Rd

Upper Deck Rd

Aney Hill Rd

Travis Rd

168

168

Bush Rd

Travis Rd

Aney Hill Rd

Hoke Rd

Puskarenko Rd

Jordanville Rd

Cemetery

24 Van Hornesville

Wiltse Hill Rd

68 Chyle Rd

FOOD

Pumpkin Hook Rd

Koenig Rd

Willsey Hill Rd

Koenig Rd

Hinds Rd

Wicks Rd

Domion Rd

FOOD

80

Texas Rd

20

Hoke Rd

Bartlett Rd

Frank Smith Rd

Springfield Center

Public Landing Rd

52

31

START!
Glimmerglass Opera

COMBINE WITH 🤝
At the Glimmerglass Opera crosswalk you may choose to combine this tour with Tours 2B,C,D; 11A,B.

23

80

Lake Otsego

0   1   2   3

.8 INCH = 1 MILE

INTERSTATE 90   STATE ROAD 20   COUNTY ROAD 33   POINTS OF INTEREST 25   BIKE SHOP BIKE SHOP   OPTION OPTION   COMBINE WITH 🤝

Cranks

Monastery Meander "B"

Start: Springfield. Glimmerglass Opera.

Miles	50	OPTION	**Tour**
Rating	**Difficult**		**25B**
Climb	**3500'** @ 69 ft/mi		

•	0.0	L	@ Crosswalk Facing Opera 🤝		0.2
	0.2	L	Bartlett Rd		1.2
	1.4	L SS	UM Hoke Rd		2.2
	3.6	L SS	㉒ ⚠		0.3
	3.9	R	Little Lakes Rd		1.4
	5.3	BL	TRO UM Little Lakes ⊘ Springer		0.8
	6.1	L	Hogsback Rd		2.7
	8.8	S SS	Cullen X ⑯⑦		2.1
	10.9	S SS	Dugan X ㉘ ⚠		1.2
	12.1	BR	TRO UM Dugan ⊘ Brighton		1.3
	13.4	BR	Prey Hill Rd ⊘ Dugan		1.1
	14.5	L SS	McKoons Rd		0.1
	14.6	BR	TRO McKoons ⊘ Richfield Hill		3.2
	17.8	S SS	Columbia Center X Jordanville		0.2
	18.0	BR	TRO Columbia Center ⊘ Spohn		1.4
	19.4	BR	TRO Columbia ⊘ Polly Miller		0.5
	19.9	L SS	㉘ ⚠		1.0
	20.9	R	Robinson Rd @ Dennison Corners		2.7
	23.6	BR	TRO UM Robinson ⊘ Mortz		0.8
•	24.4	BL	TRO UM Robinson ⊘ UM Mason		1.7
	26.1	S SS	⑯⑦		0.9
	27.0	L	Jordanville Rd ☞ R 0.5 FOOD		0.6
	27.6	L	Casler Rd		0.2
	27.8	S YS	⑯⑦		0.2
	28.0	R	Hicks Rd		0.6
	28.6	BL	Then BR TRO UM Hicks Rd		2.9
	31.5	L SS	UM Jordanville Rd		0.7
	32.2	L	Aney Hill Rd		1.7
	33.9	R	Bush Rd OPTION		1.1
	35.0	R SS	Travis Rd		1.7
	36.7	BL	TRO Travis ⊘ Puskarenko		2.0
•	38.7	R SS	㊱		0.5
	39.2	S	TRO ㊱ FOOD		0.5
•	39.7	BL	TRO ㊱ ⊘ Chyle		1.5
	41.2	L	Willsey Hill Rd		0.7
	41.9	R	Hinds Rd		1.2
	43.1	BL	TRO UM Hinds ⊘ Domion		1.4
	44.5	S SS	Griggs Rd X ㉒ ⚠		1.6
	46.1	S SS	UM ㊼		1.4
	47.5	R	Public Landing Rd		0.8
	48.3	L SS	㊱ ☞ S 0.7 ㊱ FOOD		0.1
	48.4	BR	Frank Smith Rd		0.7
	49.1	L SS	UM ㊼		0.2
	49.3	R SS	UM ㊱		1.2
	50.5	R	Opera Parking Lot		

R	Right	**S**	Straight	**SS** Stop Sign
L	Left	**TRO** To Remain On	**SL** Stop Light
BR	Bear Right	**X** Cross	**YS** Yield Sign
BL	Bear Left	**⚠** Caution	

UM Unmarked Road   **⊘** Do Not Take
㉖ County Route   ☞ Detour Off
㉘ State Route   🤝 Combine With

Points of Interest

Mile	• POINTS OF INTEREST	#
0.0	Glimmerglass Opera & Goodyear Nature Trail	㉓
25.9	Holy Trinity Russian Orthodox Monastery	㉒
39.0	Owen D. Young Marker & Nature Trail on L	㉔
39.7	Rainbow Trout Fish Hatchery ☞ BR 0.1	㉞

🤝 **Cooperstown: 2B,C,D**
@ 0.0 join Tours 2B,C,D
@ cue 9.6 L @ Crosswalk Facing Opera

🤝 **Cooperstown: 11A,B**
@ 0.0 R 0.4 To Join Tours 11A,B
@ cue 9.2 R ㉗

NOTE
People Wearing Shorts Are Not Permitted On The Monastery Premises.

NOTE
There Are Two Food Stops @ Mile 27.0 In Jordanville. They Are Both Frequently Closed On Weekends.

COUNTIES
Otsego, Herkimer

TOUR DESCRIPTION

The Monastery Meander Series explores the rolling hills and farmlands of southwestern Herkimer County. These tours purposely wander, so pay close attention to the cue sheet.

Monastery "B" is a half century ride. It adds 25 miles and a 2200 foot climb to the Monastery "A" tour. For the brave and foolhardy, an additional 8.7 mile option at mile 33.9 offers a hair-raising 6.5 mile descent followed by a gut-wrenching 600 foot additional climb in 2.2 miles.

Discover a Russian Orthodox Monastery. Hike the Nature Trails behind the Glimmerglass Opera building and the Owen D. Young Central School. Enjoy the Rainbow Trout Fish Hatchery.

OPTION
To Add 8.7 Miles And A 600 Foot Climb:

33.9	S	Aney Hill Rd	⊘ Bush	3.0
36.9	R SS	⑯⑦		0.1
37.0	S SS	TRO ⑯⑦ X ⑯⑧		0.8
37.8	R	Johnny Cake Rd		2.6
40.4	R	Travis Rd		1.7
42.1	S SS	TRO Travis X ⑯⑧		3.3
45.4	Resume @ cue 36.7 BL TRO Travis ⊘ Puskarenko			

Let us know what you think of this tour! Email: crankmail@usa.net

Climb Rating in feet per mile climbed: 0-45 = Easy, 45-60 = Moderate, 60+ = Difficult

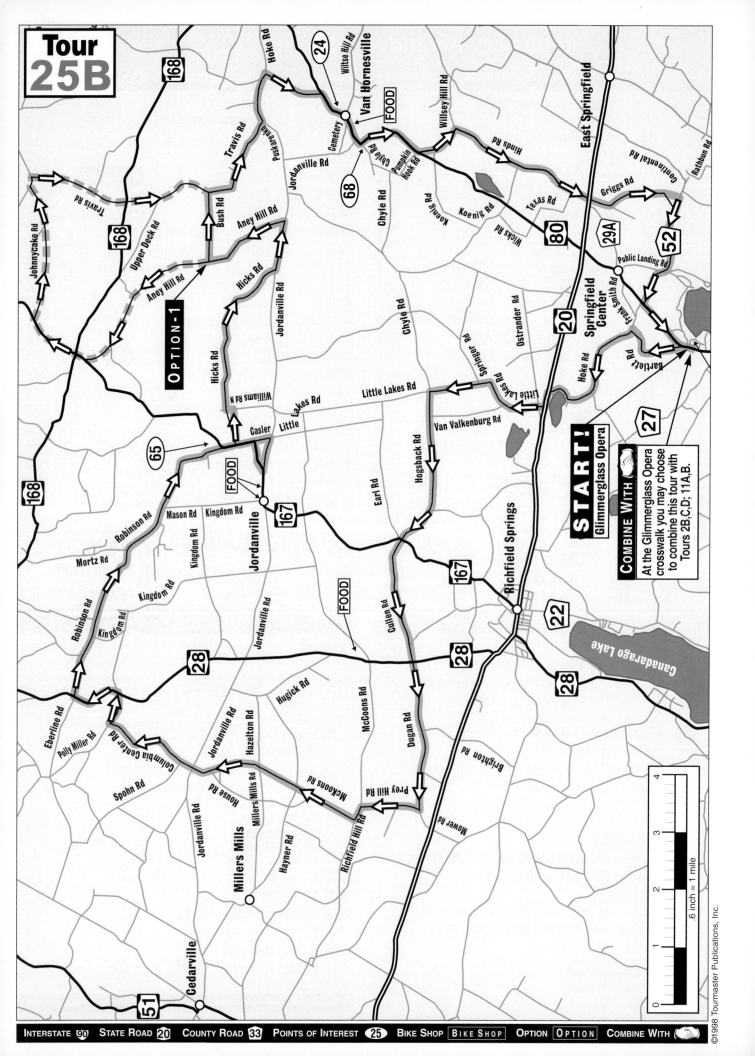

0.0	L		@ Crosswalk Facing Opera 🤝	0.2
0.2	L		Bartlett Rd	1.2
1.4	L	SS	UM Hoke Rd	2.2
3.6	L	SS	20 ⚠️	0.3
3.9	R		Little Lakes Rd	1.4
5.3	BL		TRO UM Little Lakes ⊘ Springer	0.8
6.1	L		Hogsback Rd	2.7
8.8	S	SS	Cullen X 167	2.1
10.9	S	SS	Dugan X 28 ⚠️	1.2
12.1	BR		TRO UM Dugan ⊘ Brighton	1.3
13.4	BL		TRO Dugan ⊘ Prey Hill Rd	0.4
13.8	S	SS	Mower X 20 ⚠️	0.6
14.4	L	SS	UM 24	0.8
15.2	R	SS	UM 25 Then BR ⊘ 24	3.7
18.9	BL		TRO UM 25 ⊘ UM Cole Hill Rd	2.2
21.1	L	SS	20 ⚠️	0.5
21.6	R		Sale Rd	0.7
22.3	R	SS	UM Wall St	2.5
24.8	R	SS	Toward Cedarville	0.7
25.5	R	SS	UM 51	0.1
25.6	R		TRO 51 FOOD	0.9
26.5	L		Millers Mills Rd	0.6
27.1	BR		TRO UM Millers Mills ⊘ Saxon	1.1
28.2	L	SS	TRO Millers Mills ⊘ Huxtable/Depot	0.5

28.7	BR	Y	TRO UM Millers Mills	2.4
31.1	L	SS	McKoons Rd	1.2
32.3	S	SS	Columbia Center X Jordanville	0.2
32.5	BR		TRO Columbia Center ⊘ Spohn	1.4
33.9	BR		TRO Columbia Center ⊘ Polly Miller	0.5
34.4	L	SS	28 ⚠️	0.9
35.3	R		Robinson Rd @ Dennison Corners	2.7
38.0	BR		TRO UM Robinson ⊘ Mortz	0.8
38.8	BL		TRO UM Robinson ⊘ UM Mason	1.7
40.5	S	SS	167	0.3
40.8	L		Hicks Rd ☞ S 1.1 167 FOOD	0.6
41.4	BL		Then BR TRO UM Hicks	2.9
44.3	L	SS	UM Jordanville Rd	0.8
45.1	L		Aney Hill Rd	1.6
46.7	R		Bush Rd **OPTION**	1.1
47.8	R	SS	Travis Rd	1.7
49.5	BL		TRO Travis ⊘ Puskarenko	2.0
51.5	S		80	0.5
52.0	S		TRO 80 FOOD	0.5
52.5	BL		TRO 80 ⊘ Chyle	1.5
54.0	L		Willsey Hill Rd	0.6
54.6	L		Hinds Rd	1.2
55.8	BL		TRO UM Hinds ⊘ Domion	1.4
57.2	S	SS	Griggs Rd X 20 ⚠️	1.7

R	Right	S	Straight	
L	Left	TRO	To Remain On	
BR	Bear Right	X	Cross	
BL	Bear Left	⚠️	Caution	
SS	Stop Sign	UM	Unmarked Road	⊘ Do Not Take
SL	Stop Light	26	County Route	☞ Detour Off
YS	Yield Sign	28	State Route	🤝 Combine With

...Tour Cues Continued

58.9	R	SS	UM 52	2.0
60.9	L	SS	UM 80	1.2
62.1	R		Opera Parking Lot	

Points of Interest

Mile	•Points of Interest	#
0.0	Glimmerglass Opera & Goodyear Nature Trail	23
28.7	Millers Mills Ice Harvest	66
40.3	Holy Trinity Russian Orthodox Monastery	65
51.8	Owen D. Young Marker & Nature Trail on L	24
52.5	Rainbow Trout Fish Hatchery ☞ BR 0.1	68

NOTE
People Wearing Shorts Are Not Permitted On The Monastery Premises.

NOTE
There Are Two Food Stops @ Mile 40.8 In Jordanville. They Are Both Frequently Closed On Weekends.

COUNTIES
Otsego, Herkimer

Tour Description

Due to space limitations, see Tour Description on reverse side...

🤝 **Cooperstown: 2B,C,D**
@ 0.0 join Tours 2B,C,D
@ cue 9.6 L @ Crosswalk Facing Opera

🤝 **Cooperstown: 11A,B**
@ 0.0 R 0.4 To Join Tours 11A,B
@ cue 9.2 R 27

OPTION
To Add 8.7 Miles And A 600 Foot Climb:

46.7	S		Aney Hill Rd ⊘ Bush	3.0
49.7	R	SS	167	0.1
49.8	S	SS	TRO 167 X 168	0.8
50.6	R		Johnny Cake Rd	2.6
53.2	R		Travis Rd	1.7
54.9	S	SS	TRO Travis X 168	3.3
58.2	Resume @ cue 49.5 BL TRO Travis ⊘ Puskarenko			

Let us know what you think of this tour! Email: crankmail@usa.net

Climb Rating in feet per mile climbed: 0-45 = Easy, 45-60 = Moderate, 60+ = Difficult

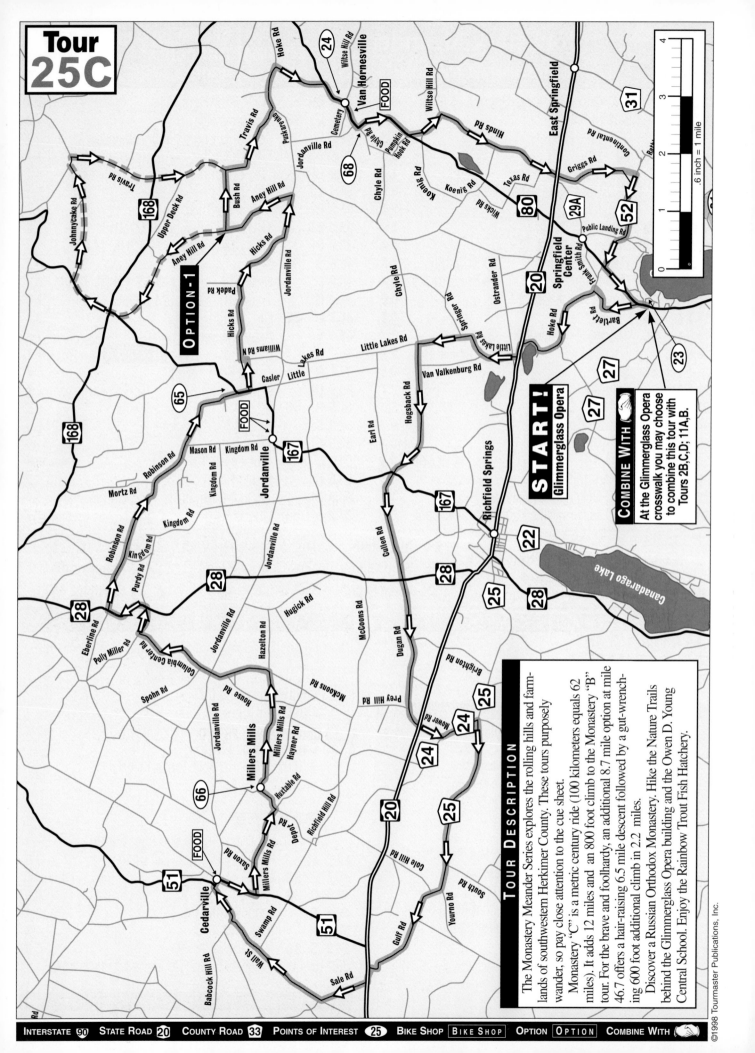

Tour 25C

OPTION-1

START!
Glimmerglass Opera

COMBINE WITH
At the Glimmerglass Opera crosswalk you may choose to combine this tour with Tours 2B,C,D; 11A,B.

TOUR DESCRIPTION

The Monastery Meander Series explores the rolling hills and farmlands of southwestern Herkimer County. These tours purposely wander, so pay close attention to the cue sheet. Monastery "C" is a metric century ride (100 kilometers equals 62 miles). It adds 12 miles and an 800 foot climb to the Monastery "B" tour. For the brave and foolhardy, an additional 8.7 mile option at mile 46.7 offers a hair-raising 6.5 mile descent followed by a gut-wrenching 600 foot additional climb in 2.2 miles.

Discover a Russian Orthodox Monastery. Hike the Nature Trails behind the Glimmerglass Opera building and the Owen D. Young Central School. Enjoy the Rainbow Trout Fish Hatchery.

Scale: .6 inch = 1 mile

INTERSTATE 90 STATE ROAD 20 COUNTY ROAD 33 POINTS OF INTEREST 25 BIKE SHOP OPTION COMBINE WITH

Van Hornesville · East Springfield · Springfield Center · Richfield Springs · Jordanville · Millers Mills · Cedarville · Canadarago Lake

FOOD

Monastery Meander "D"

Start: Springfield. Glimmerglass Opera.

Miles	75 [handshake] OPTION	Tour
Rating	Difficult	**25D**
Climb	5100' @ 68 ft/mi	

	Mile	Dir		Description		Dist
•	0.0	L		@ Crosswalk Facing Opera [handshake]		0.2
	0.2	L		Bartlett Rd		1.2
	1.4	L	SS	UM Hoke Rd		2.2
	3.6	L	SS	[20] [!]		0.3
	3.9	R		Little Lakes Rd		1.4
	5.3	BL		TRO UM Little Lakes ⊘ Springer		0.8
	6.1	L		Hogsback Rd		2.7
	8.8	S	SS	Cullen X [167]		2.1
	10.9	S	SS	Dugan X [28] [!]		1.2
	12.1	BR		TRO UM Dugan ⊘ Brighton		1.3
	13.4	BL		TRO Dugan ⊘ Prey Hill Rd		0.4
	13.8	S	SS	Mower X [20] [!]		0.6
	14.4	L	SS	UM [24]		0.8
	15.2	R	SS	UM [25] Then BR ⊘ [24]		3.7
	18.9	BL		TRO UM [25] ⊘ UM Cole Hill Rd		2.2
	21.1	L	SS	[20] [!]		0.5
	21.6	R		Sale Rd		0.7
	22.3		SS	UM Wall St		2.5
	24.8	R	SS	Toward Cedarville		0.7
	25.5	R	SS	UM [51]		0.1
	25.6	R		TRO [51] FOOD		0.9
	26.5	L		Millers Mills Rd		0.6
	27.1	BR		TRO UM Millers Mills ⊘ Saxon		1.1
	28.2	L	SS	TRO Millers Mills ⊘ Huxtable/Depot		0.5
	28.7	BR	Y	TRO UM Millers Mills		2.4
	31.1	R	SS	McKoons Rd		1.8
	32.9	BL		TRO McKoons ⊘ Richfield Hill		0.3
	33.2	BL		TRO McKoons ⊘ Prey Hill Rd		2.5
	35.7	L	SS	[28] [!] FOOD		0.5
	36.2	BL		UM Hugick Rd [!]		2.0
	38.2	L	SS	UM Jordanville Rd		1.6
	39.8	R	SS	Columbia Center Rd		0.2
	40.0	L		Spohn Rd		2.4
	42.4	R	SS	Brewer Rd		1.1
	43.5			Polly Miller Rd ⊘ Eberline		1.4
	44.9	BL		To YS Then S Columbia Center Rd		0.6
	45.5	L	SS	[28] [!]		0.9
	46.4	R		Robinson Rd @ Dennison Corners		2.7
	49.1	BR		TRO UM Robinson ⊘ Mortz		0.8
	49.9	BL		TRO UM Robinson ⊘ UM Mason		1.7
•	51.6	S	SS	[167]		0.9
	52.5	L		Jordanville Rd [pointer] R 0.5 FOOD		0.5
	53.0	L		Casler Rd		0.3
	53.3	S	YS	[167]		0.2
	53.5	R		Hicks Rd		0.6
	54.1	BL		Then BR TRO UM Hicks Rd		2.9
	57.0	L	SS	UM Jordanville Rd		0.8
	57.8	L		Aney Hill Rd		1.6

Legend

R Right	**S** Straight	**SS** Stop Sign	**UM** Unmarked Road	⊘ Do Not Take
L Left	**TRO** To Remain On	**SL** Stop Light	[26] County Route	[pointer] Detour Off
BR Bear Right	**X** Cross	**YS** Yield Sign	[28] State Route	[handshake] Combine With
BL Bear Left	[!] Caution			

...TOUR CUES CONTINUED

Mile	Dir		Description		Dist
59.4	R		Bush Rd **OPTION**		1.1
60.5	R	SS	Travis Rd		1.7
62.2	BL		TRO Travis ⊘ Puskarenko		2.0
64.2	R	SS	[80]		0.5
64.7	S		TRO [80] FOOD		0.5
65.2	BL		TRO [80] ⊘ Chyle		1.5
66.7	L		Willsey Hill Rd		0.6
67.3	R		Hinds Rd		1.2
68.5	BL		TRO UM Hinds ⊘ Domion		1.4
69.9	S	SS	Griggs Rd X [20] [!]		1.7
71.6	R	SS	UM [52]		2.0
73.6	L	SS	UM [80]		1.3
74.9	R		Opera Parking Lot		

Mile	•POINTS OF INTEREST	#
0.0	Glimmerglass Opera & Goodyear Nature Trail	(23)
28.7	Millers Mills Ice Harvest	(66)
51.4	Holy Trinity Russian Orthodox Monastery	(65)
64.5	Owen D. Young Marker & Nature Trail on L	(24)
65.2	Rainbow Trout Fish Hatchery [pointer] BR 0.1	(68)

COUNTIES

Otsego, Herkimer

TOUR DESCRIPTION

Due to space limitations, see Tour Description on reverse side...

NOTE People Wearing Shorts Are Not Permitted On The Monastery Premises.

NOTE The Two Food Stops @ Mile 52.6 In Jordanville Are Frequently Closed On Weekends.

[handshake] **Cooperstown: 2B,C,D**
@ 0.0 join Tours 2B,C,D
@ cue 9.6 L @ Crosswalk Facing Opera

[handshake] **Cooperstown: 11A,B**
@ 0.0 R 0.4 To Join Tours 11A,B
@ cue 9.2 R (27)

OPTION

To Add 8.7 Miles And A 600 Foot Climb:

Mile	Dir		Description		Dist
59.4	S		Aney Hill Rd ⊘ Bush		3.0
62.4	R	SS	[167]		0.1
62.5	S	SS	TRO [167] X [168]		0.8
63.3	R		Johnny Cake Rd		2.6
65.9	R		Travis Rd		1.7
67.6	S	SS	TRO Travis X [168]		3.3
70.9			Resume @ cue 62.2 BL TRO Travis ⊘ Puskarenko		

Let us know what you think of this tour! Email: crankmail@usa.net

Climb Rating in feet per mile climbed: 0-45 = Easy, 45-60 = Moderate, 60+ = Difficult

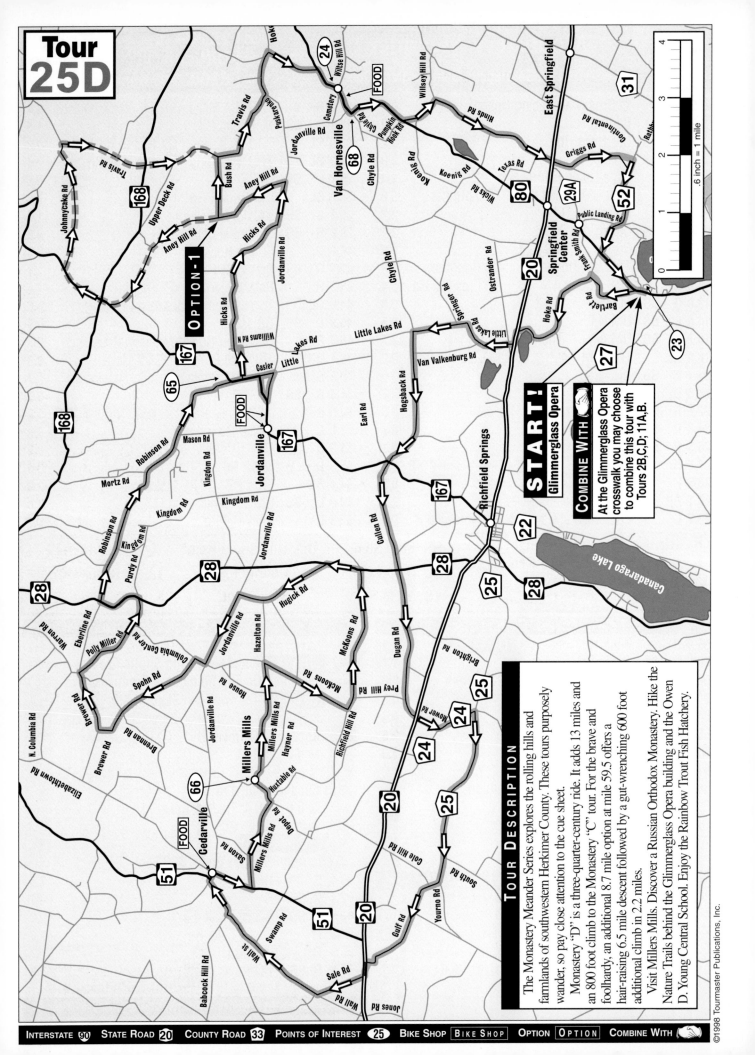

Tour 25D

TOUR DESCRIPTION

The Monastery Meander Series explores the rolling hills and farmlands of southwestern Herkimer County. These tours purposely wander, so pay close attention to the cue sheet.

Monastery "D" is a three-quarter-century ride. It adds 13 miles and an 800 foot climb to the Monastery "C" tour. For the brave and foolhardy, an additional 8.7 mile option at mile 59.5 offers a hair-raising 6.5 mile descent followed by a gut-wrenching 600 foot descent followed by a gut-wrenching 600 foot additional climb in 2.2 miles.

Visit Millers Mills. Discover a Russian Orthodox Monastery. Hike the Nature Trails behind the Glimmerglass Opera building and the Owen D. Young Central School. Enjoy the Rainbow Trout Fish Hatchery.

START!
Glimmerglass Opera

COMBINE WITH
At the Glimmerglass Opera crosswalk you may choose to combine this tour with Tours 2B,C,D; 11A,B.

OPTION-1

FOOD

.6 inch = 1 mile

 **Cranks**

Monastery Meander "E"

Start: Springfield. Glimmerglass Opera.

Miles	100  OPTION	Tour
Rating	Difficult	**25E**
Climb	6500' @ 65 ft/mi	

• 0.0	L		@ Crosswalk Facing Opera 🤝	0.2
0.2	L		Bartlett Rd	1.2
1.4	L	SS	UM Hoke Rd	2.2
3.6	L	SS	20 ⚠	0.3
3.9	R		Little Lakes Rd	1.4
5.3	BL		TRO UM Little Lakes ⊘ Springer	0.8
6.1	L		Hogsback Rd	2.7
8.8	S	SS	Cullen X 167	2.1
10.9	S	SS	Dugan X 28 ⚠	1.2
12.1	BR		TRO UM Dugan ⊘ Brighton	1.3
13.4	BL		TRO Dugan ⊘ Prey Hill Rd	0.4
13.8	S	SS	Mower X 20 ⚠	0.6
14.4	L	SS	UM 24	0.8
15.2	R	SS	UM 25 Then BR ⊘ 24	3.7
18.9	BL		TRO UM 25 ⊘ UM Cole Hill Rd	2.2
21.1	R	SS	20 ⚠	0.4
21.5	L		51 ⚠	1.8
23.3	L		Swamp Rd	1.1
24.4	L	SS	UM Wall St	2.5
26.9	S	SS	TRO Wall St X Stone Rd	0.1
27.0	S	SS	Jones Rd X 20 ⚠	0.7
27.7	BR		TRO UM Jones ⊘ Twomey (Dead End)	0.3
28.0	R	SS	Burrows Rd	1.2
29.2	R		South St (UM 51)	0.3

29.5	S	SL	UM N. Winfield Rd X 20 FOOD	1.1
30.6	S	SS	TRO N. Winfield Rd X Stone Rd	1.2
31.8	BL		TRO N. Winfield ⊘ Brace Rd	1.3
33.1	S		Albany Rd X Babcock Hill Rd	1.9
35.0	BL		TRO Albany ⊘ Suncody	0.6
35.6	BL		Then L SS Rider Rd	0.9
36.5	R		Camp Rd	0.8
37.3	S	SS	Rasbach Rd X UM Goodier Rd	1.5
38.8	S	SS	Jerusalem Hill ☞ L 0.1 FOOD	0.1
38.9	BR		TRO Jerusalem Hill ⊘ Ball Rd	2.1
41.0			Berberick Rd	3.5
44.5	S	SS	Brace Rd X Babcock Hill	0.7
45.2	L		Cross Rd	0.5
45.7	BL		Then L SS UM Meeting House Rd	1.8
47.5	R	SS	Babcock Hill Rd	0.3
47.8	S	SS	Toward Cedarville	0.7
48.5	R	SS	UM 51	0.2
48.7	R		51 FOOD	0.8
49.5	L		Millers Mills Rd	0.6
50.1	BR		TRO UM Millers Mills ⊘ Saxon	1.2
51.3	L	SS	TRO Millers Mills ⊘ Huxtable/Depot	0.4
• 51.7	BR		TRO UM Millers Mills	2.4
54.1	R	SS	McKoons Rd	1.8
55.9	BL		TRO McKoons ⊘ Richfield Hill	0.2

R	Right		**S**	Straight	**SS**	Stop Sign
L	Left		**TRO**	To Remain On	**SL**	Stop Light
BR	Bear Right		**X**	Cross	**YS**	Yield Sign
BL	Bear Left		⚠	Caution		

UM	Unmarked Road	⊘ Do Not Take
26	County Route	☞ Detour Off
28	State Route	🤝 Combine With

...Tour Cues Continued

56.1	BL		TRO McKoons ⊘ Prey Hill Rd	2.5
58.6	L	SS	28 ⚠ FOOD	0.6
59.2	BL		UM Hugick Rd ⚠	2.0
61.2	L	SS	UM Jordanville Rd	1.5
62.7	R	SS	Columbia Center Rd	0.2
62.9	L		Spohn Rd	2.5
65.4	L	SS	Brewer Rd	1.0
66.4	R	SS	Elizabethtown Rd	0.9
67.3	R		N. Columbia Rd	1.9
69.2	R	SS	Warren Rd	0.1
69.3	L		Polly Miller Rd ⊘ Eberline	1.4
70.7	BL		To YS Then S Columbia Center Rd	0.6
71.3	L	SS	28 ⚠	0.9
72.2	R		Robinson Rd @ Dennison Corners	2.7
74.9	BR		TRO UM Robinson ⊘ Mortz	0.8
• 75.7	BL		TRO UM Robinson ⊘ UM Mason	1.7
77.4	S	SS	167	0.9
78.3	L		Jordanville Rd ☞ R 0.5 FOOD	0.5
78.8	L		Casler Rd	0.3
79.1	S	YS	167	0.2
79.3	R		Hicks Rd	0.6

...Tour Cues Continued

79.9	BL		Then BR TRO UM Hicks Rd	2.9
82.8	L	SS	UM Jordanville Rd	0.8
83.6	L		Aney Hill Rd	1.6
85.2	R		Bush Rd OPTION	1.1
86.3	R	SS	Travis Rd	1.7
88.0	BL		TRO Travis ⊘ Puskarenko	2.0
• 90.0	R	SS	80	0.5
90.5	S		TRO 80 FOOD	0.5
• 91.0	BL		TRO 80 ⊘ Chyle	1.5
92.5	L		Willsey Hill Rd	0.6
93.1	R		Hinds Rd	1.2
94.3	BL		TRO UM Hinds ⊘ Domion	1.4
95.7	S	SS	Griggs Rd X 20 ⚠	1.7
97.4	R	SS	UM 52	2.0
99.4	L	SS	UM 80	1.2
100.6	R		Opera Parking Lot	

COUNTIES
Otsego, Herkimer

THIS TOUR CONTINUES ON NEXT PAGE ☞

Let us know what you think of this tour! Email: crankmail@usa.net

Climb Rating in feet per mile climbed: 0-45 = Easy, 45-60 = Moderate, 60+ = Difficult

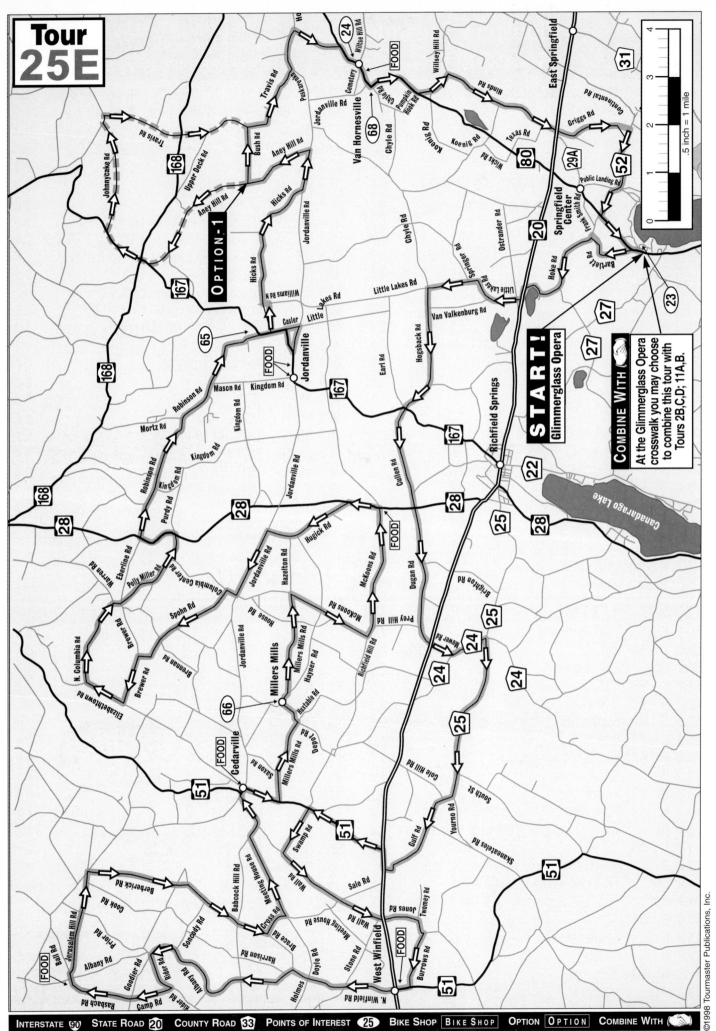

Tour 25E

OPTION-1

START!
Glimmerglass Opera

COMBINE WITH
At the Glimmerglass Opera crosswalk you may choose to combine this tour with Tours 2B,C,D; 11A,B.

Canadarago Lake

East Springfield
Springfield Center
Van Hornesville
Richfield Springs
Jordanville
Millers Mills
Cedarville
West Winfield

.5 inch = 1 mile

Monastery Meander "E"

. . . CONTINUED

Miles	100
Rating	Difficult
Climb	6500' @ 65 ft/mi

Tour 25E

Mile	• Points of Interest	#
0.0	Glimmerglass Opera & Goodyear Nature Trail	23
51.7	Millers Mills Ice Harvest	66
77.2	Holy Trinity Russian Orthodox Monastery	65
90.3	Owen D. Young Marker & Nature Trail on L	24
91.0	Rainbow Trout Fish Hatchery ☞ BR 0.1	68

Tour Description

The Monastery Meander Series explores the rolling hills and farmlands of southwestern Herkimer County. These tours purposely wander, so pay close attention to the cue sheet.

Monastery "E" is a century ride. It adds 25 miles and a 1400 foot climb to the Monastery "D" tour. For the brave and foolhardy, an additional 8.7 mile option at mile 85.2 offers a hair-raising 6.5 mile descent followed by a gut-wrenching 600 foot additional climb in 2.2 miles.

Visit Millers Mills. Discover a Russian Orthodox Monastery. Hike the Nature Trails behind the Glimmerglass Opera building and the Owen D. Young Central School. Enjoy the Rainbow Trout Fish Hatchery.

NOTE **People Wearing Shorts Are Not Permitted On The Monastery Premises.**

NOTE The Two Food Stops @ Mile 78.3 In Jordanville Are Frequently Closed On Weekends.

Cooperstown: 2B,C,D
@ 0.0 join Tours 2B,C,D
@ cue 9.6 L @ Crosswalk Facing Opera

Cooperstown: 11A,B
@ 0.0 R 0.4 To Join Tours 11A,B
@ cue 9.2 R 27

Option

To Add 8.7 Miles And A 600 Foot Climb:

85.2	S	Aney Hill Rd ⊘ Bush	3.0
88.2	R SS	167	0.1
88.3	S SS	TRO 167 X 168	0.8
89.1	R	Johnny Cake Rd	2.6
91.7	R	Travis Rd	1.7
93.4	S SS	TRO Travis X 168	3.3
96.7	Resume	@ cue 88.0 BL TRO Travis ⊘ Puskarenko	

INTERSTATE 90 STATE ROAD 20 COUNTY ROAD 33 POINTS OF INTEREST 25 BIKE SHOP BIKE SHOP OPTION OPTION COMBINE WITH

Let's Get Cranking!

Cranks from Cooperstown is the Perfect Gift...

for people...
- *who bike*
- *who used to bike*
- *who ought to bike*
- *who want to bike, but don't know how*
- *who need exercise that's fun*

it's also the Perfect Gift for people...
- *who live in Cooperstown*
- *who want to live in Cooperstown*
- *who plan to visit Cooperstown*

it's even the Perfect Gift for people...
- *who tour by motorized vehicle*

So don't delay! Place your order today!

Complete this form to place an order.

By Phone: **607-547-CRANK** (607-547-2726)
888-49-CRANK (888-492-7265)
By Fax: **607-547-CRANK** (607-547-2726)
888-59-CRANK (888-592-7265)
By Email: *crankmail@usa.net*
By Mail: **Tourmaster Publications**
P.O. Box 568
Cooperstown, NY 13326

NAME (PLEASE PRINT): _____

SHIPPING ADDRESS: _____

_____

CITY:_____ STATE _____ ZIP_____

HOME PHONE:_____ WORK_____

FAX_____ EMAIL_____

Please send _____ copies of
Cranks from Cooperstown @ $19.95 ea $_____

Shipping & Handling (in the continental U.S.) $4.95 ea $_____

Sub-Total $_____

NY Residents add Sales Tax (county_____)
_____% $_____

| Your satisfaction is guaranteed. | TOTAL $_____ |

Let's Get Cranking!

I AM PAYING BY: _____CHECK _____MONEY ORDER _____VISA _____MASTERCARD

CARD# | | | | | | | | | | | | | | | | | |

EXPIRATION DATE____/____ *WE MUST HAVE YOUR EXPIRATION DATE TO PROCESS YOUR ORDER*

SIGNATURE_____

If you'd like your local bike shop or book store to carry Cranks from Cooperstown, let us know.

Your Tour Log

TOUR #	DATE BIKED	MILES BIKED	COMMENTS

Fix the Facts: *The roads won't change, but the road signs may. In the northeast, snowplows eat road signs for breakfast in the winter. Hunters shoot them in the fall. And teenagers tear them down in the summer. If you notice any changes or errors in this book, please contact the publisher so that future editions can be corrected.*

Let us know what you think of the tours! Email: crankmail@usa.net

Cranks from Cooperstown is the Perfect Gift...

for people...
- *who bike*
- *who used to bike*
- *who ought to bike*
- *who want to bike, but don't know how*
- *who need exercise that's fun*

it's also the Perfect Gift for people...
- *who live in Cooperstown*
- *who want to live in Cooperstown*
- *who plan to visit Cooperstown*

it's even the Perfect Gift for people...
- *who tour by motorized vehicle*

So don't delay! Place your order today!

Complete this form to place an order.

By Phone: **607-547-CRANK (607-547-2726)**
888-49-CRANK (888-492-7265)
By Fax: **607-547-CRANK (607-547-2726)**
888-59-CRANK (888-592-7265)
By Email: crankmail@usa.net
By Mail: **Tourmaster Publications**
P.O. Box 568
Cooperstown, NY 13326

NAME (PLEASE PRINT): _____

SHIPPING ADDRESS: _____

_____

CITY:_____ STATE _____ ZIP_____

HOME PHONE:_____WORK_____

FAX_____ EMAIL_____

Please send _____ copies of
Cranks from Cooperstown @ $19.95 ea $_____

Shipping & Handling (in the continental U.S.) $4.95 ea $_____

Sub-Total $_____

NY Residents add Sales Tax (county_____)
_____% $_____

| Your satisfaction is guaranteed. | TOTAL | $_____ |

Let's Get Cranking!➤

I AM PAYING BY: _____CHECK _____MONEY ORDER _____VISA _____MASTERCARD

CARD# | | | | | | | | | | | | | | | | | | |

EXPIRATION DATE____/____ *WE MUST HAVE YOUR EXPIRATION DATE TO PROCESS YOUR ORDER*

SIGNATURE_____

If you'd like your local bike shop or book store to carry Cranks from Cooperstown, let us know.